Steve Vai – Real Illus...

5	Building The Church
23	Dying For Your Love
31	Glorious
48	K'm-Pee-Du-Wee
57	Firewall
68	Freak Show Excess
102	Lotus Feet
113	Yai Yai
120	Midway Creatures
133	I'm Your Secrets
142	Under It All
174	Guitar Notation Legend

Photography by Larry DiMarzio

Music transcriptions by David Stocker

ISBN-13: 978-1-4234-2318-8
ISBN-10: 1-4234-2318-6

7777 W. BLUEMOUND RD. P.O. BOX 13819 MILWAUKEE, WI 53213

For all works contained herein:
Unauthorized copying, arranging, adapting,
recording or public performance is an infringement of copyright.
Infringers are liable under the law.

Visit Hal Leonard Online at
www.halleonard.com

Building the Church

By Steve Vai

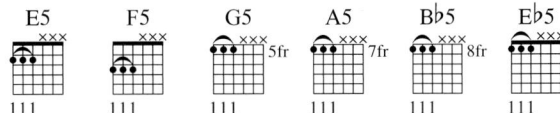

Drop D tuning, down 1 step:
(low to high) C-G-C-F-A-D

Moderately slow ♩ = 94

**Em11

*Gtr. 1

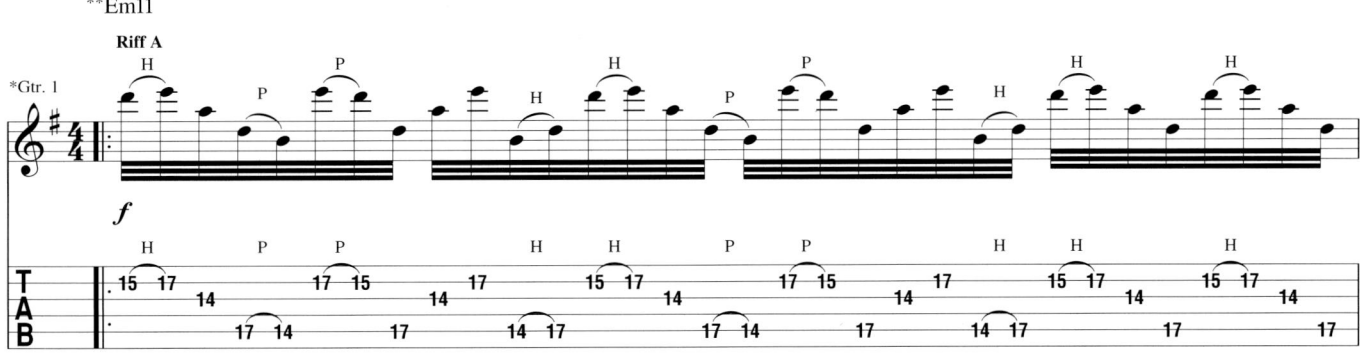

*Analog synth. arr. for gtr.
**Chord symbols reflect overall harmony.

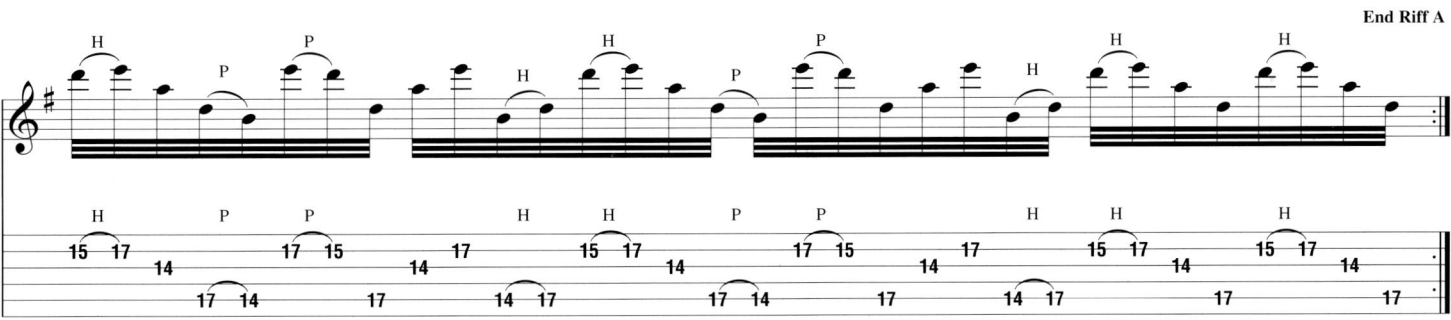

Gtr. 1: w/ Riff A (1 1/2 times)

Em11

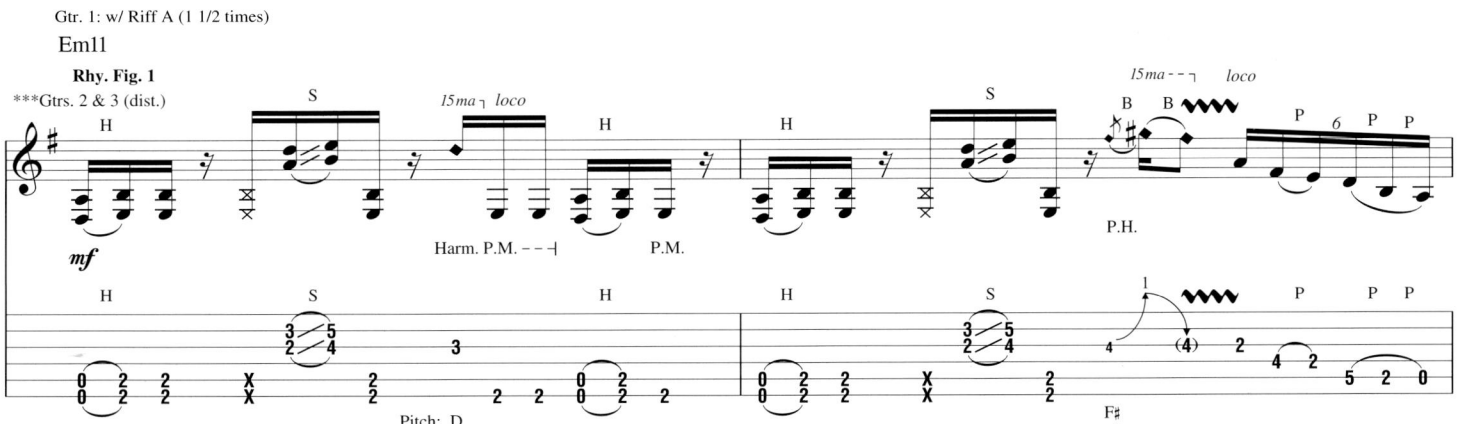

***Composite arrangement

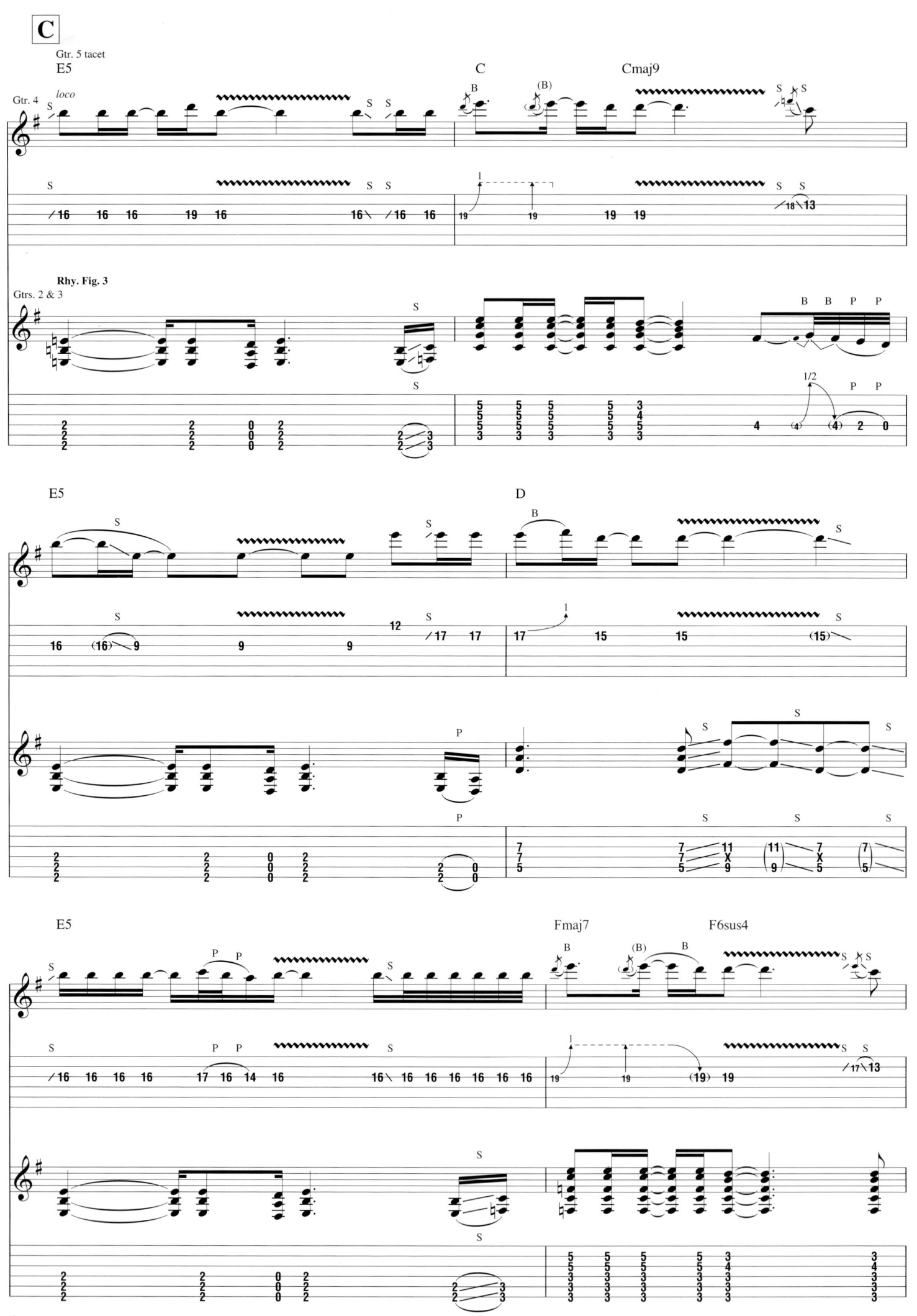

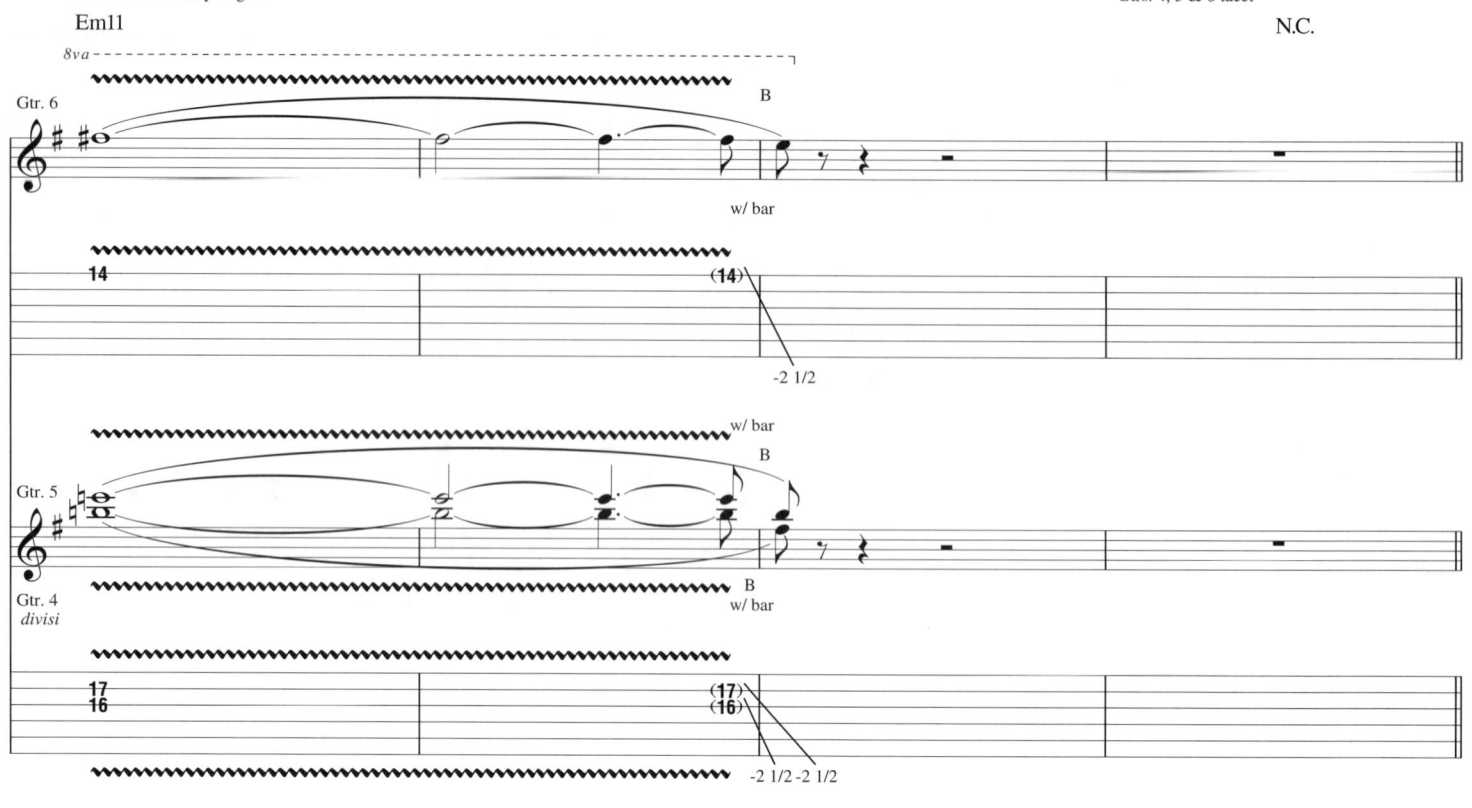

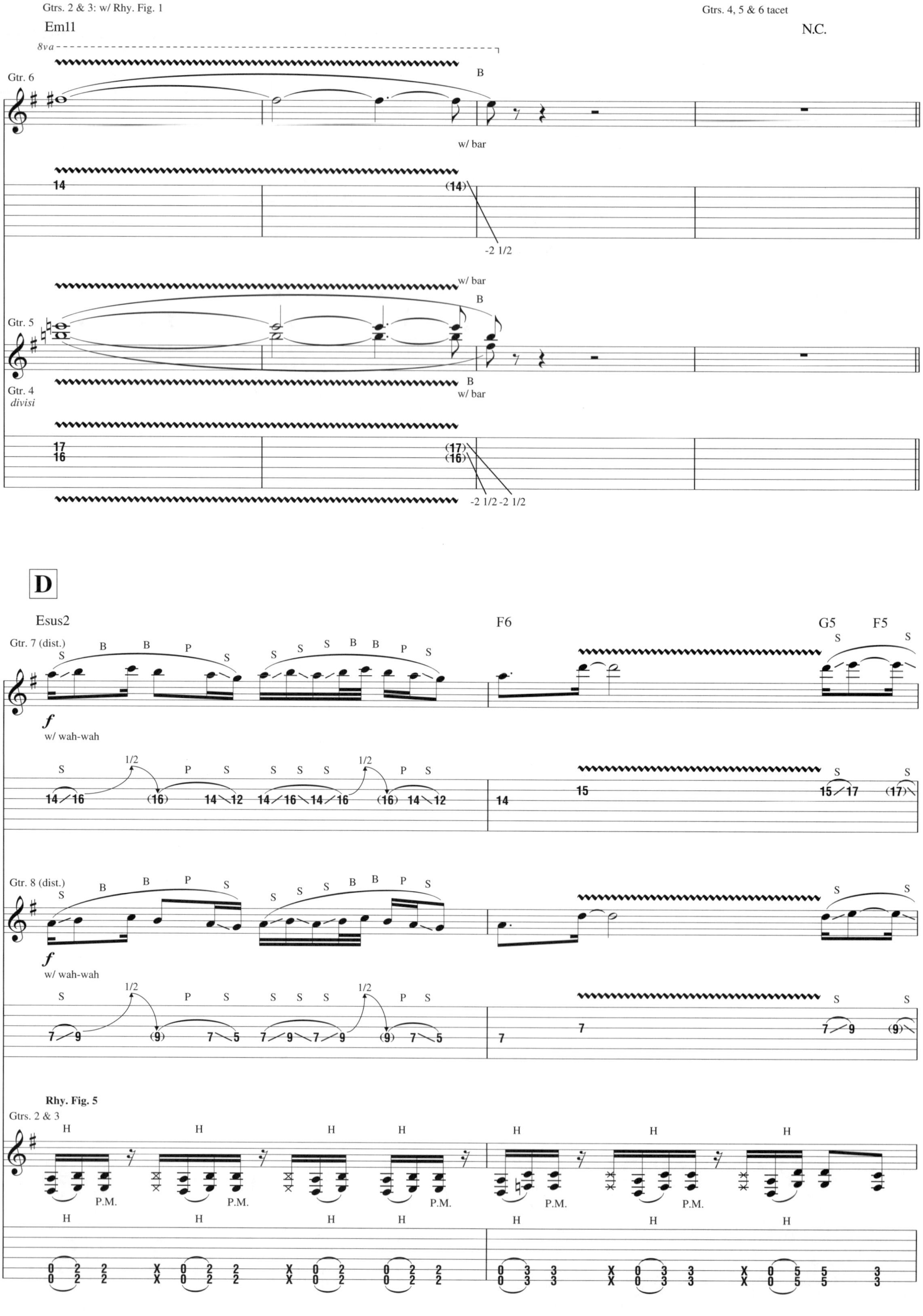

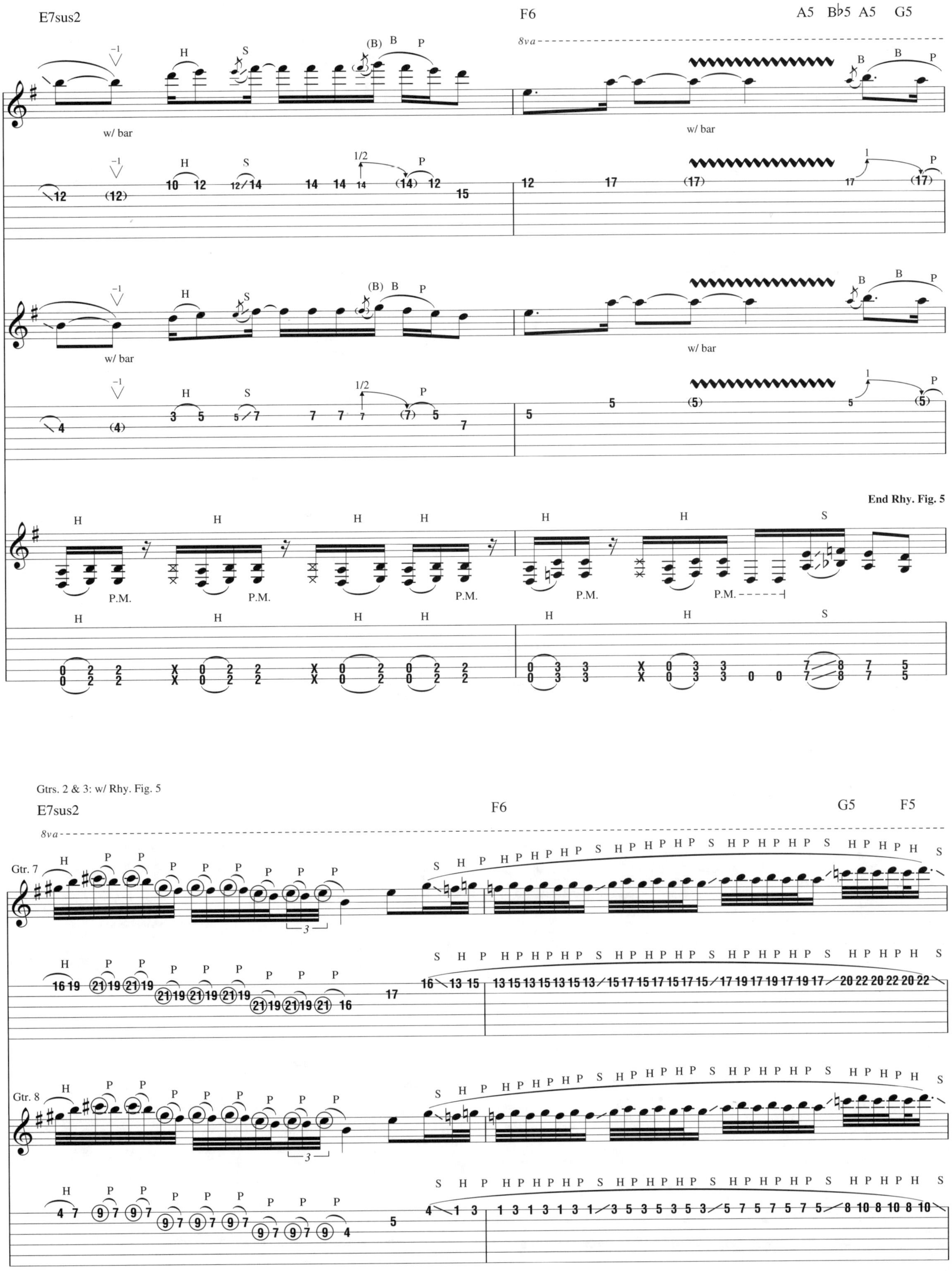

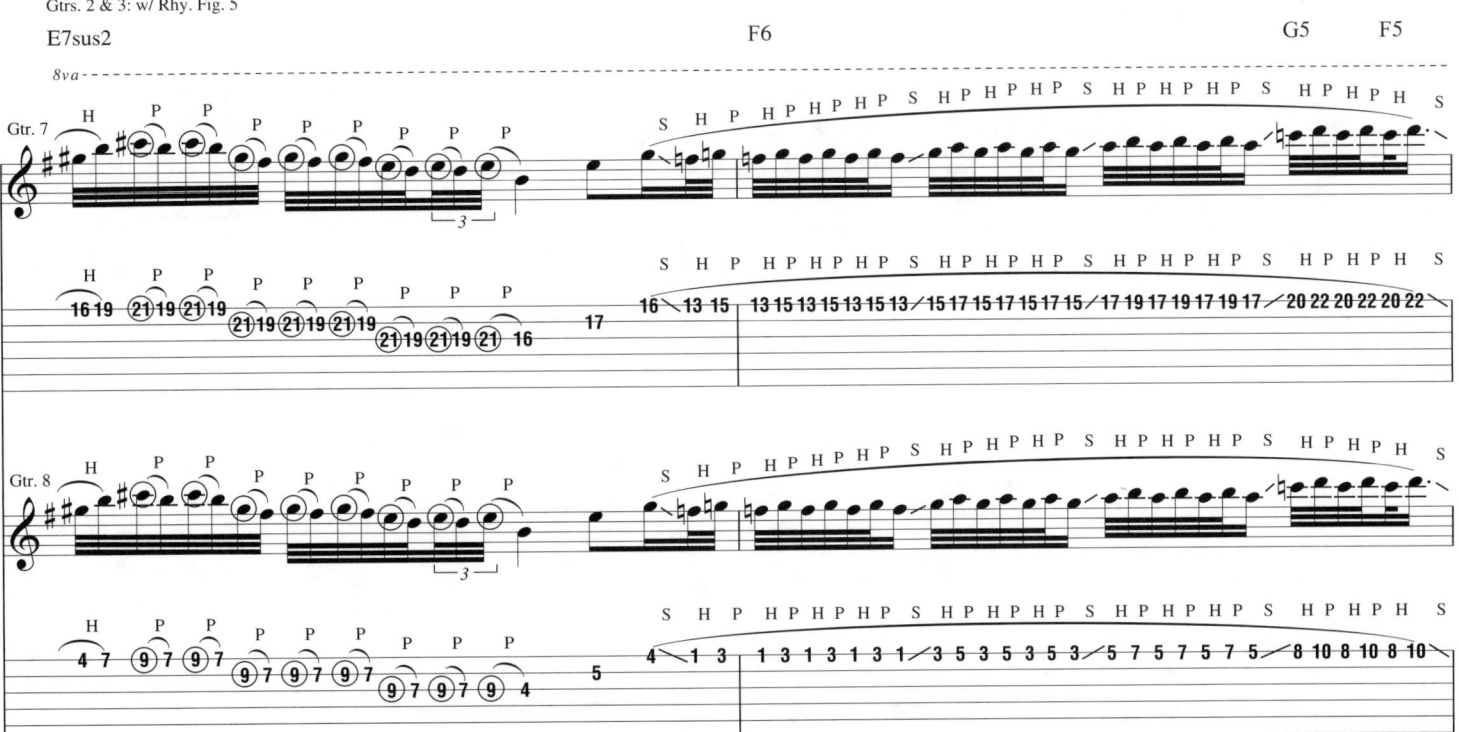

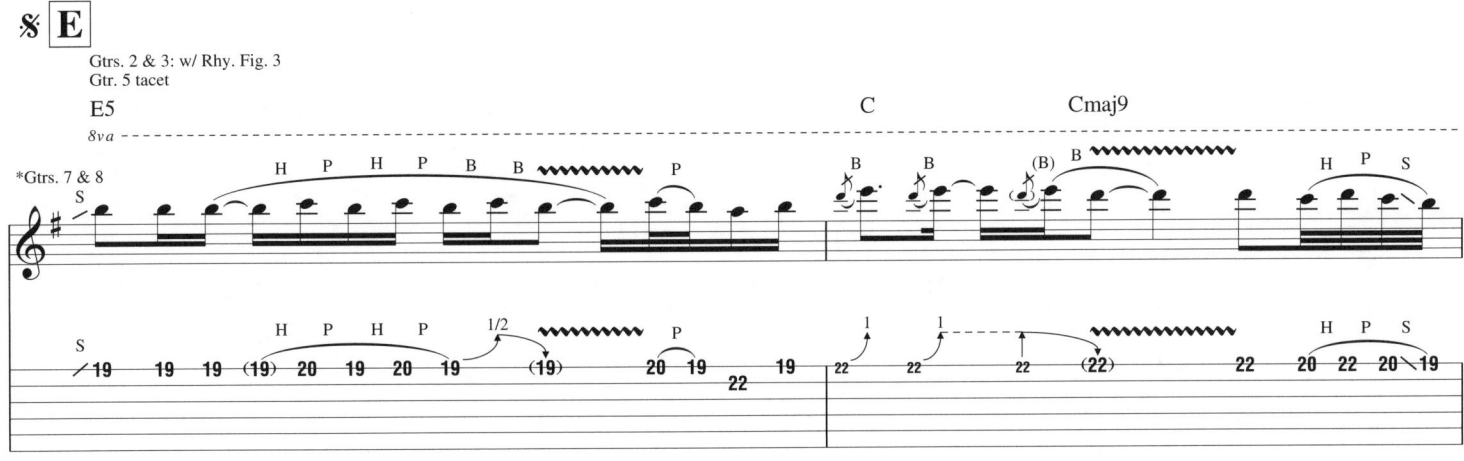
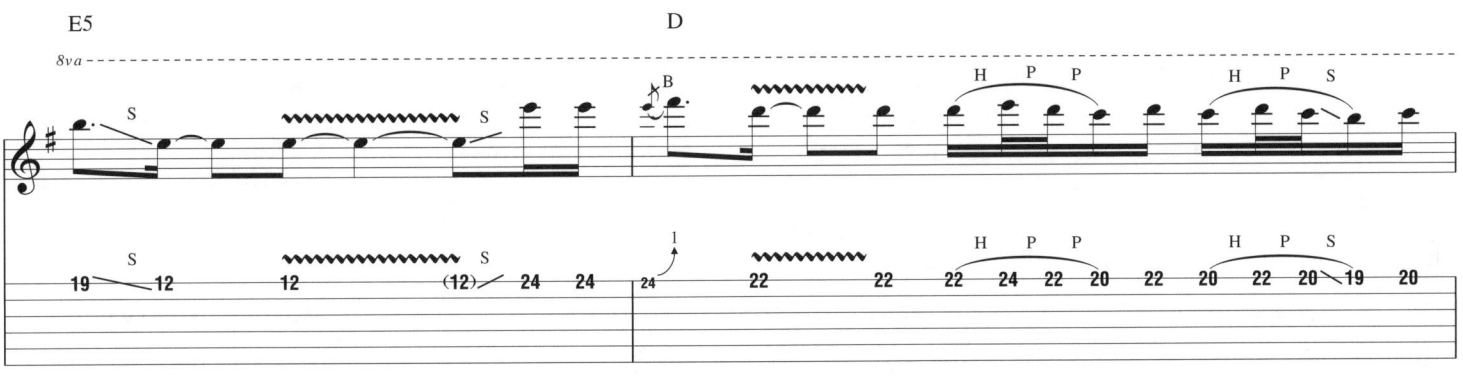
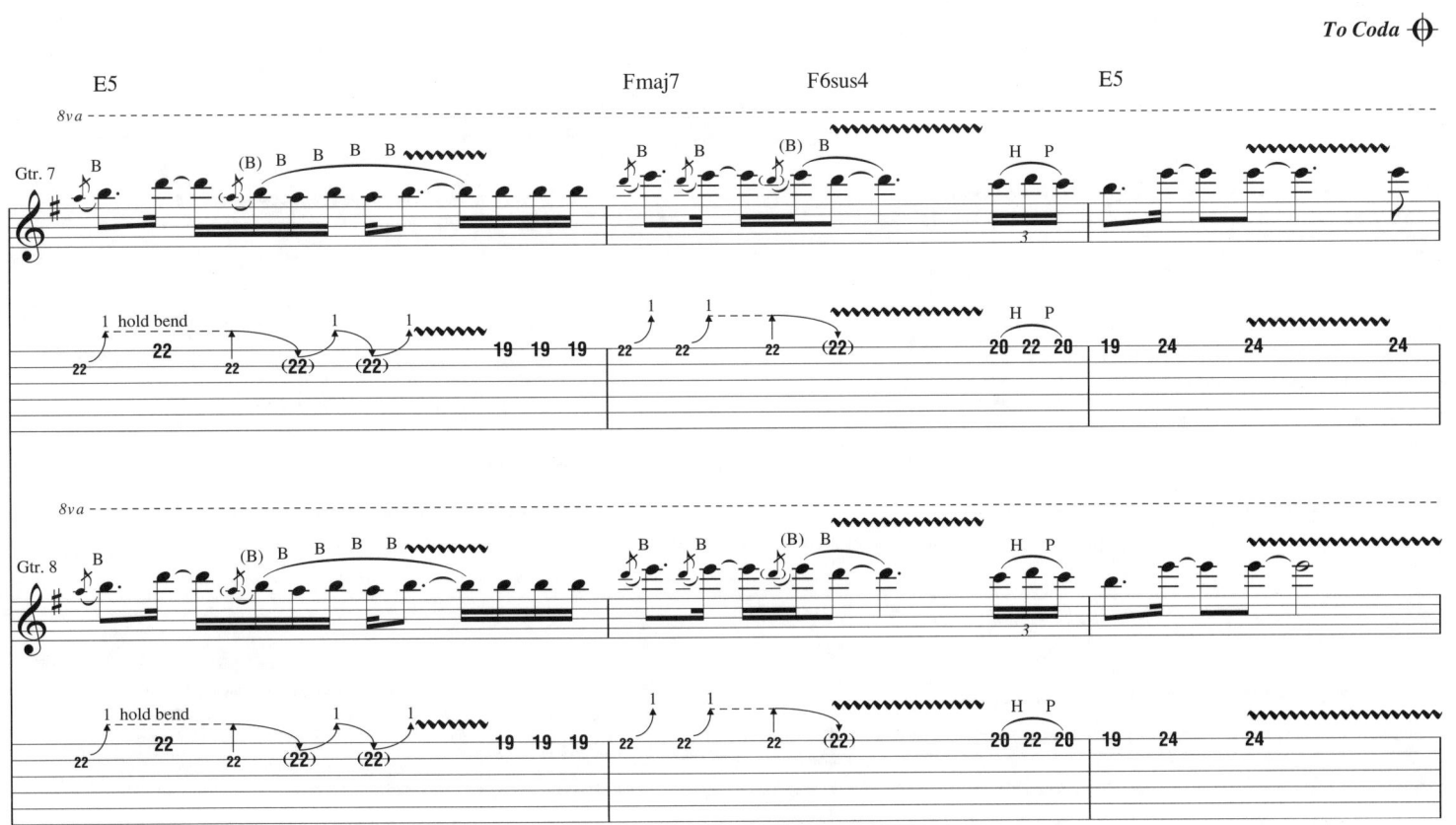

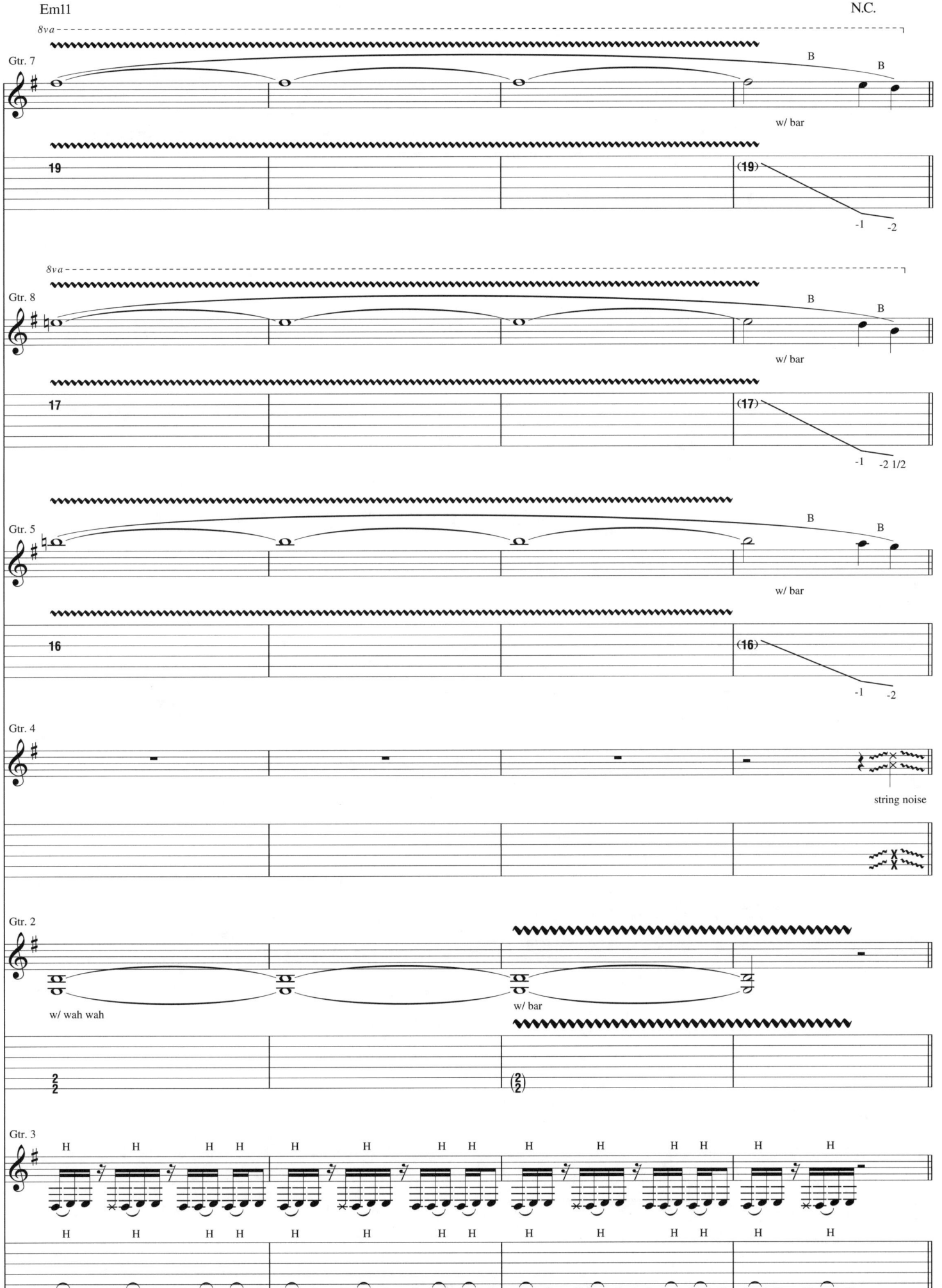

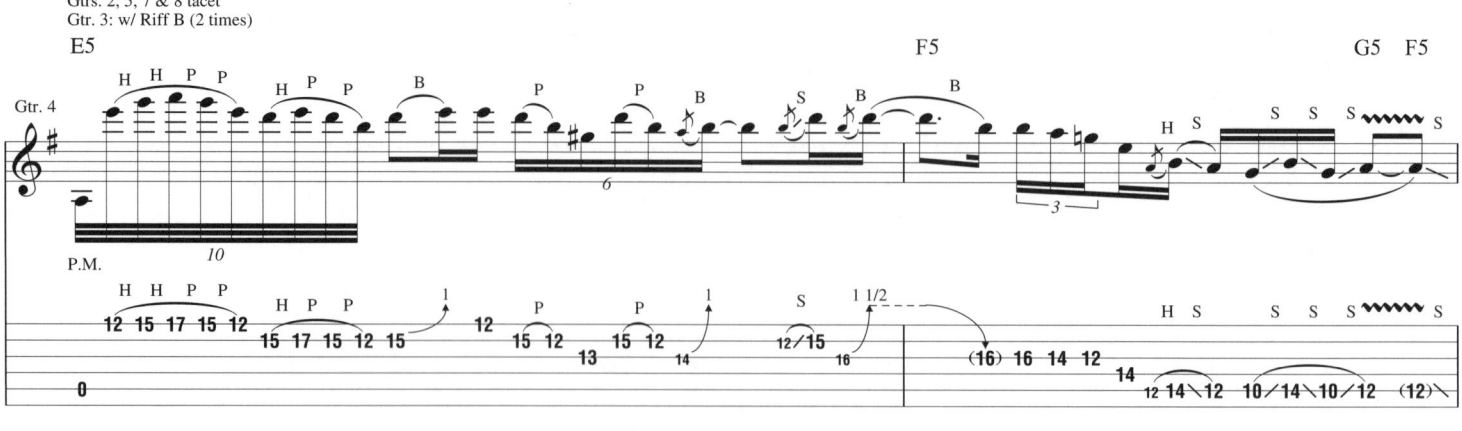
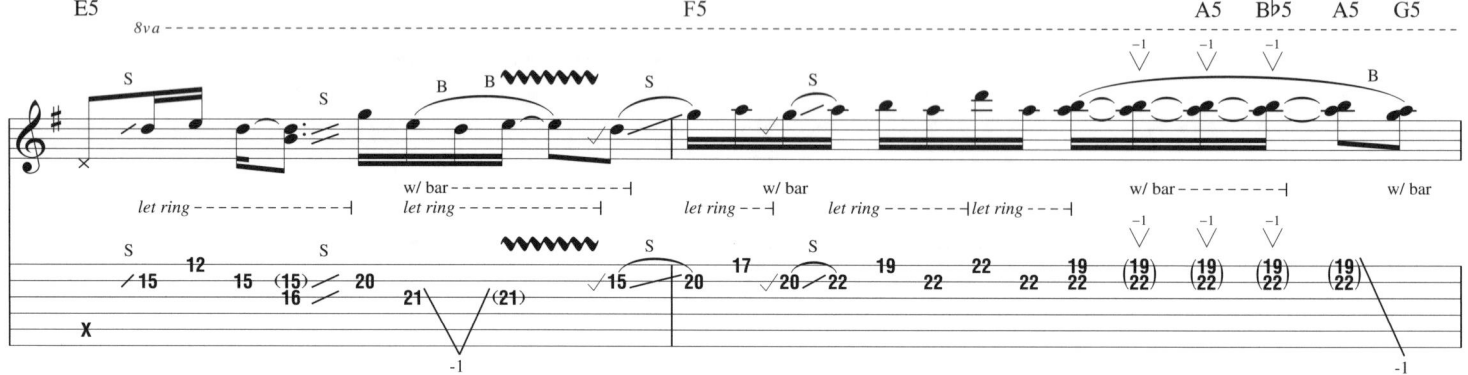
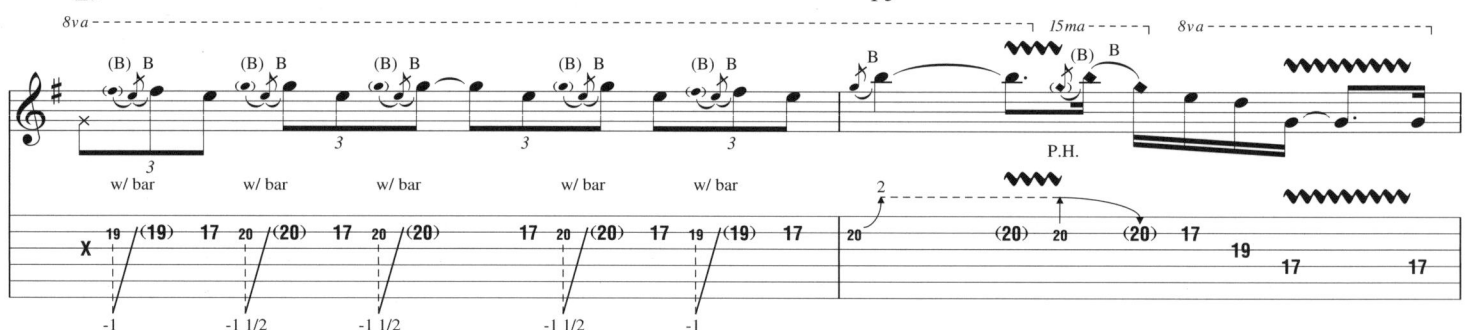
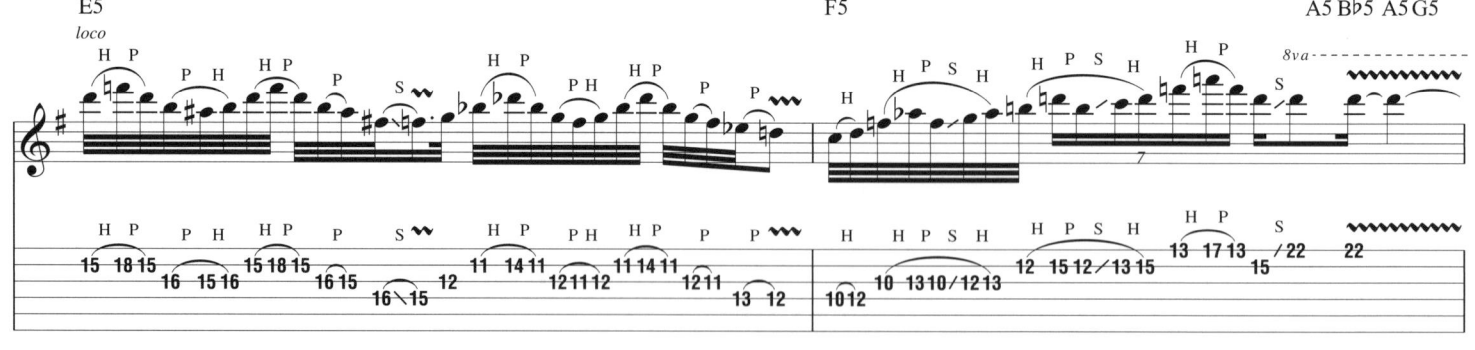
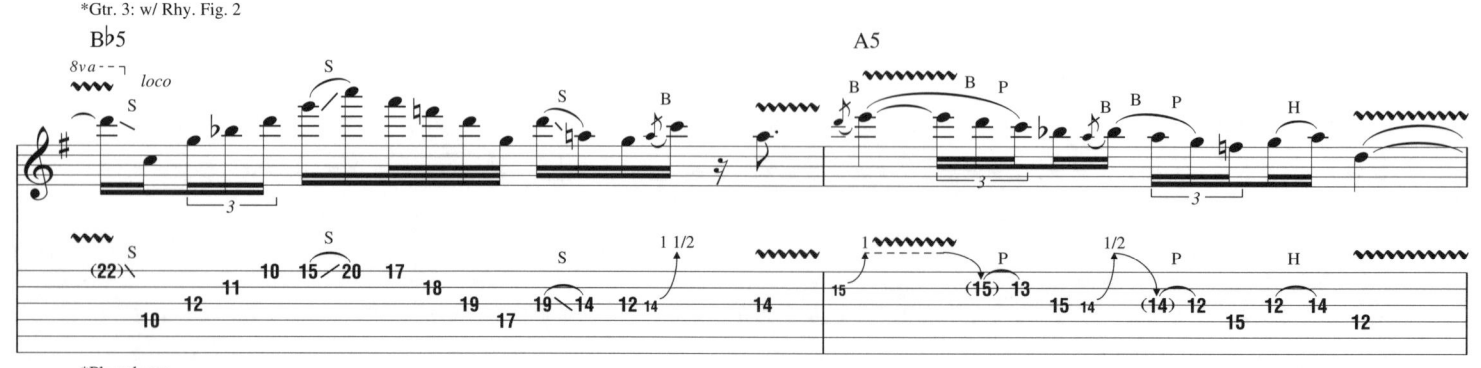

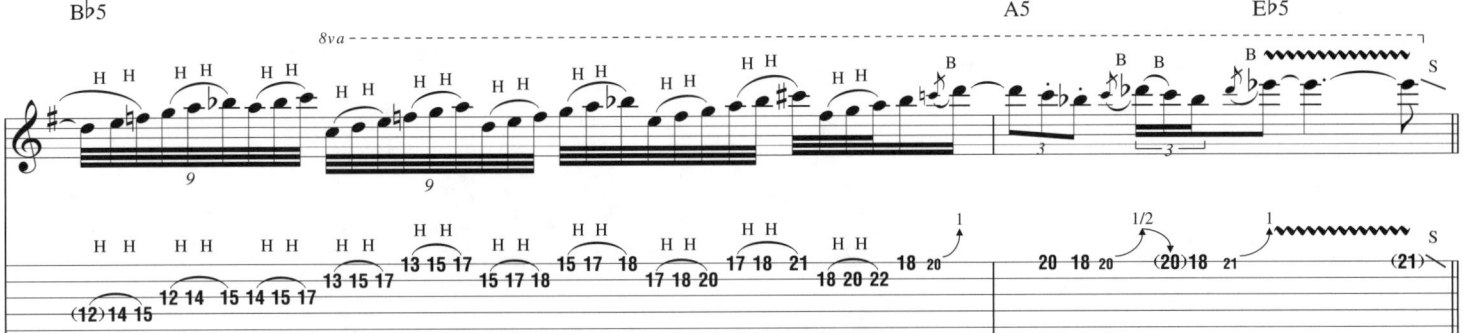

G

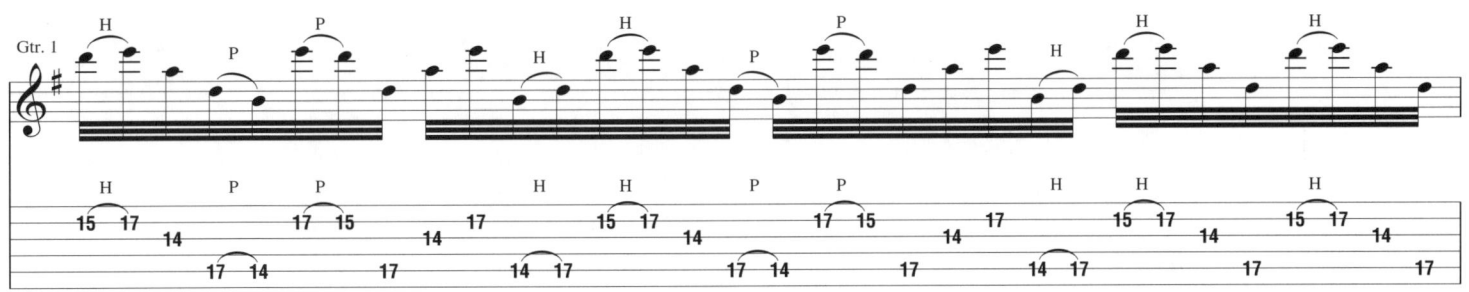

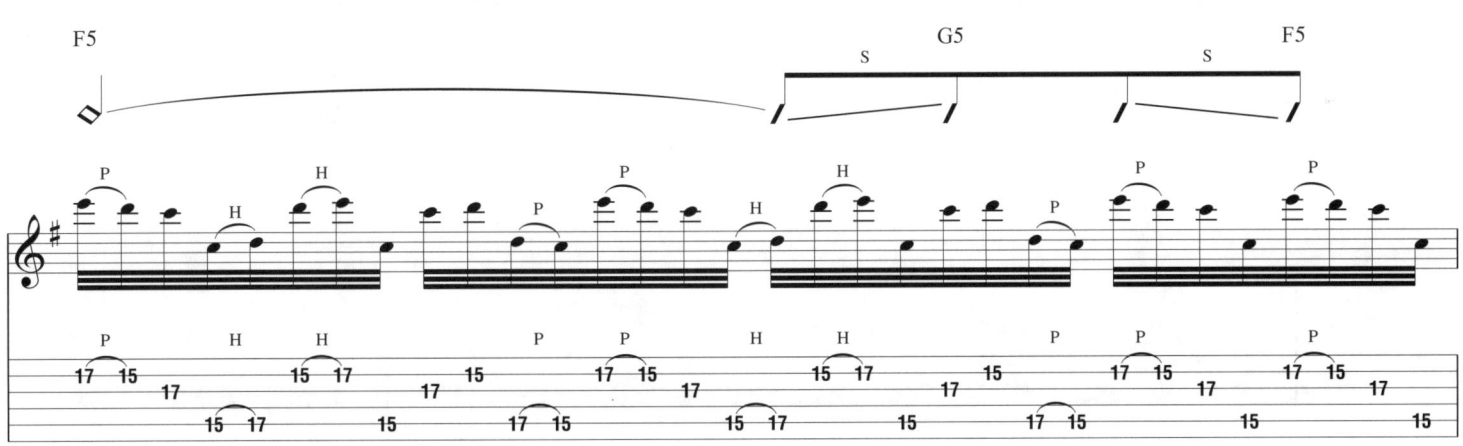

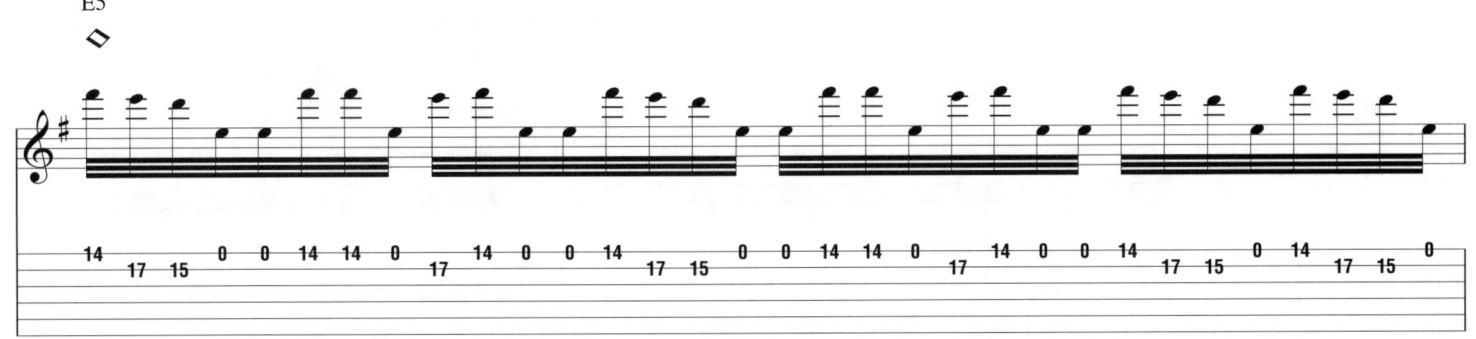

17

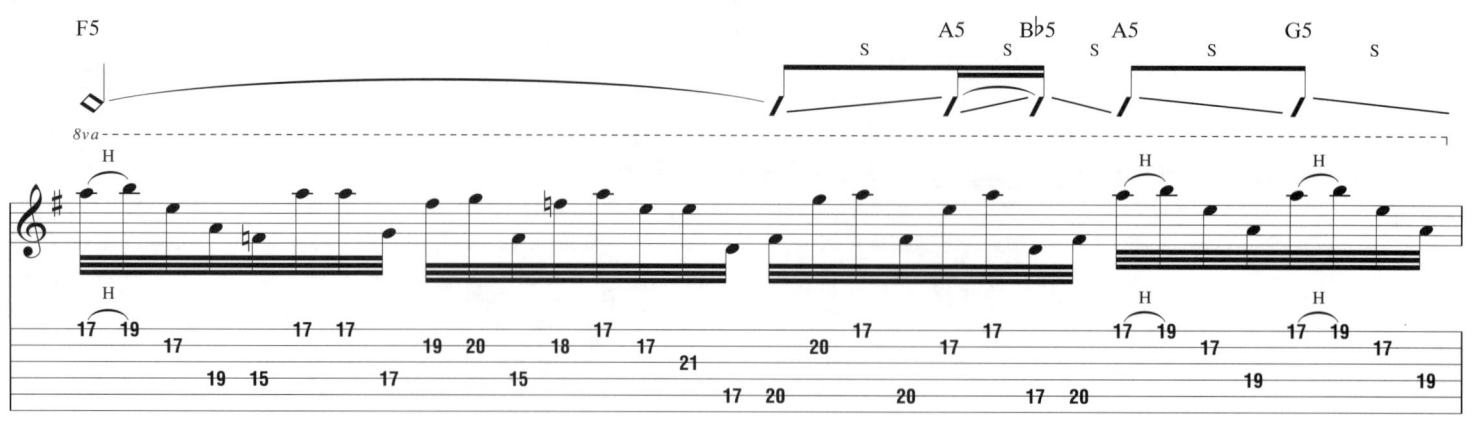
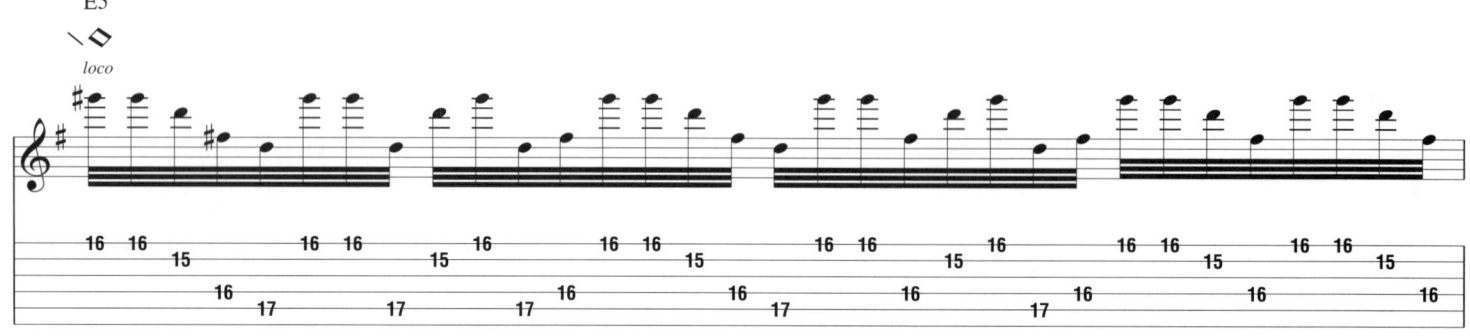
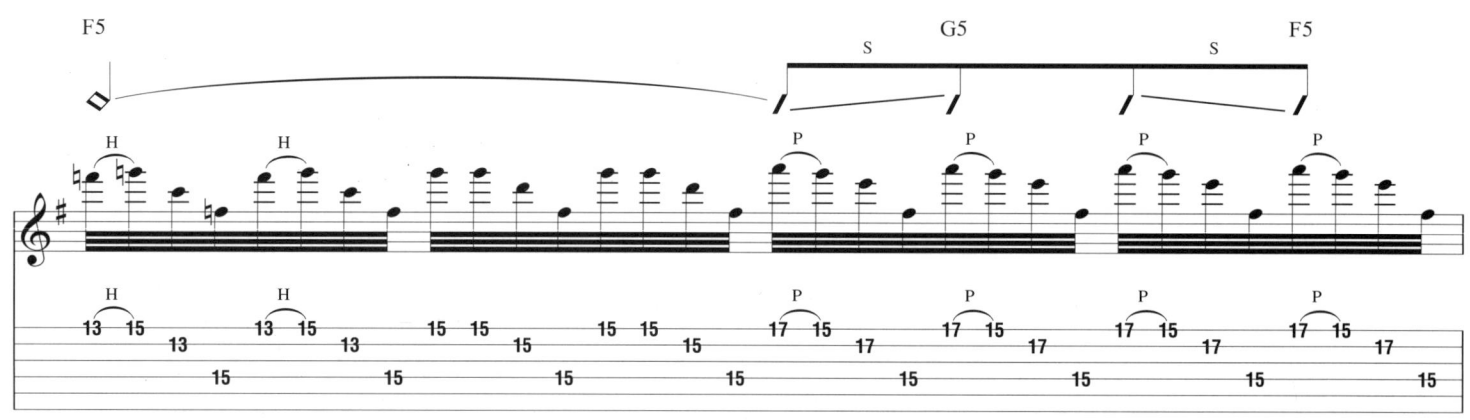
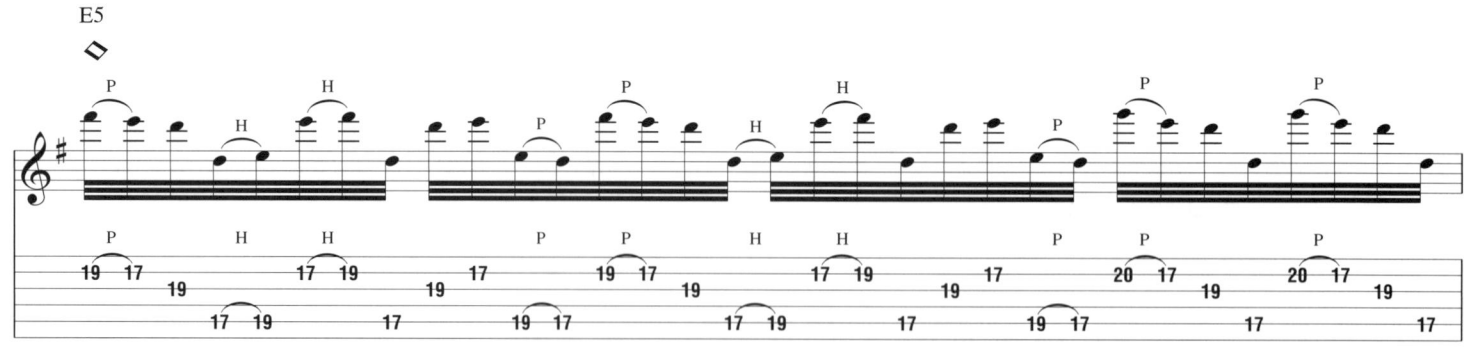
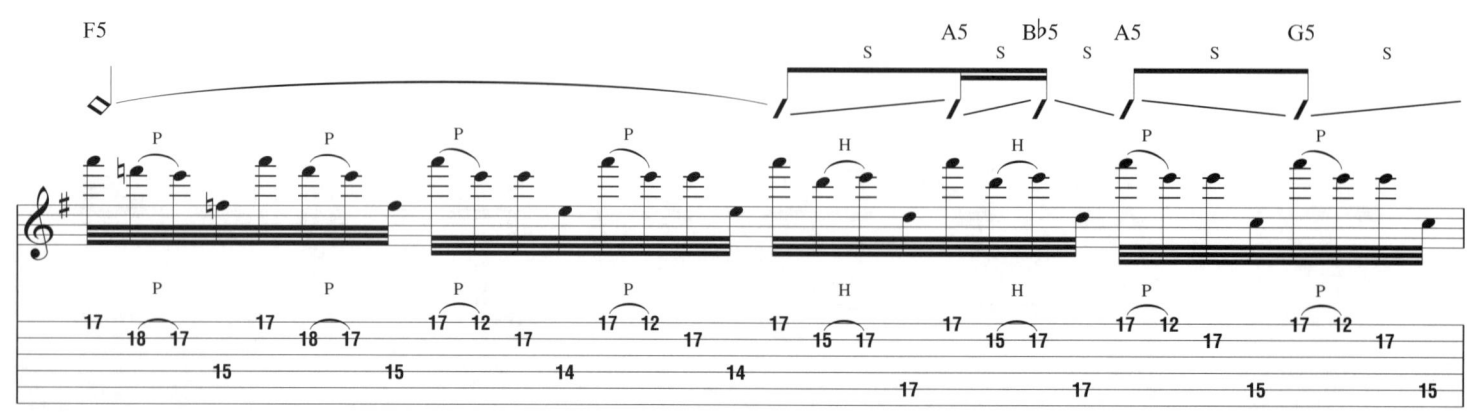

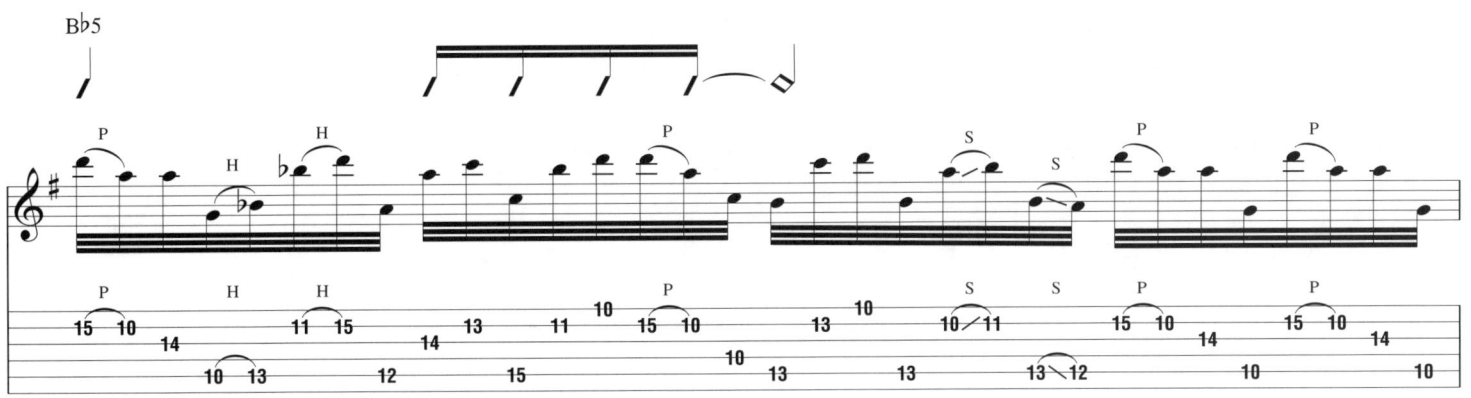

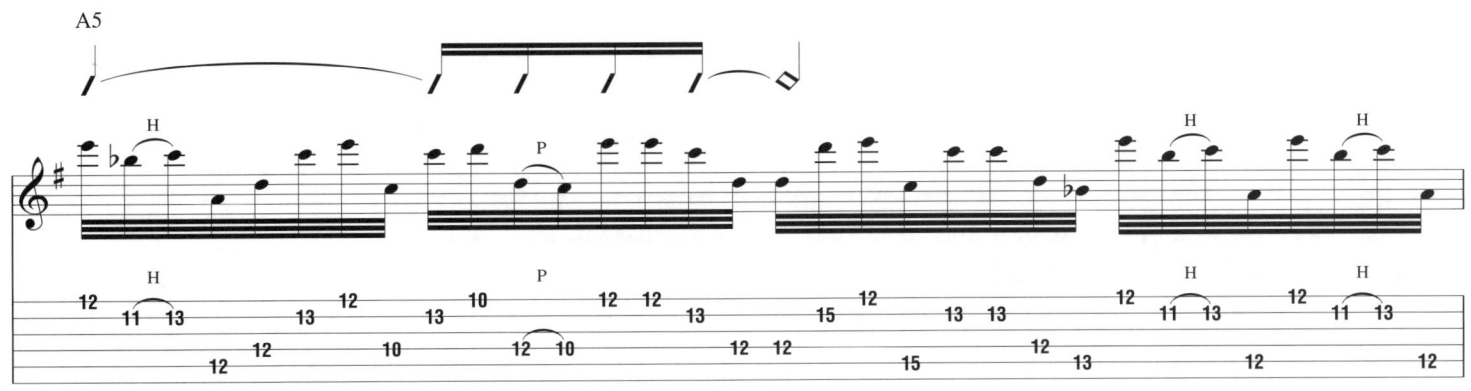

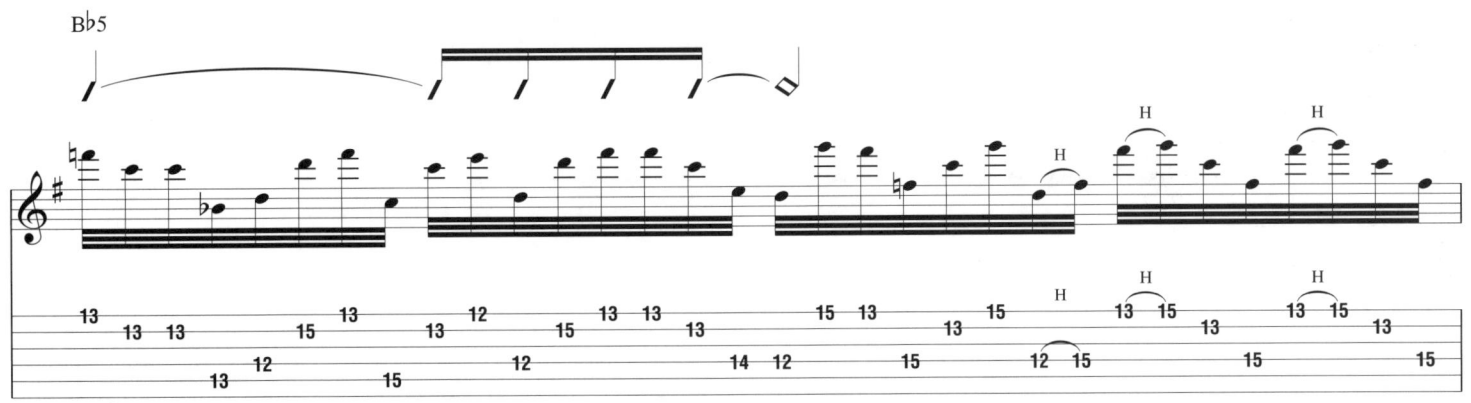

D.S. al Coda

⊕ **Coda**

Gtrs. 2 & 3: w/ Rhy. Fig. 4
Gtrs. 5, 7 & 8: w/ Riffs C, C1 & C2

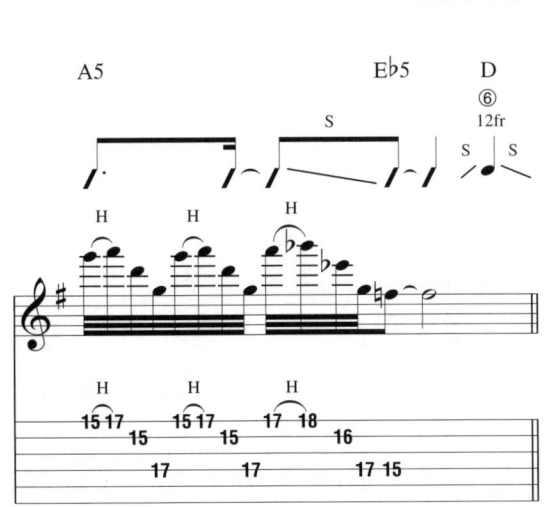

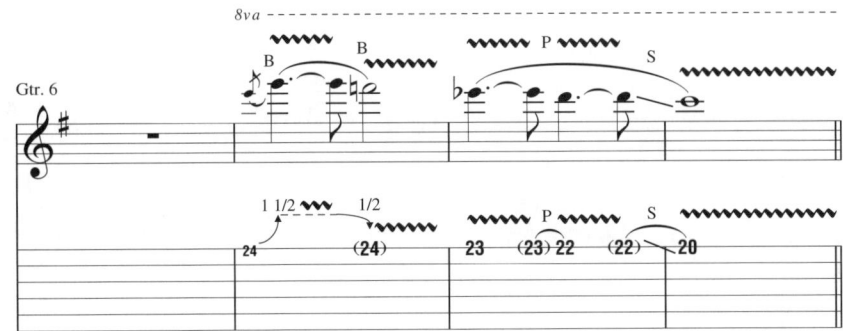

19

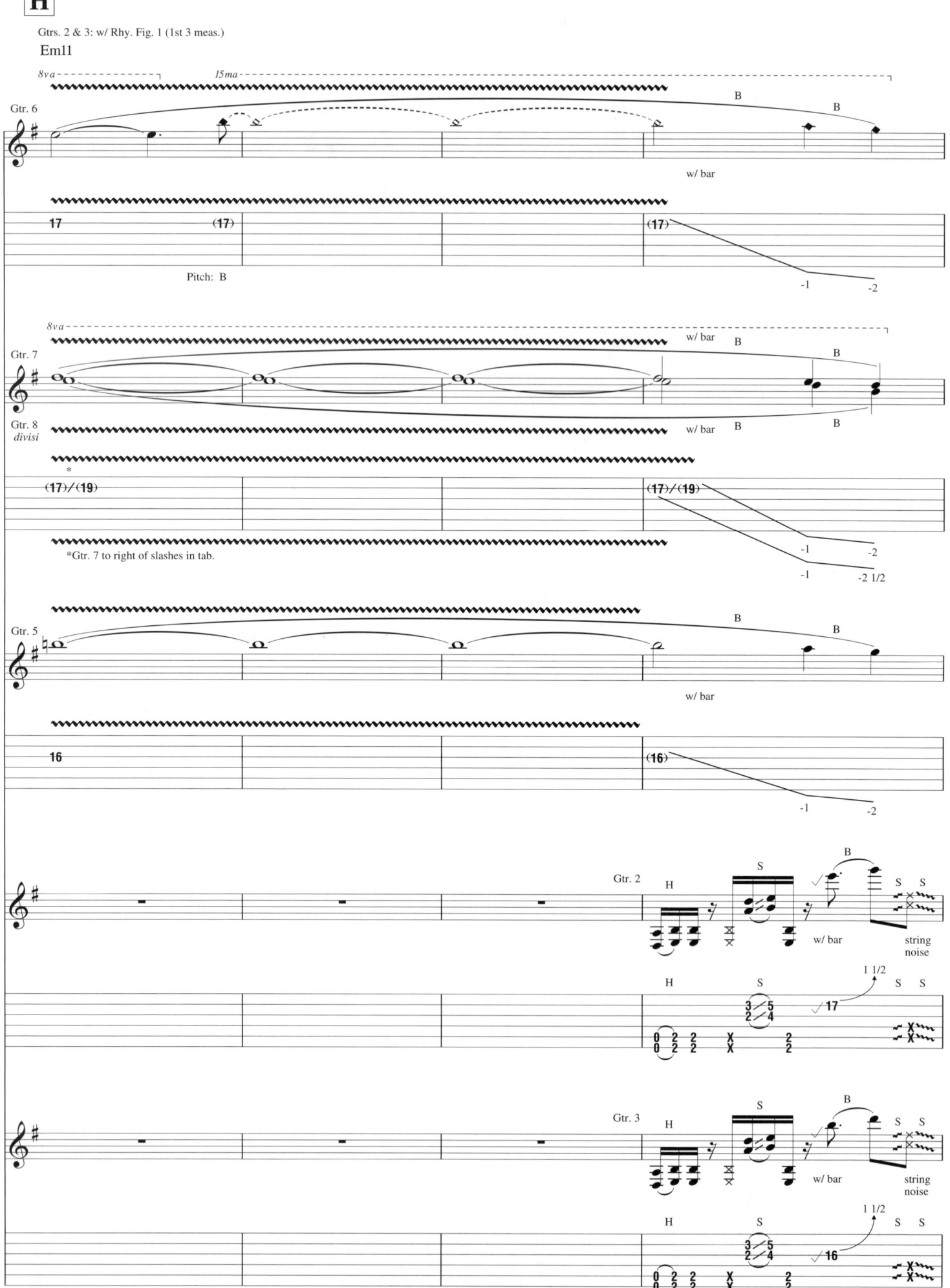

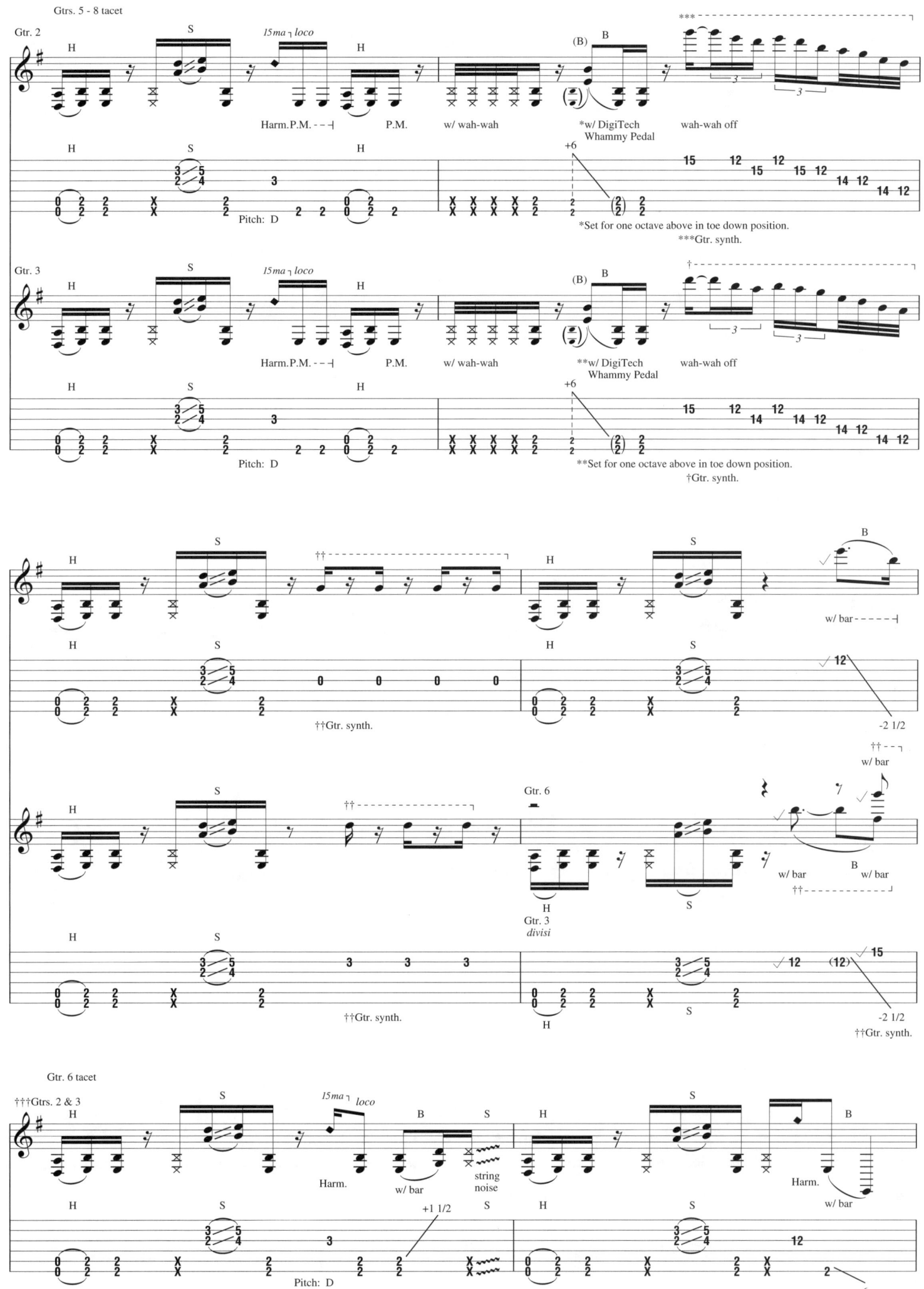

Dying for Your Love
By Steve Vai

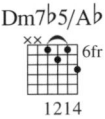

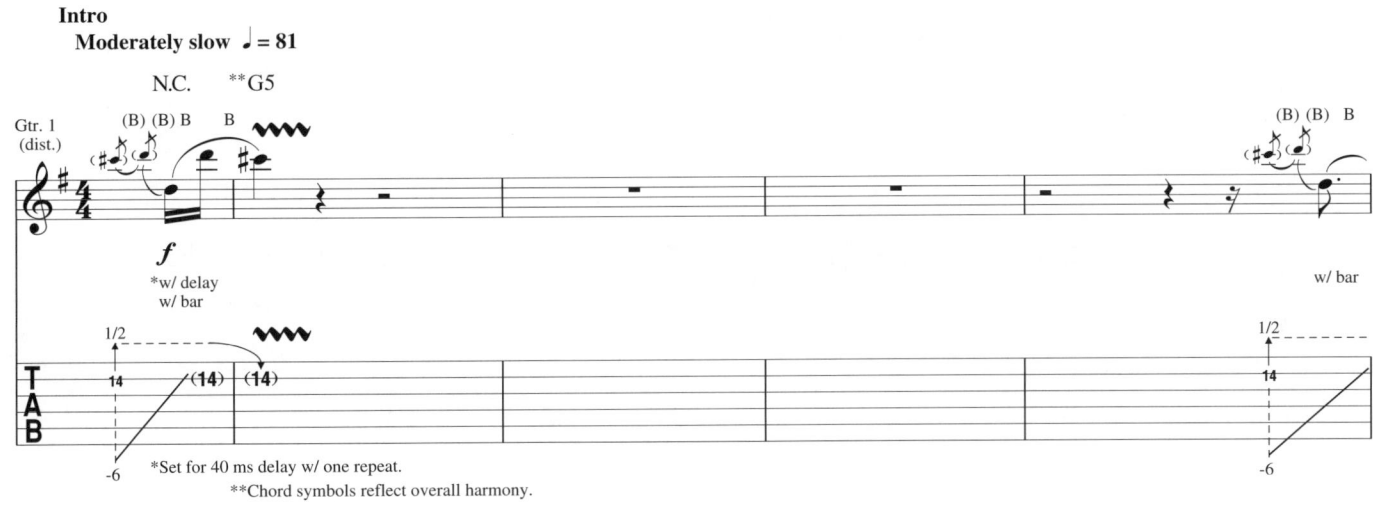

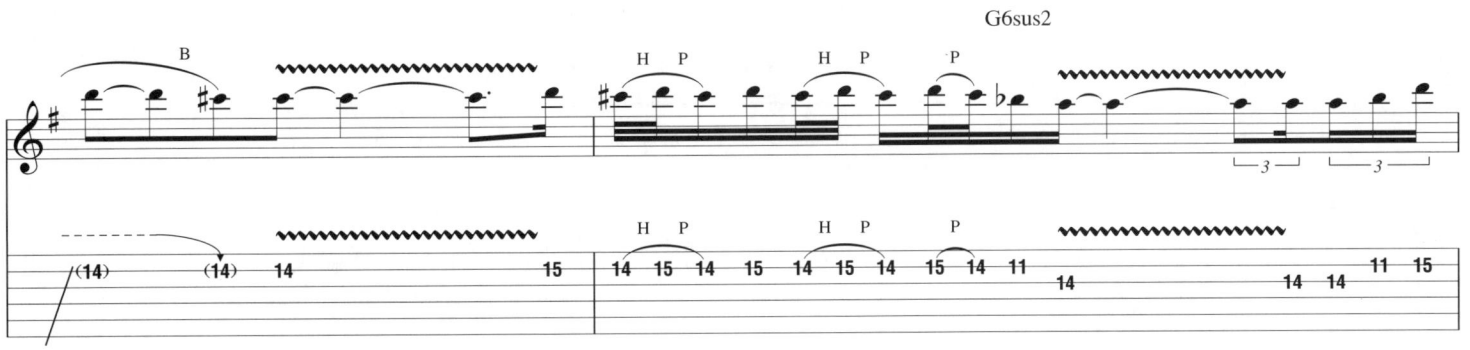

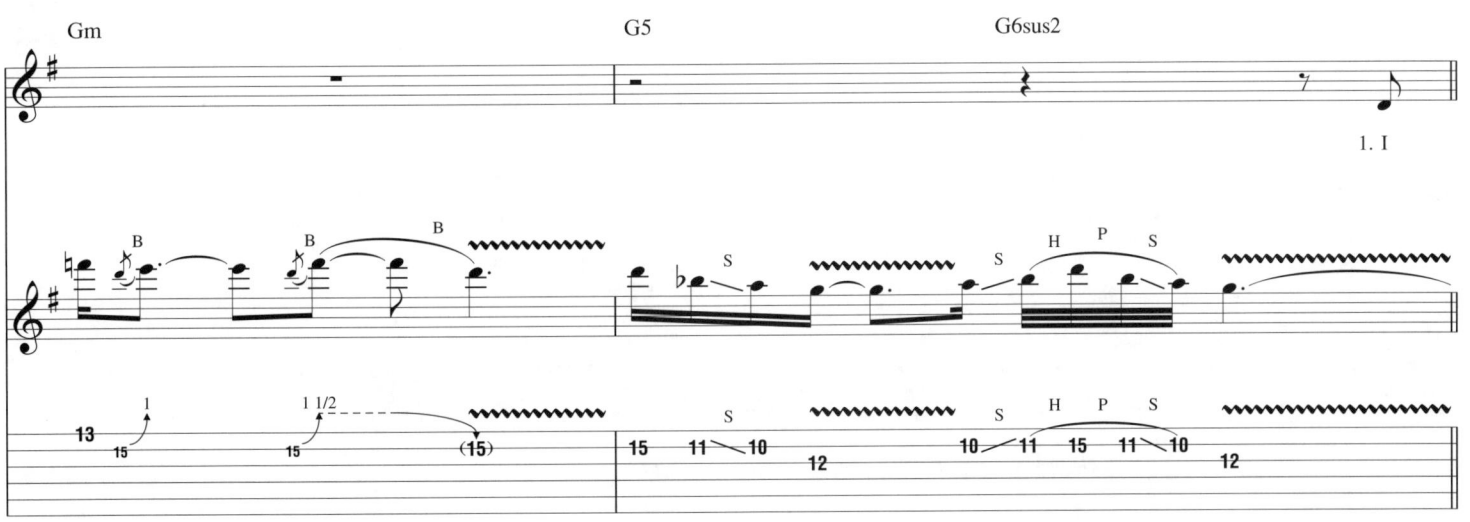

Copyright © 2005 Sy Vy Music (ASCAP)
International Copyright Secured   All Rights Reserved

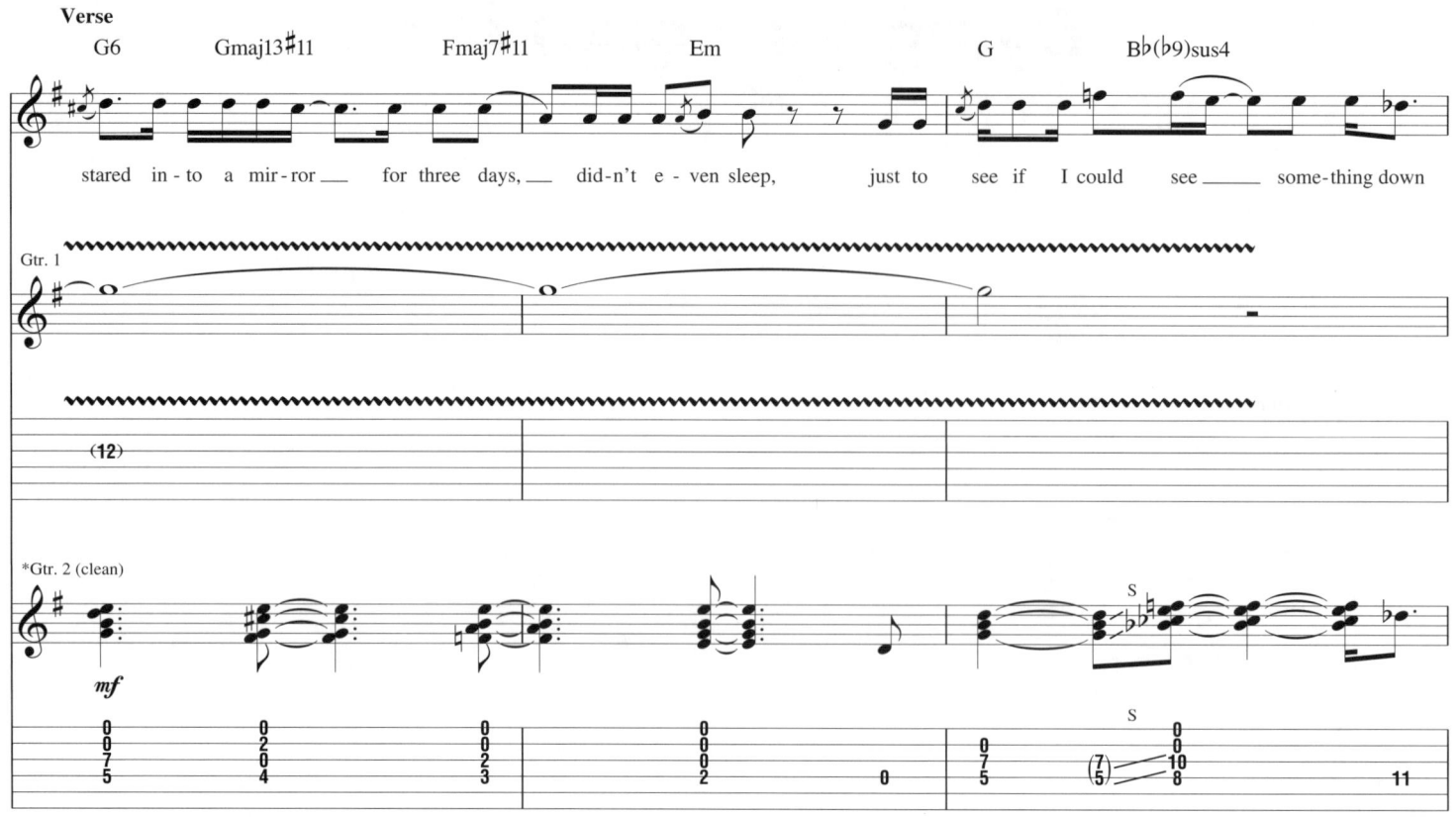
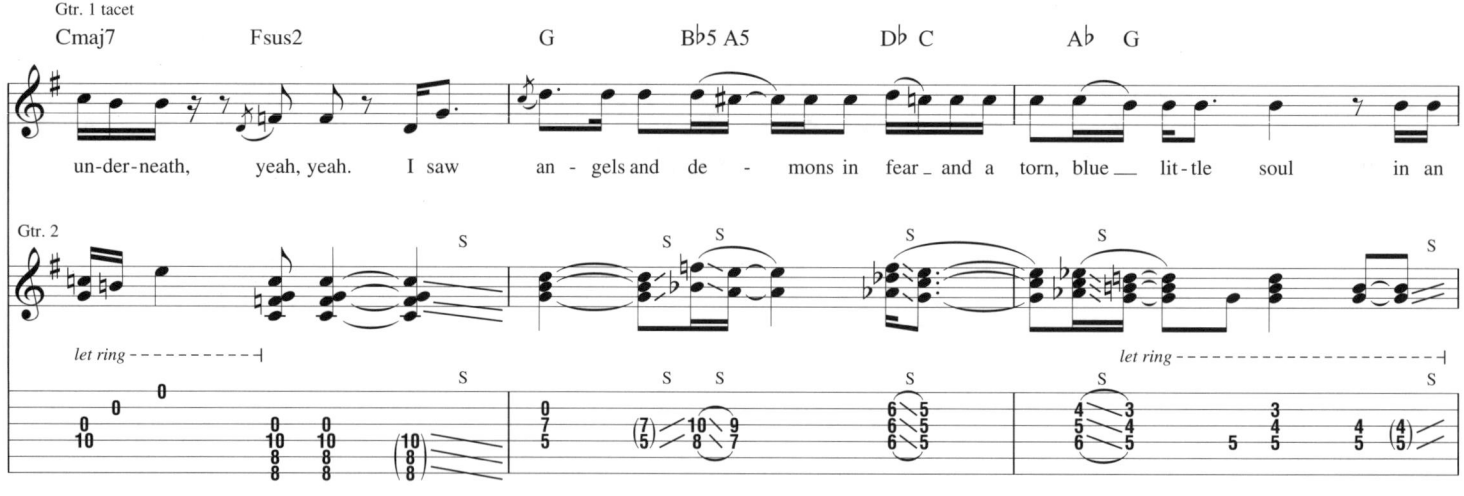
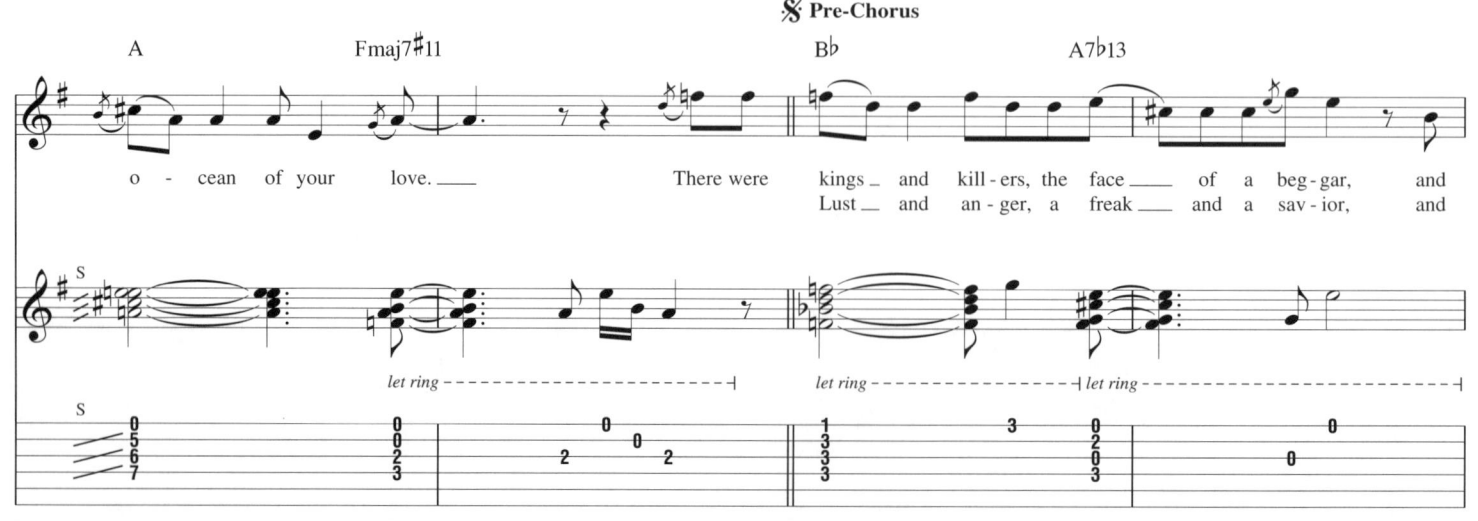

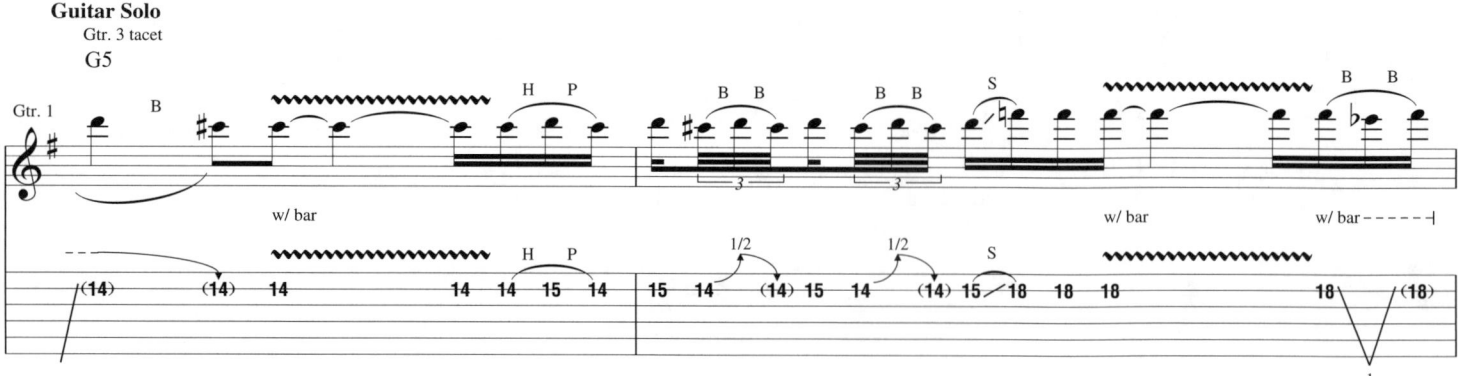
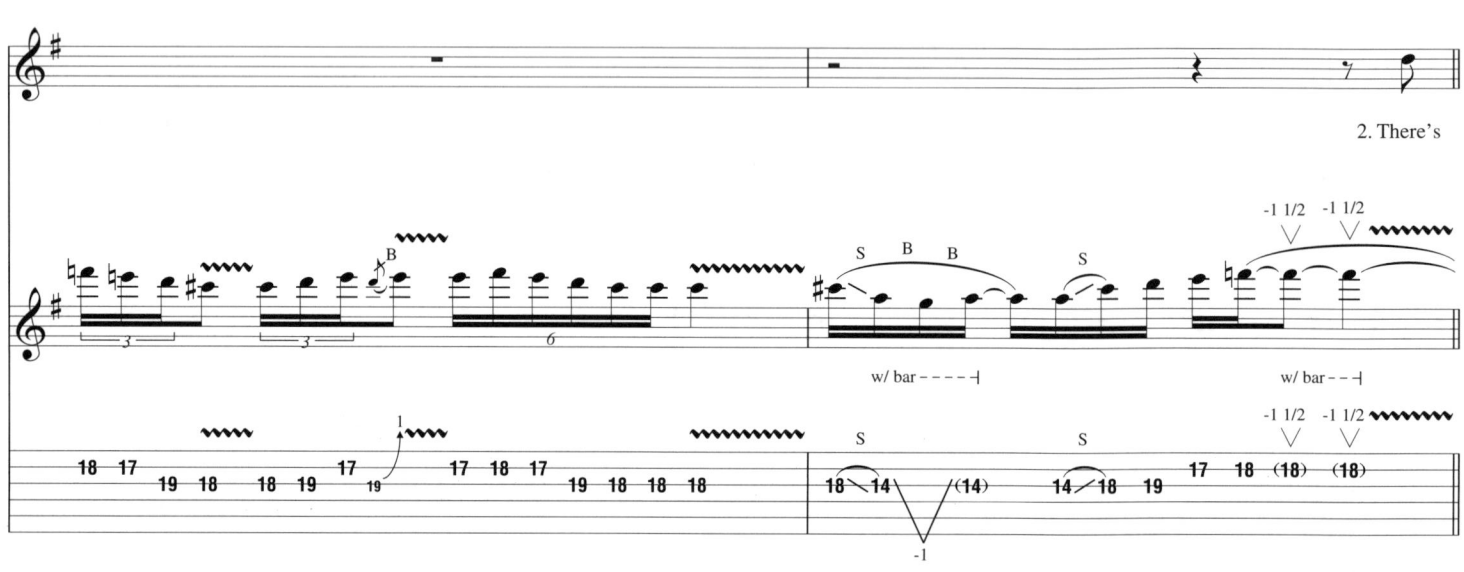
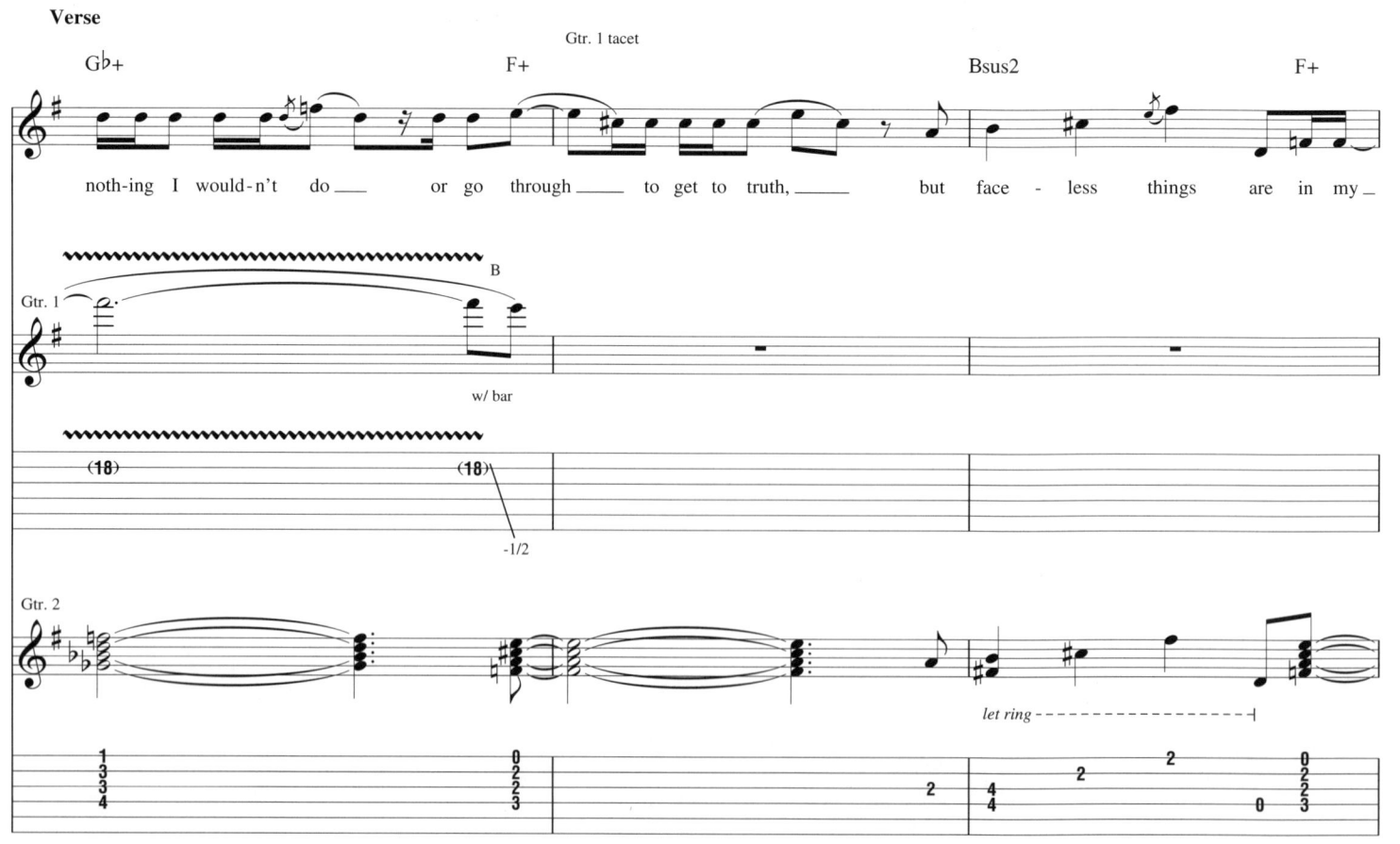

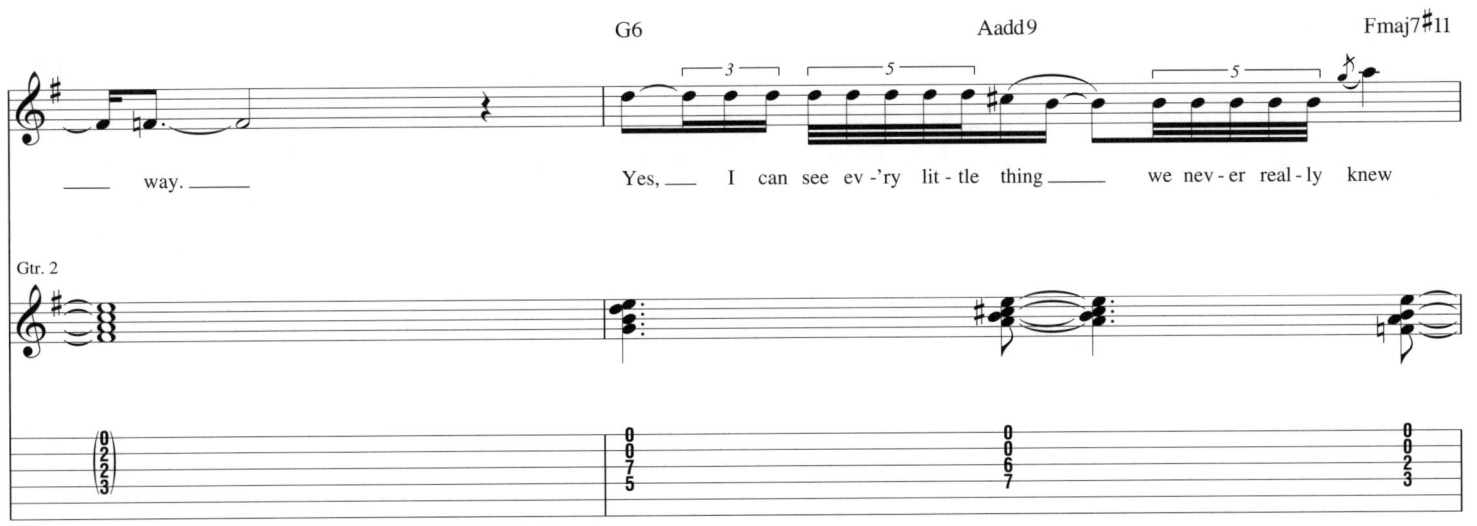

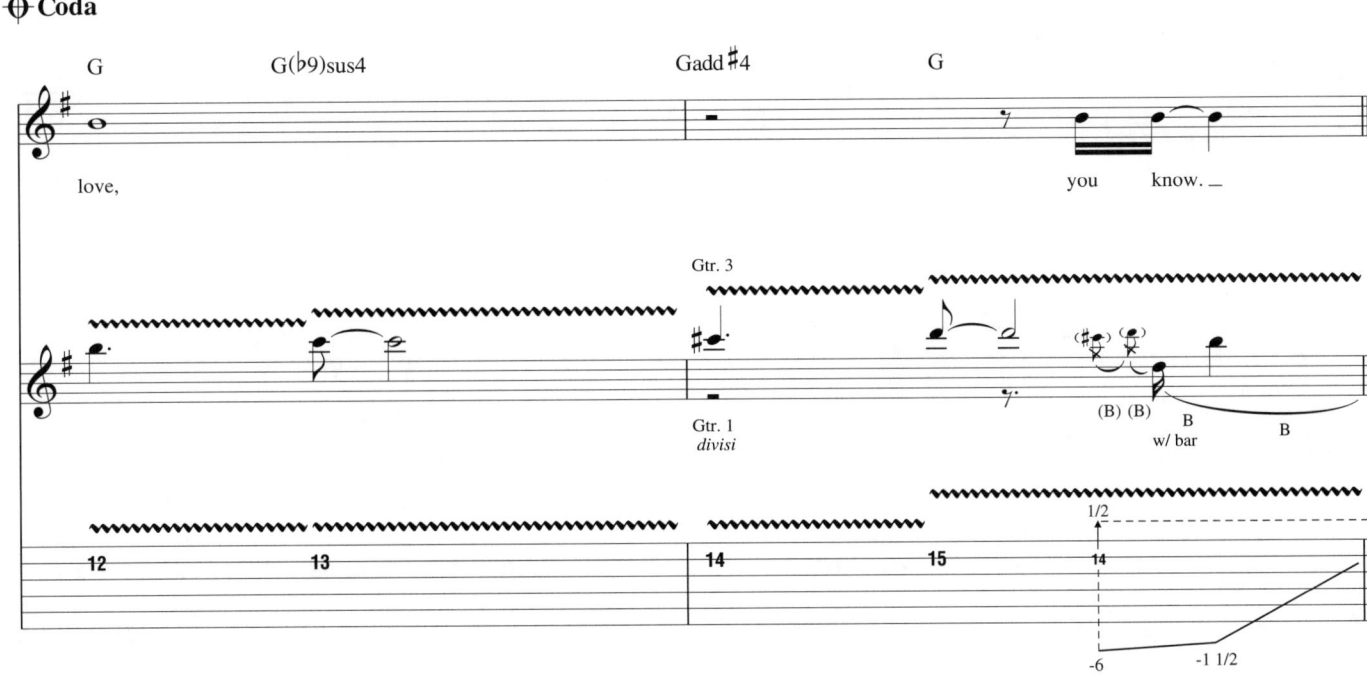

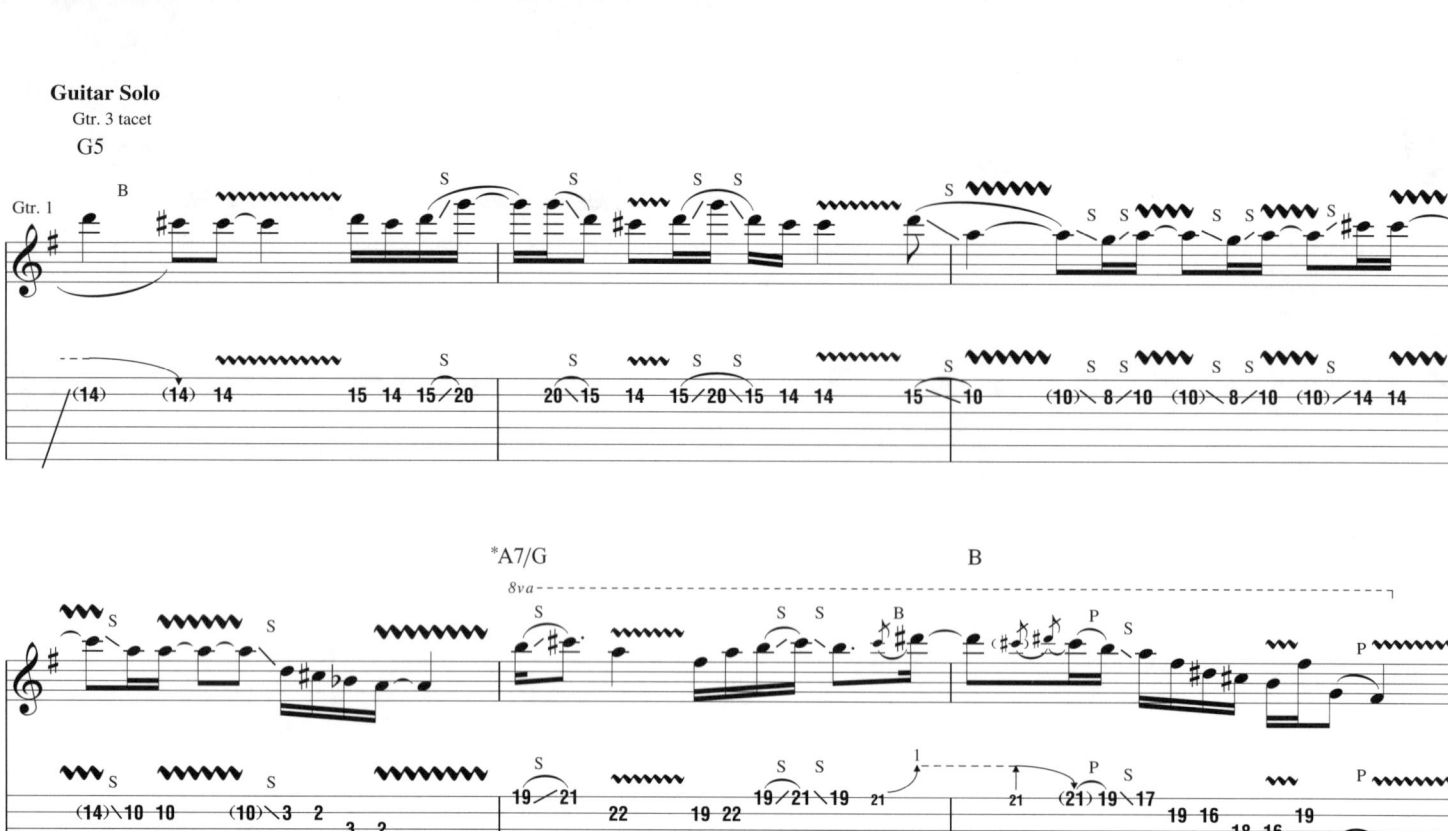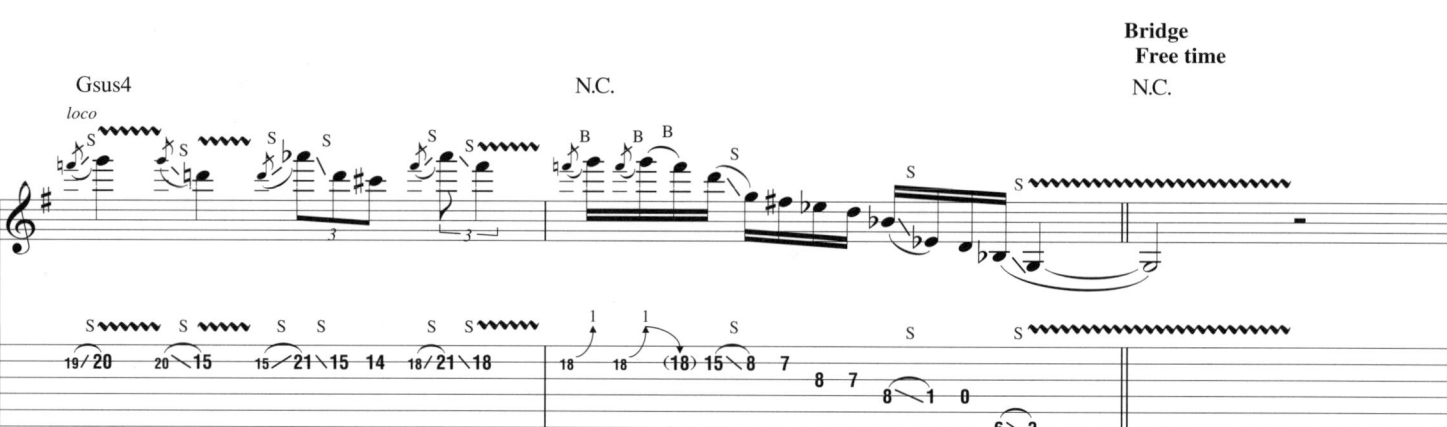

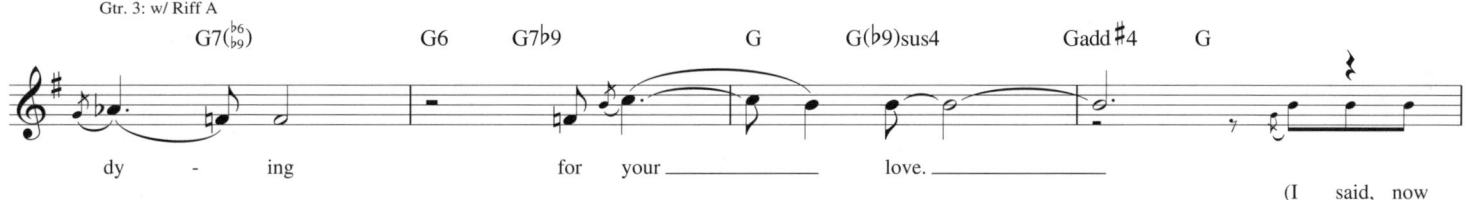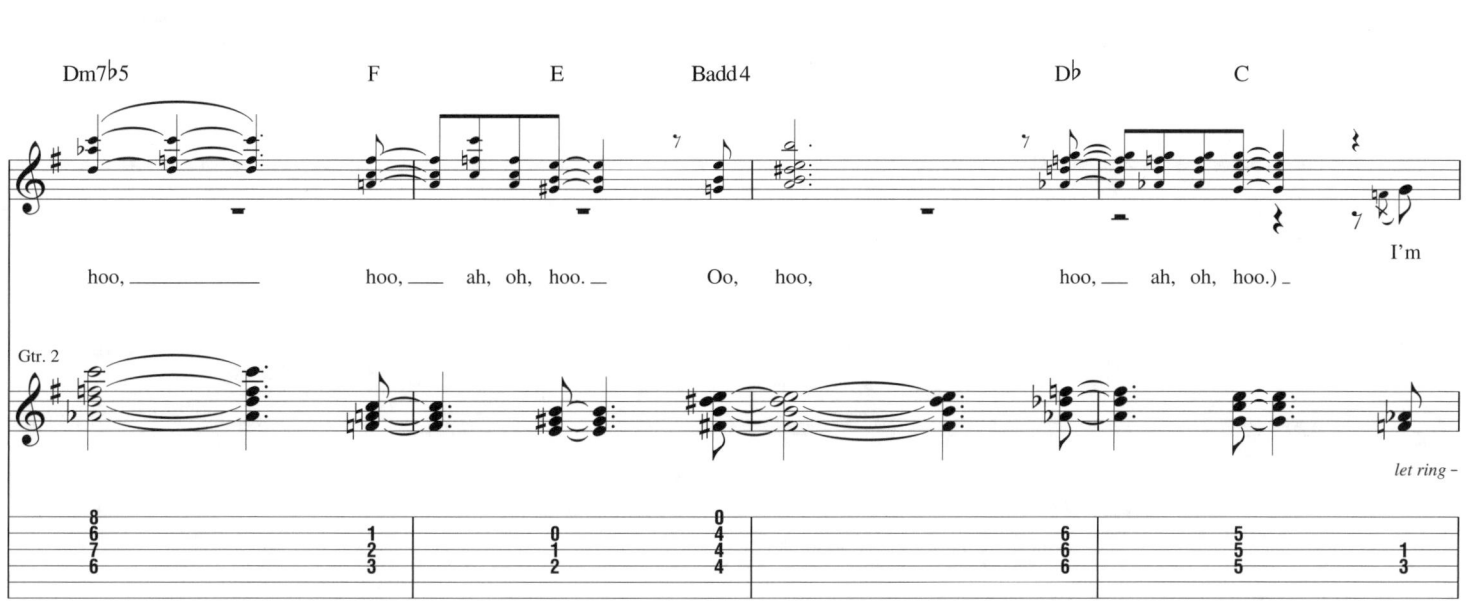

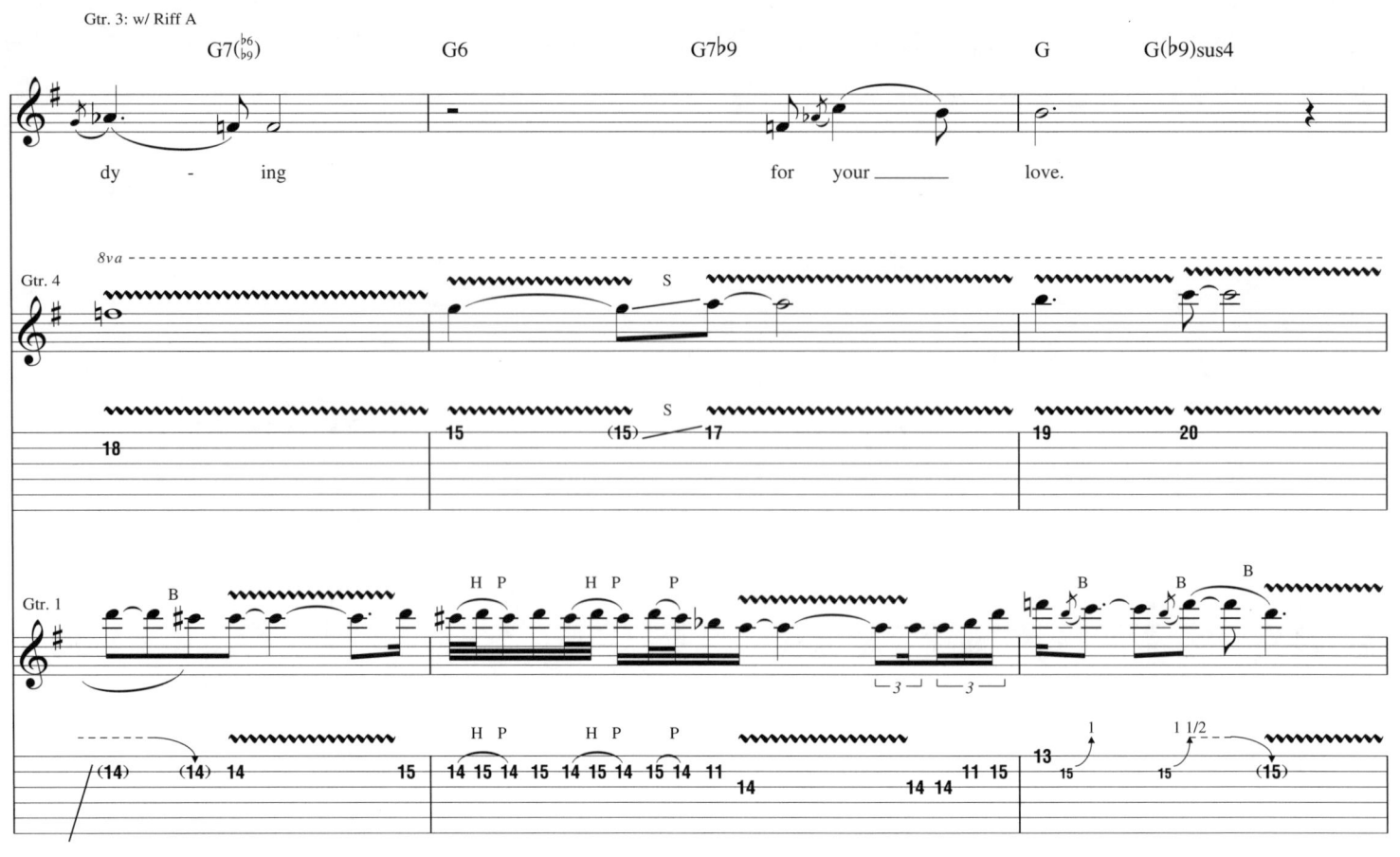

Glorious

By Steve Vai

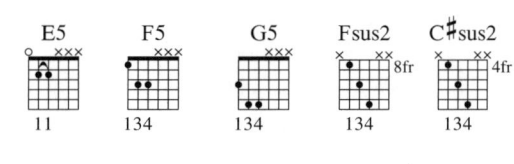

Tune down 1 step:
(low to high) D-G-C-F-A-D

Fast ♩ = 200

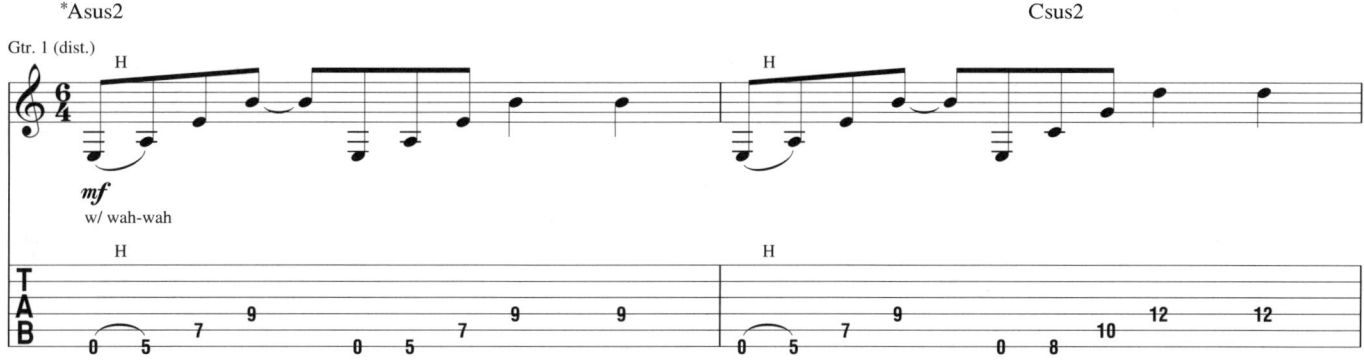

*Chord symbols reflect implied harmony.

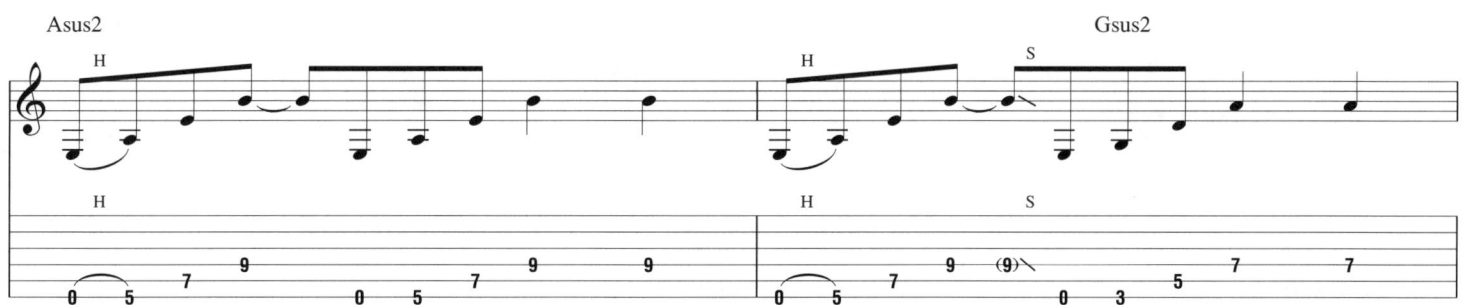

Gtr. 1 tacet

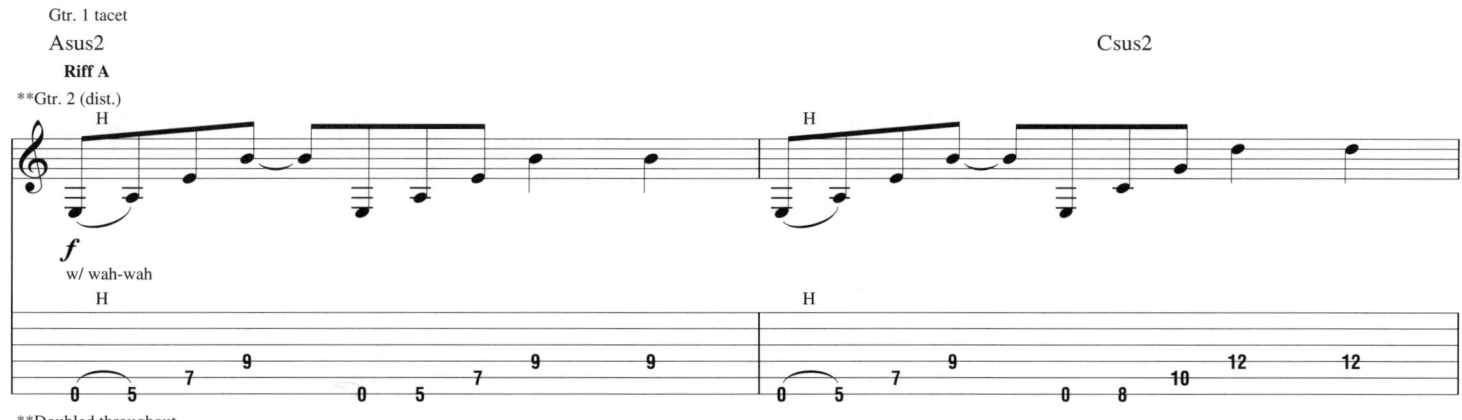

**Doubled throughout

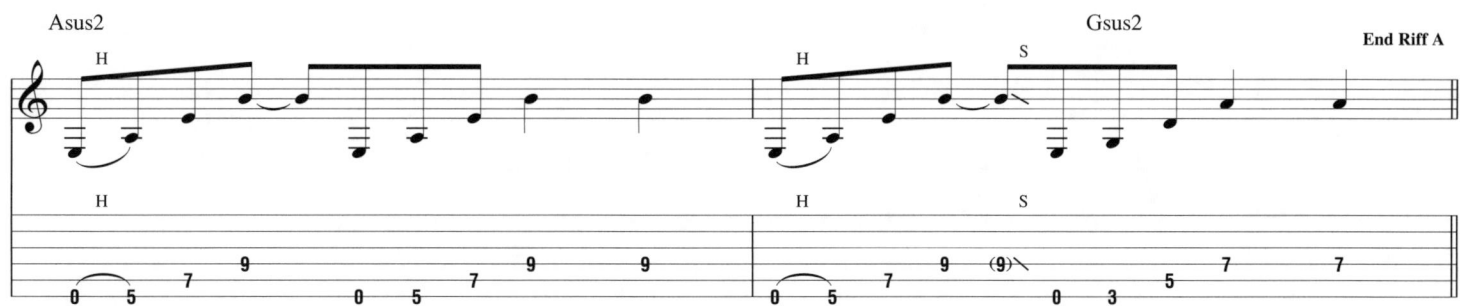

Copyright © 2005 Sy Vy Music (ASCAP)
International Copyright Secured   All Rights Reserved

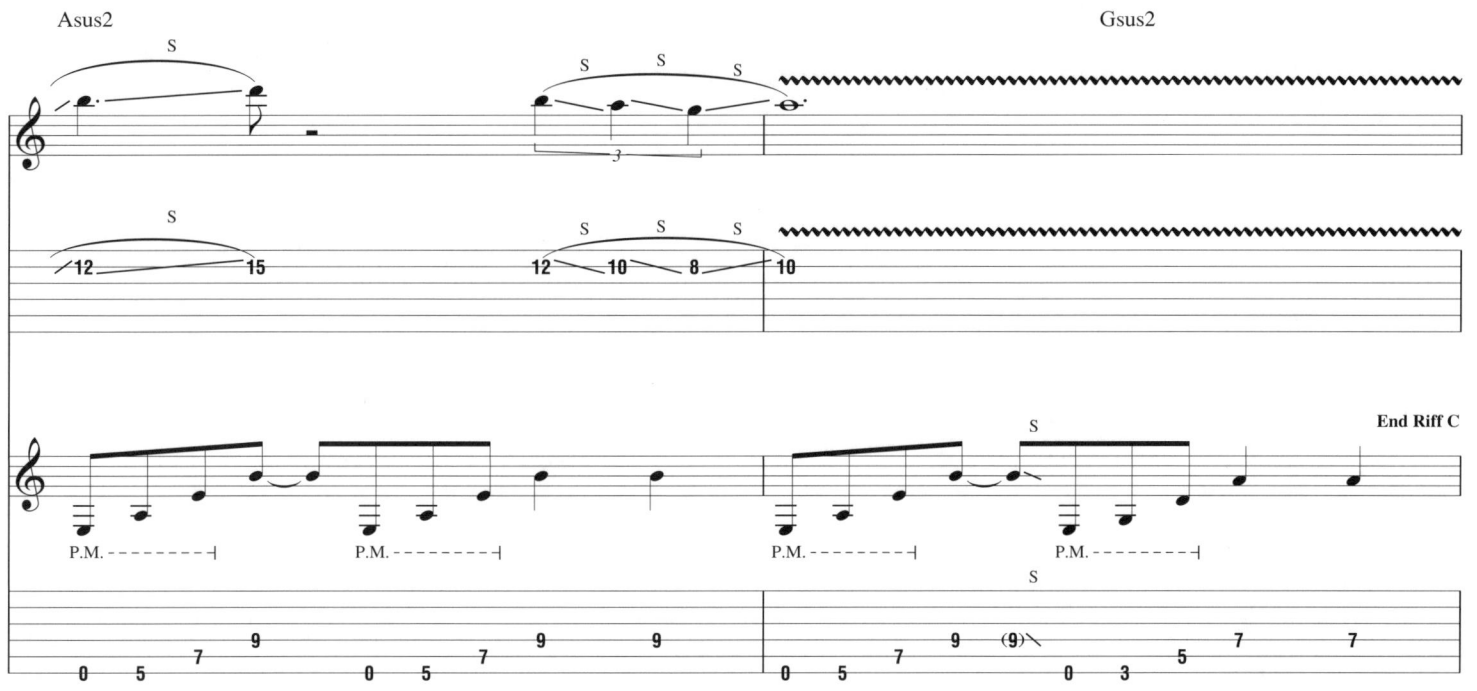
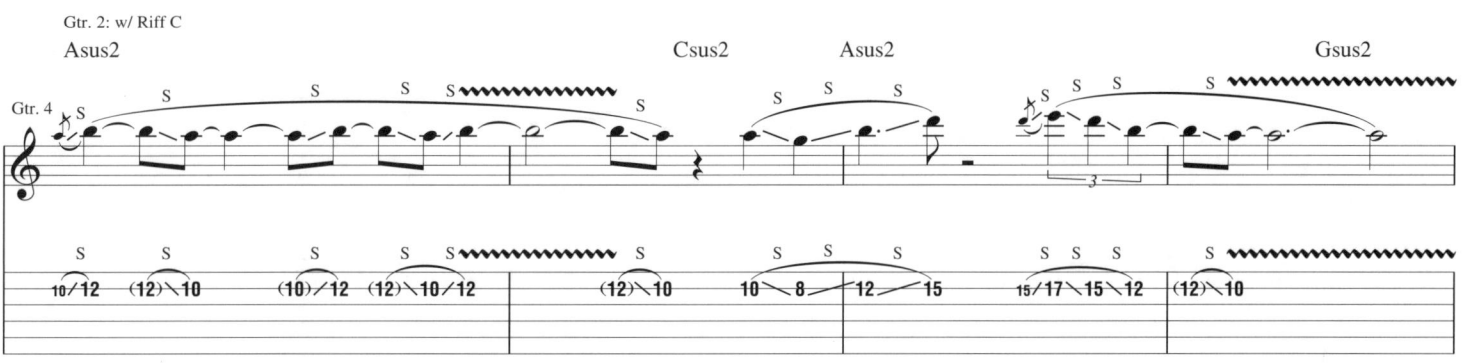
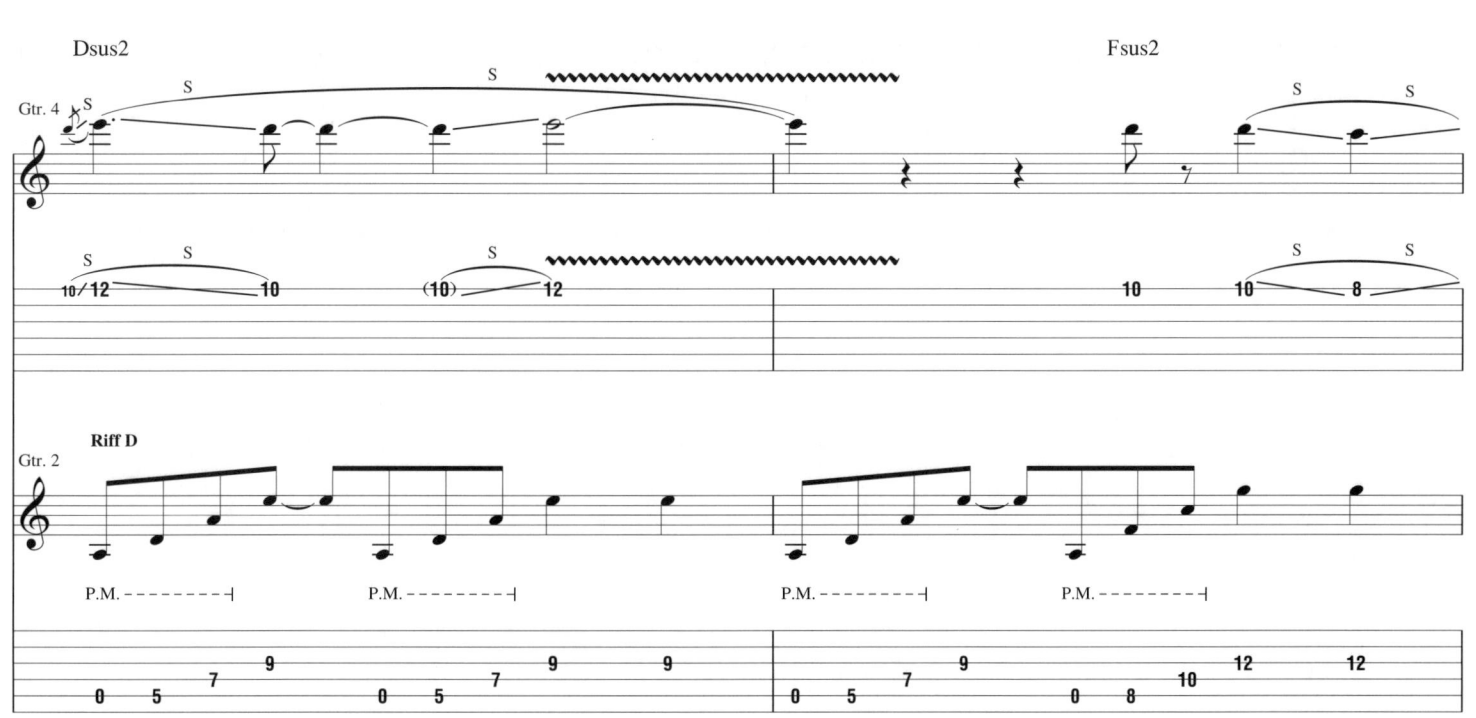

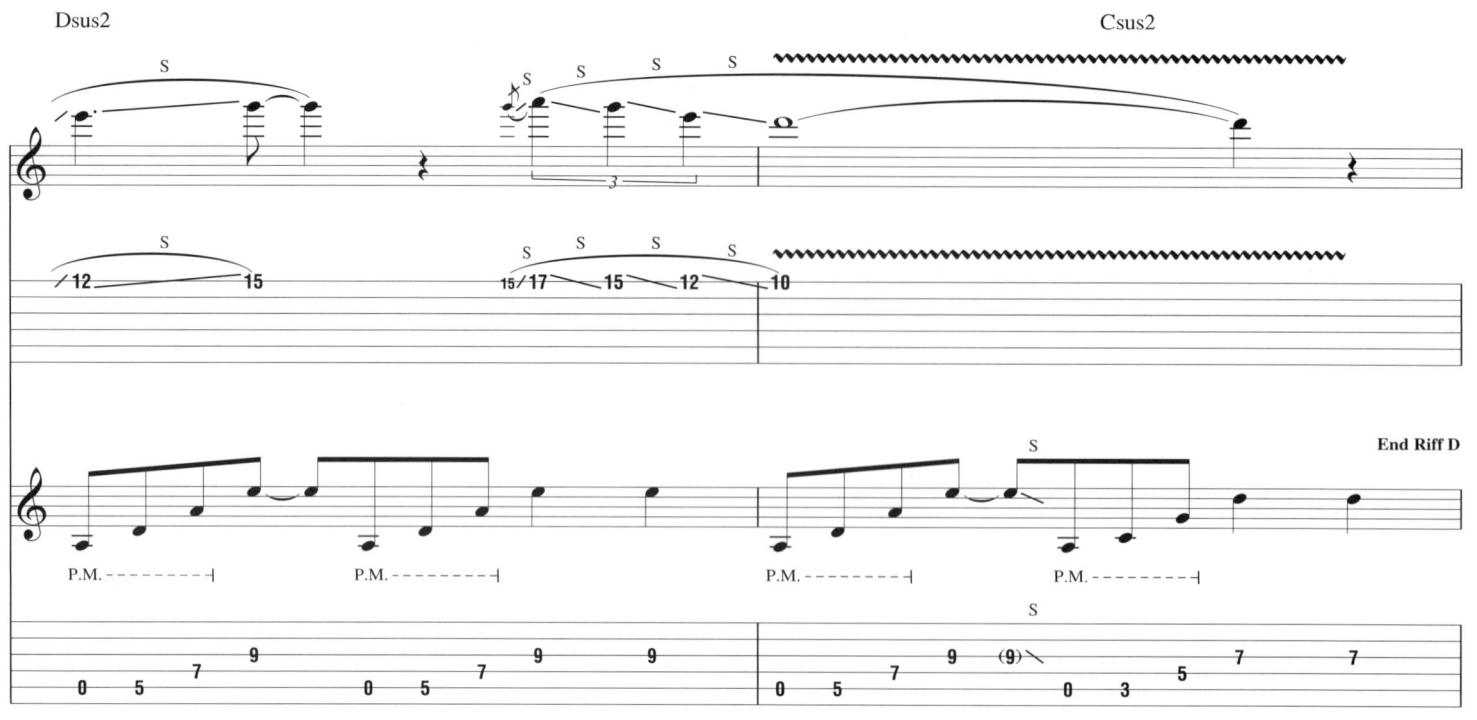
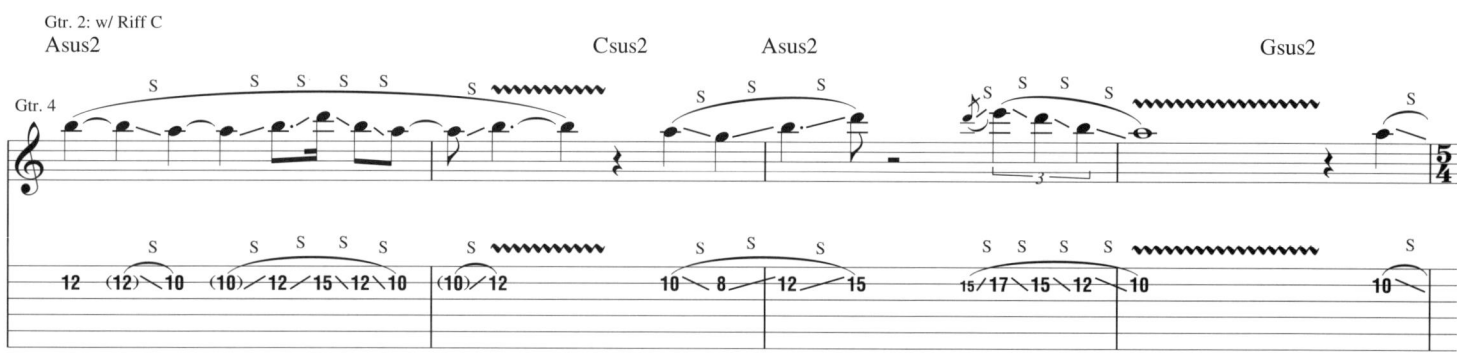
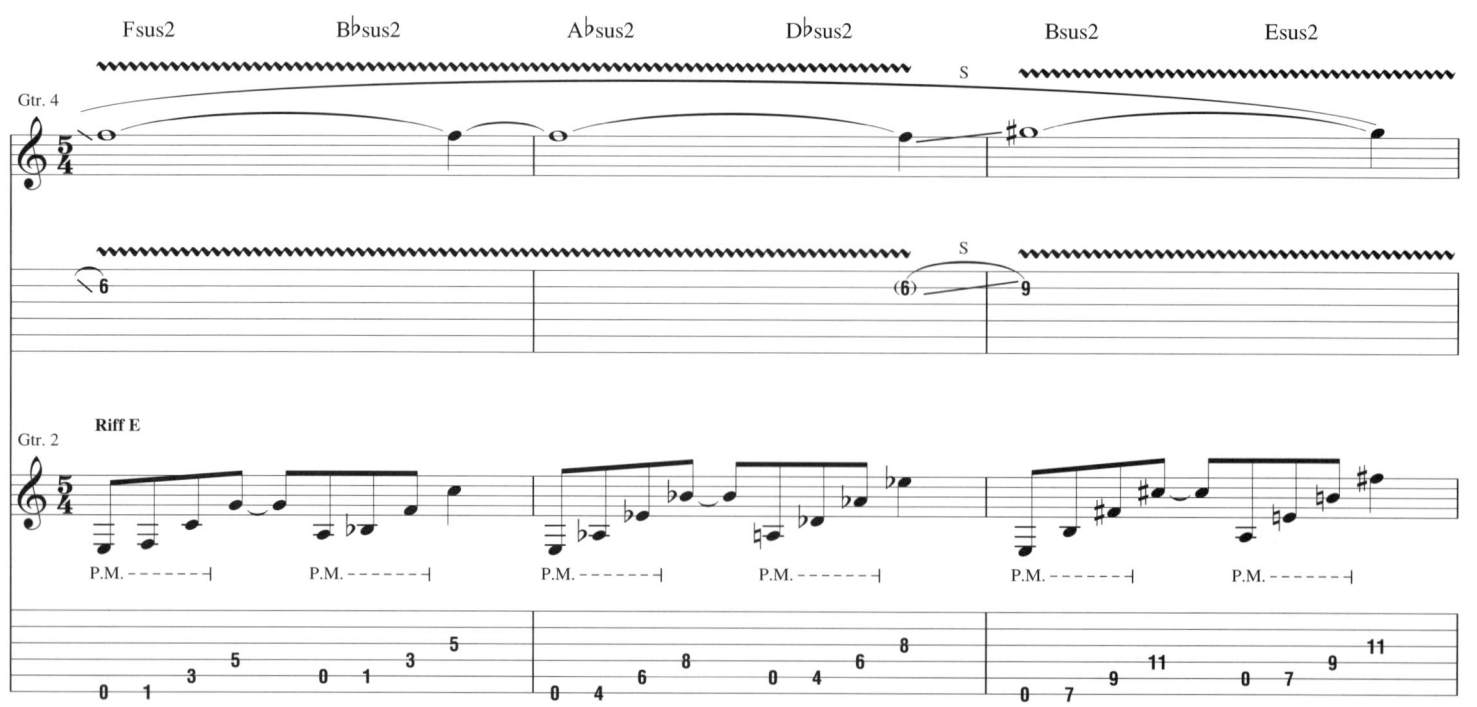

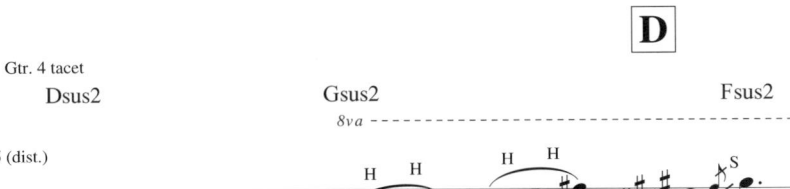

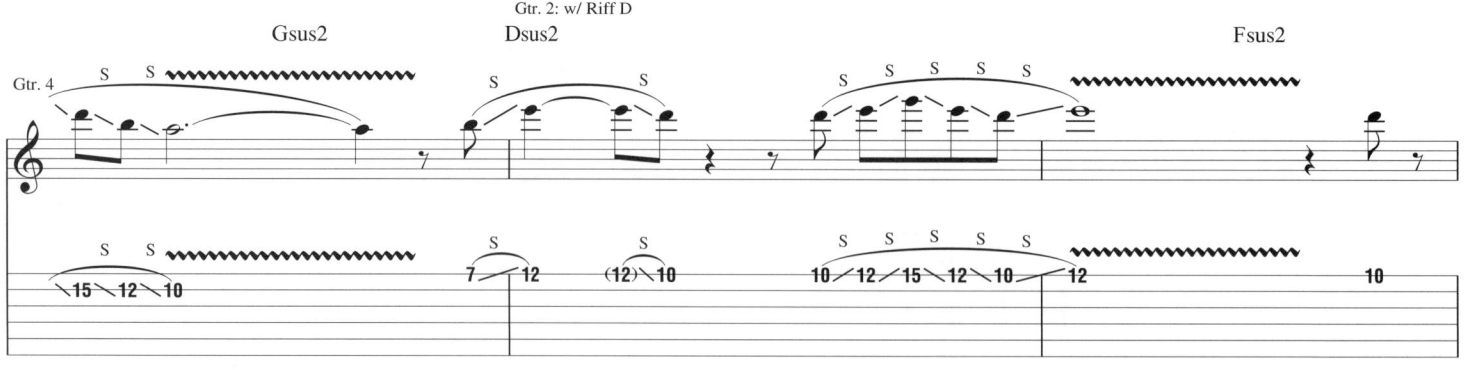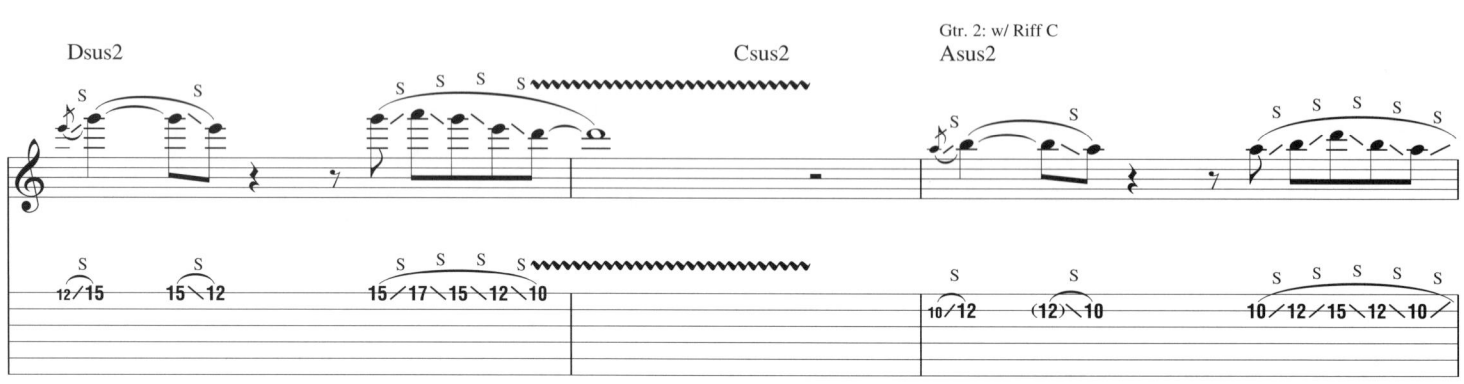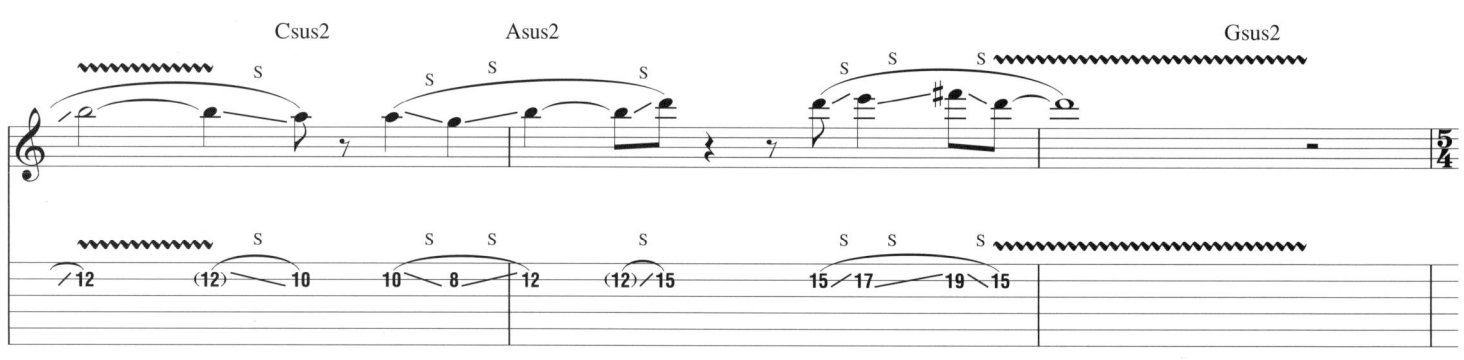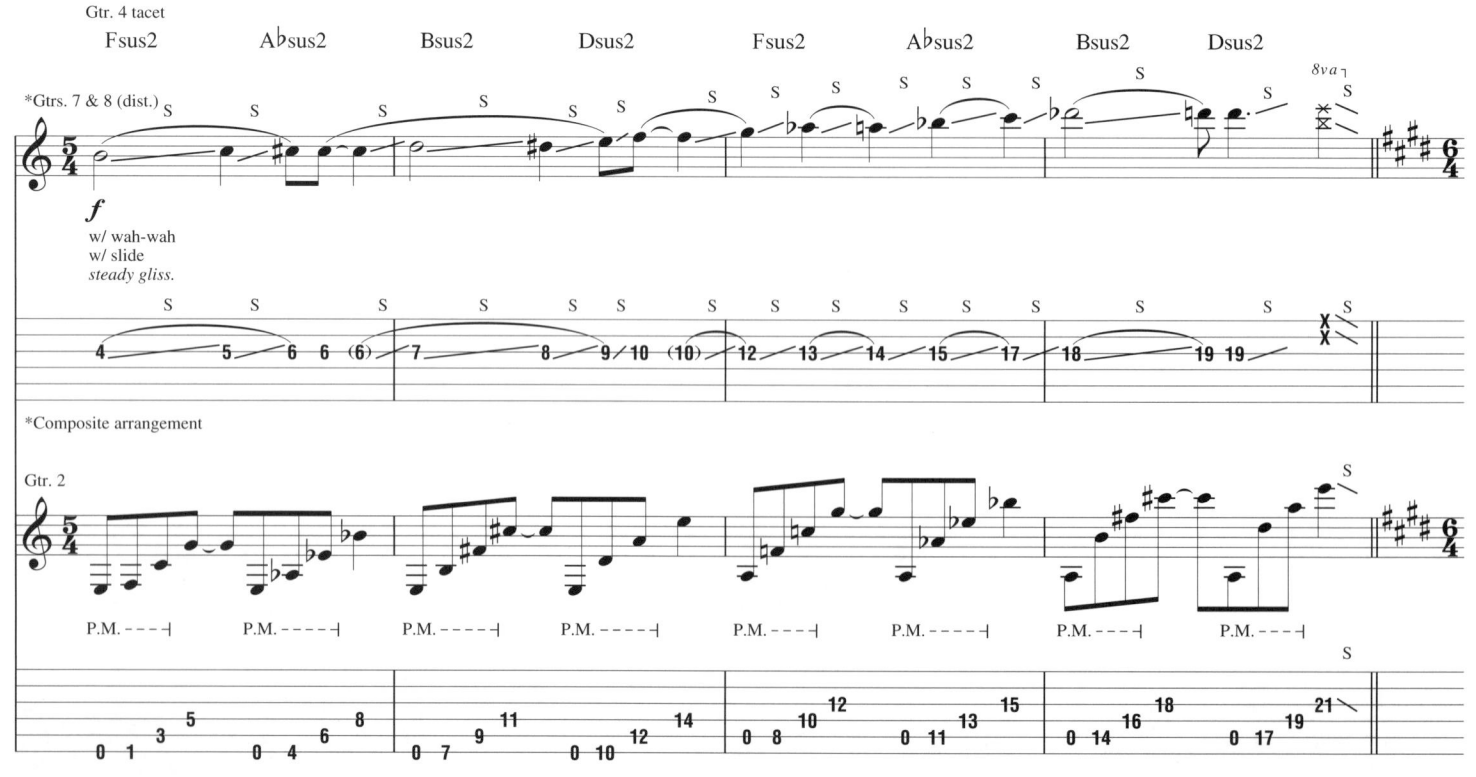

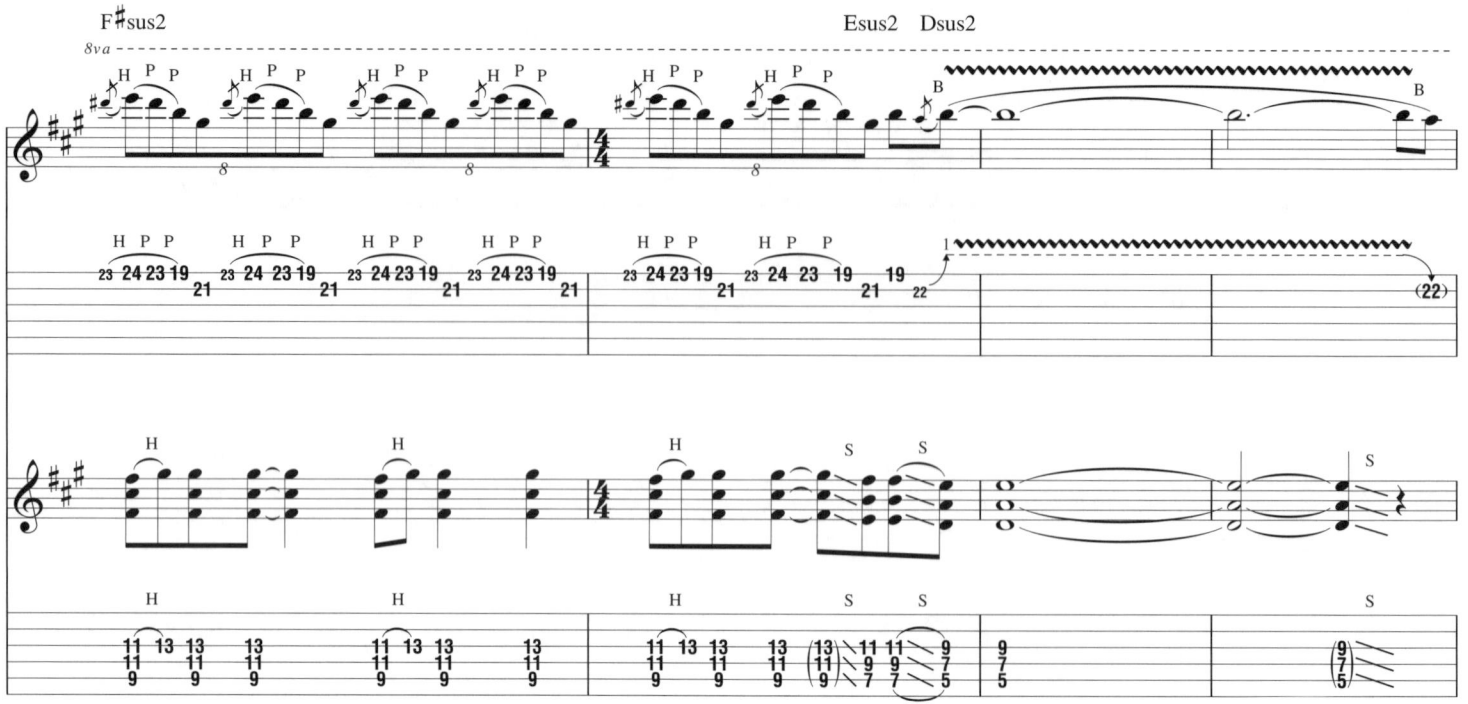

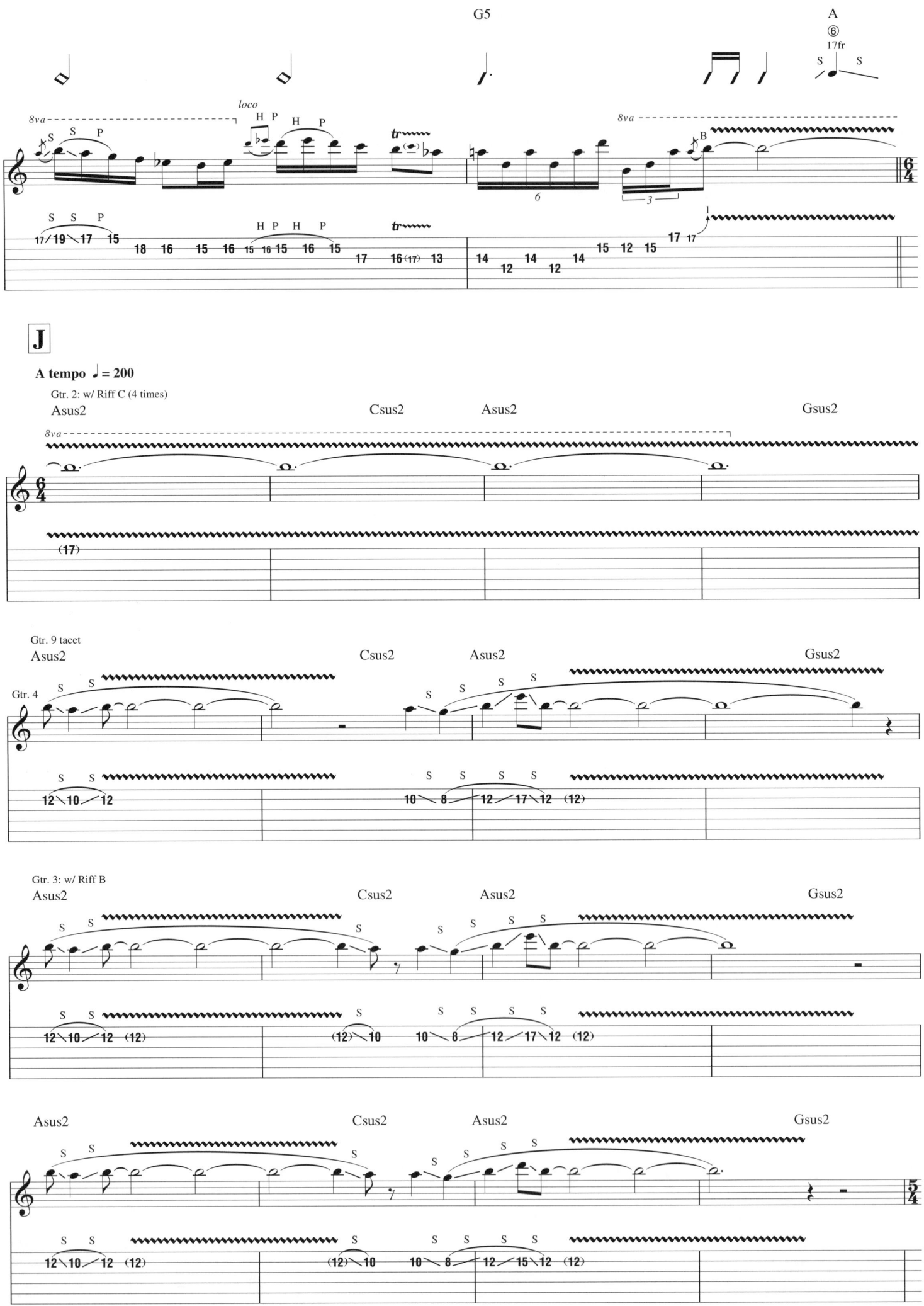

K'm-Pee-Du-Wee

By Steve Vai

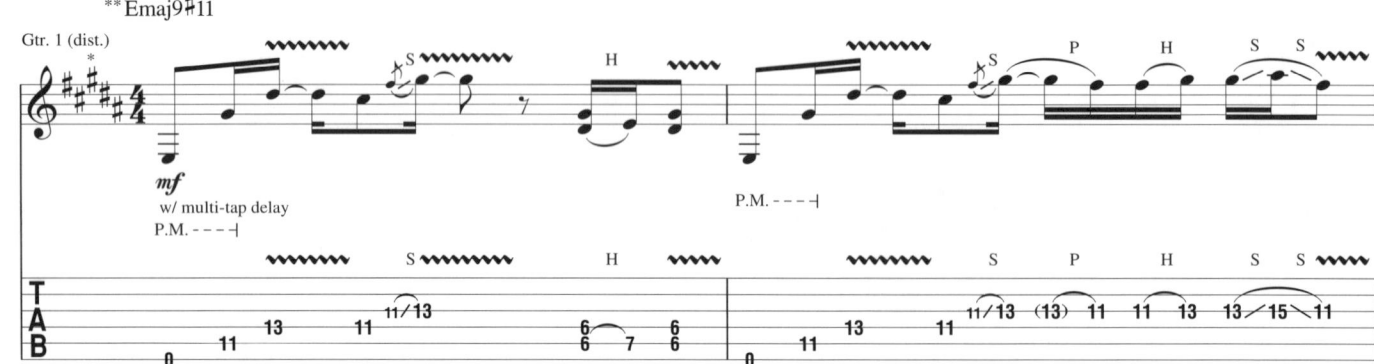

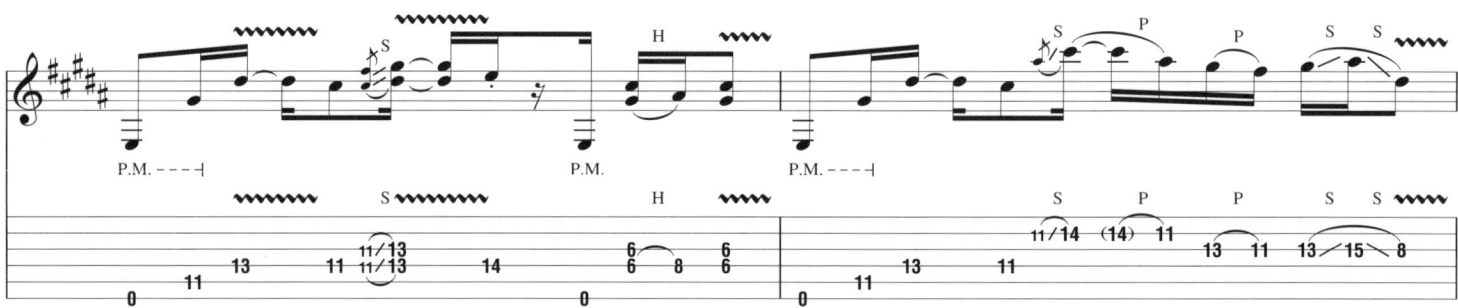

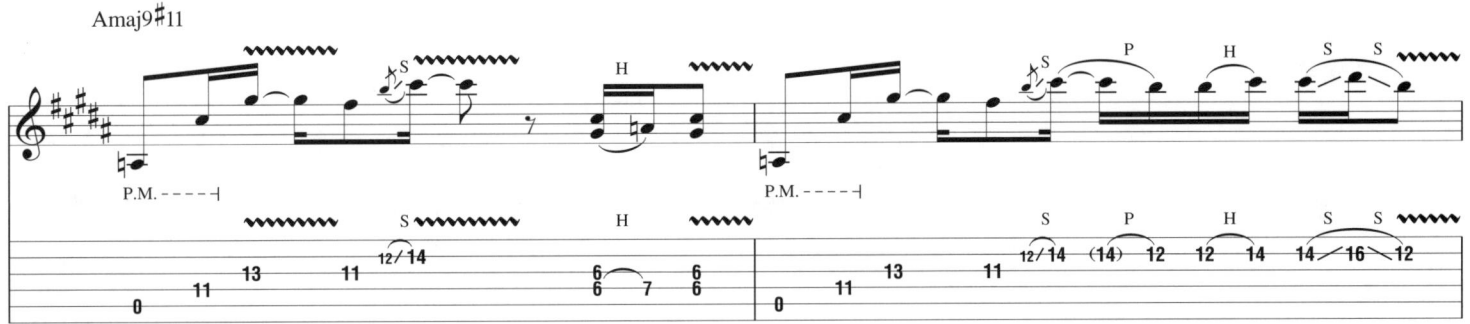
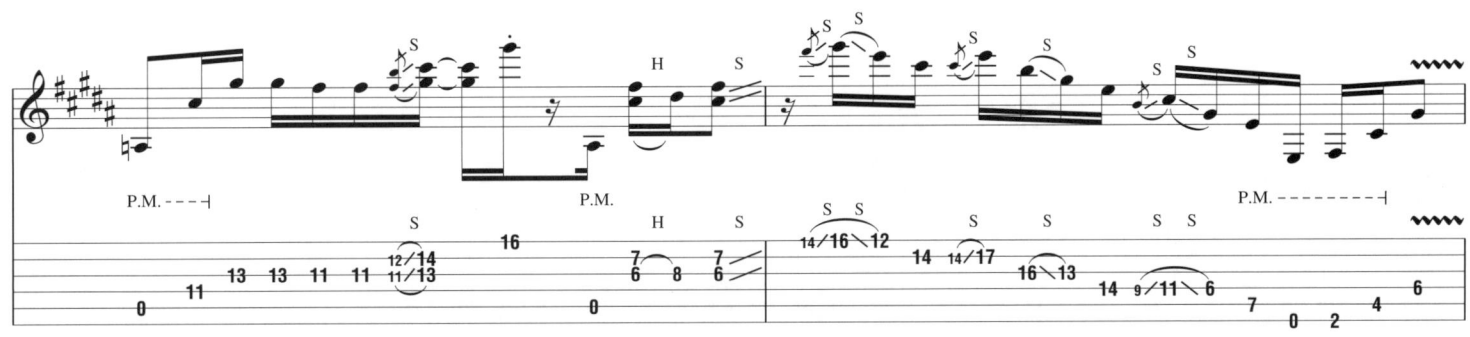
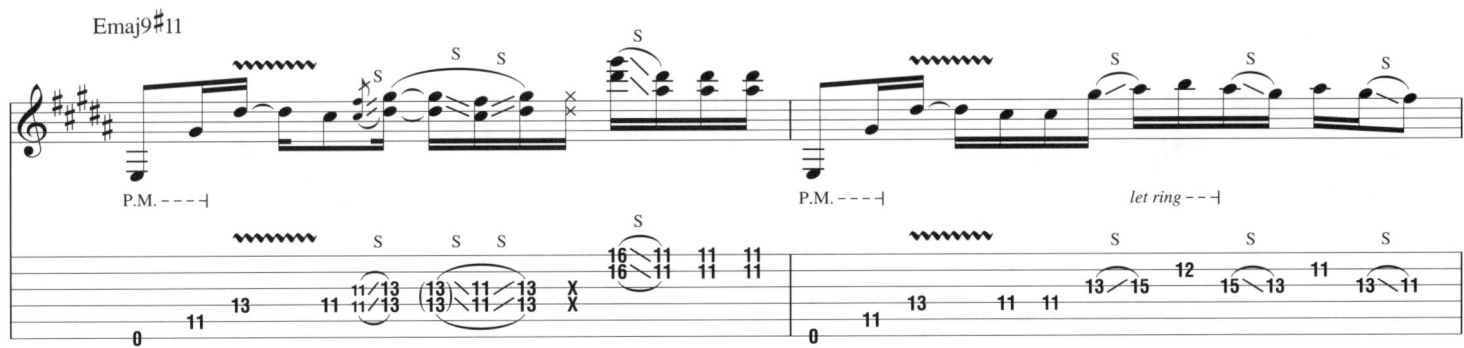
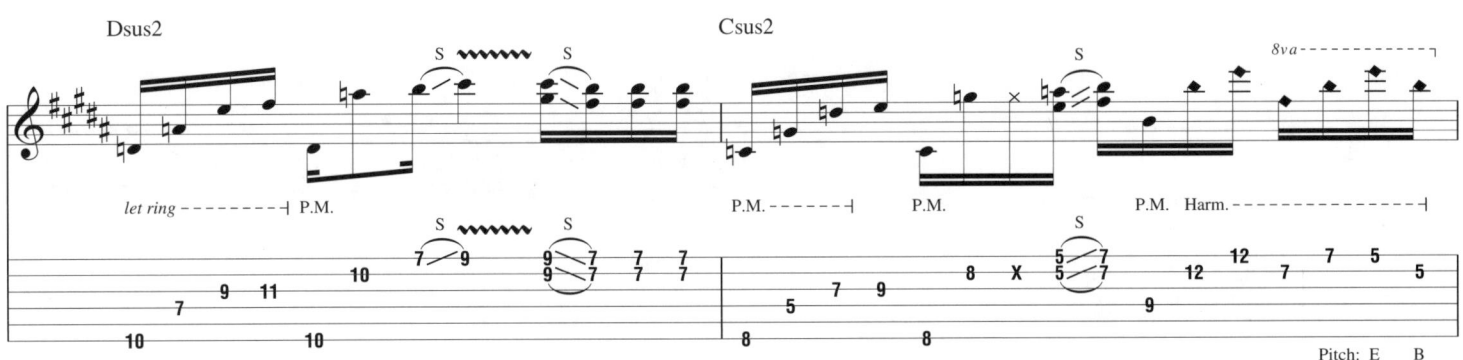
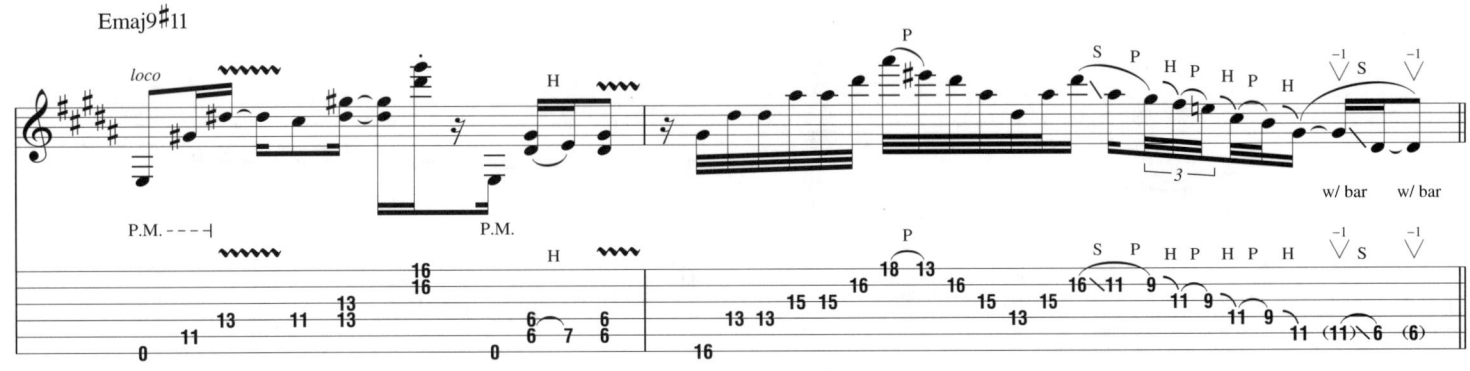

49

Emaj9#11

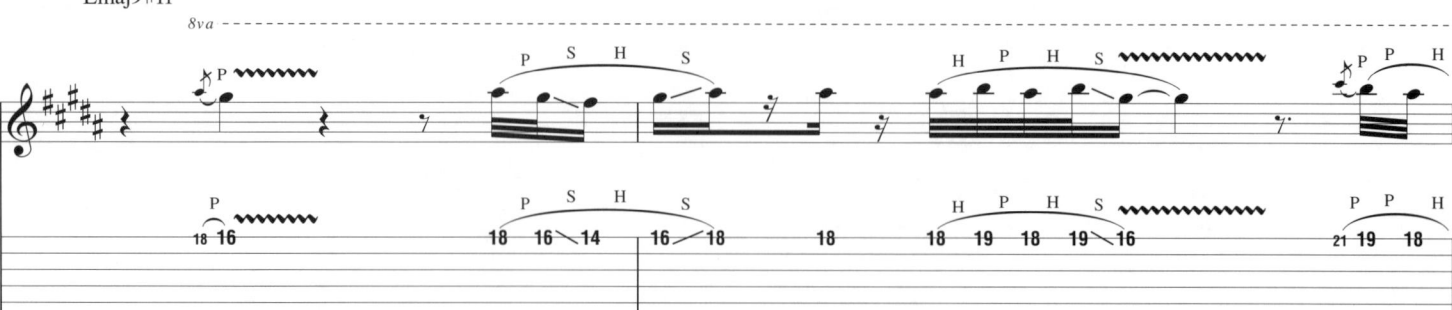
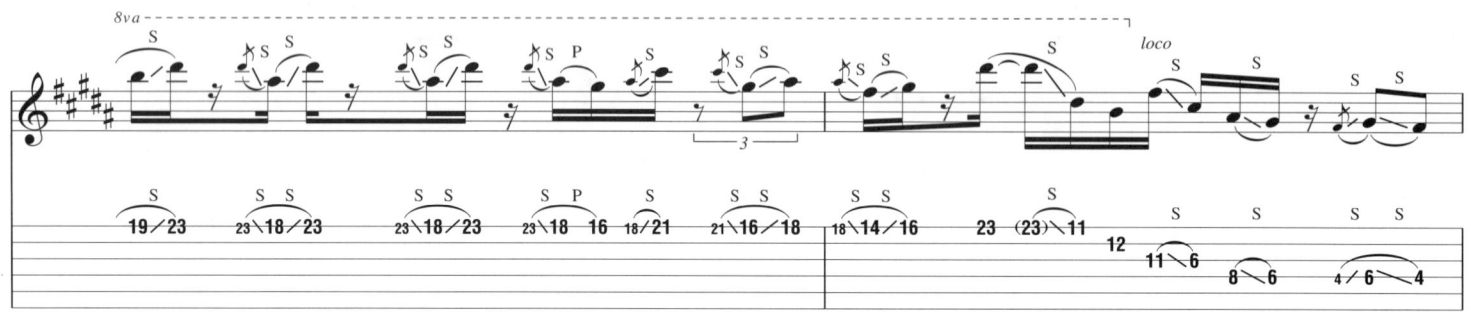
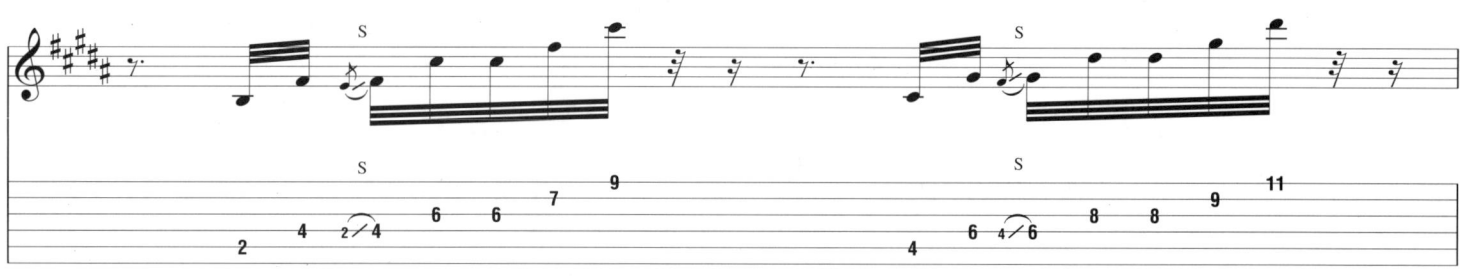
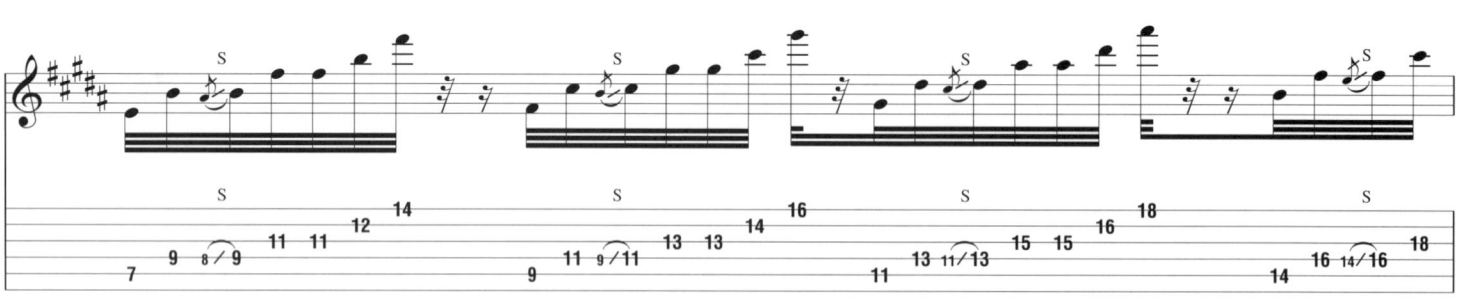
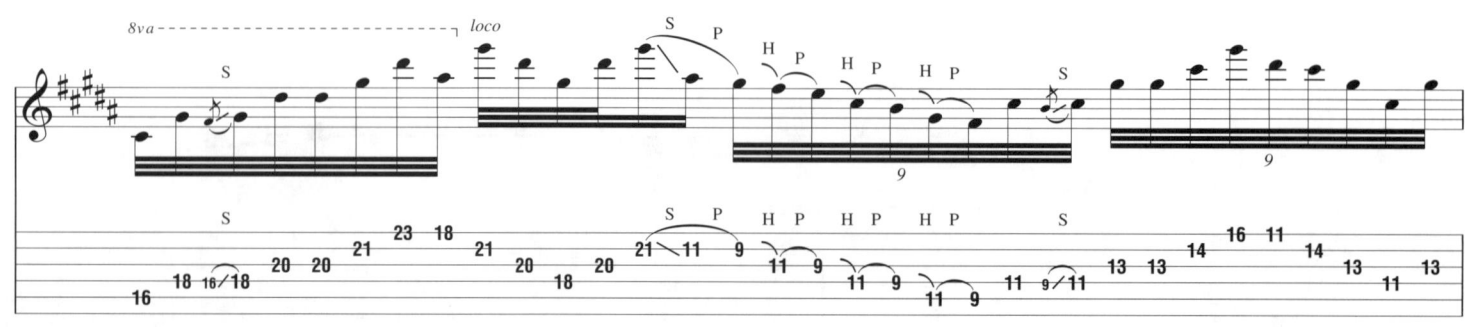

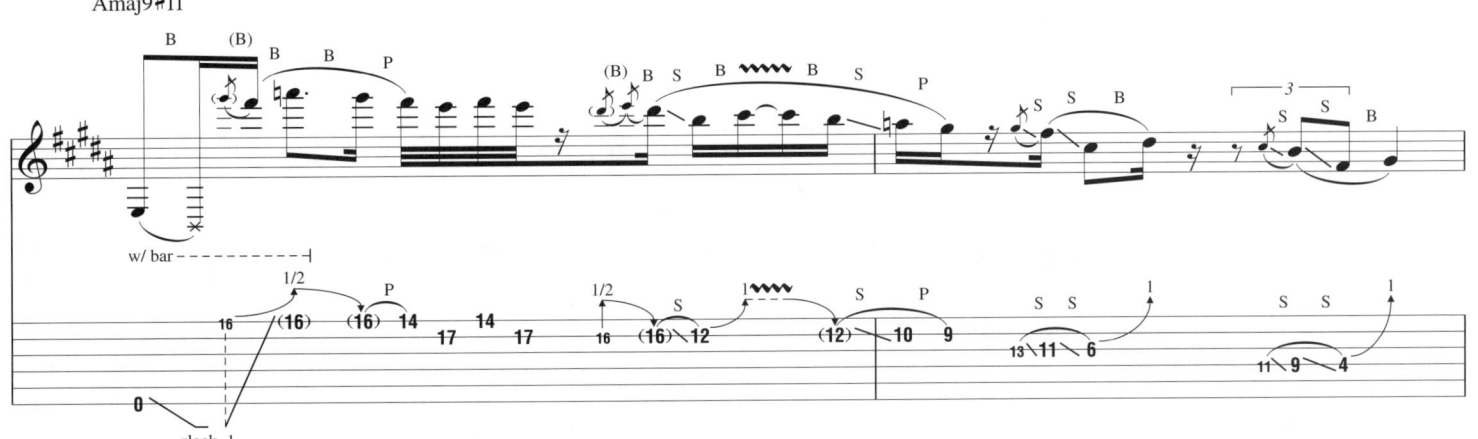
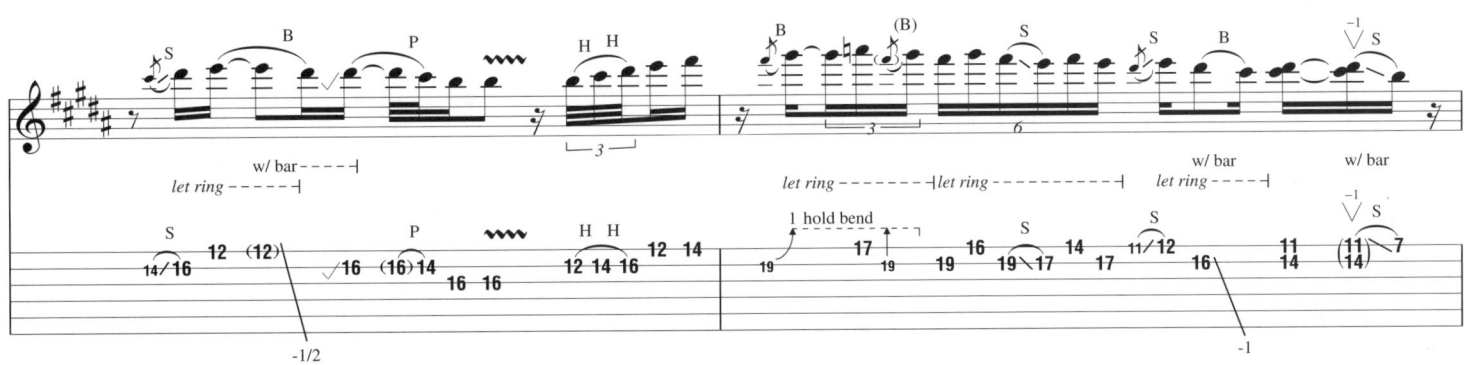
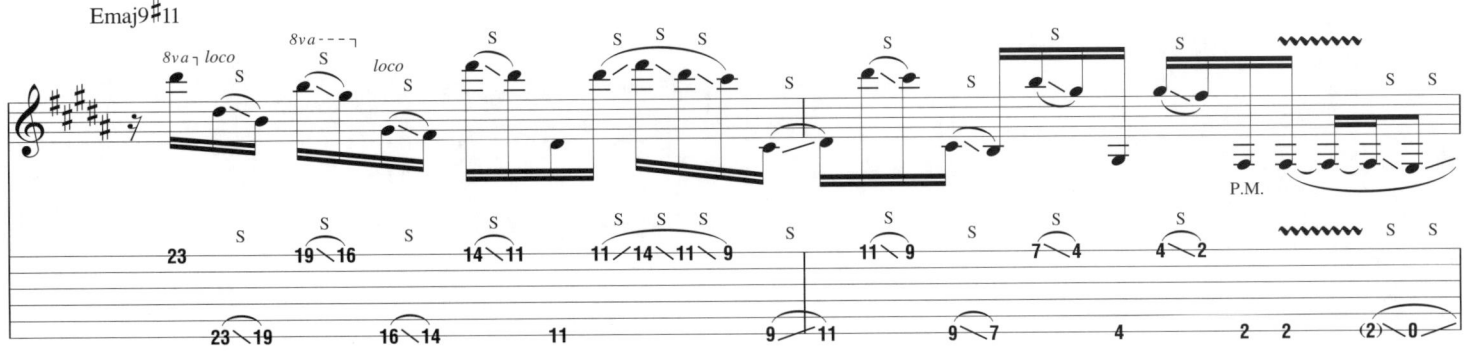
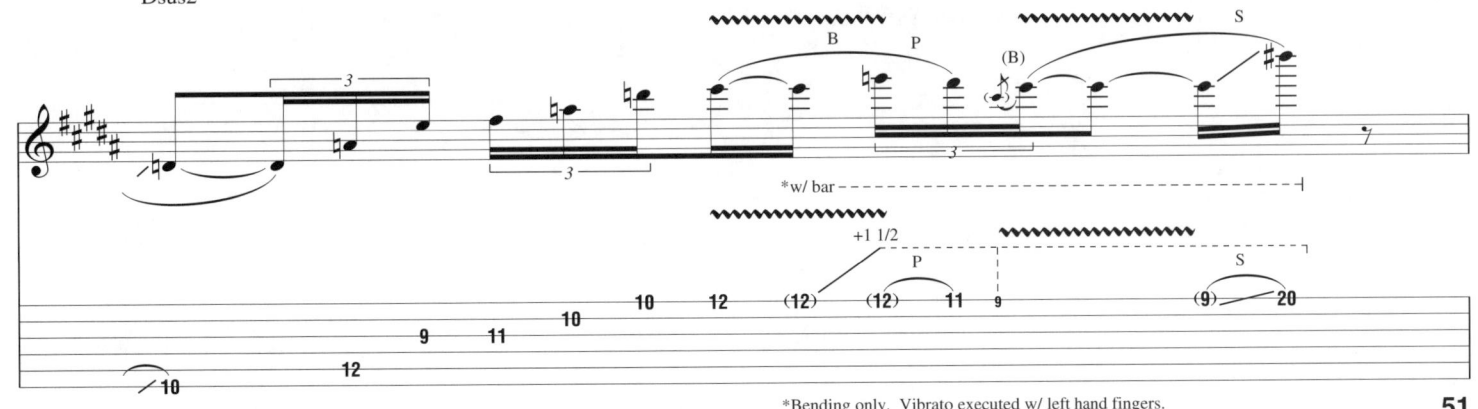

*Bending only. Vibrato executed w/ left hand fingers.

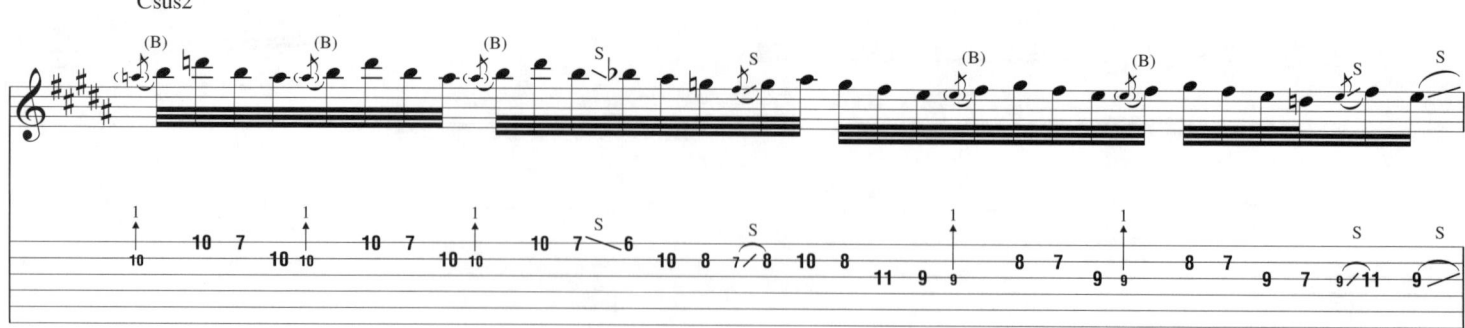
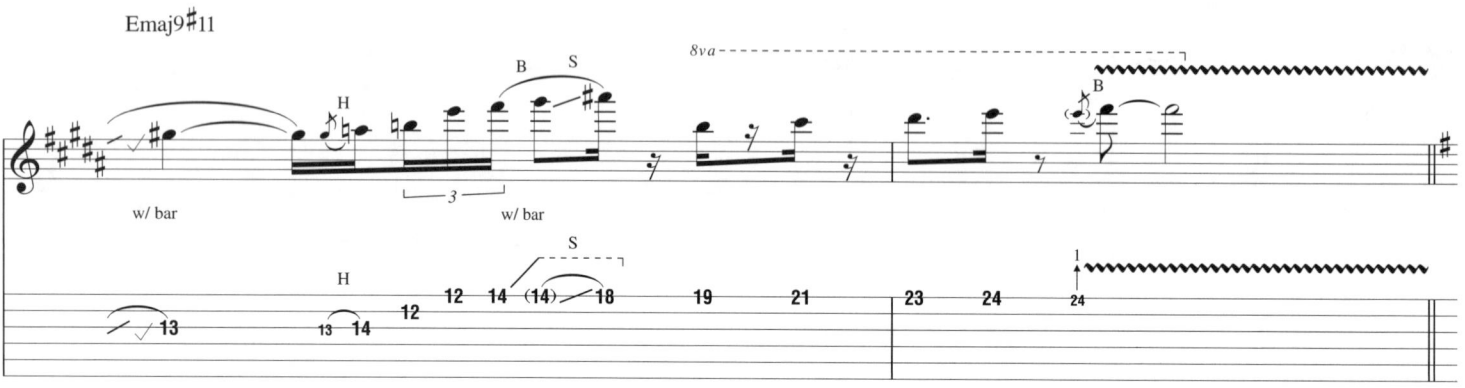
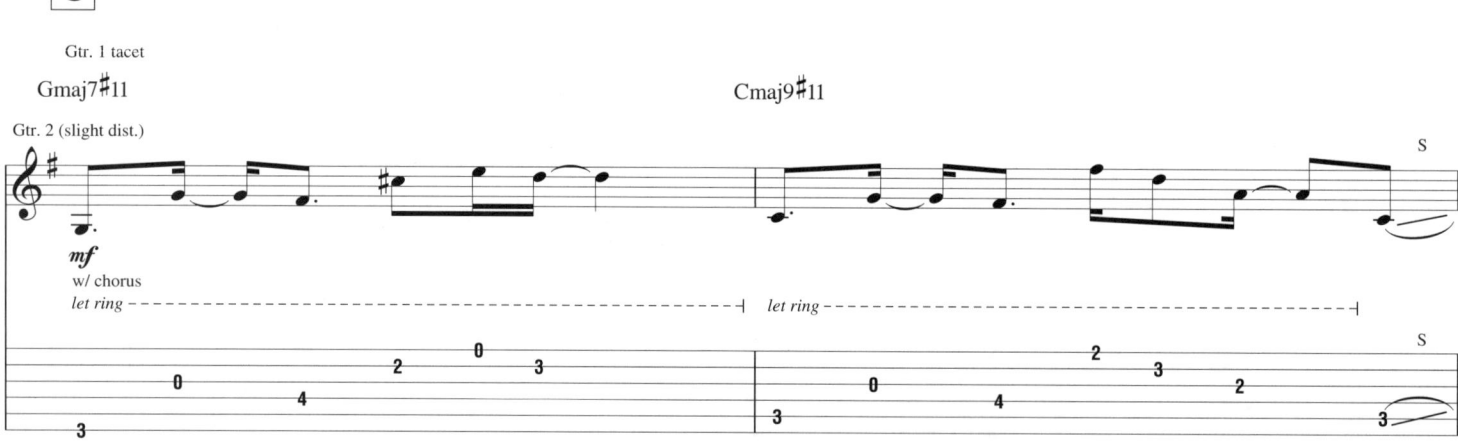
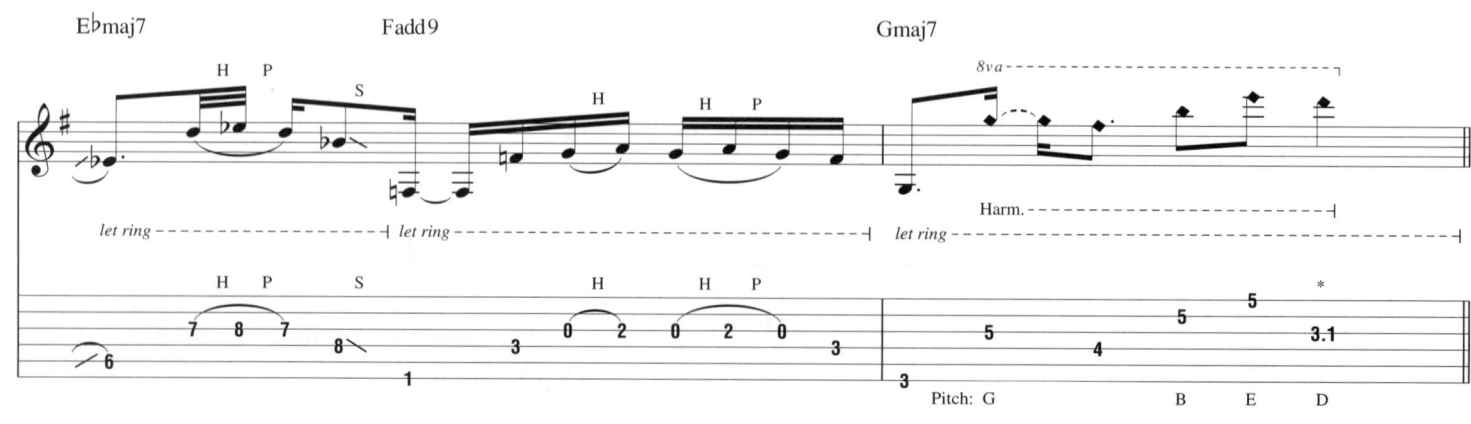

*Harmonic located approx. one-tenth the distance between the 3rd & 4th frets.

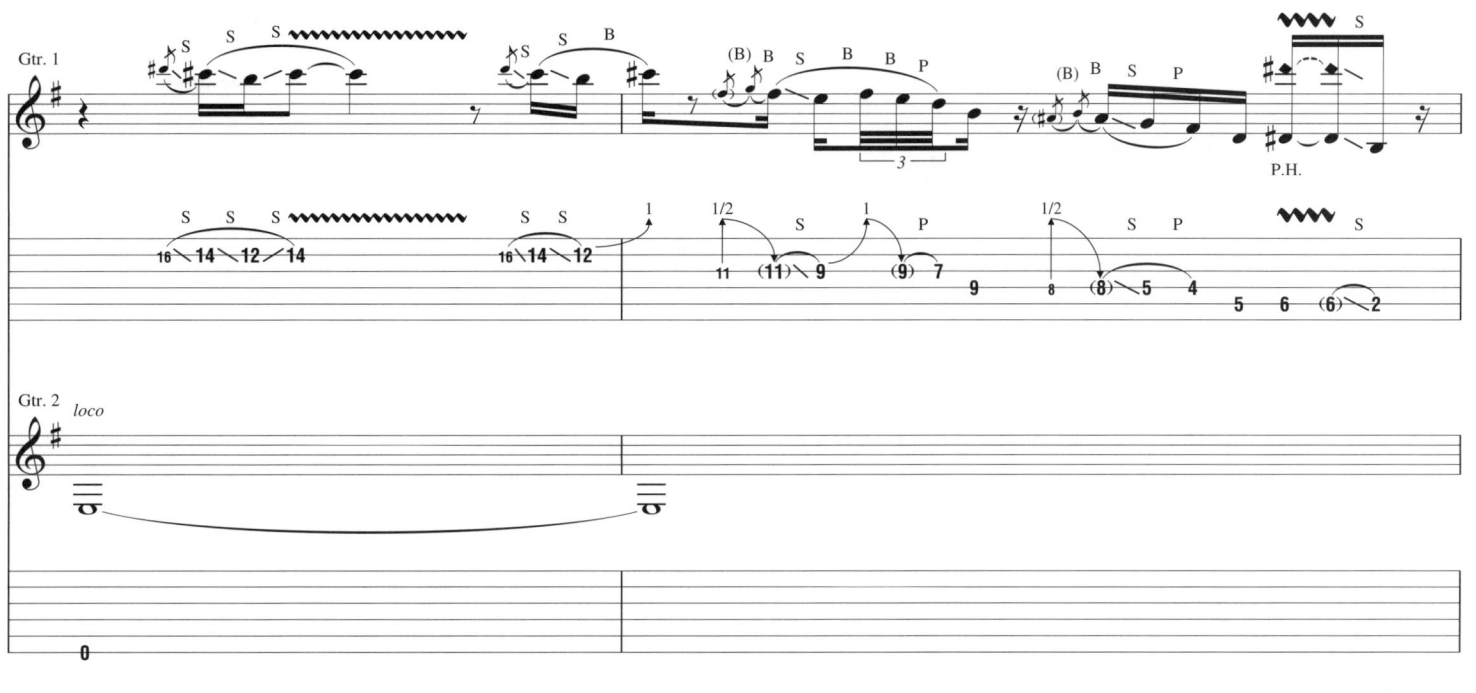

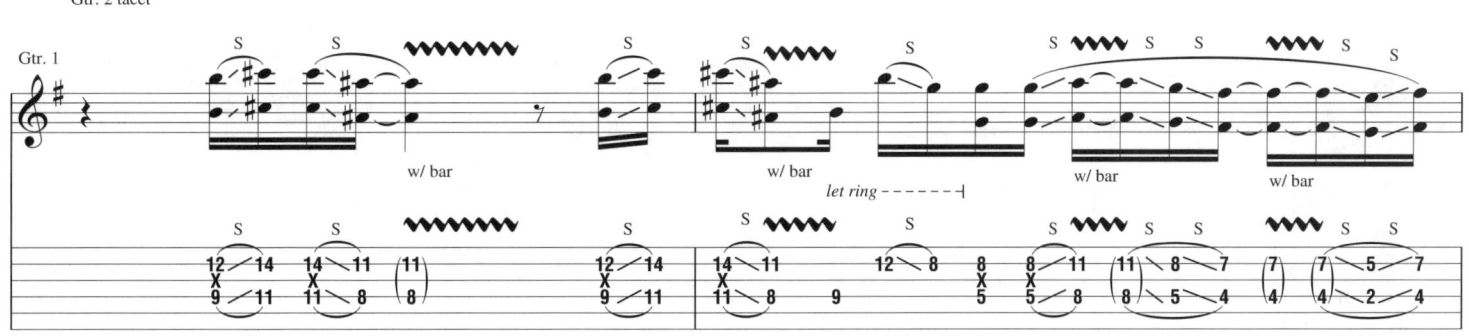

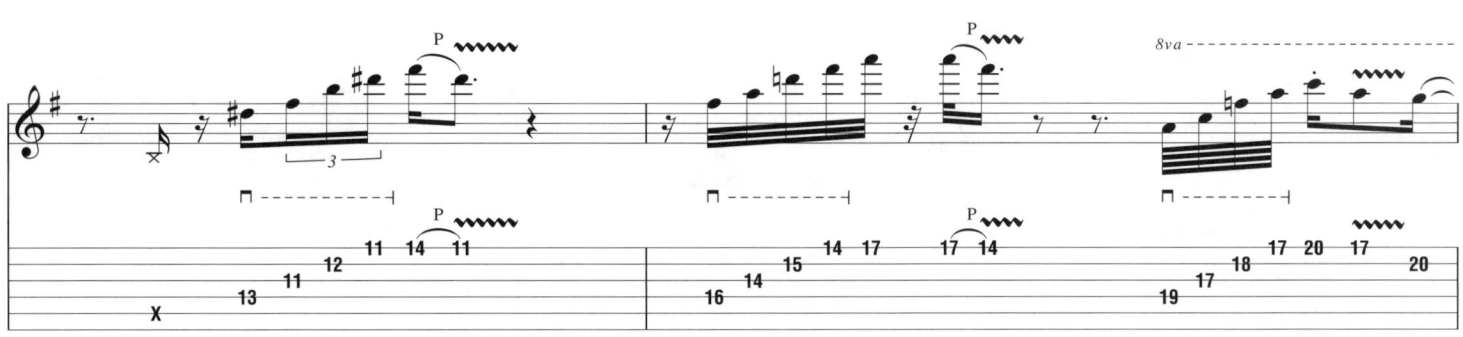

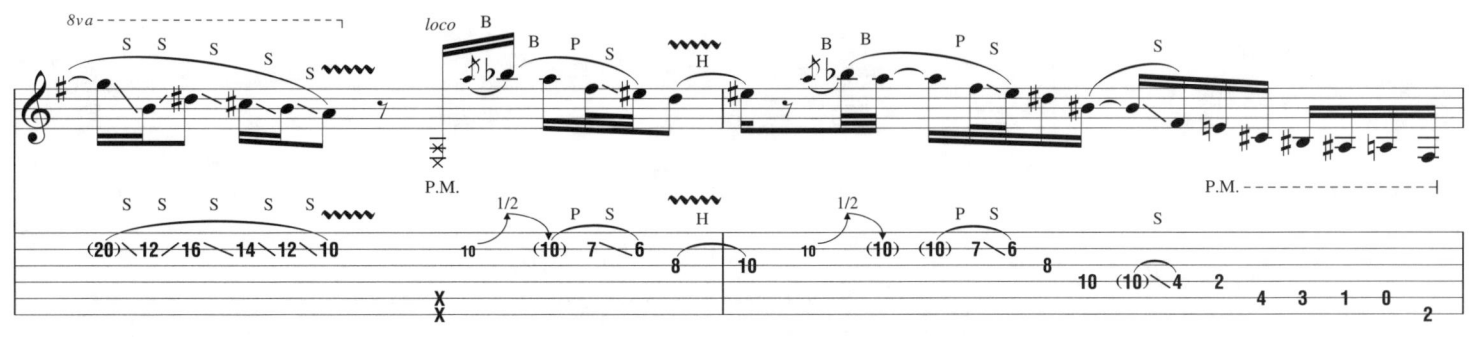

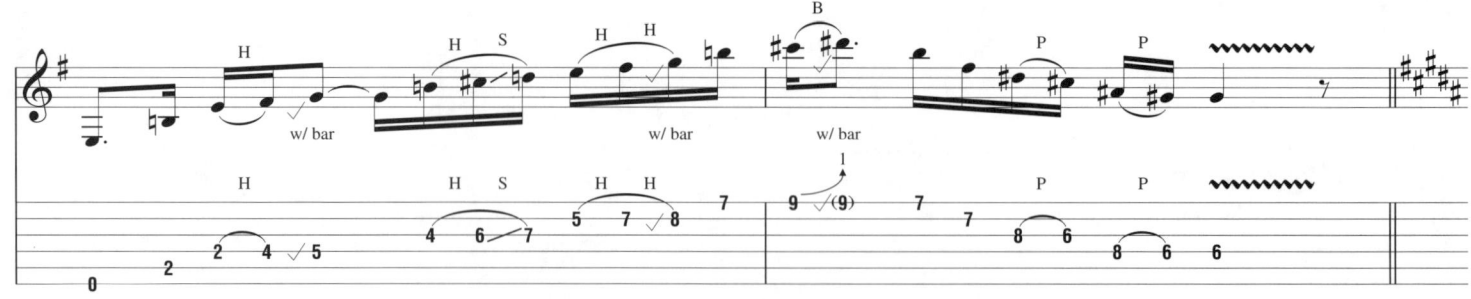

E

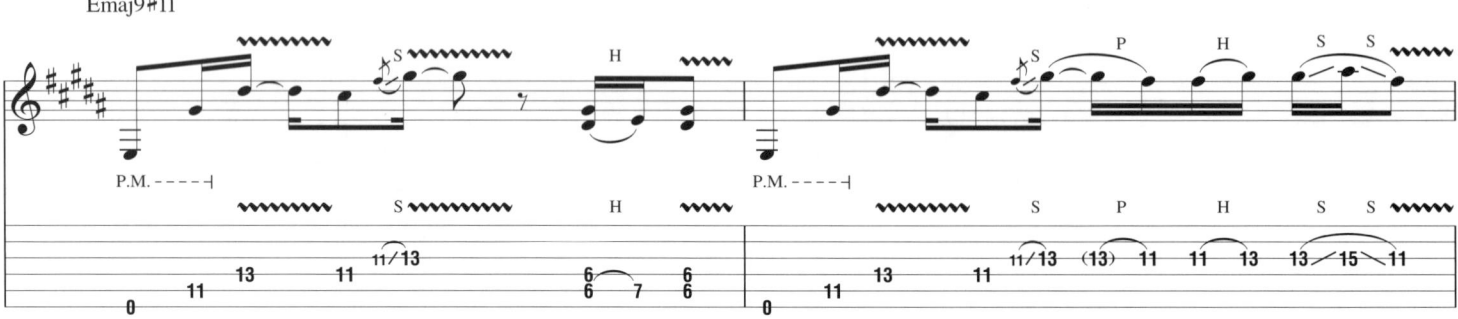

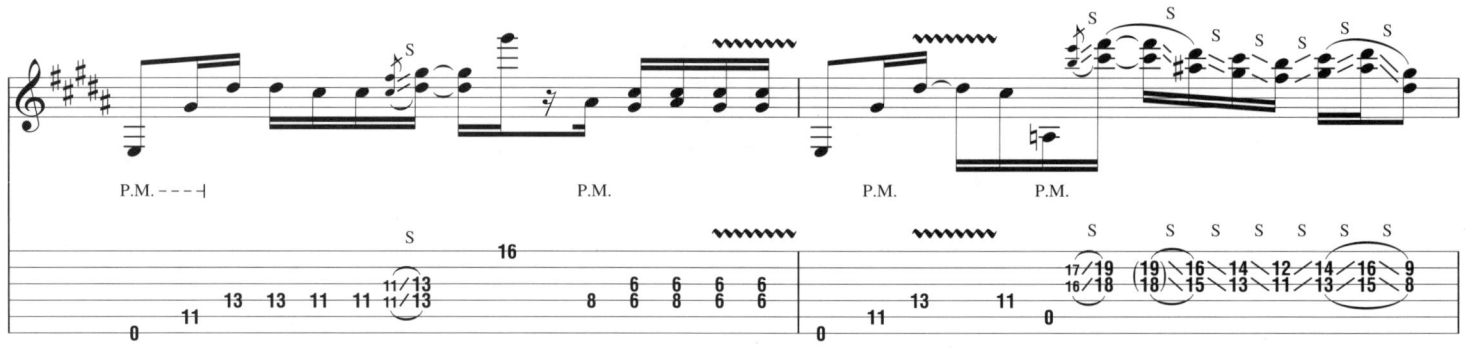

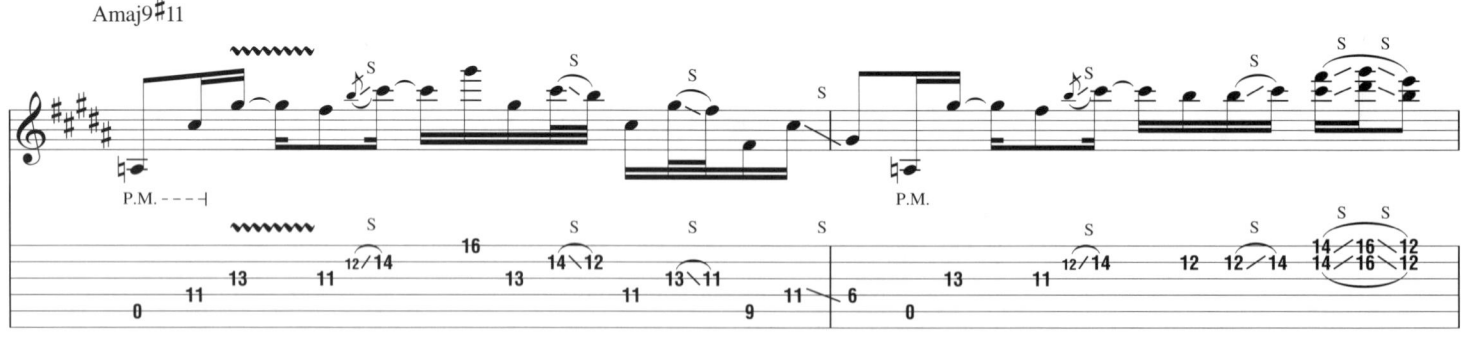

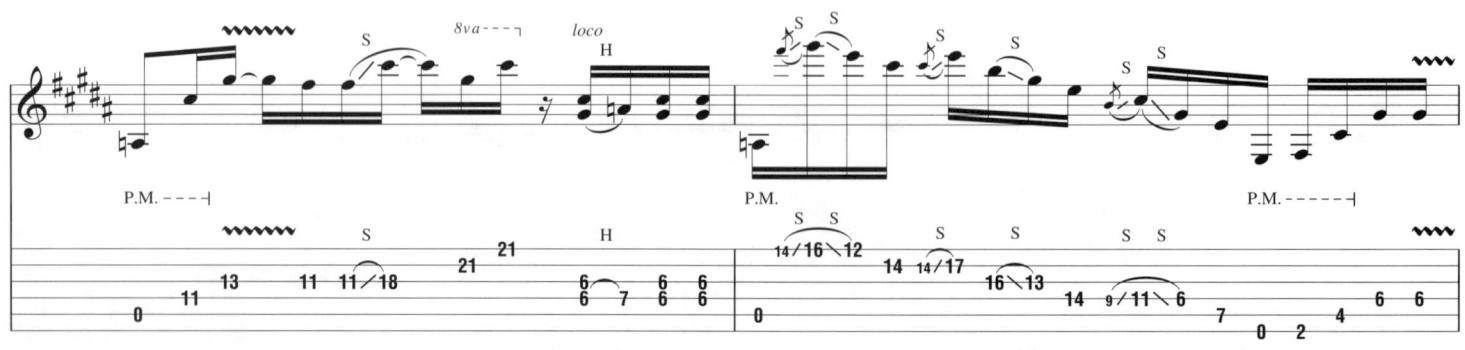

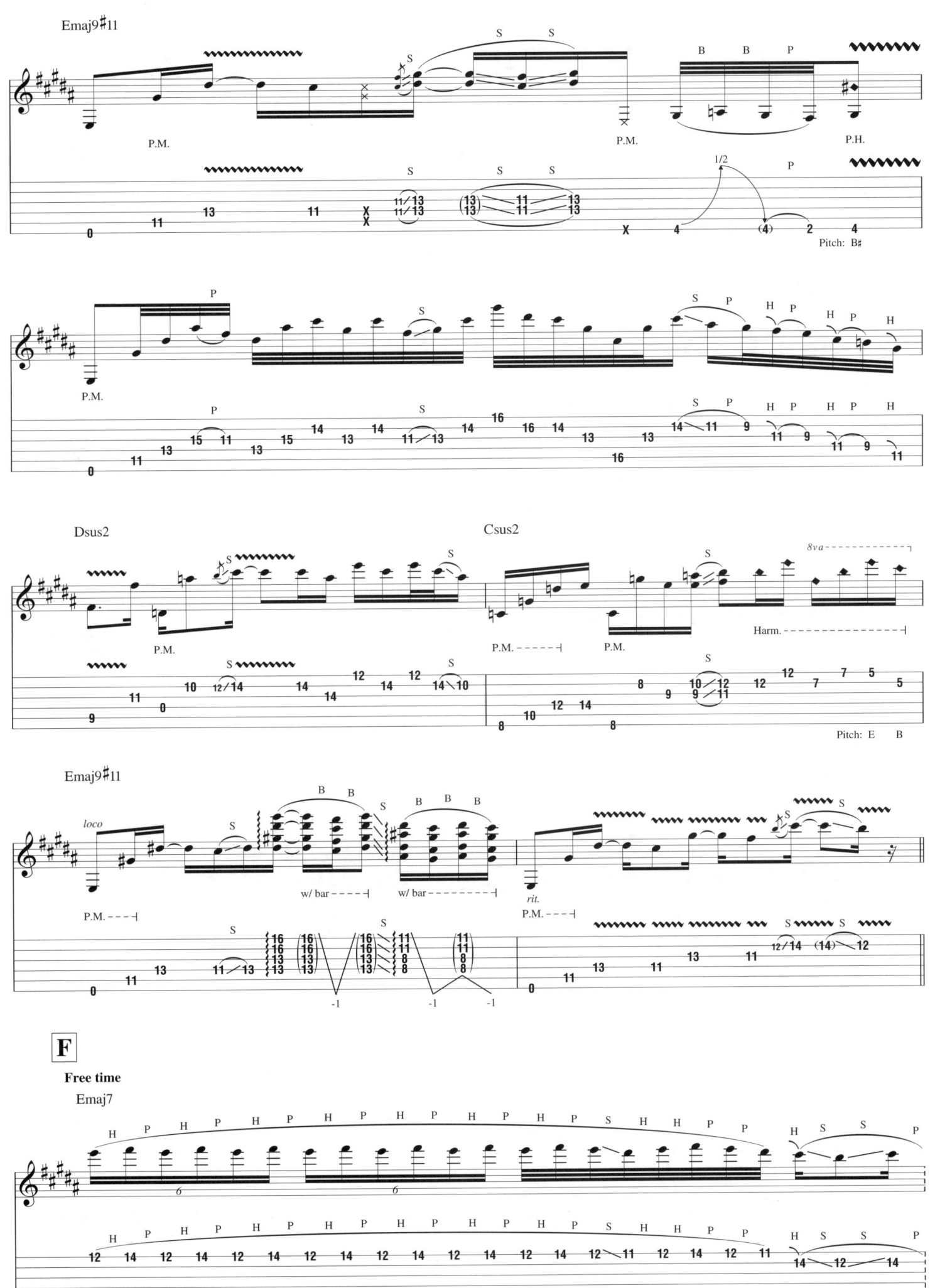

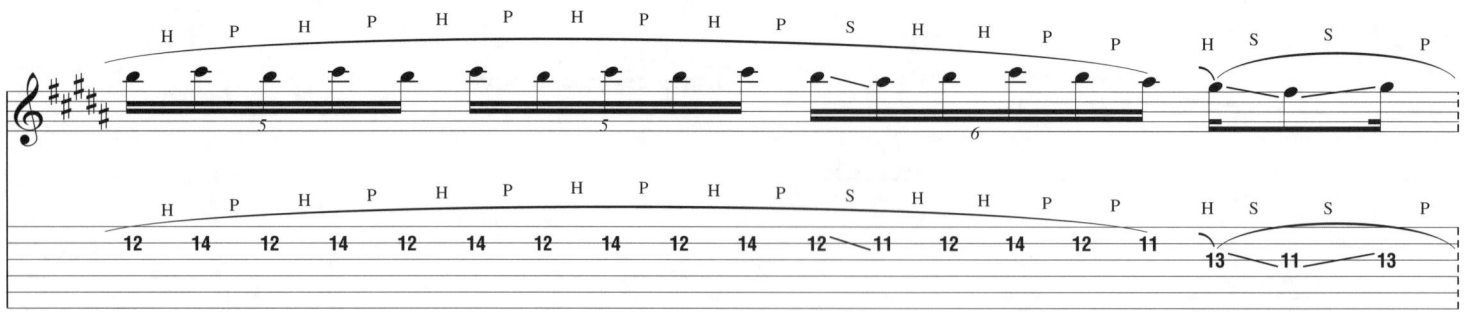
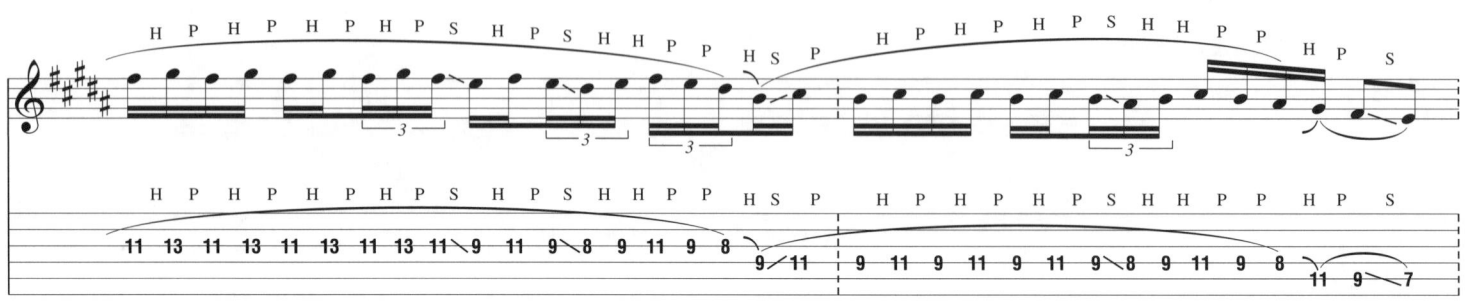
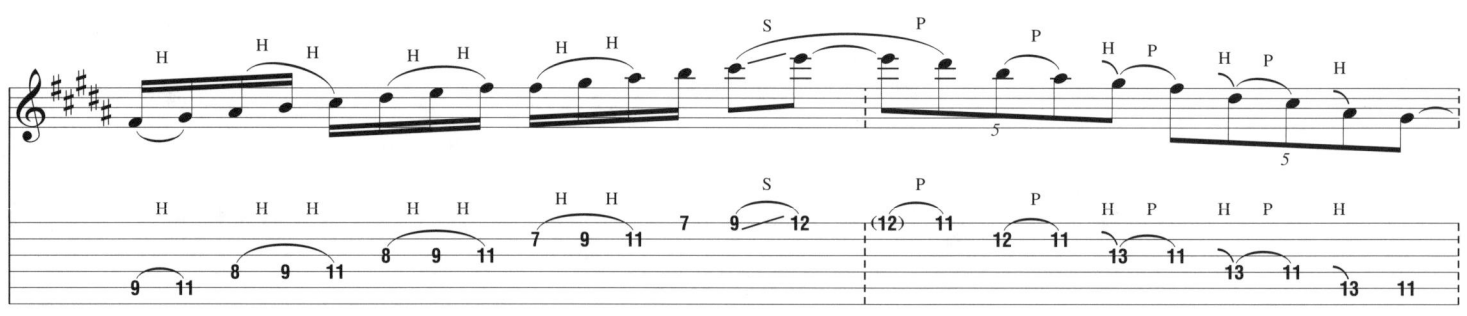
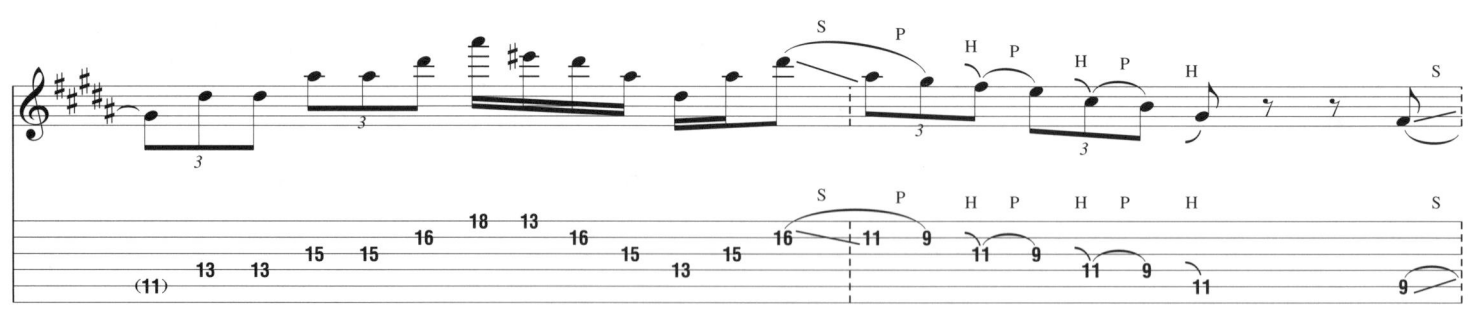
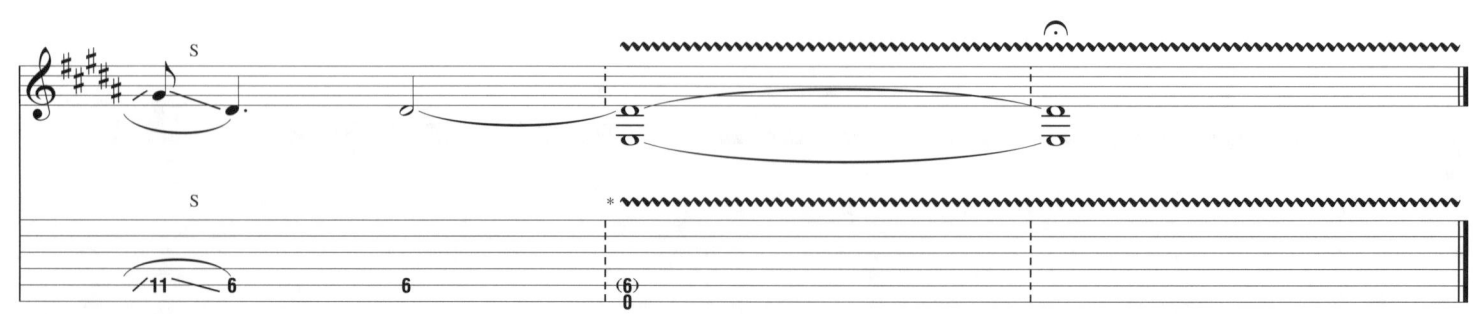

*6th fret of 4th str. gets bumped periodically due to vibrato.

Firewall

By Steve Vai

Tune down 1 step:
(low to high) D-G-C-F-A-D

Intro
Moderately ♩ = 128

N.C.

(Boom, shi - ka - boom, _ shi - ka, ba - ka - tu - ka, boom, shi - ka doo - ba - boom - ba - tack - a - choo - ka.

Boom, _ shi - ka, boom, boom, chi - ka, ba - koom - ta, shi - ka - ba - ku - ta, brrr, chi - ka, bu - kum - ta.

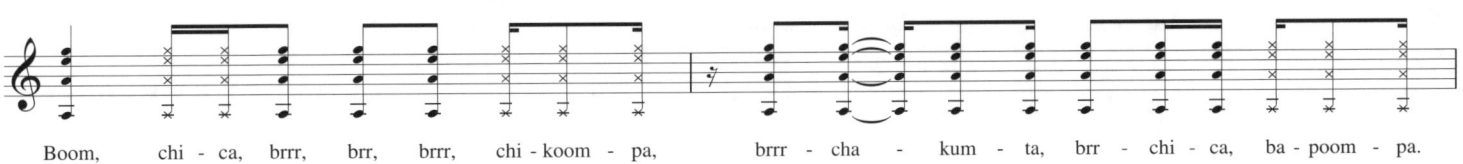
Boom, chi - ca, brrr, brr, brrr, chi - koom - pa, brrr - cha - kum - ta, brr - chi - ca, ba - poom - pa.

End Voc. Fig. 1

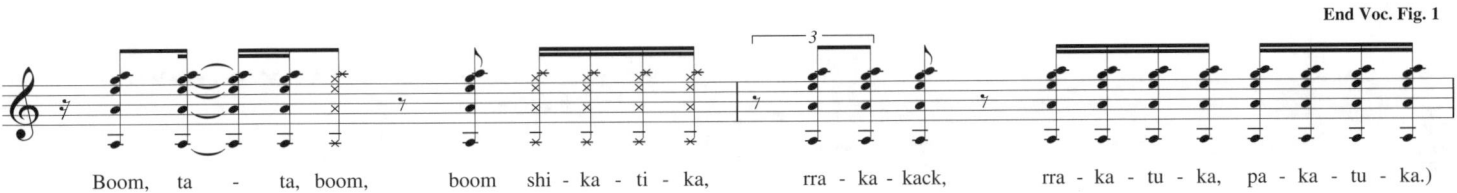
Boom, ta - ta, boom, boom shi - ka - ti - ka, rra - ka - kack, rra - ka - tu - ka, pa - ka - tu - ka.)

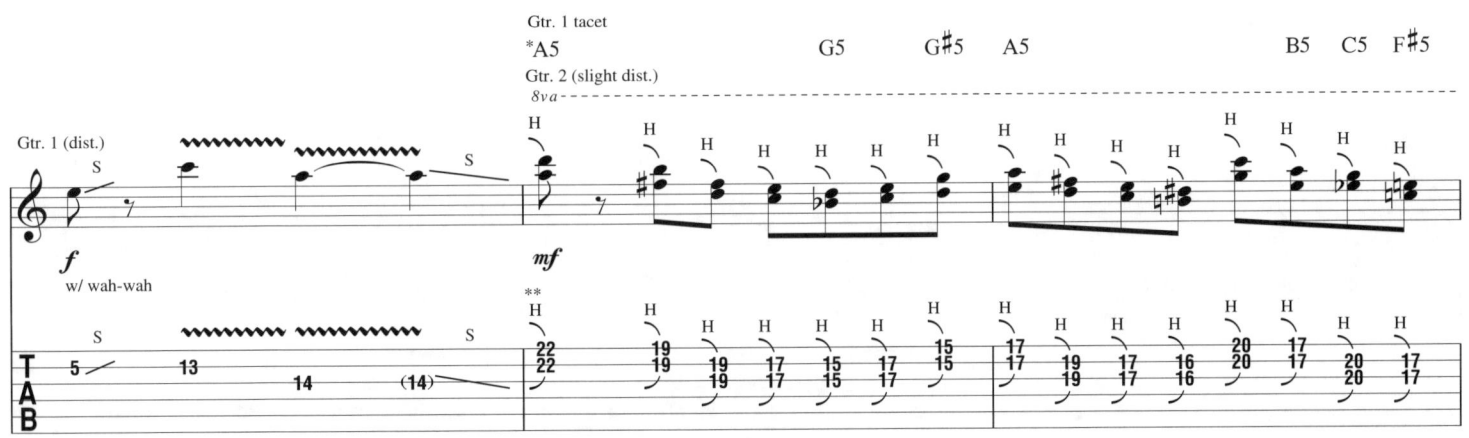

*Chord symbols reflect overall harmony.
**Notes sounded by tapping pick against fretboard (next 5 meas.).

Copyright © 2005 Sy Vy Music (ASCAP)
International Copyright Secured   All Rights Reserved

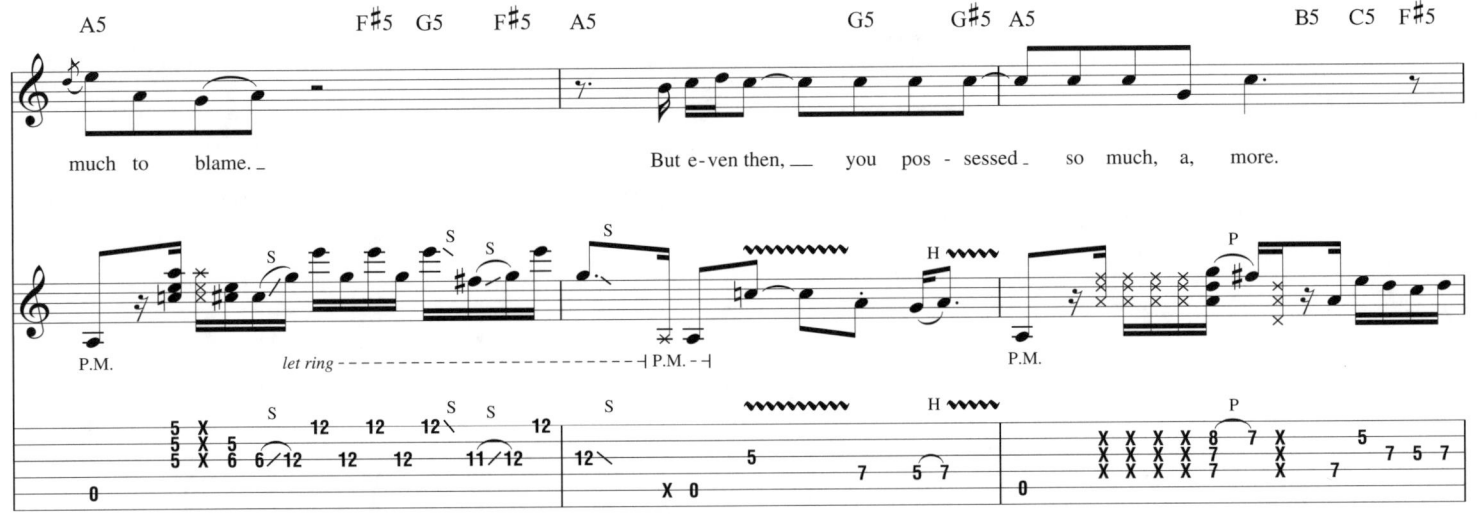
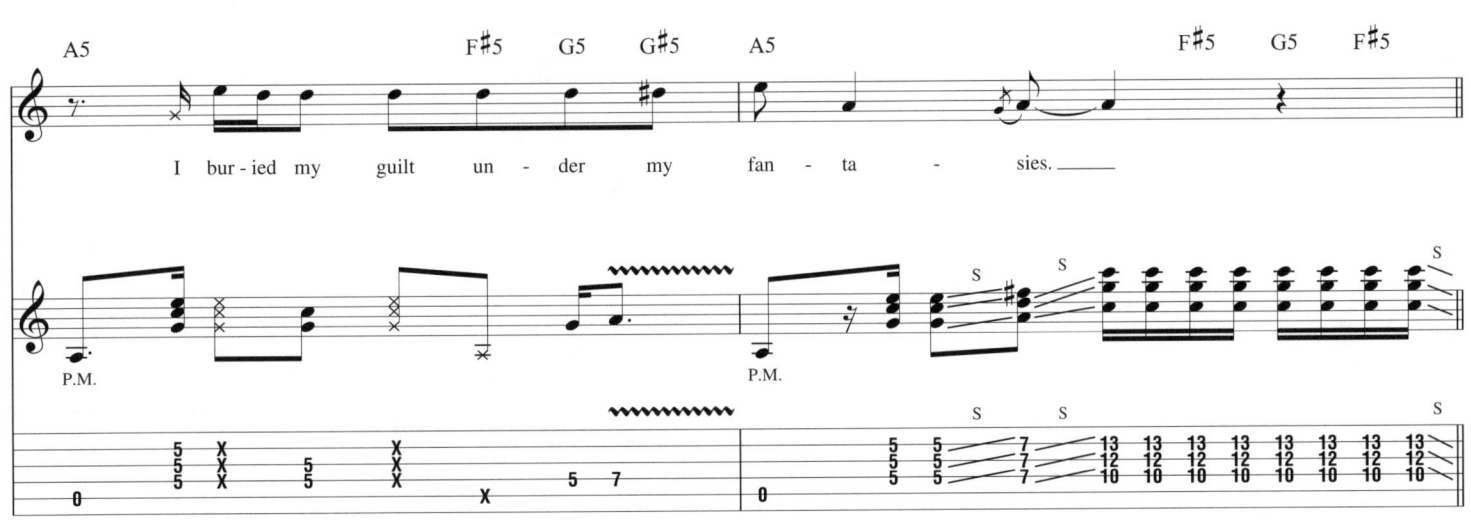
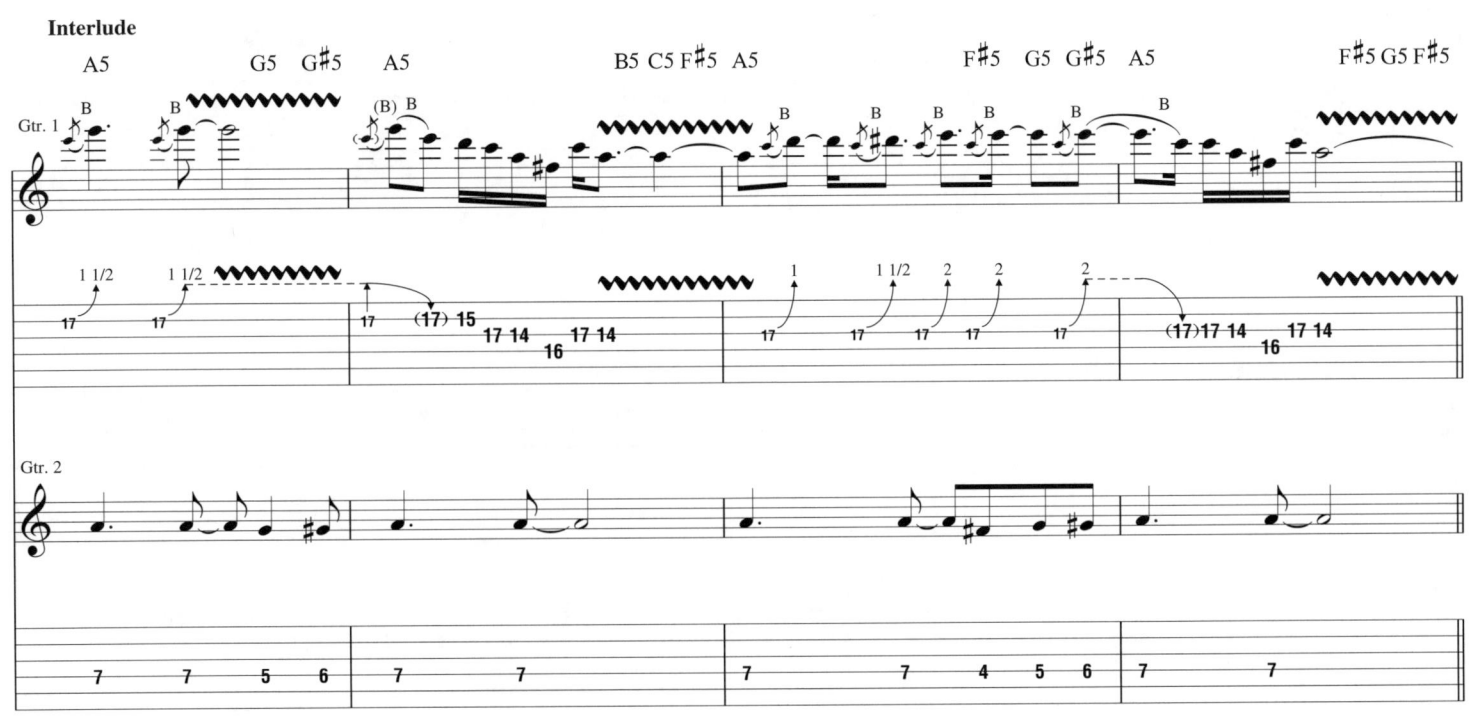

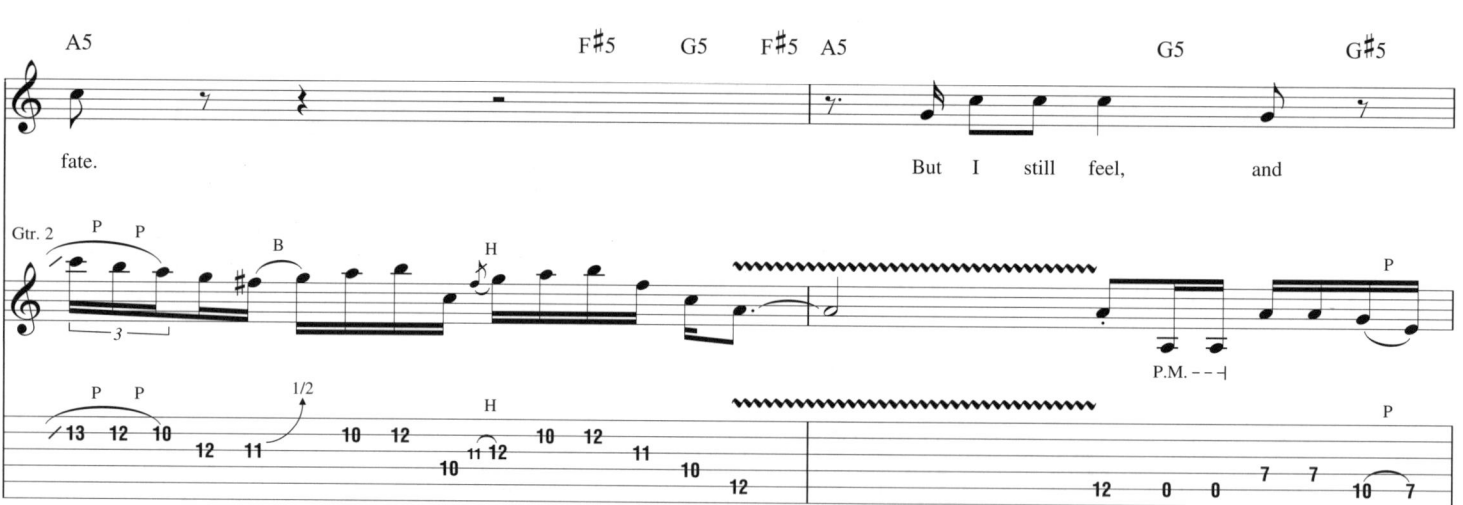
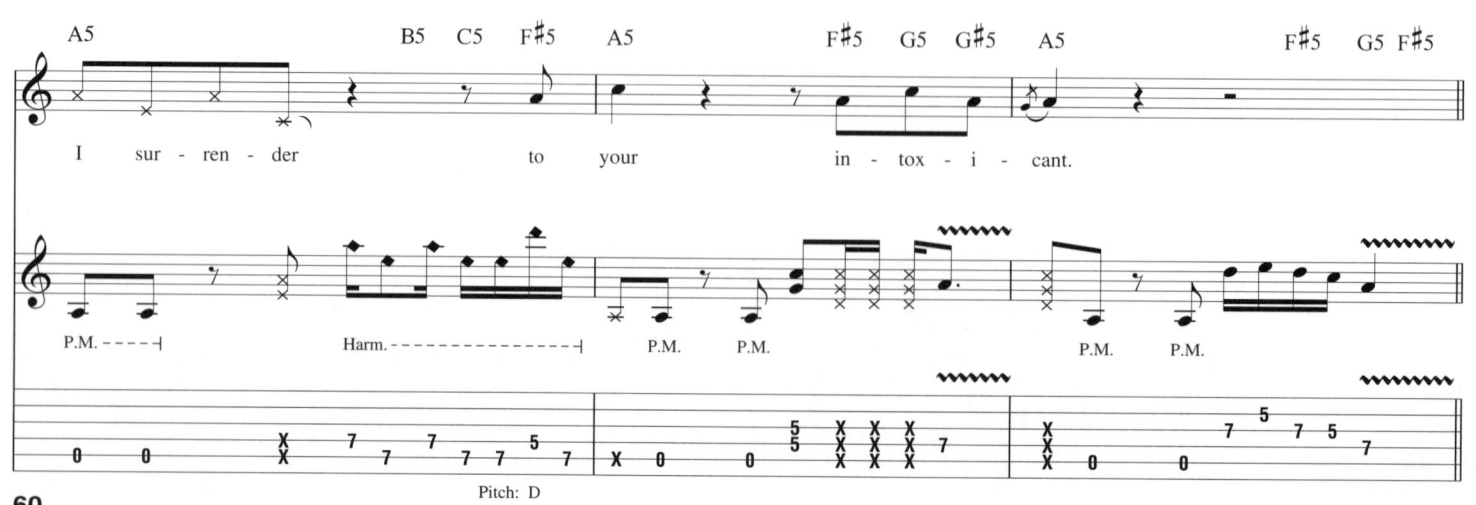

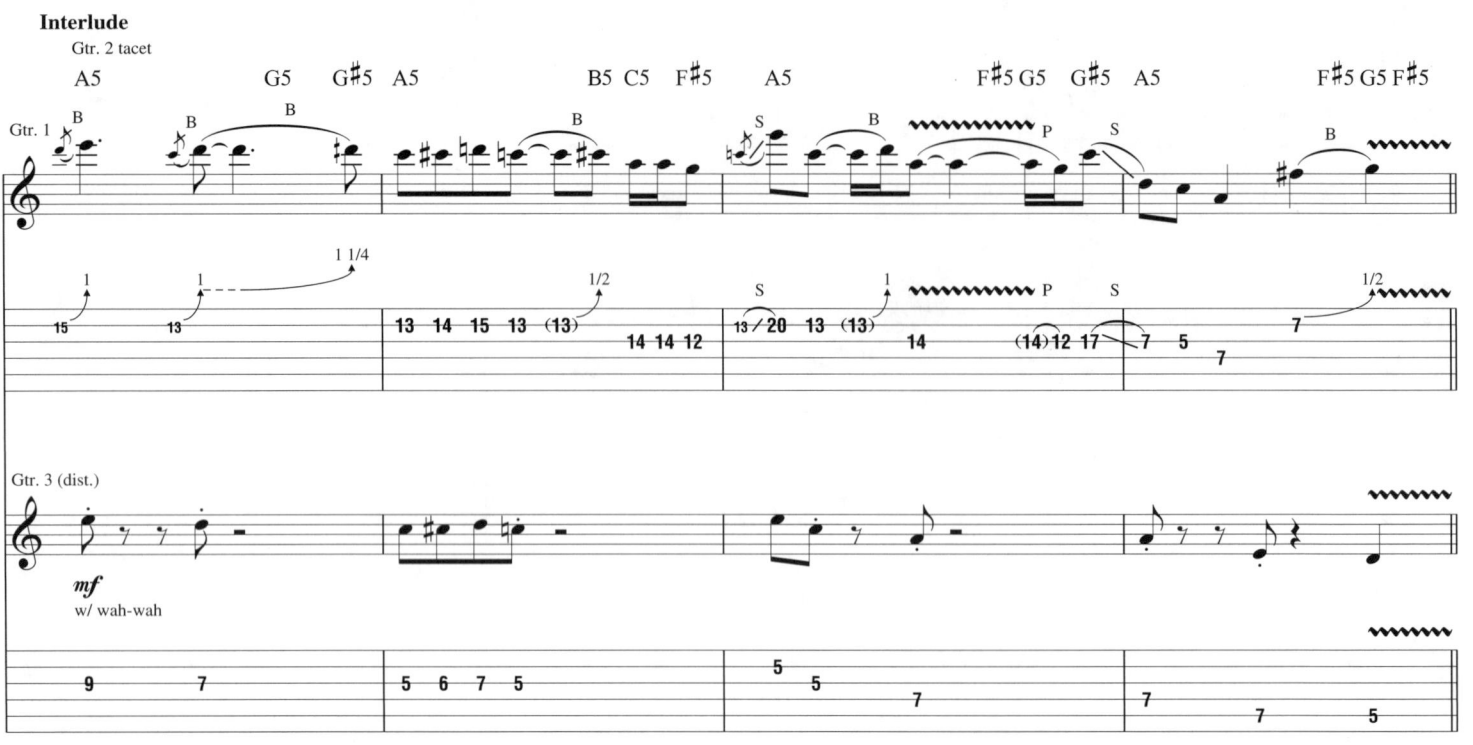
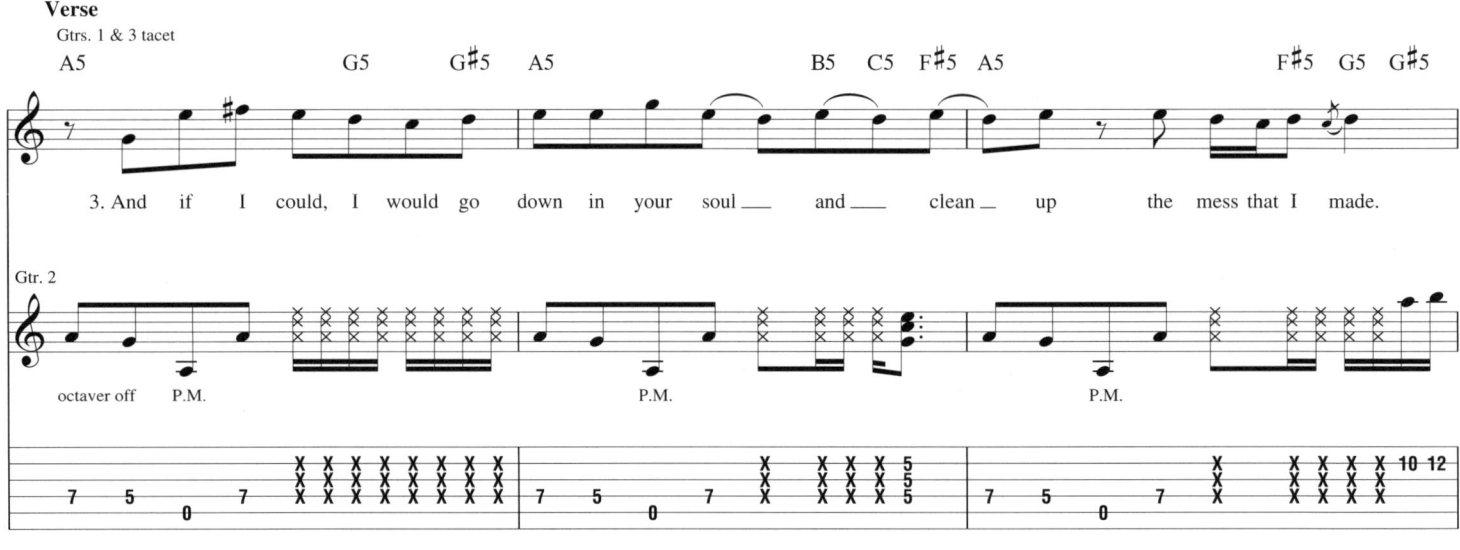
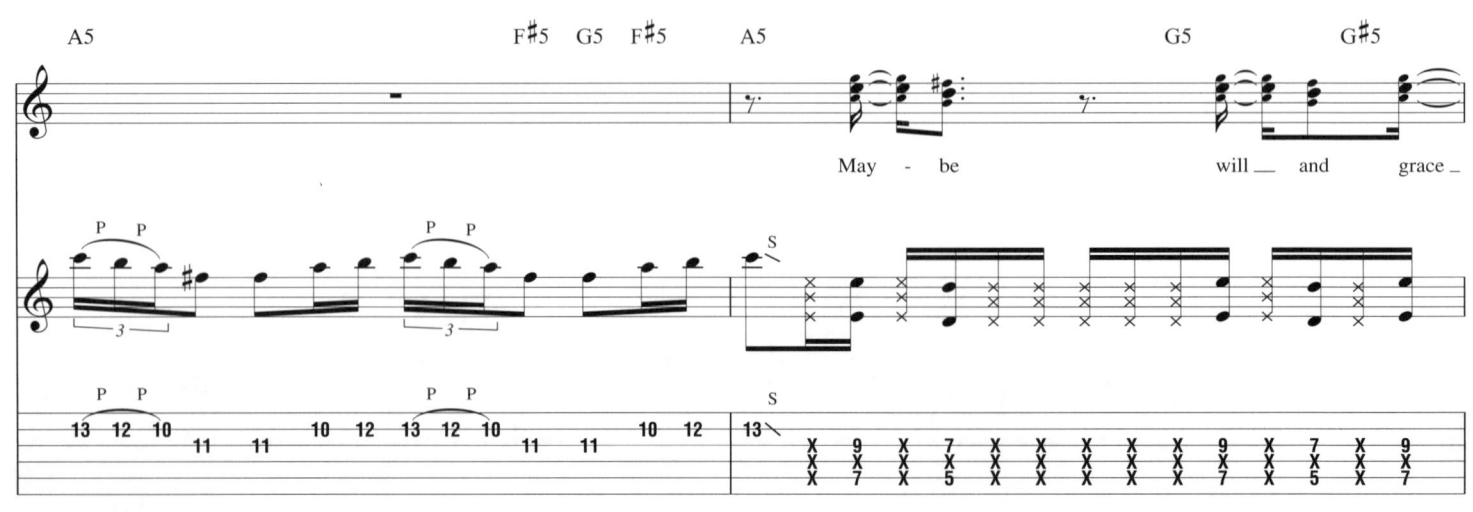

Guitar Solo

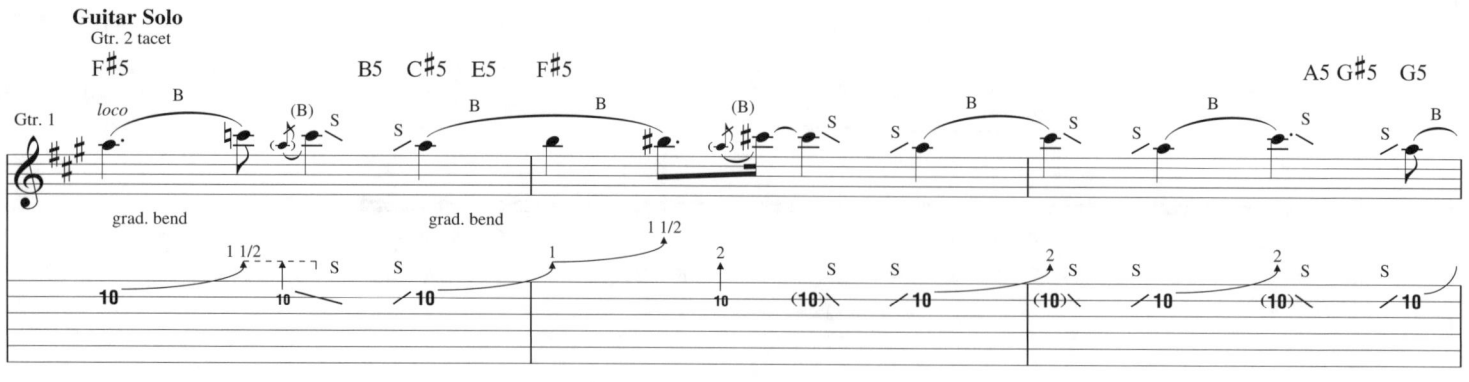

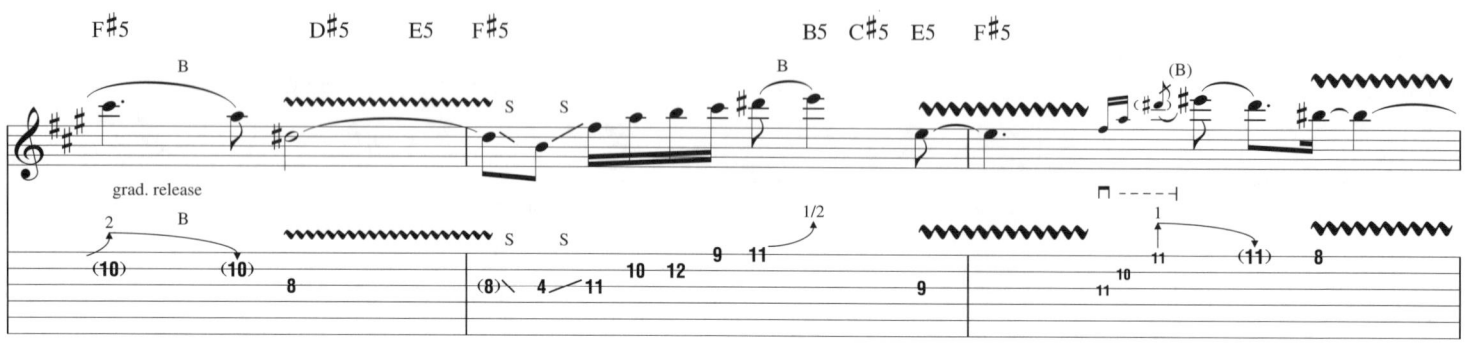

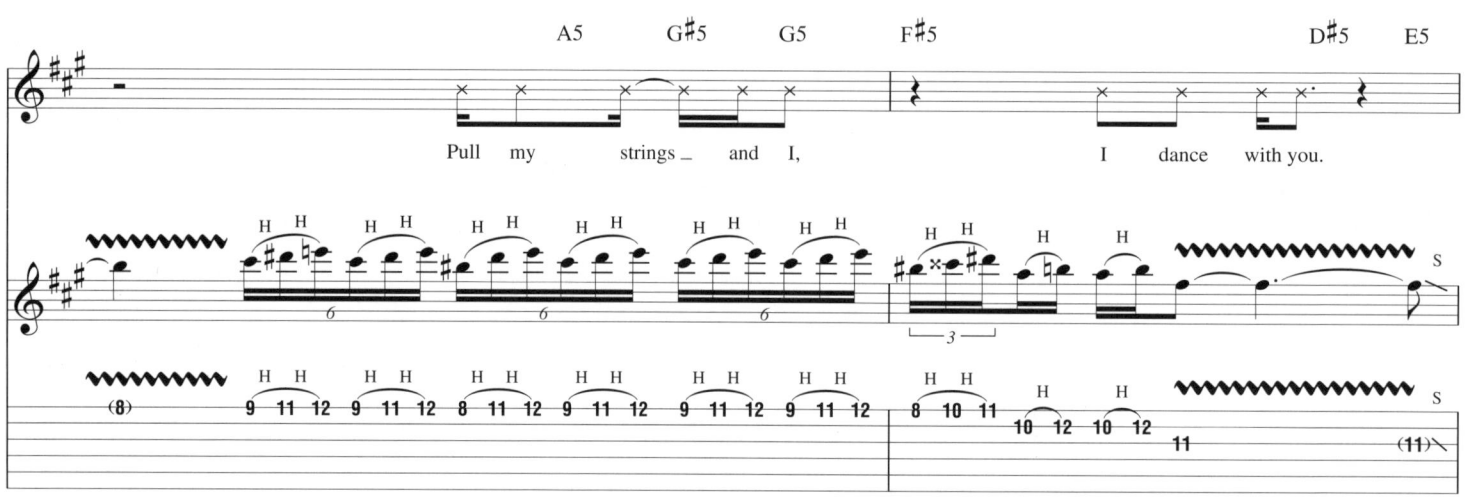

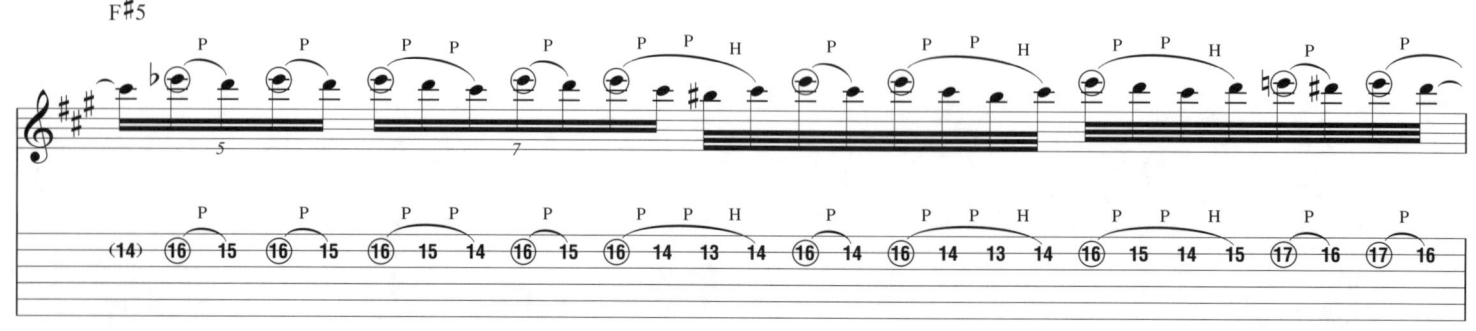

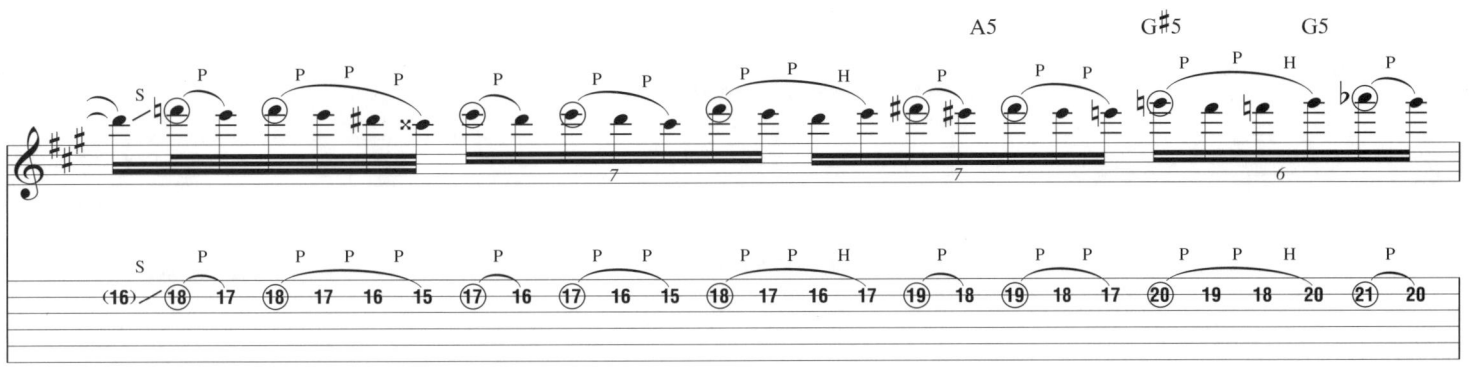
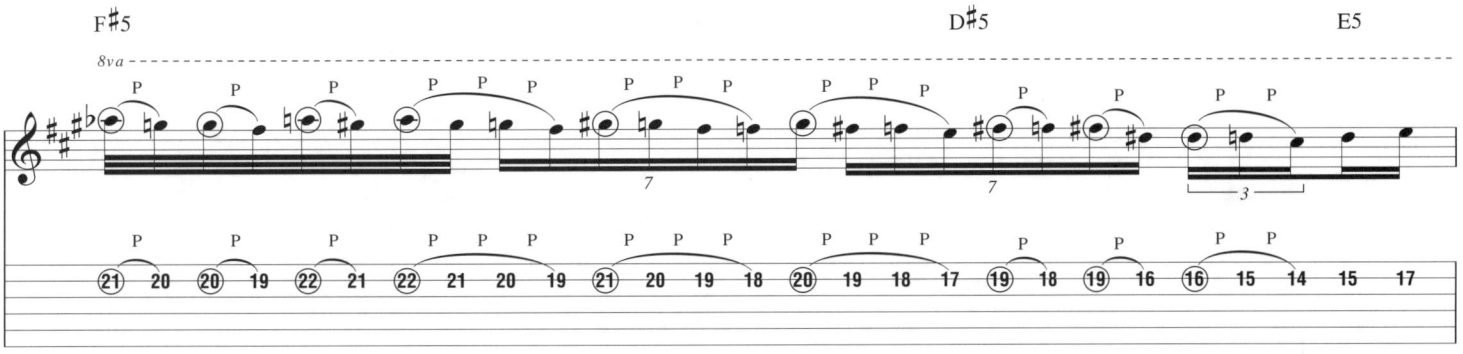
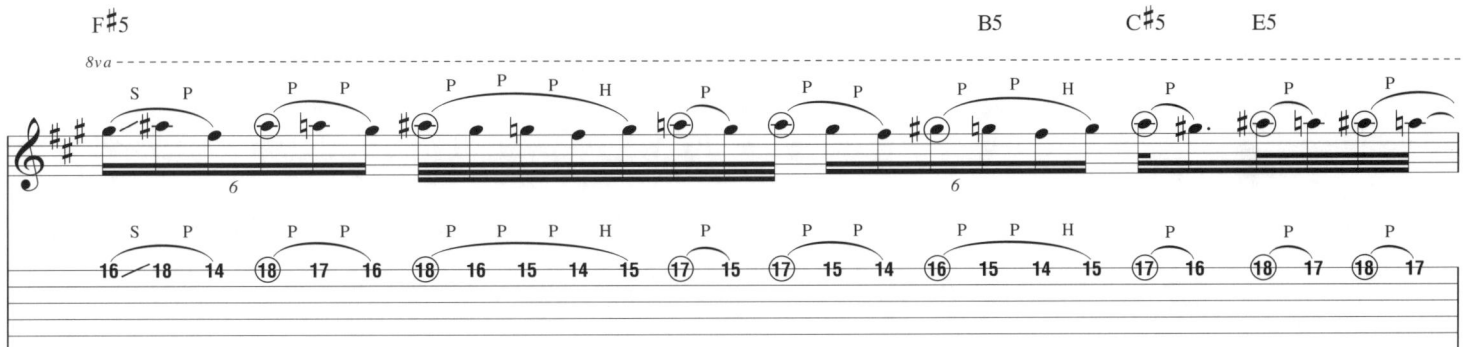
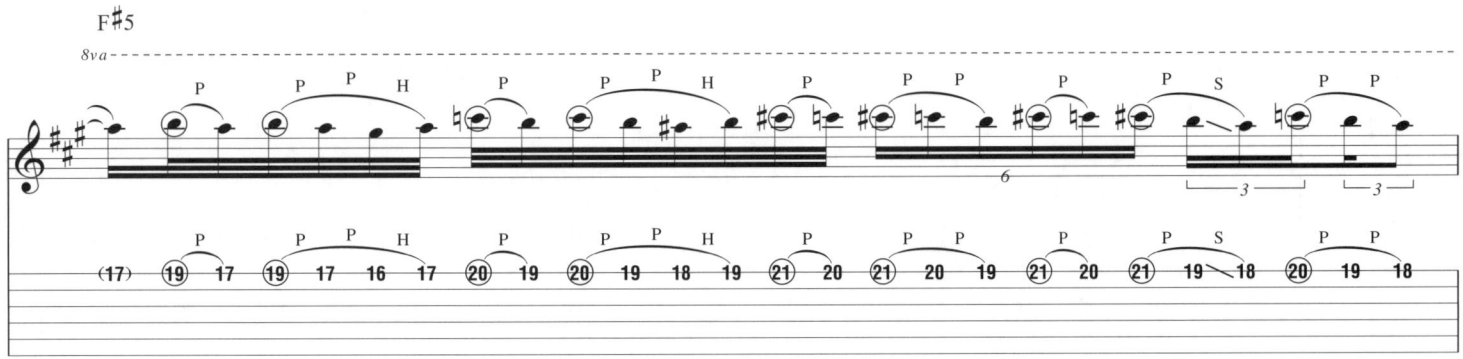
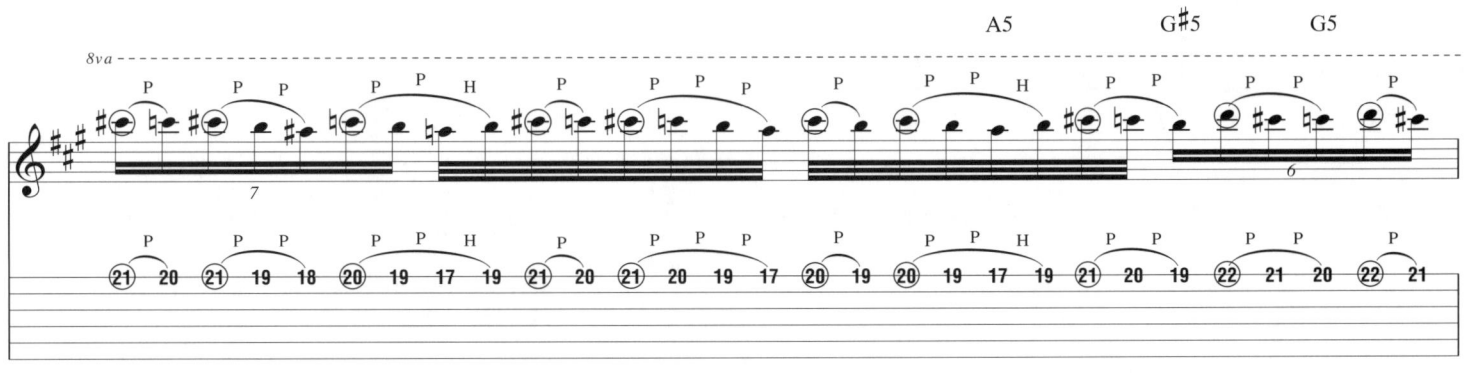

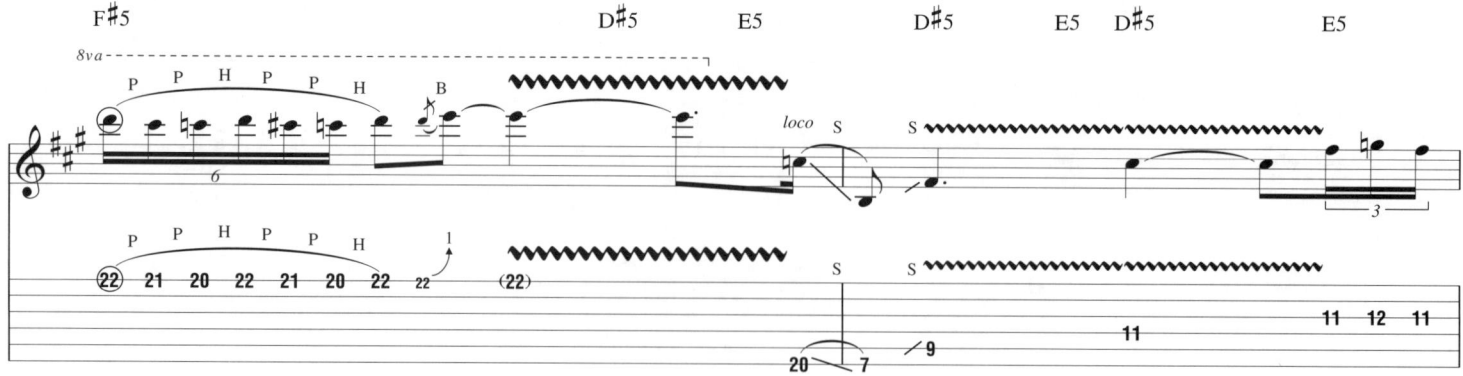

Interlude

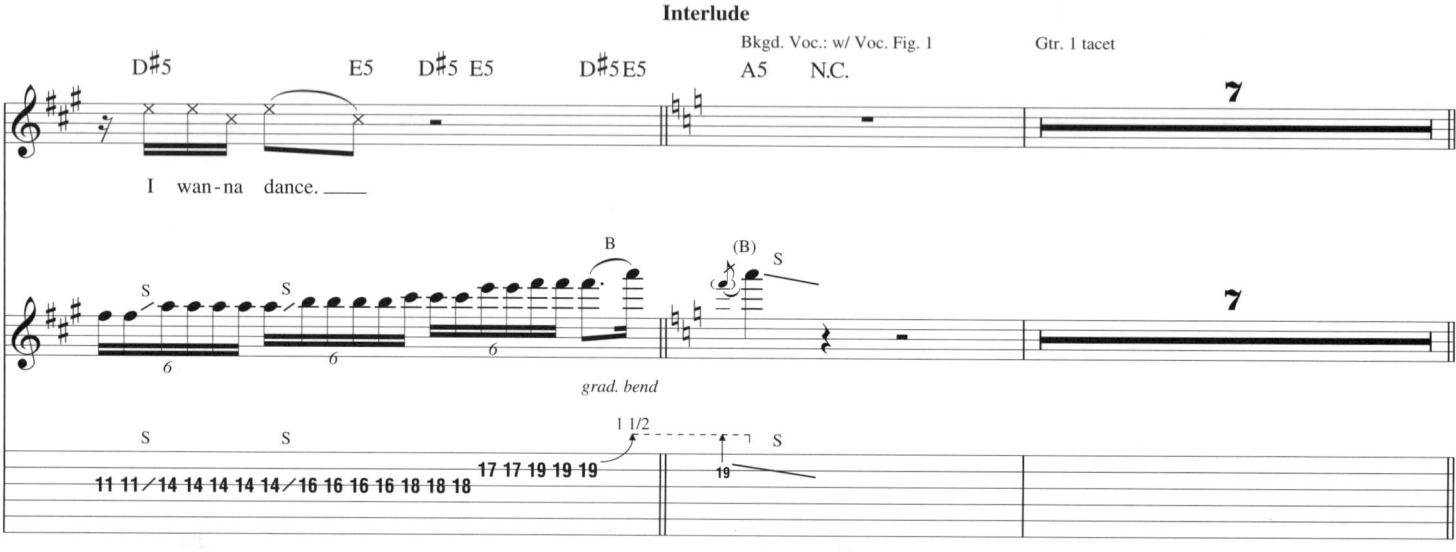

I wan-na dance.

Chorus

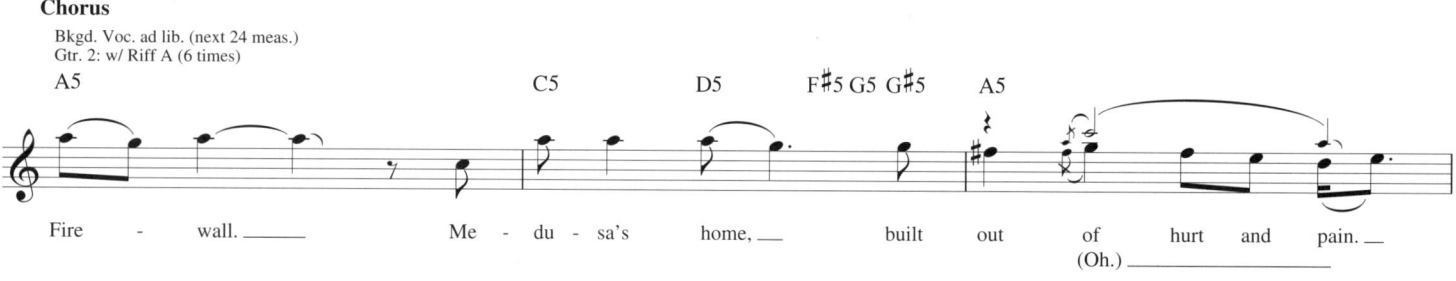

Fire-wall. Me-du-sa's home, built out of hurt and pain. (Oh.)

Wel-come to the fire-wall. If I get too close, I

will go down in flames. A vic-tim of your fire-wall.
(Oh.)

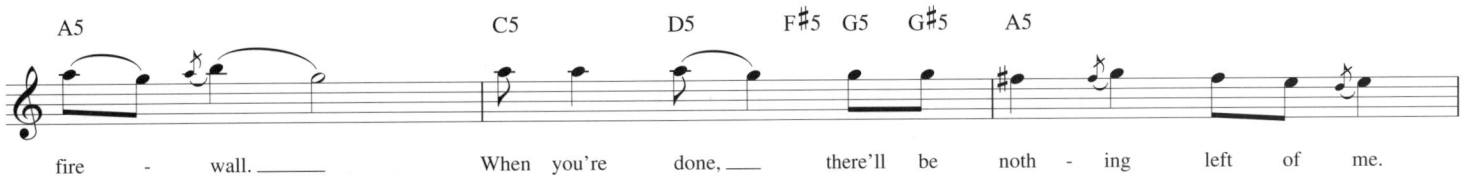

*Bkgd. vocs. are female.

Freak Show Excess

By Steve Vai

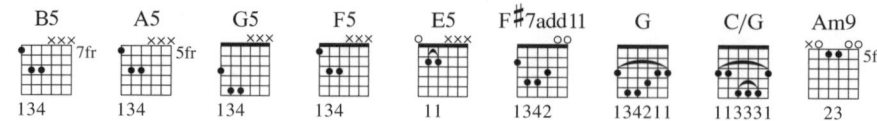

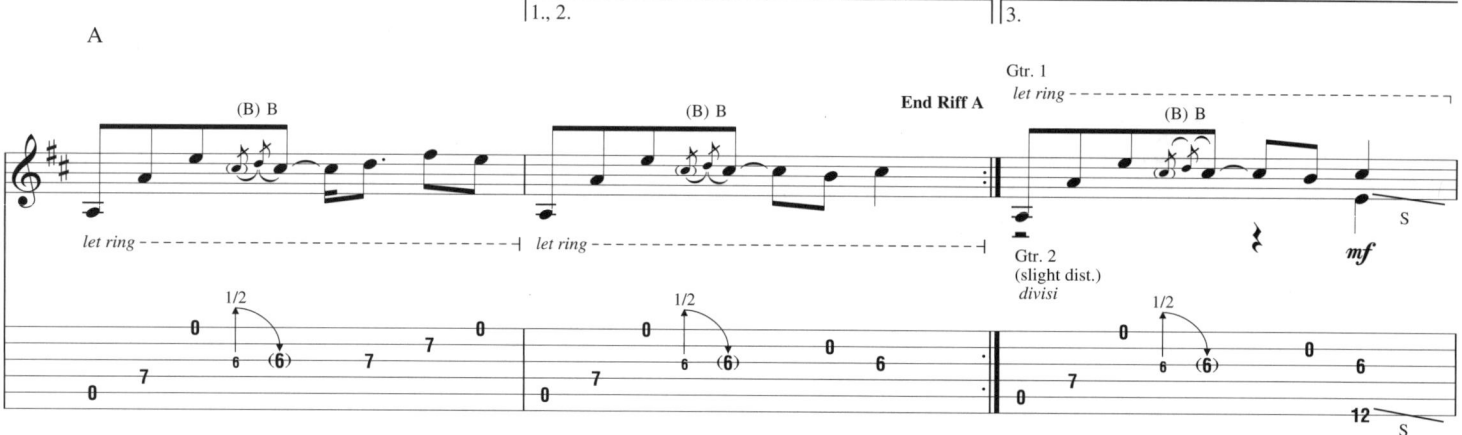
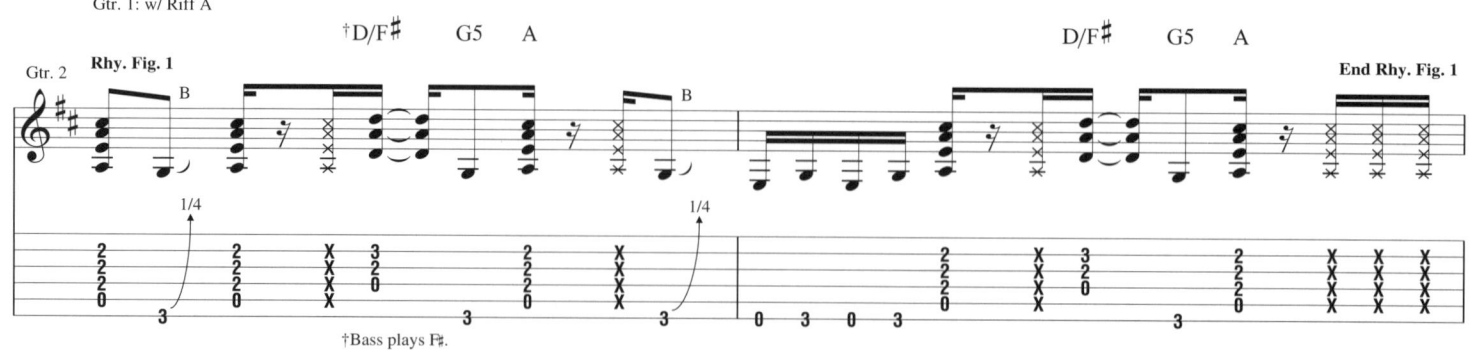
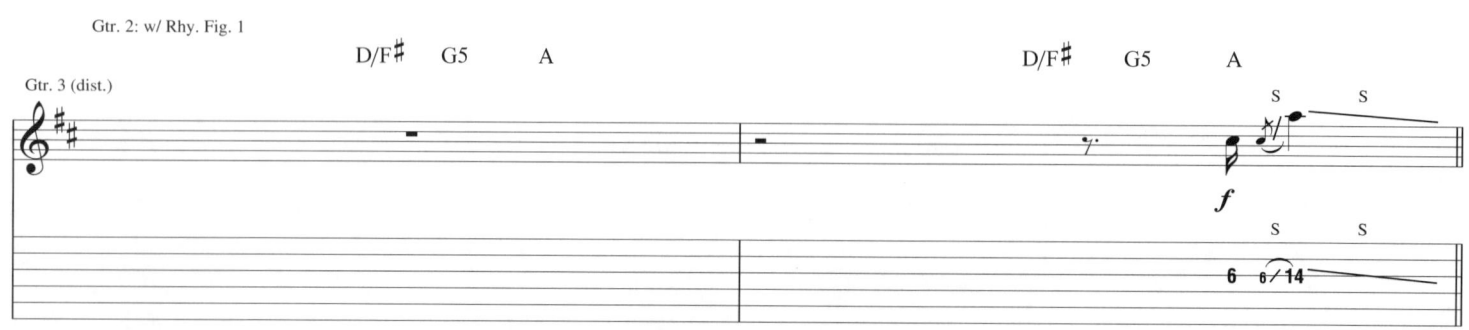

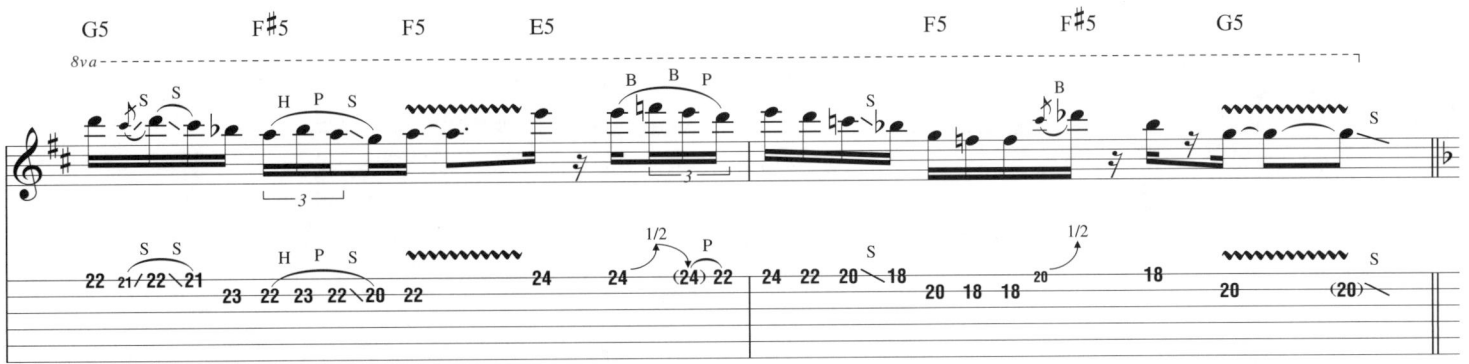
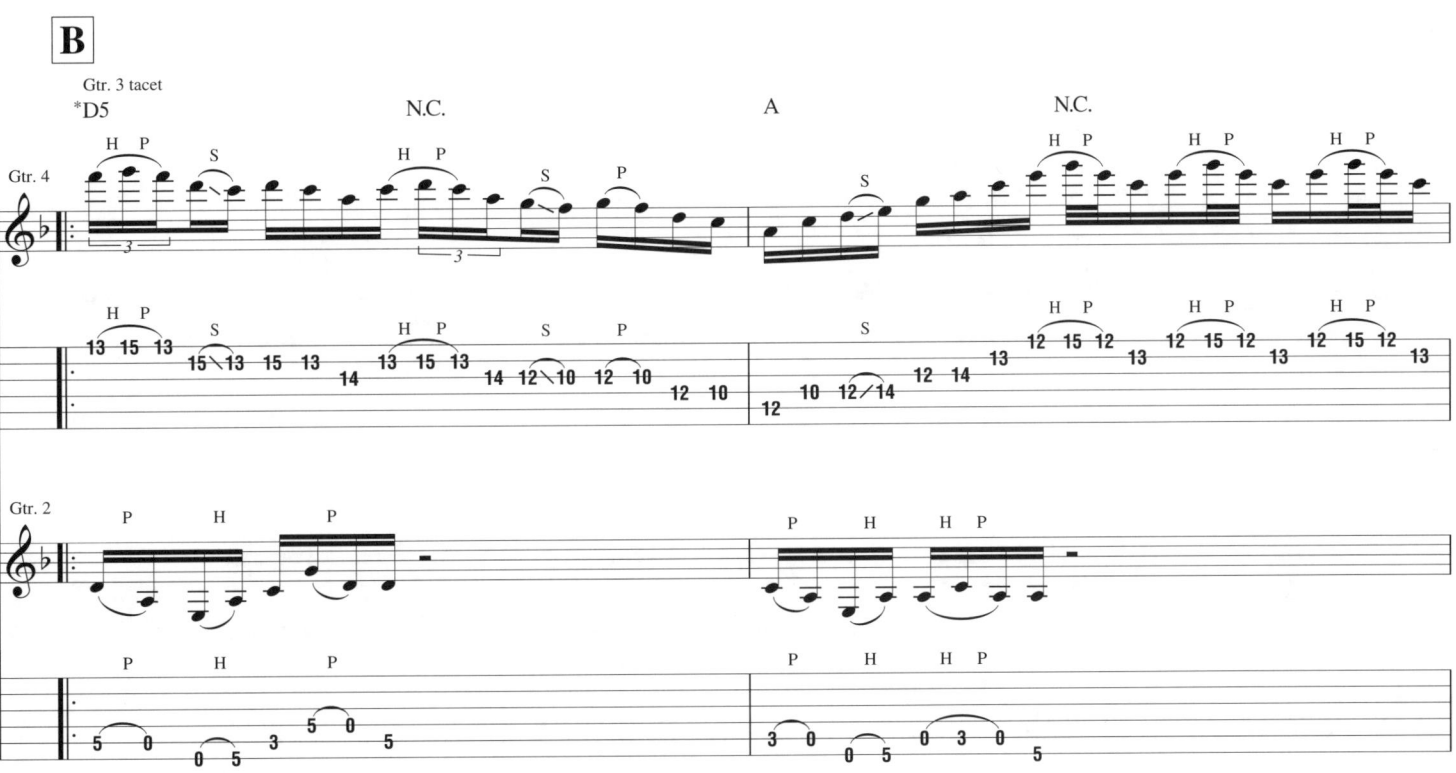
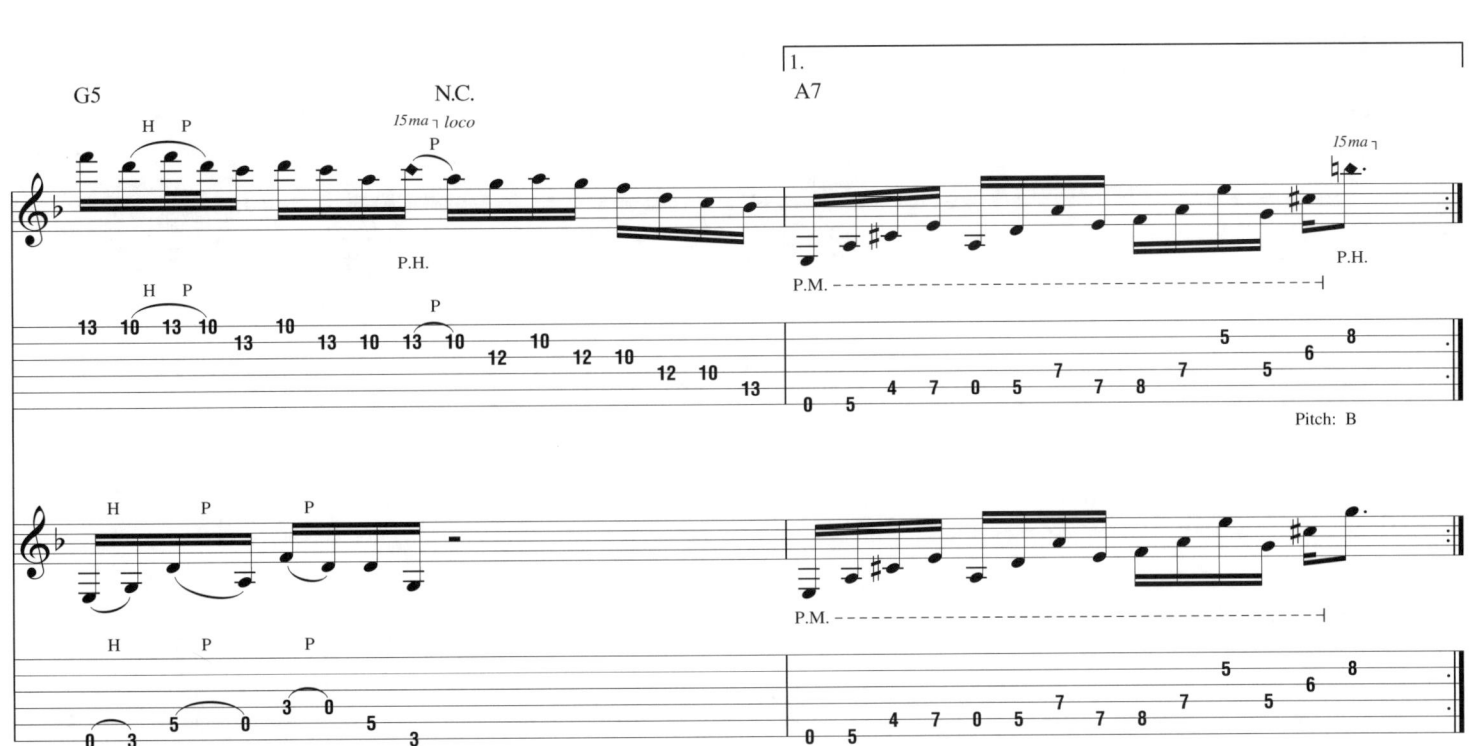

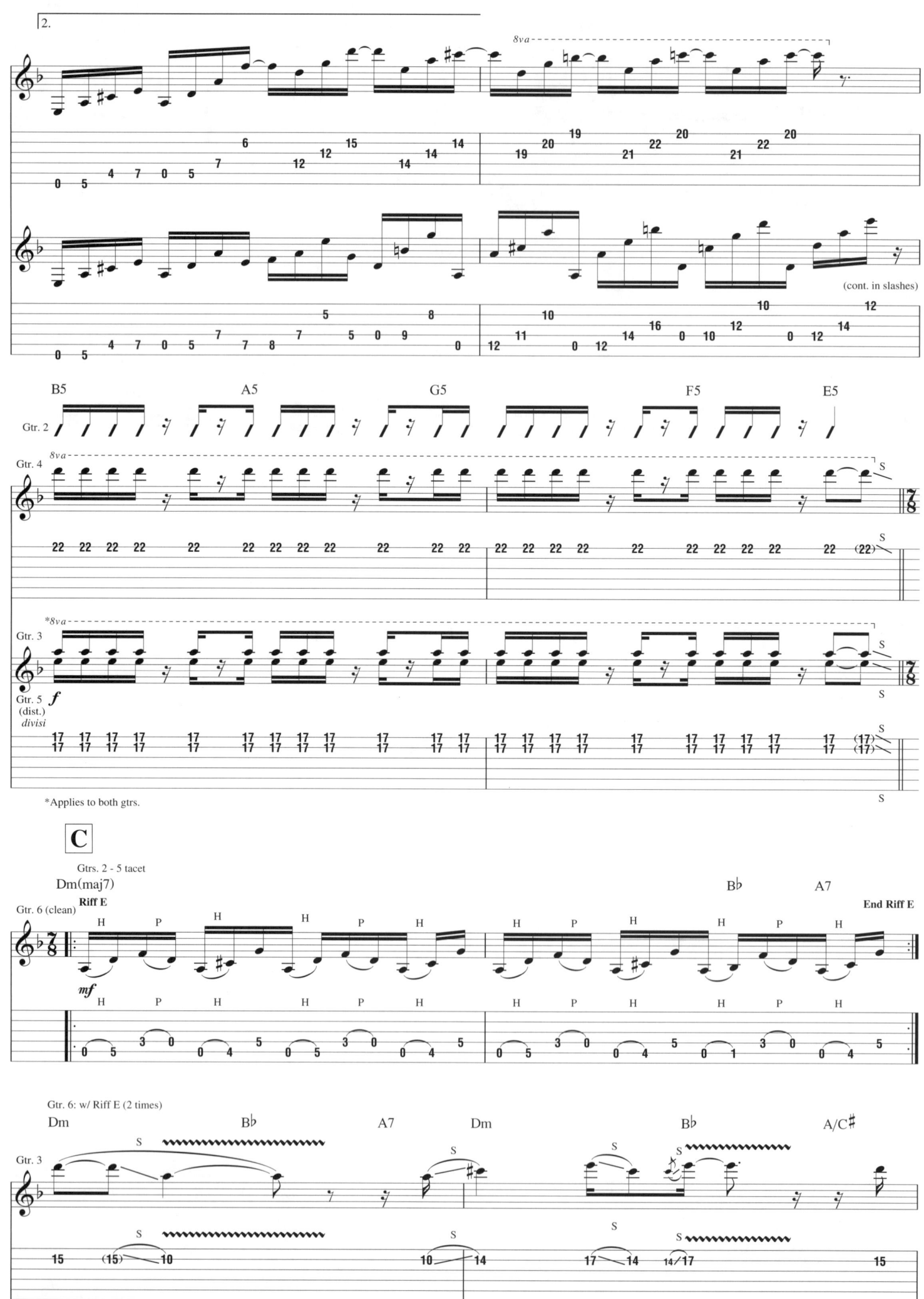

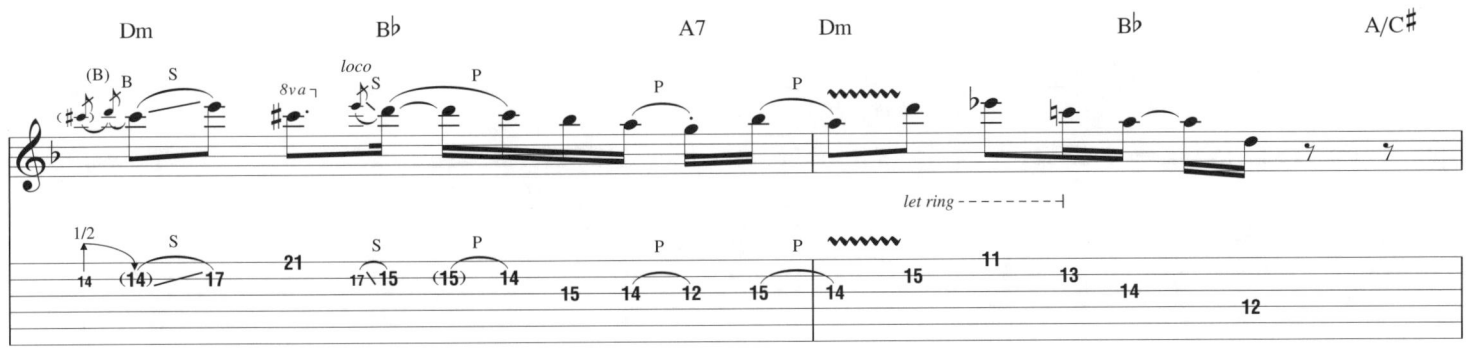
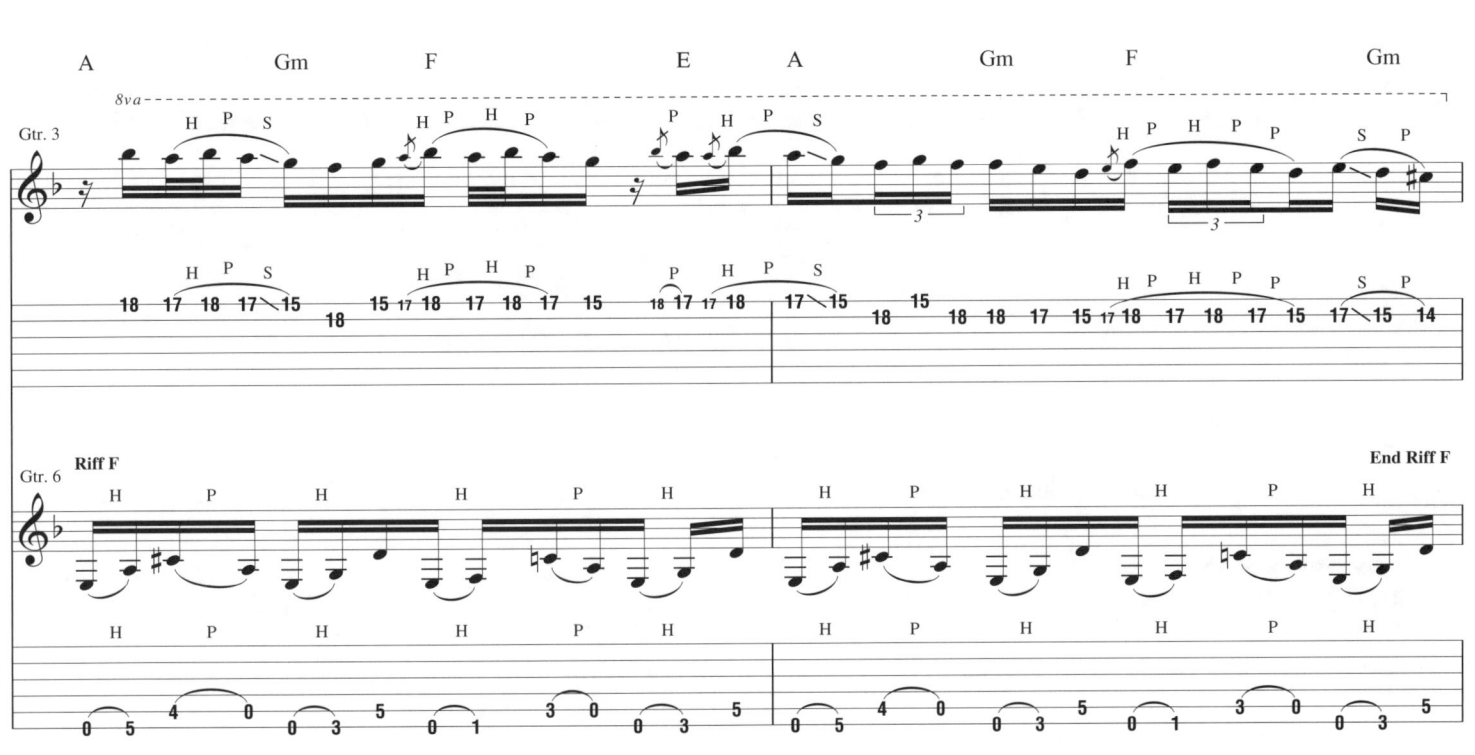
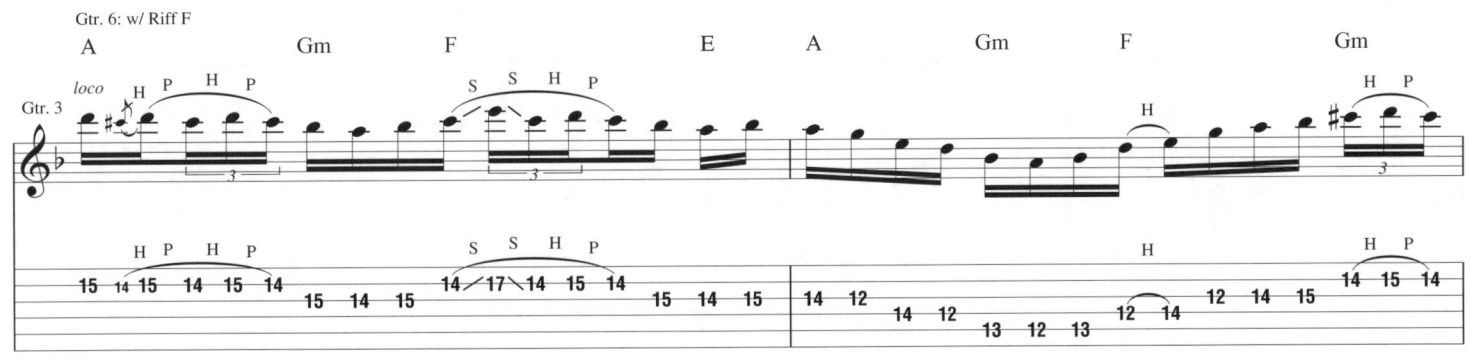
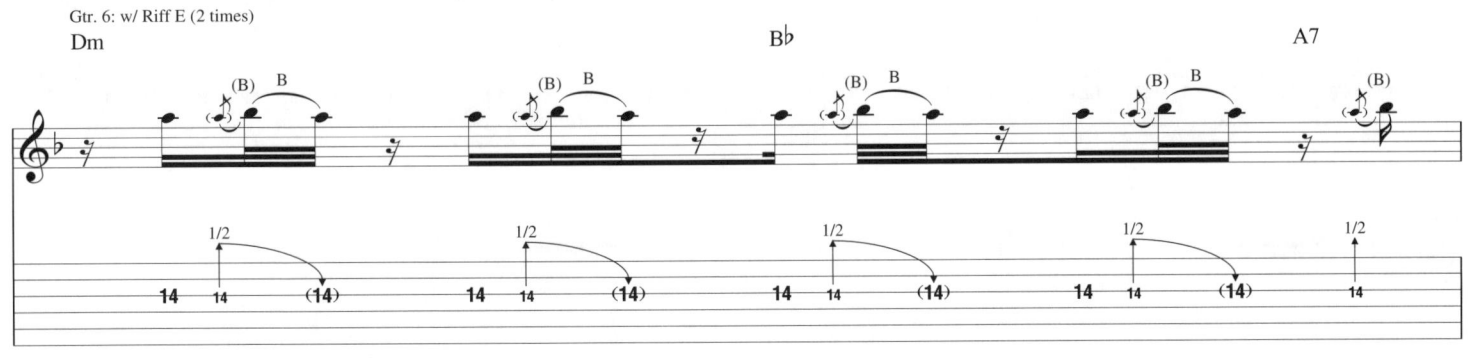

73

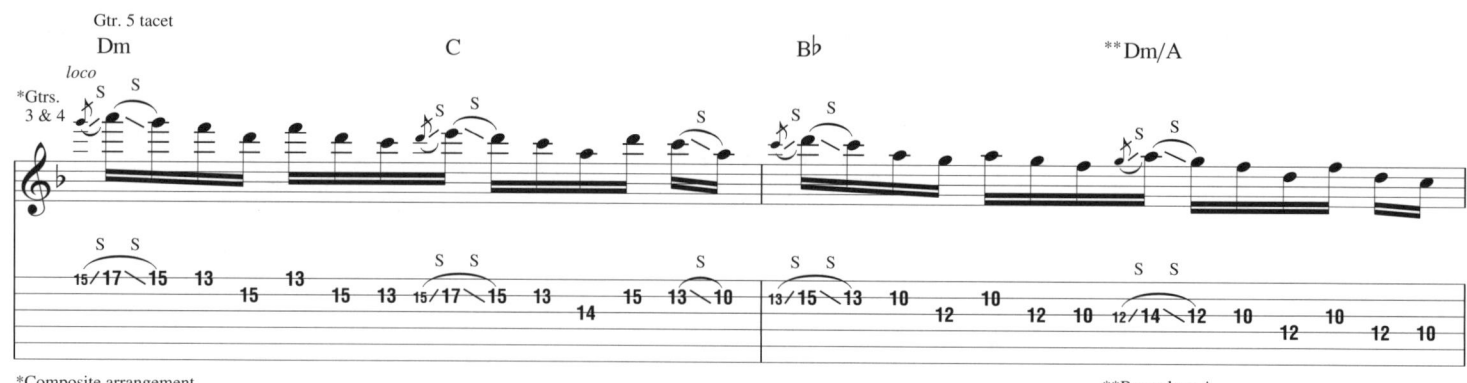
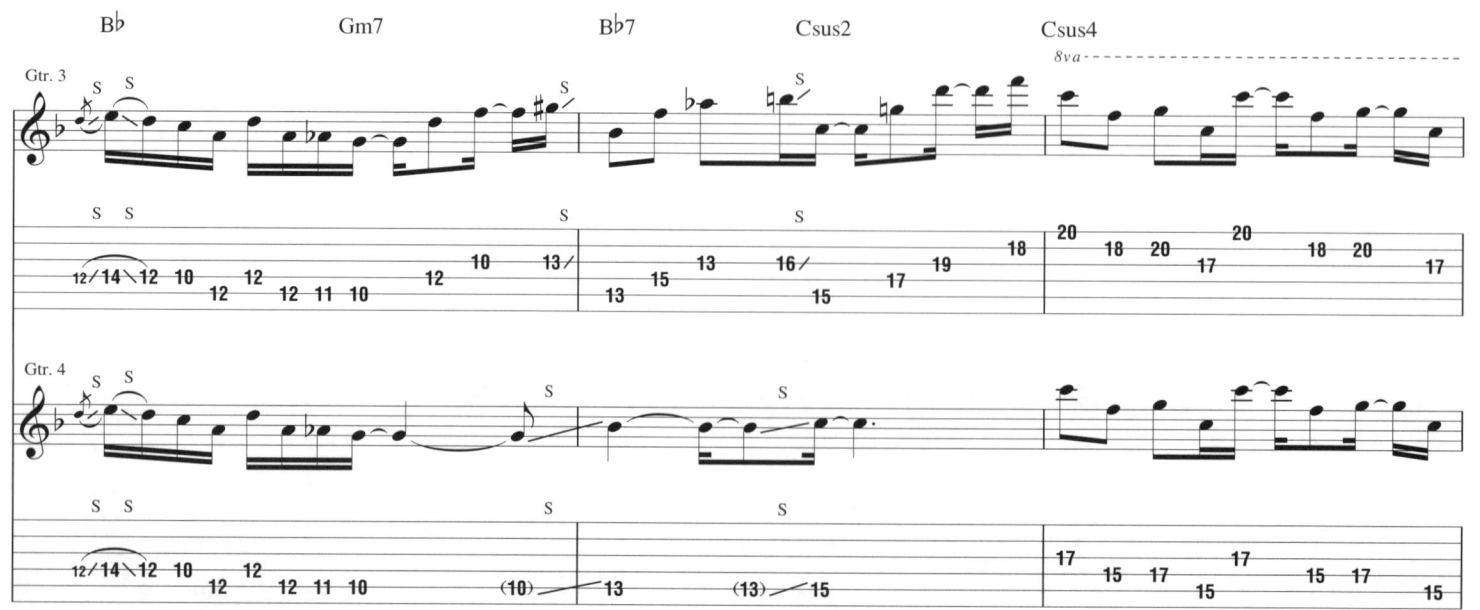

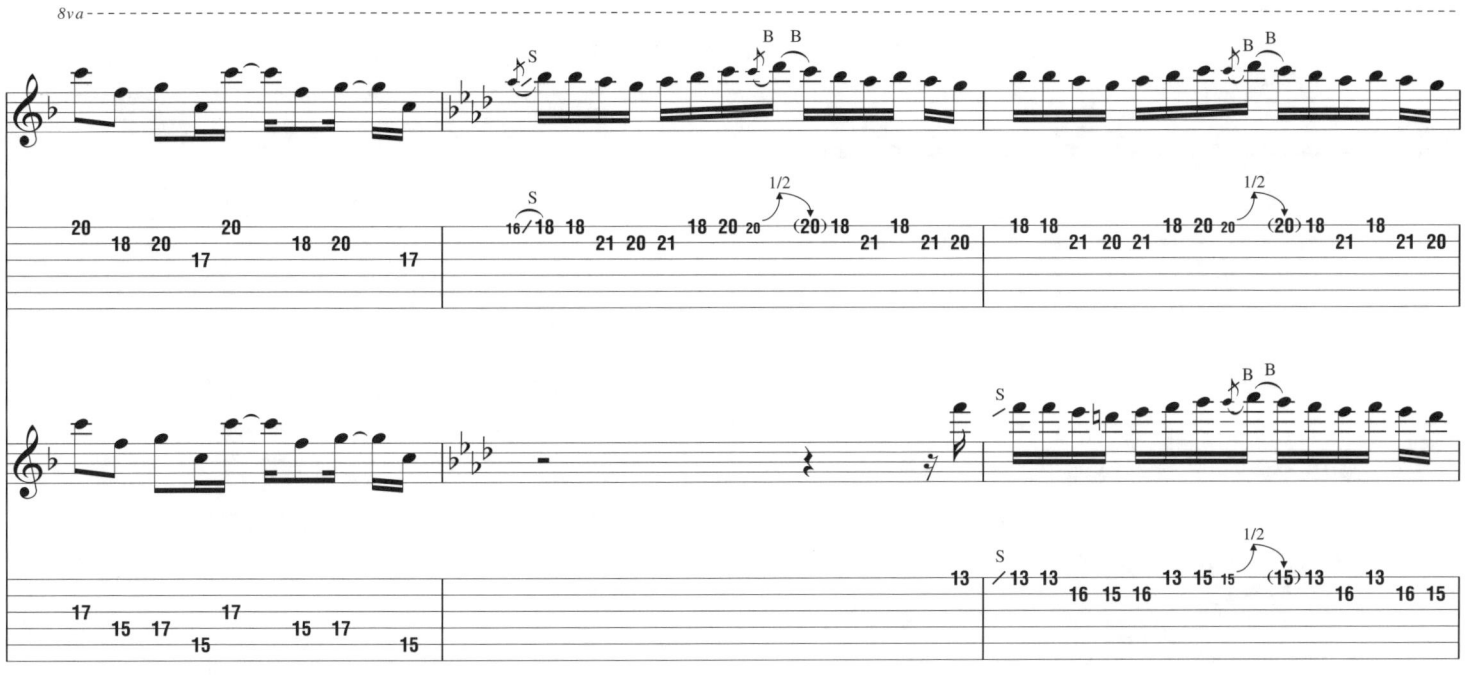

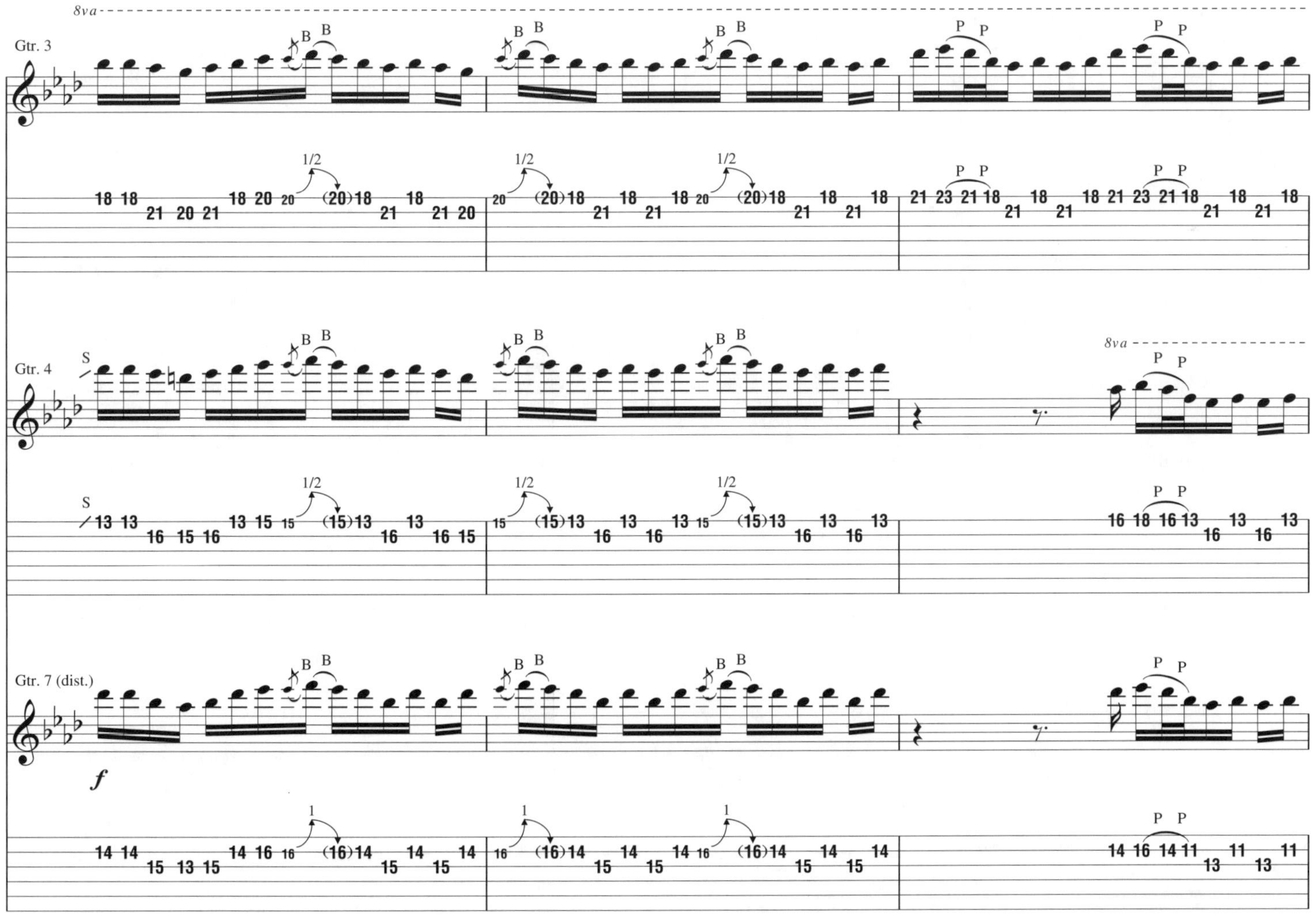

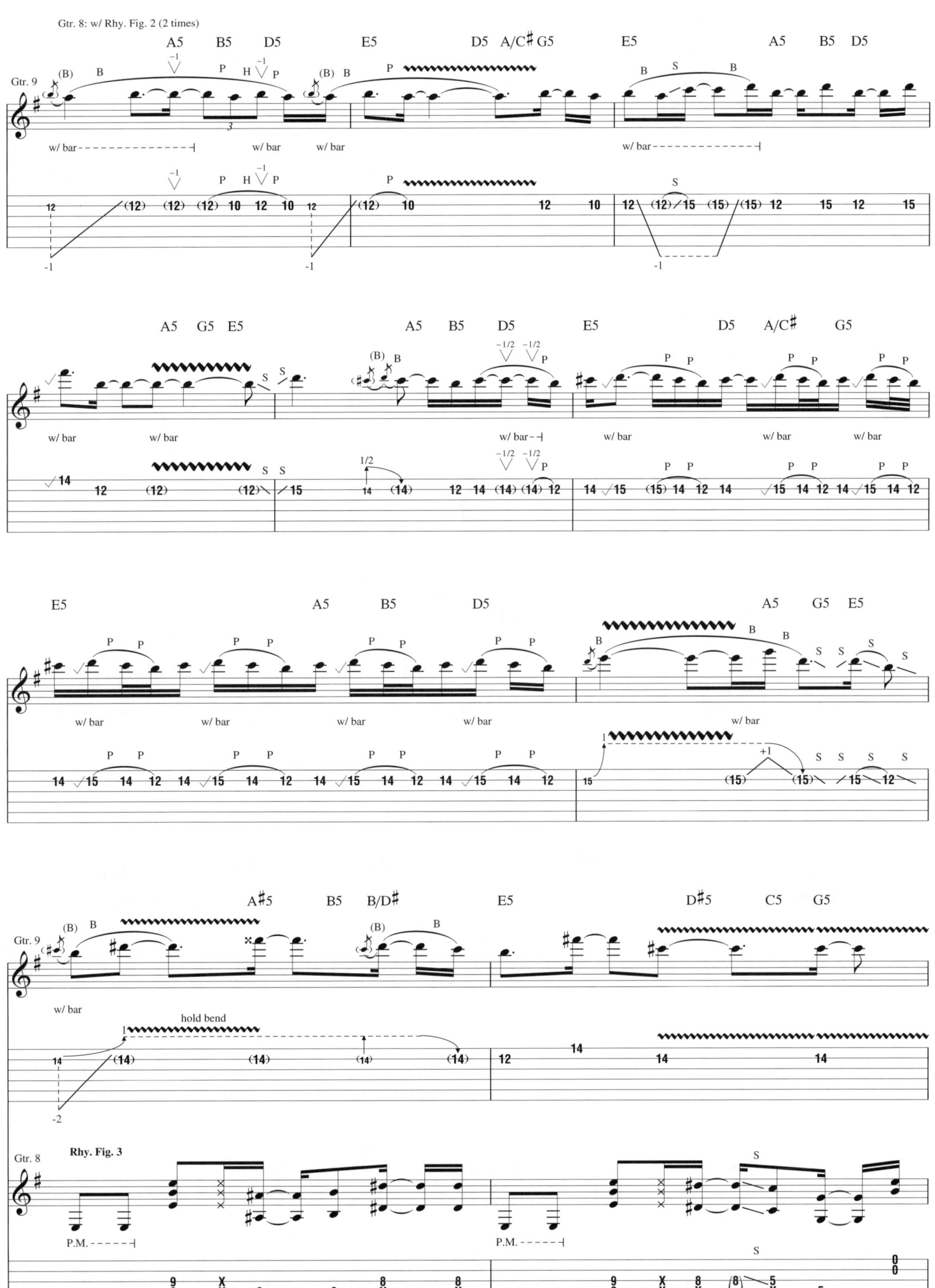

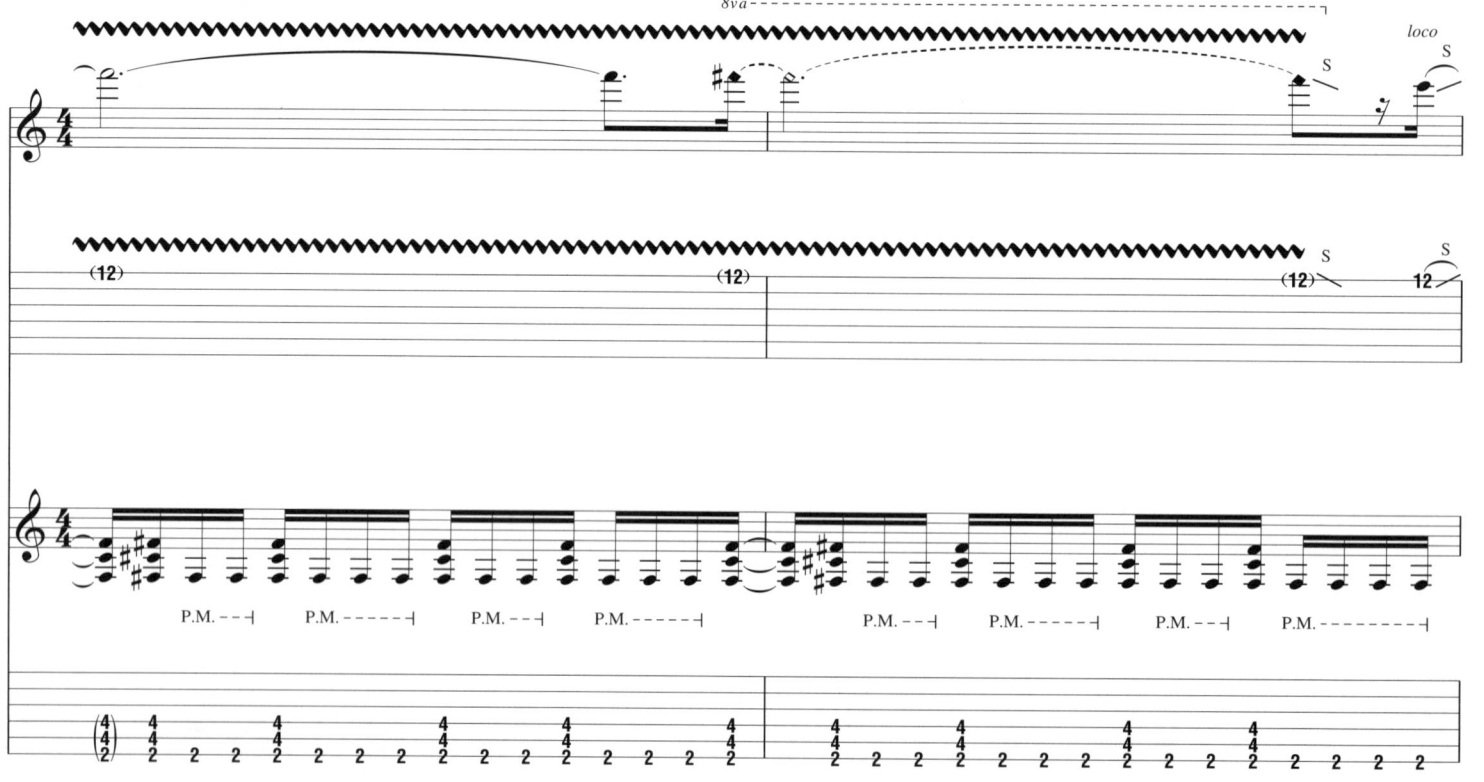

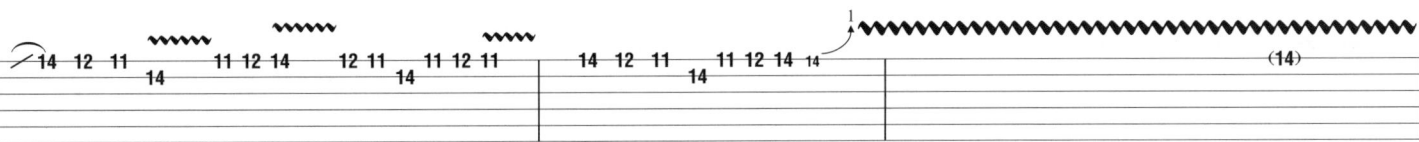

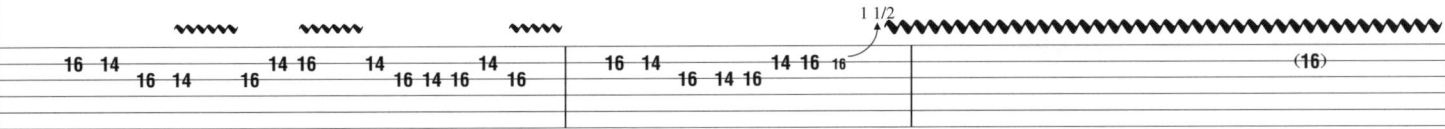

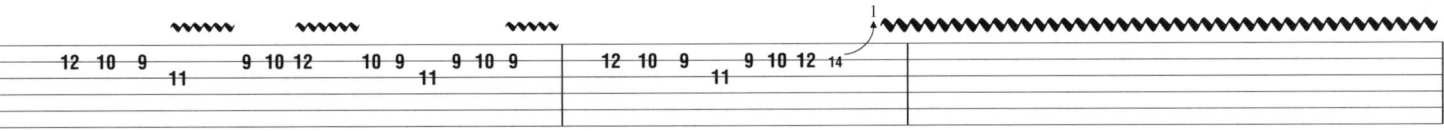

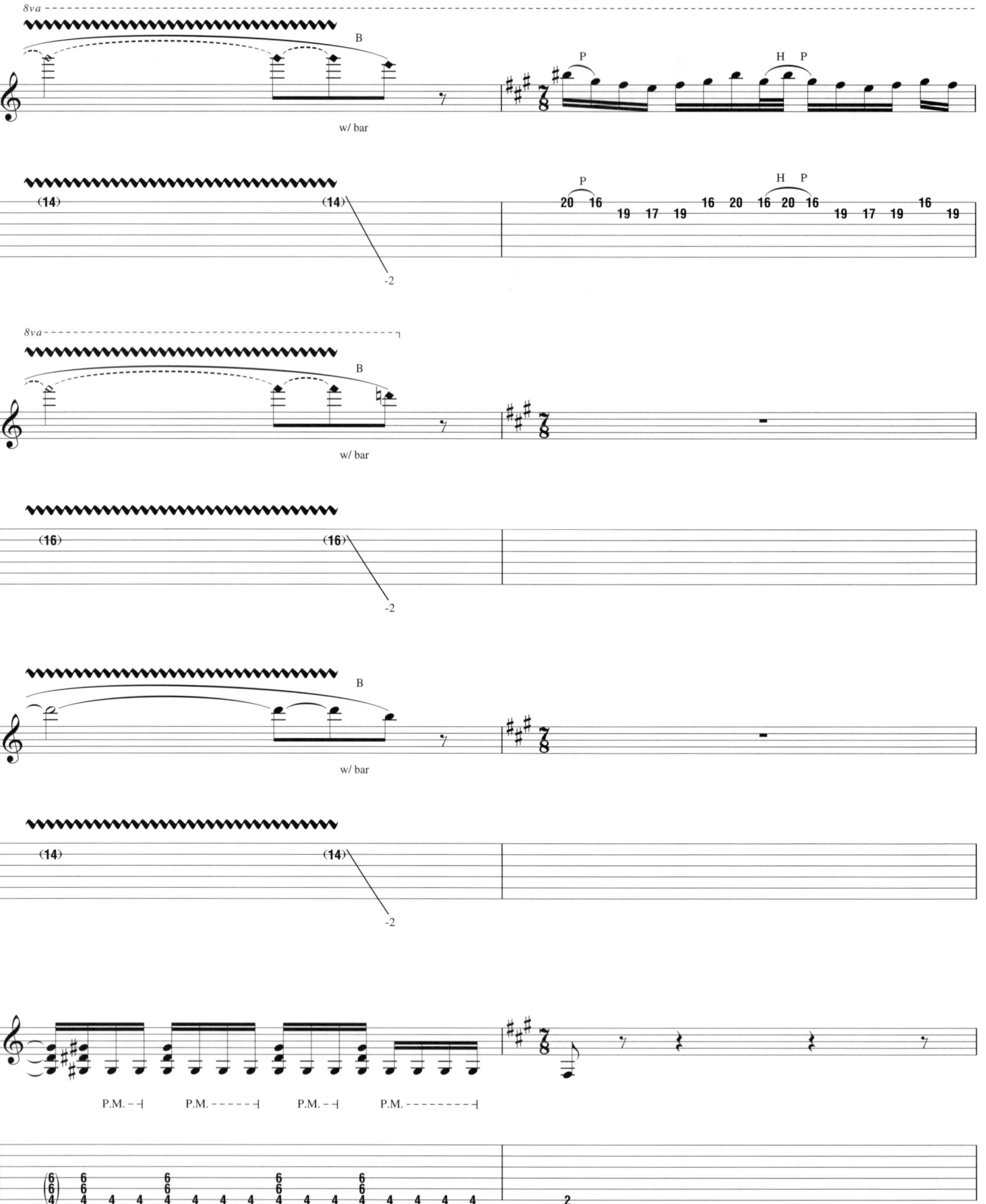

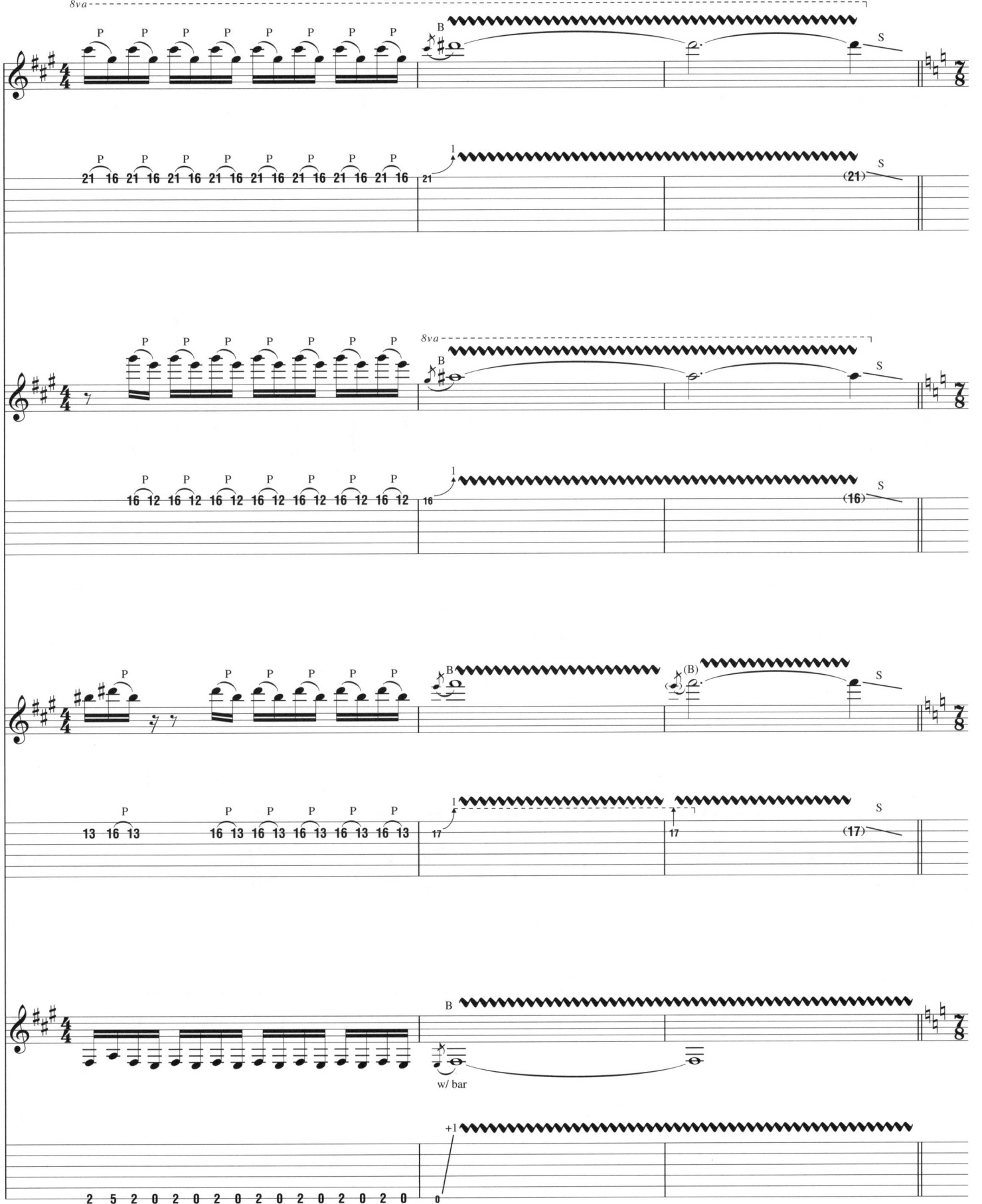

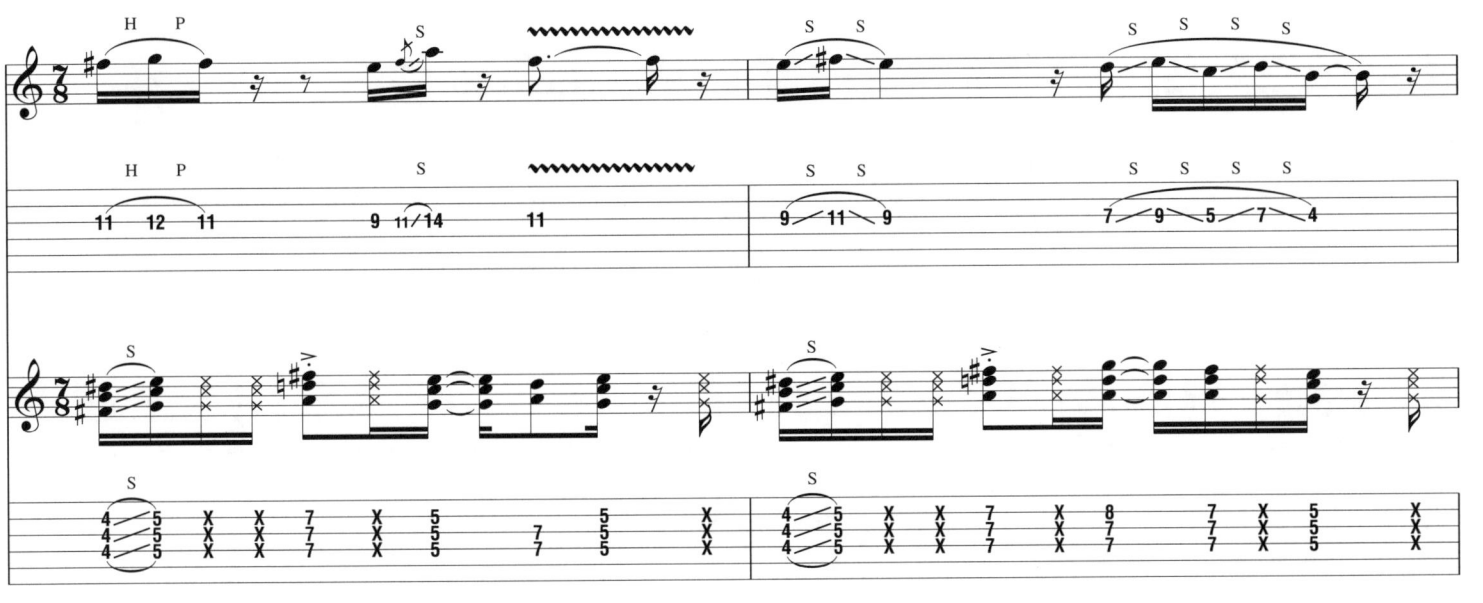

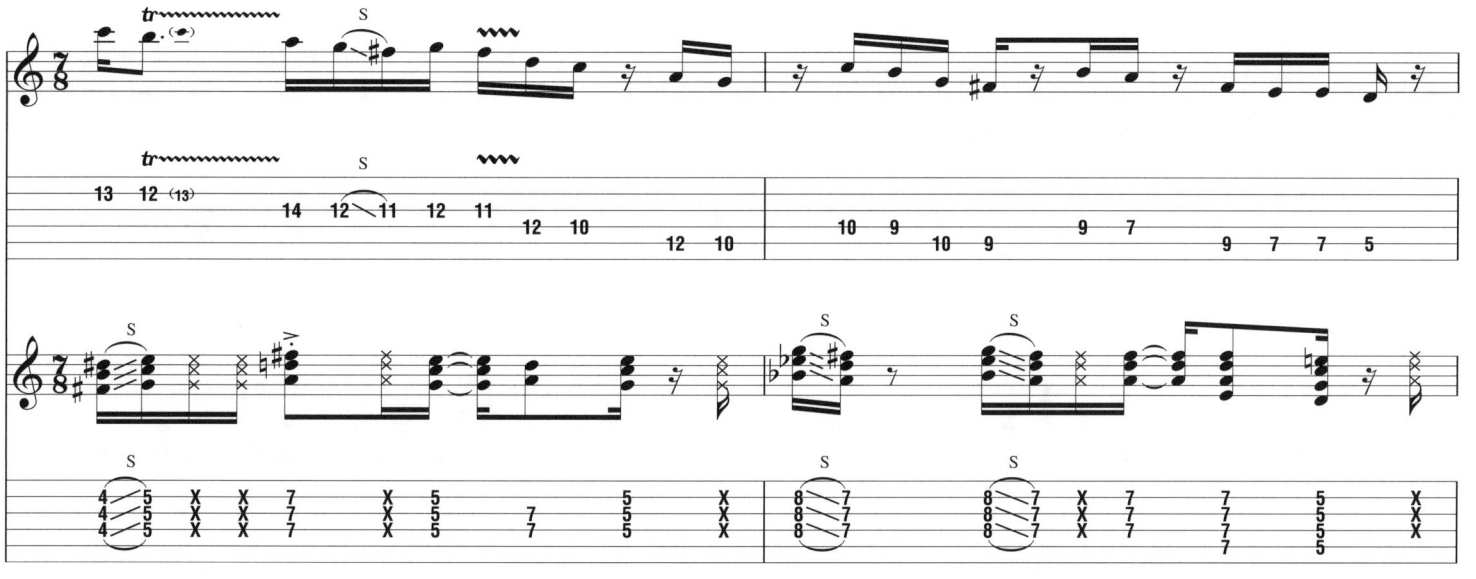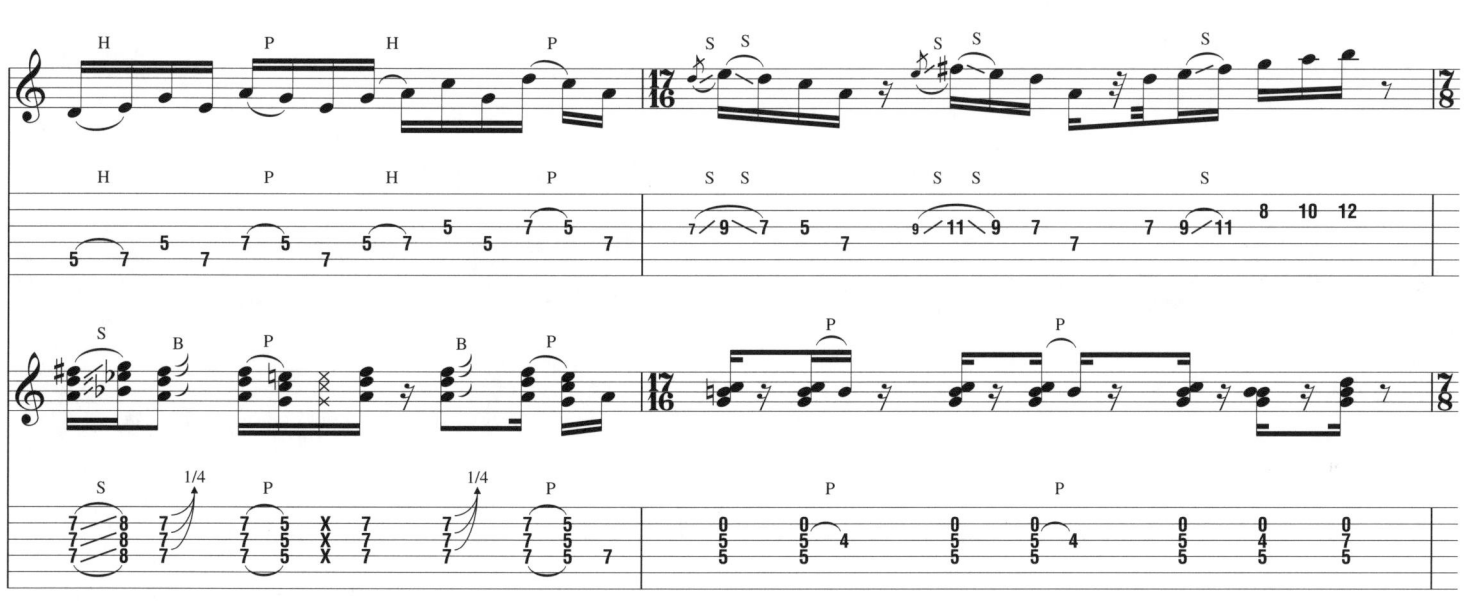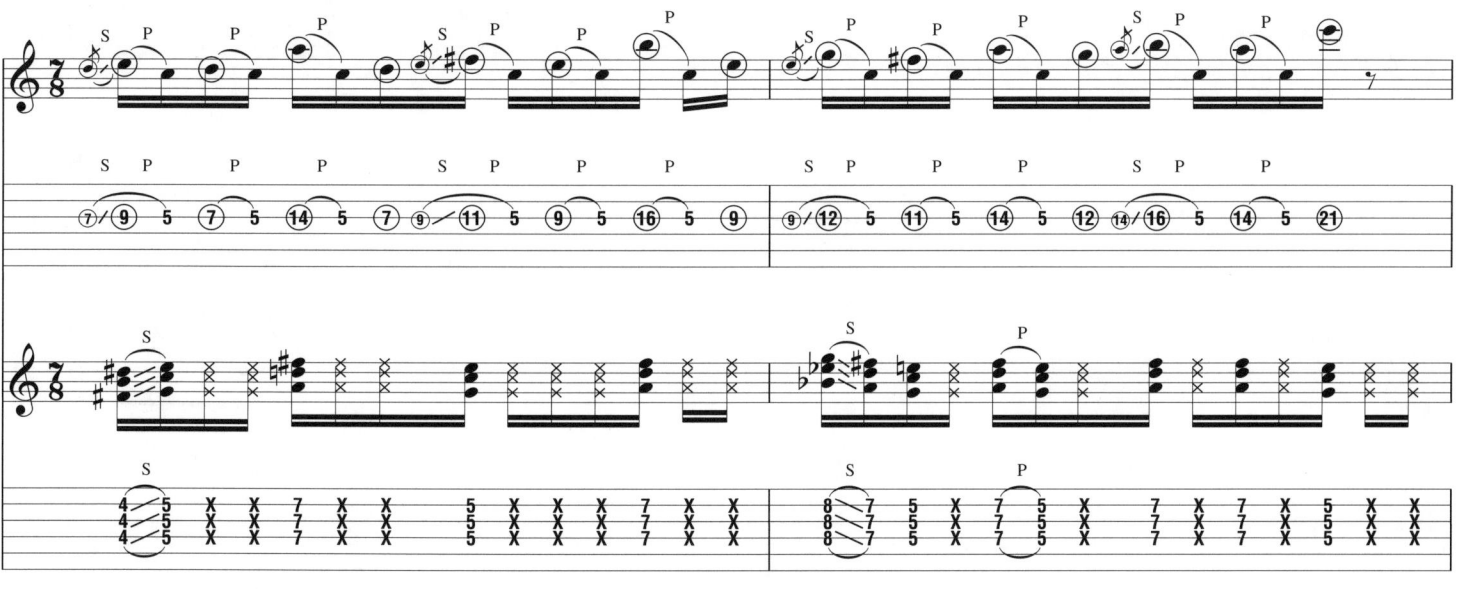

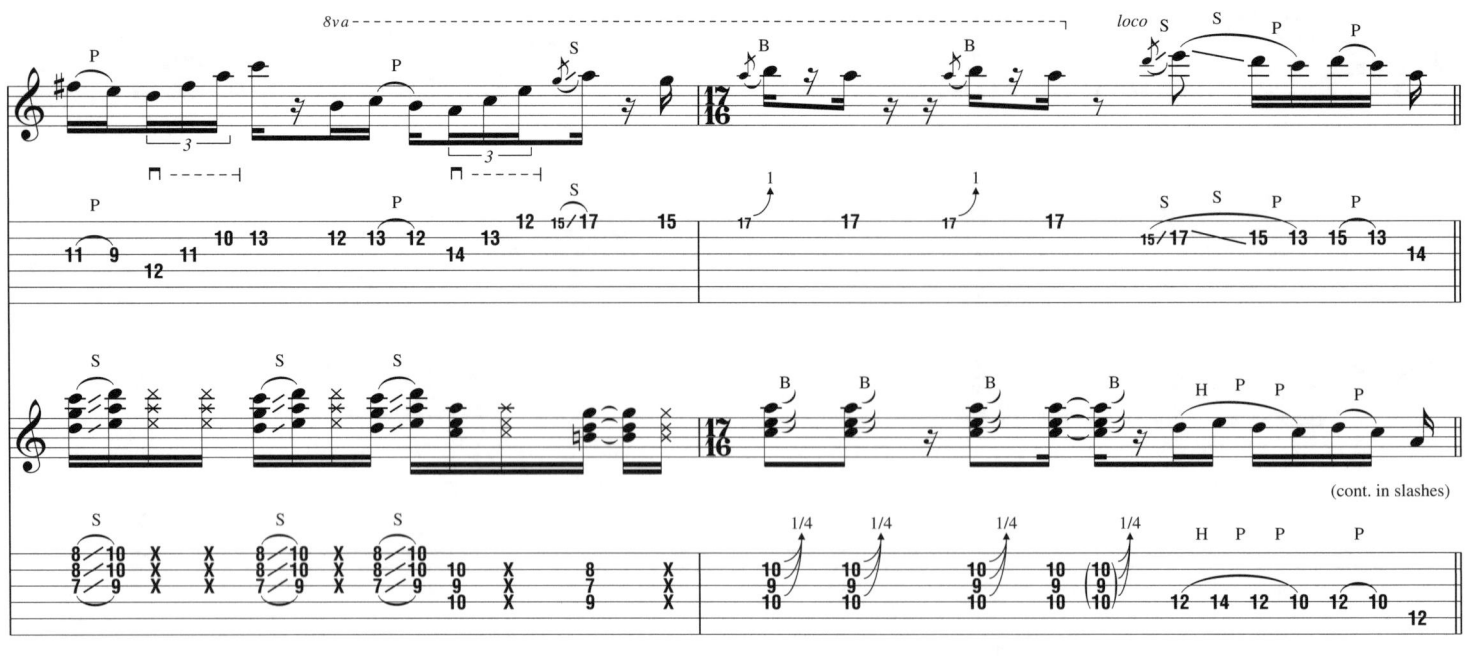

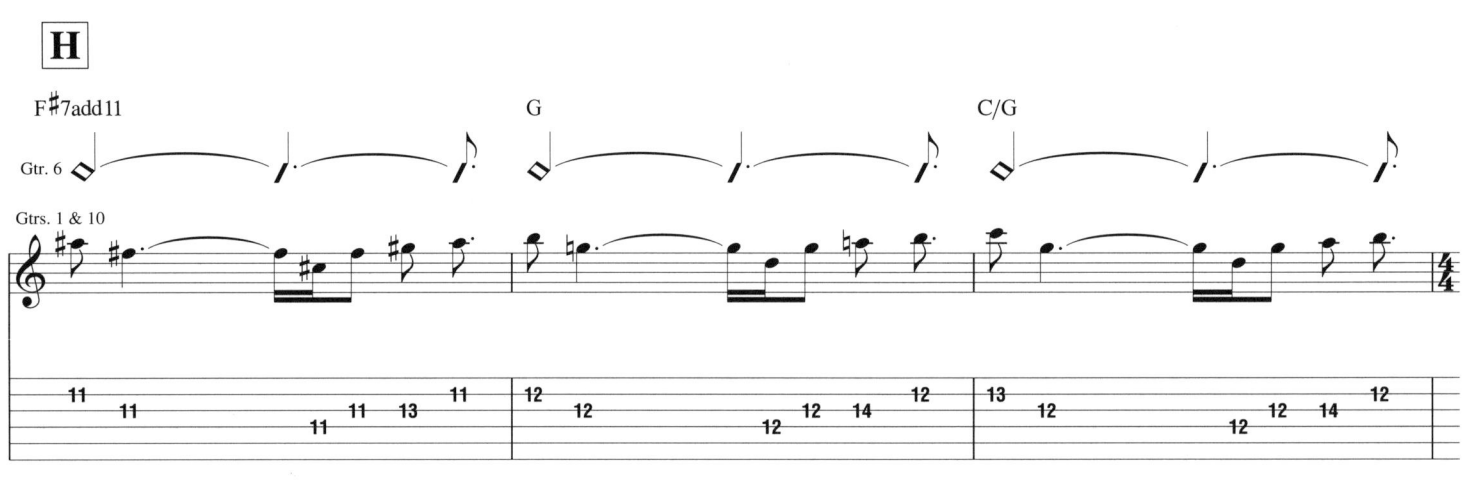

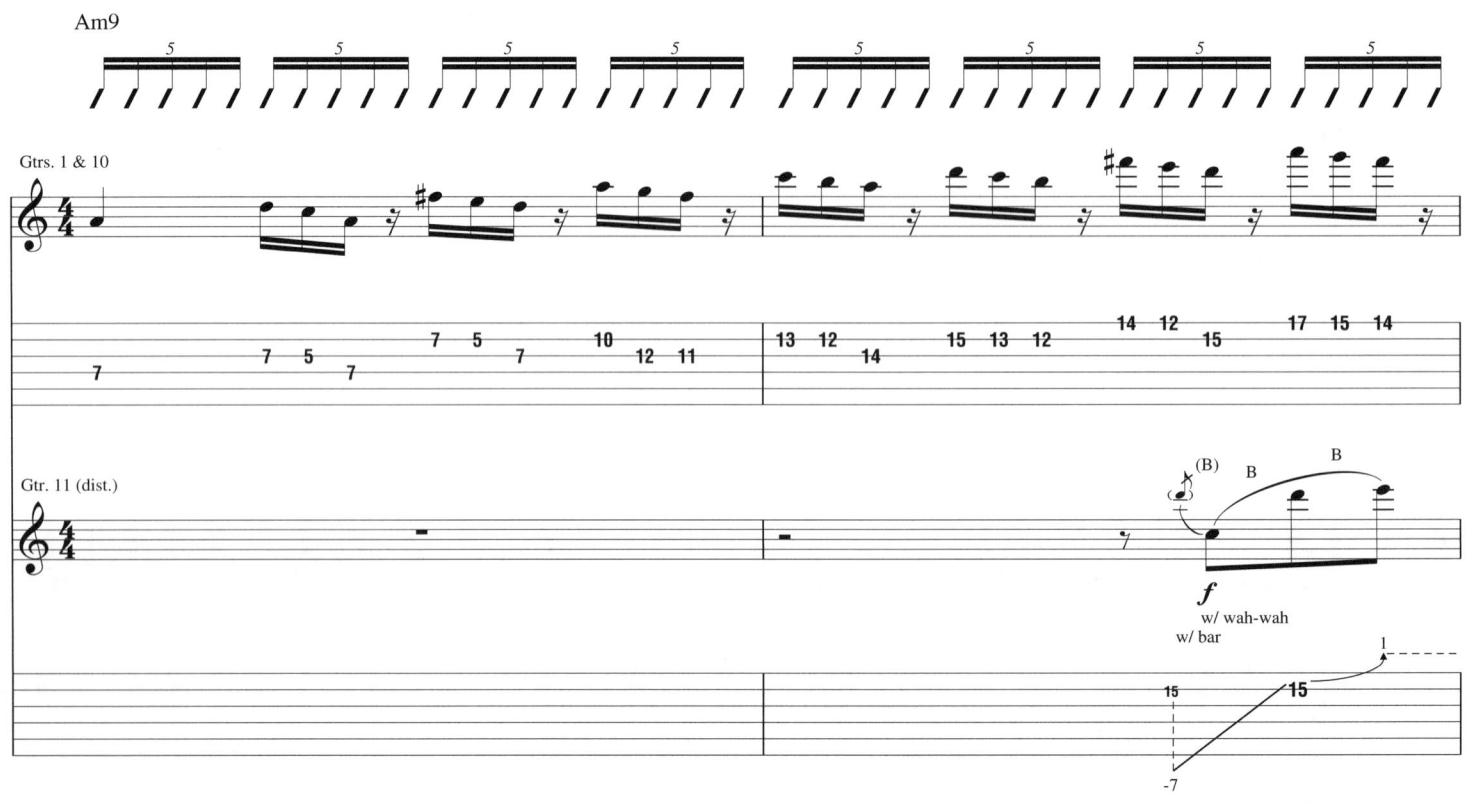

94

Free time

Gtrs. 1, 6 & 10 tacet
N.C.

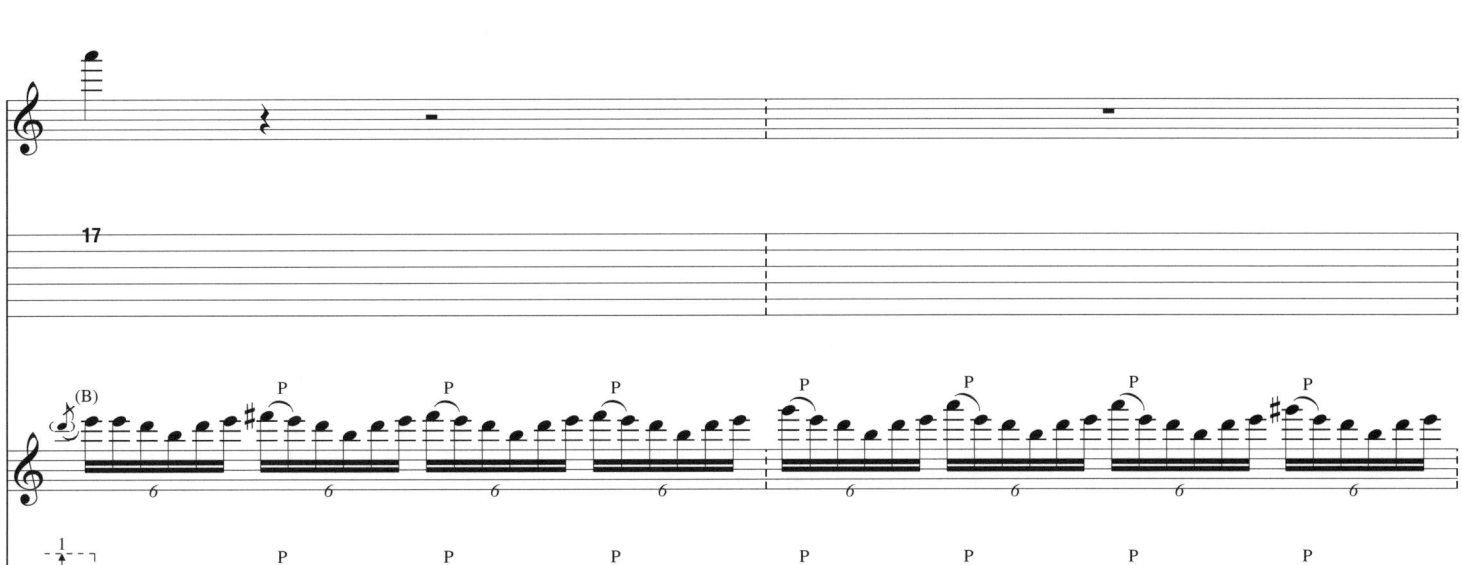

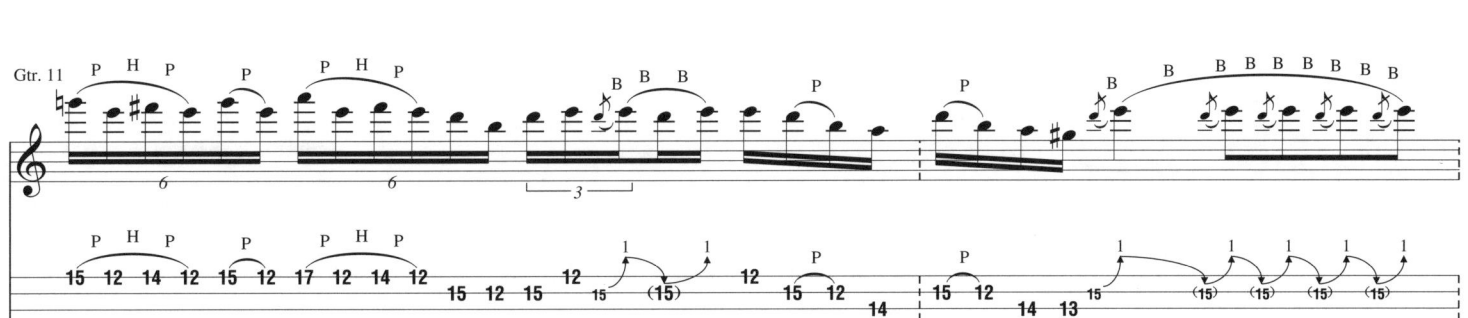

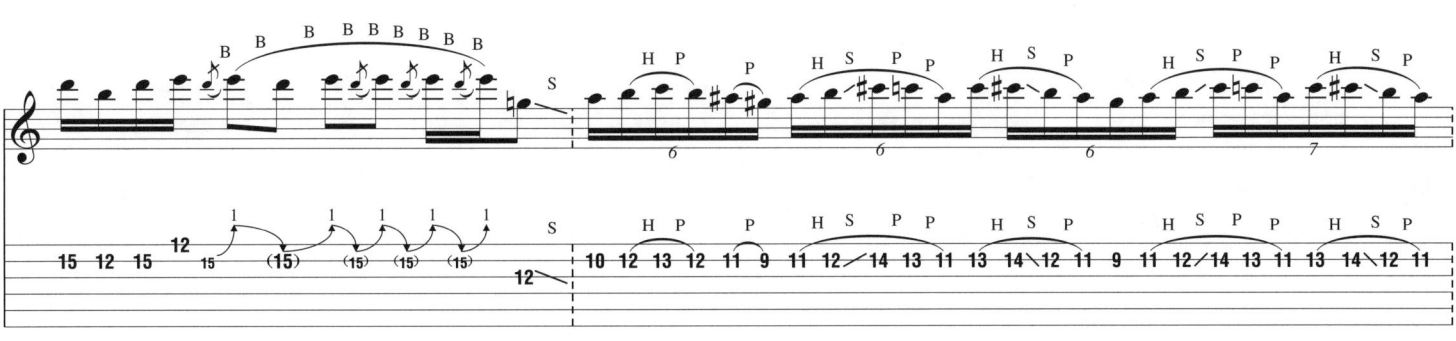

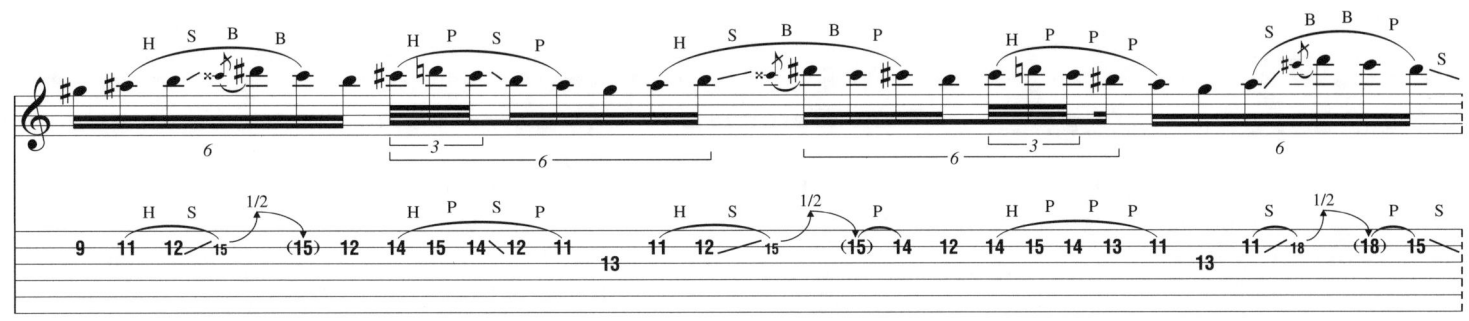

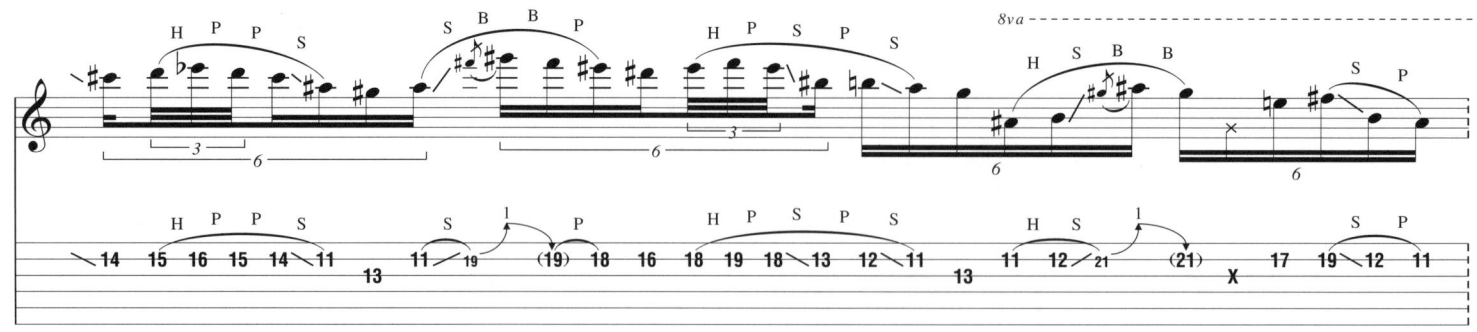
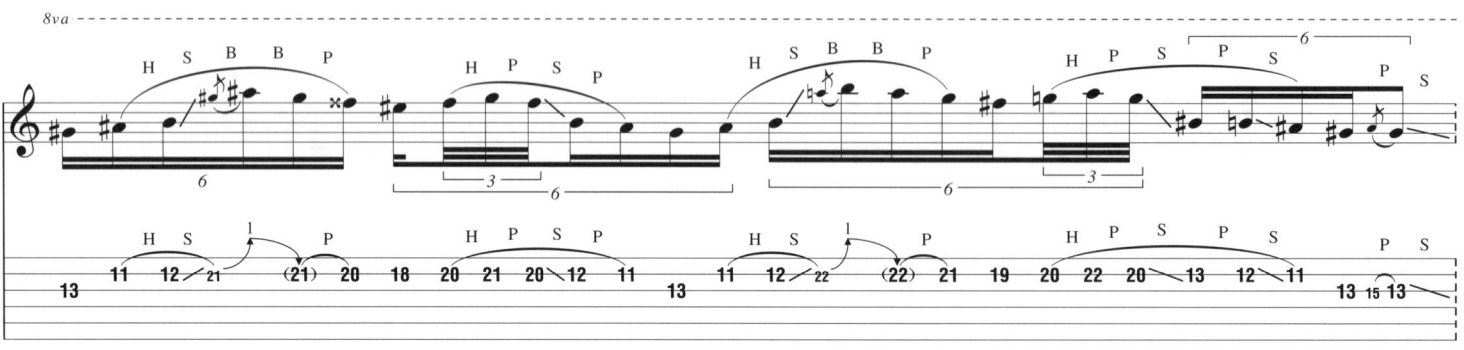
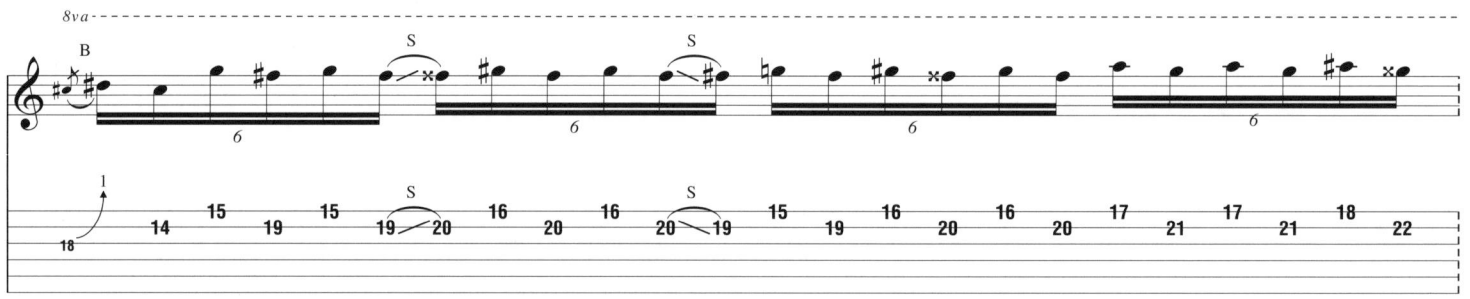

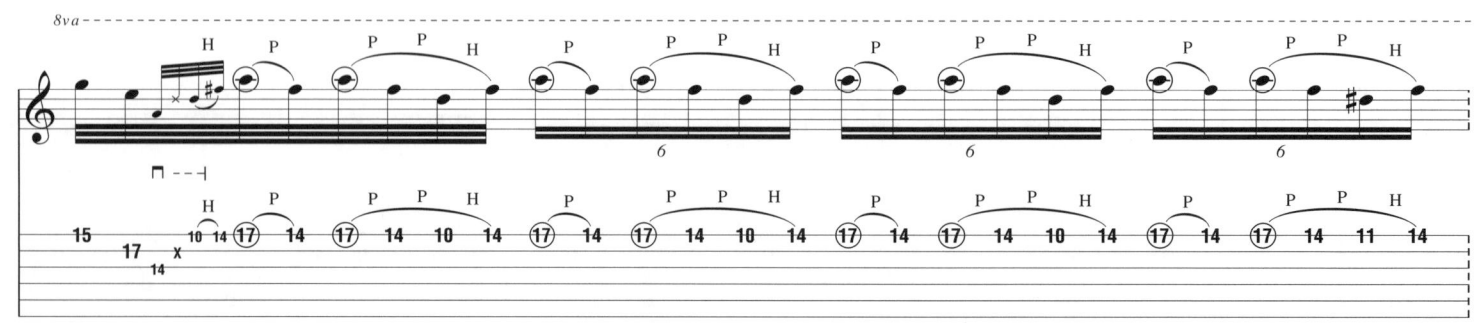

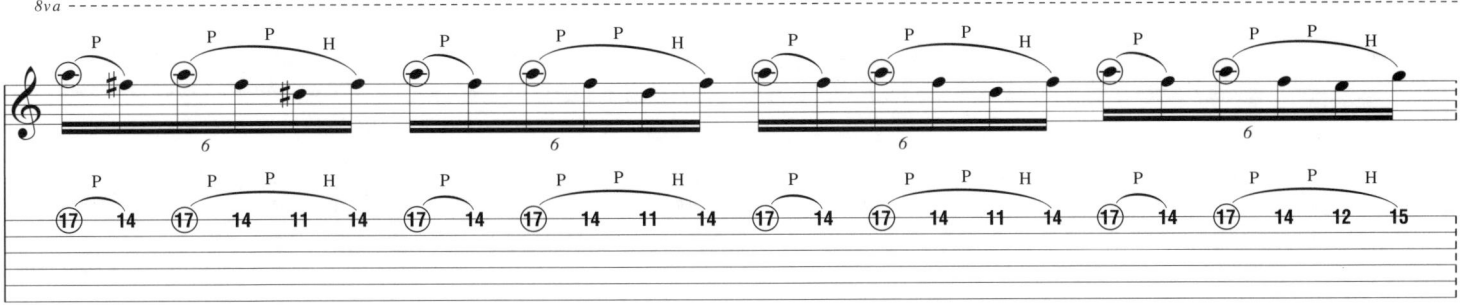
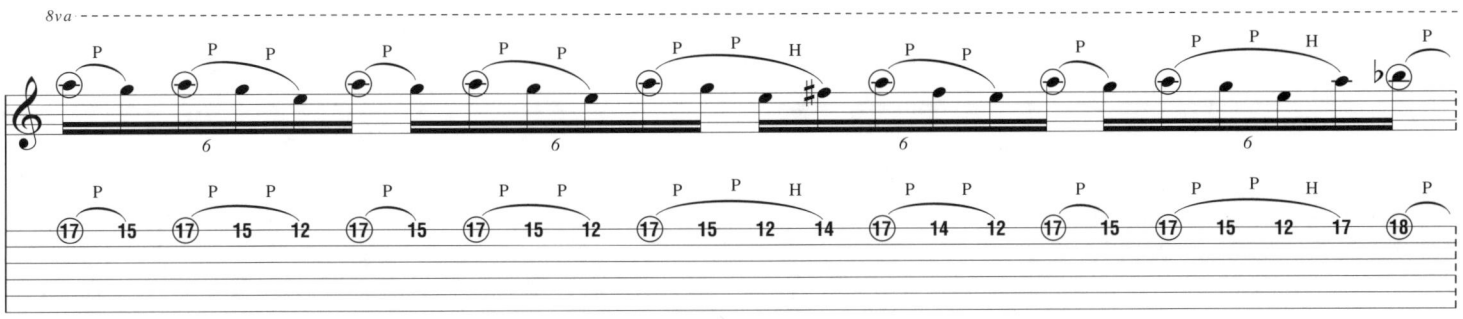
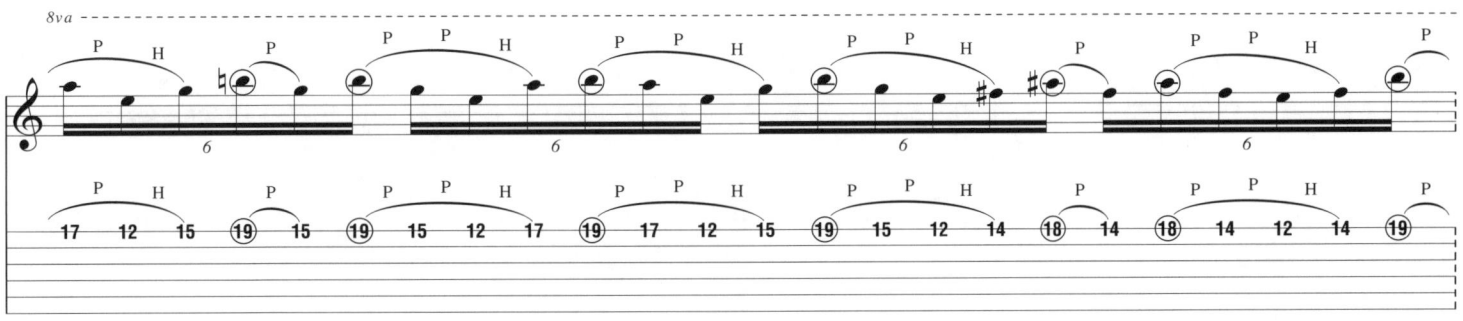
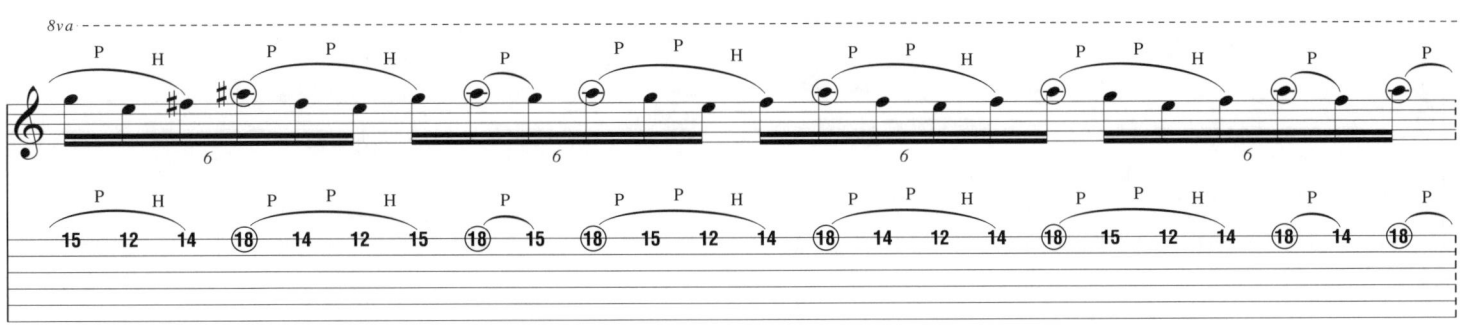
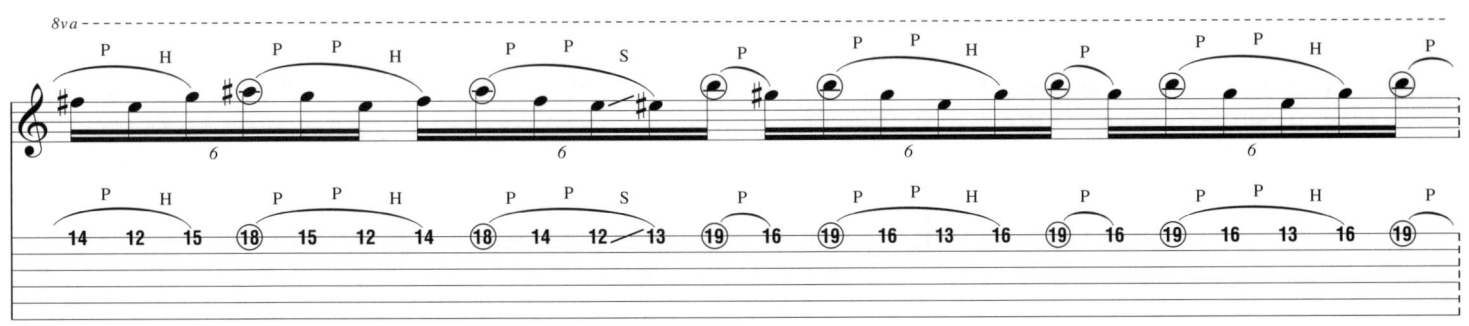

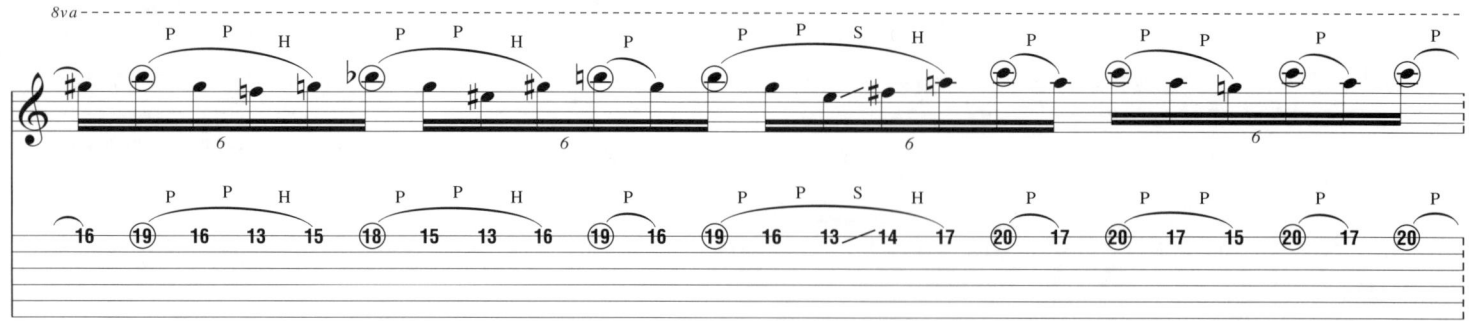
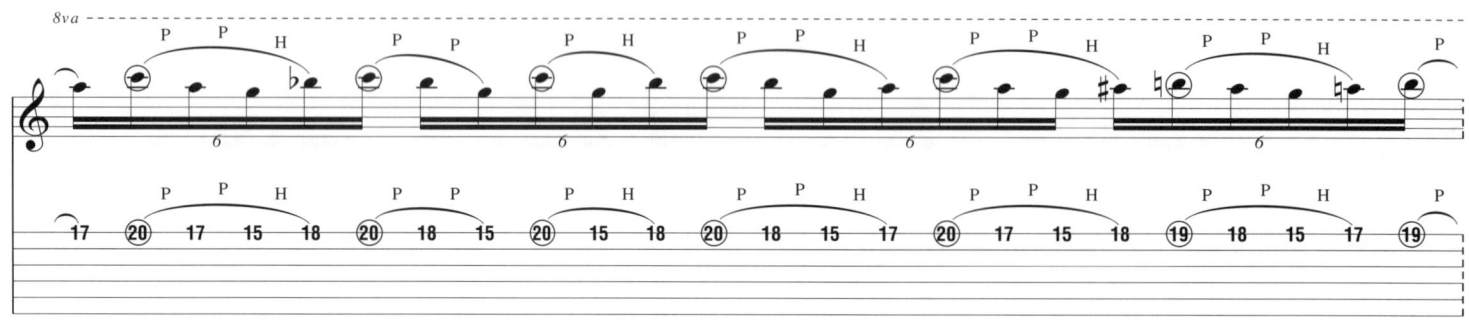
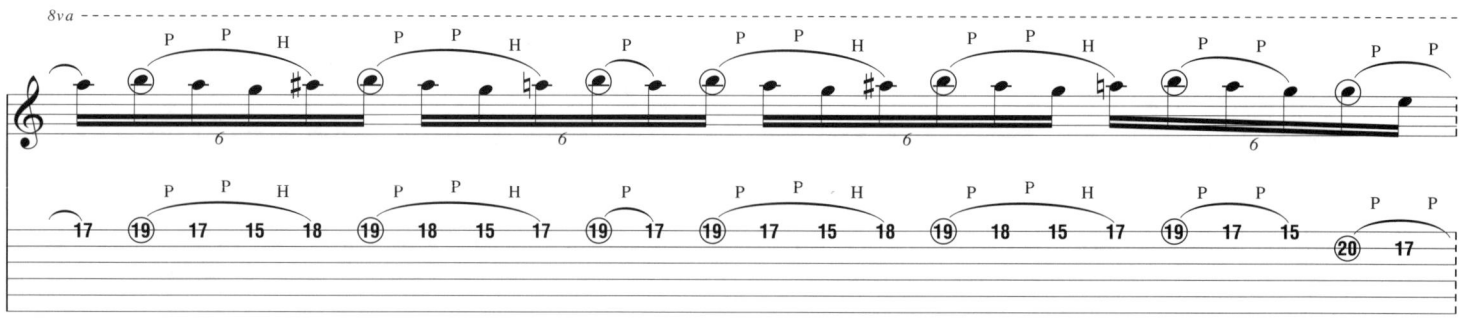
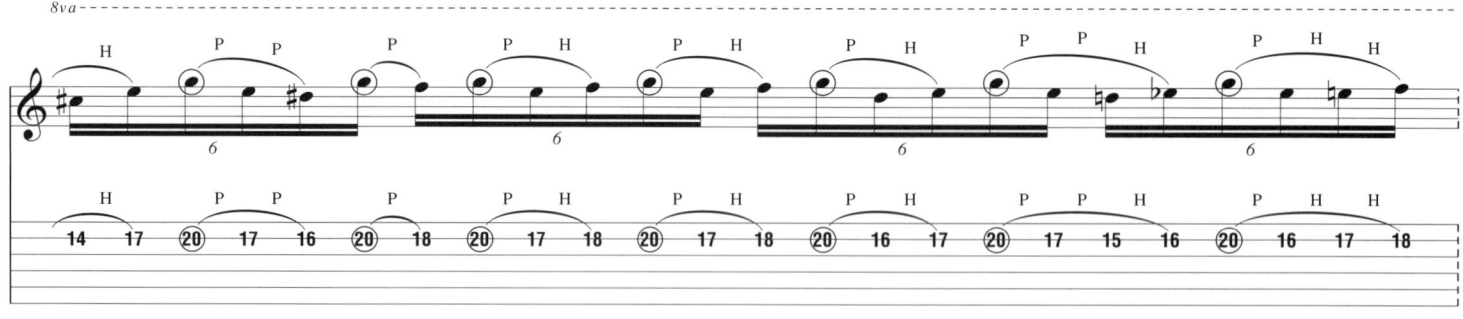
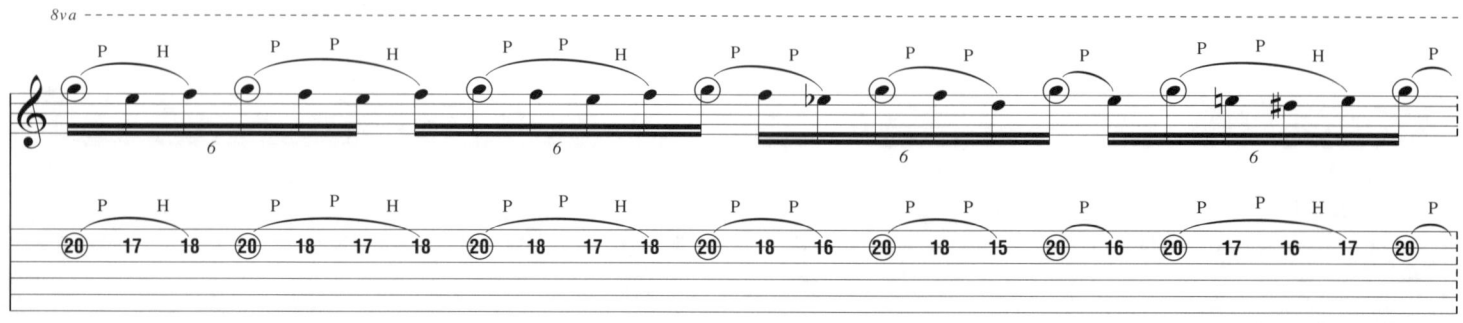

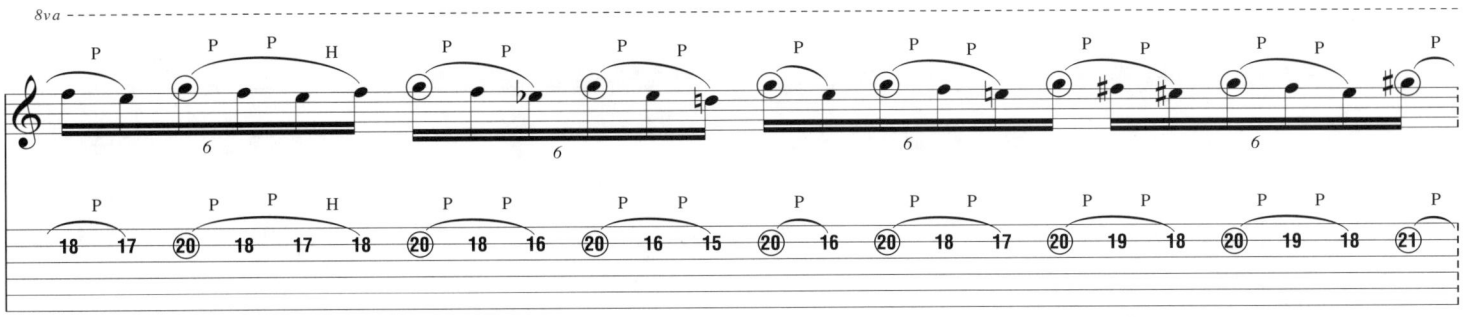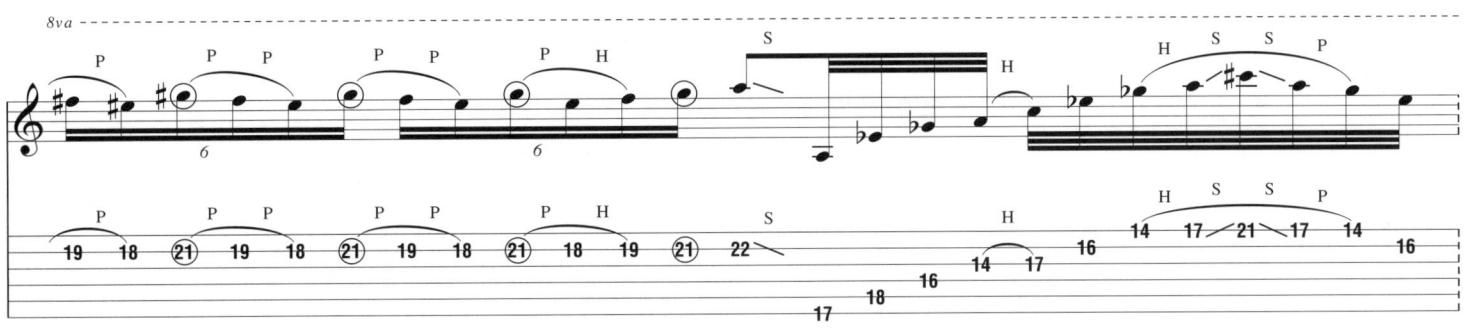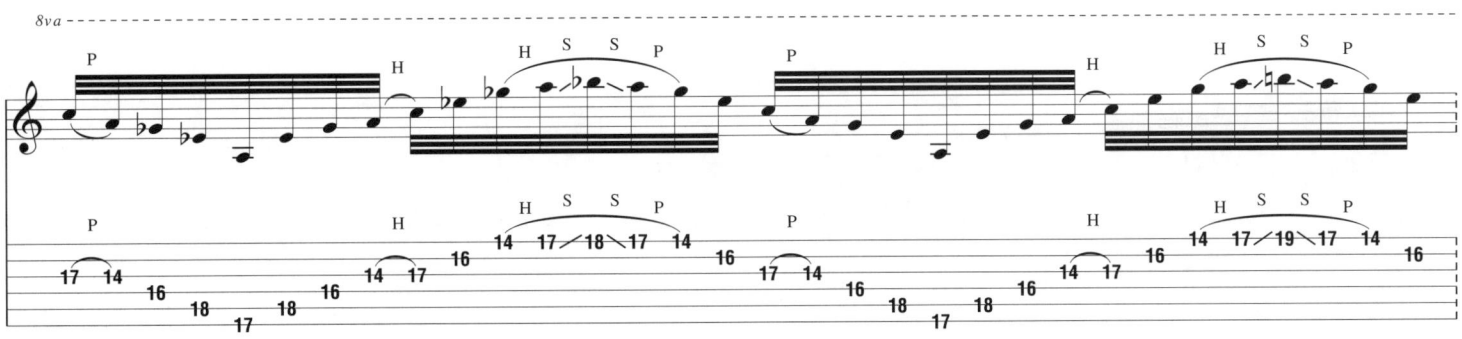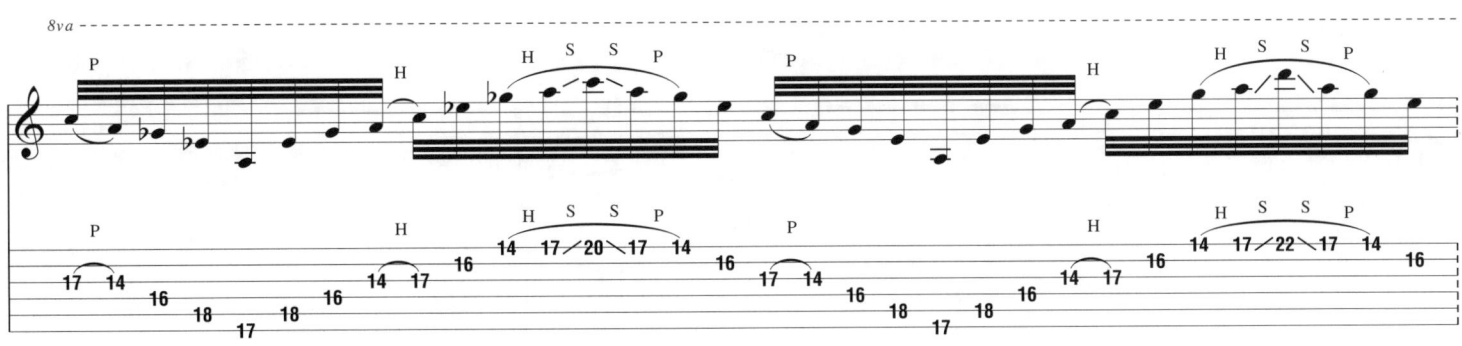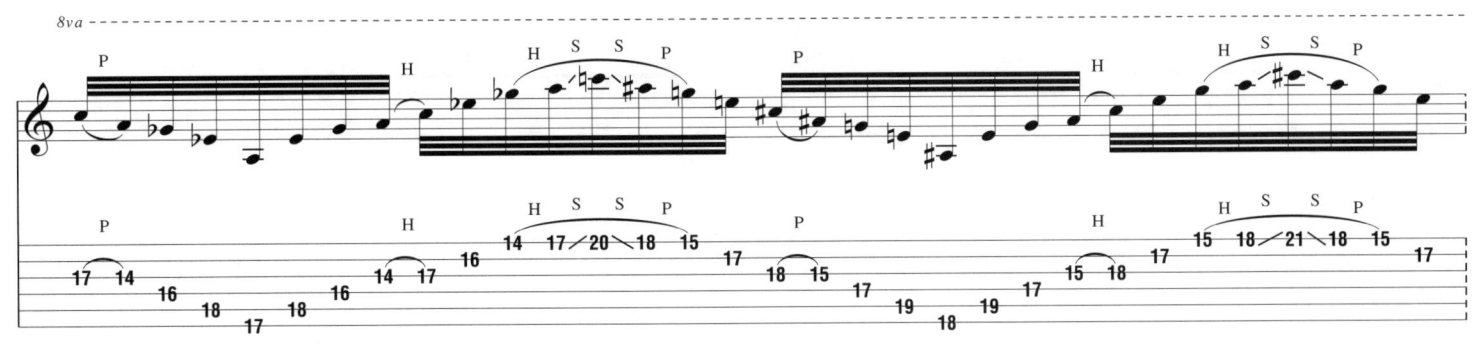

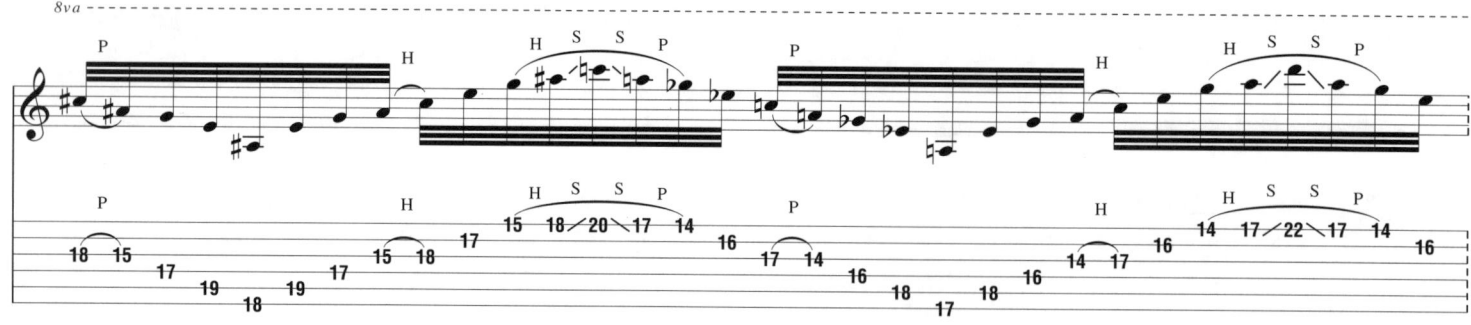

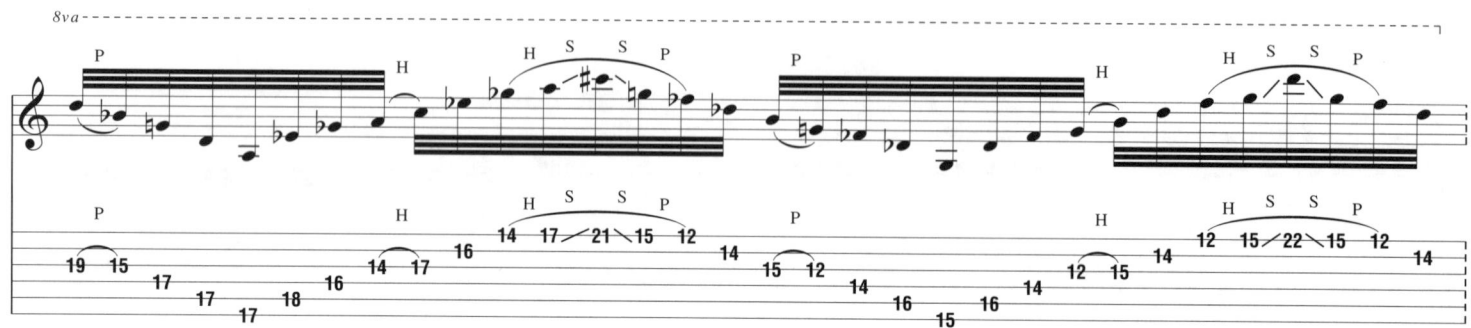

Spoken: Alright. That's enough of that nonsense.

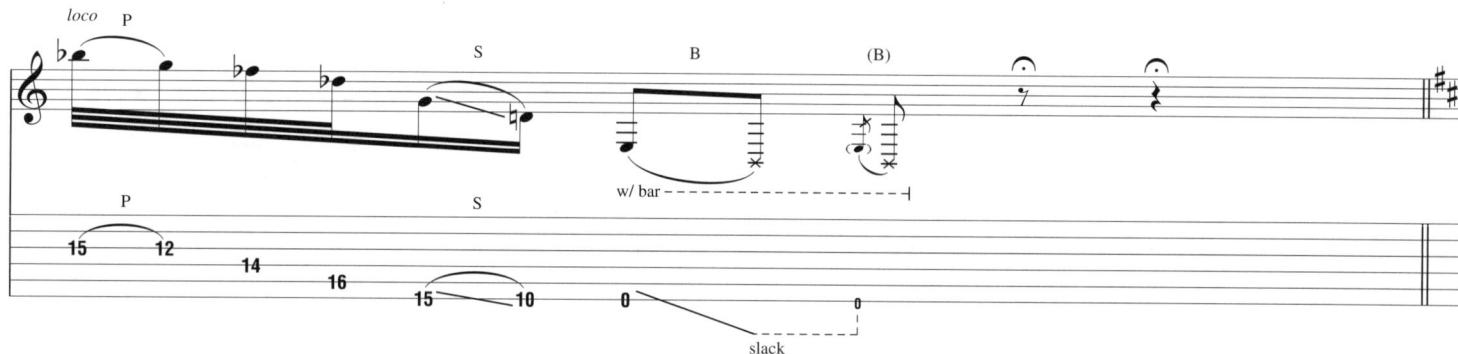

I

A tempo

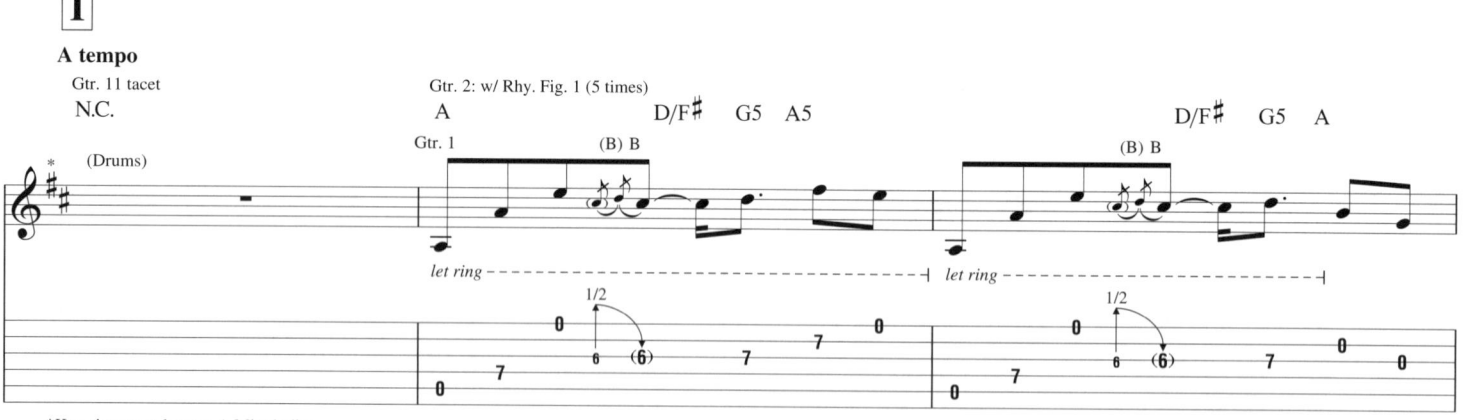

*Key signature denotes A Mixolydian.

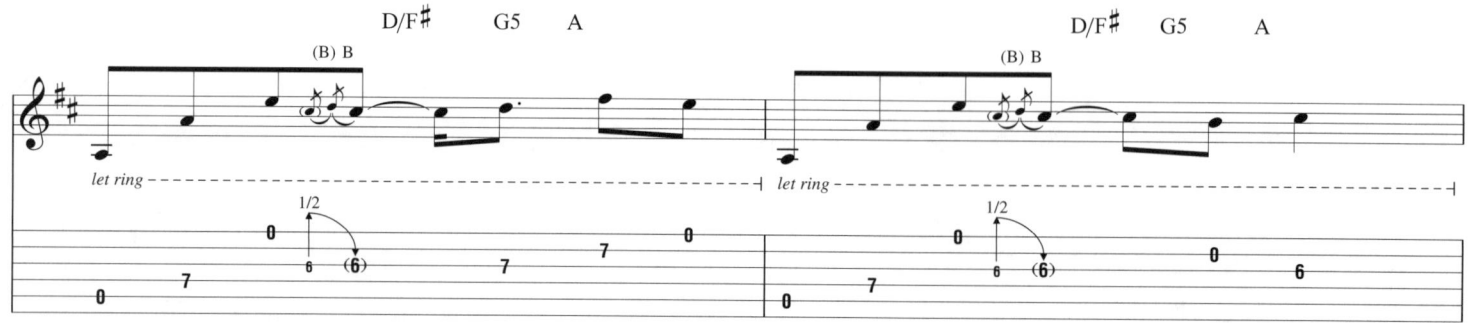

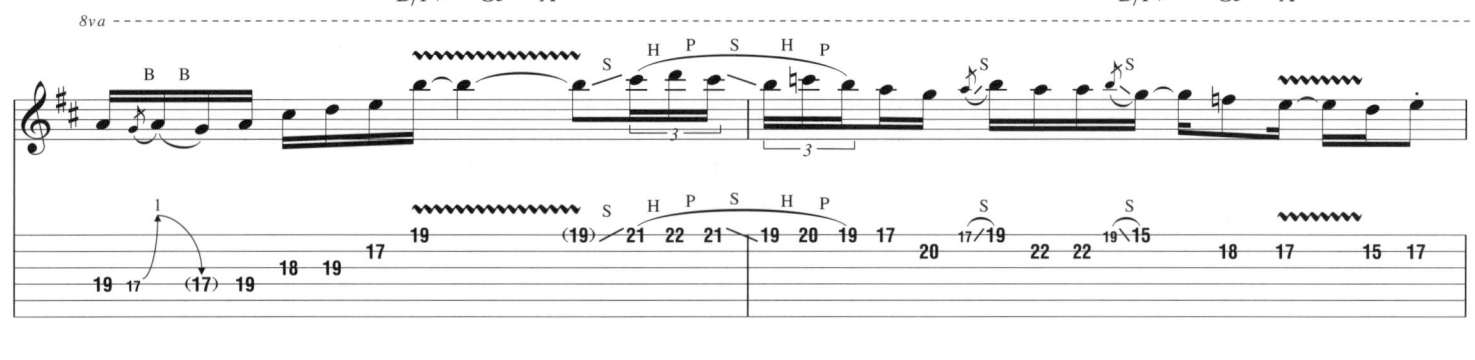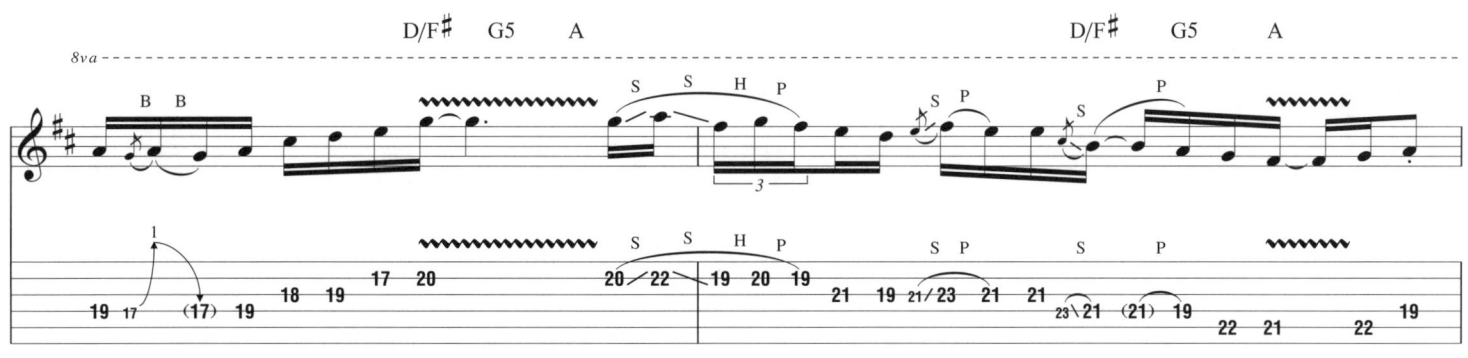

101

Lotus Feet

By Steve Vai

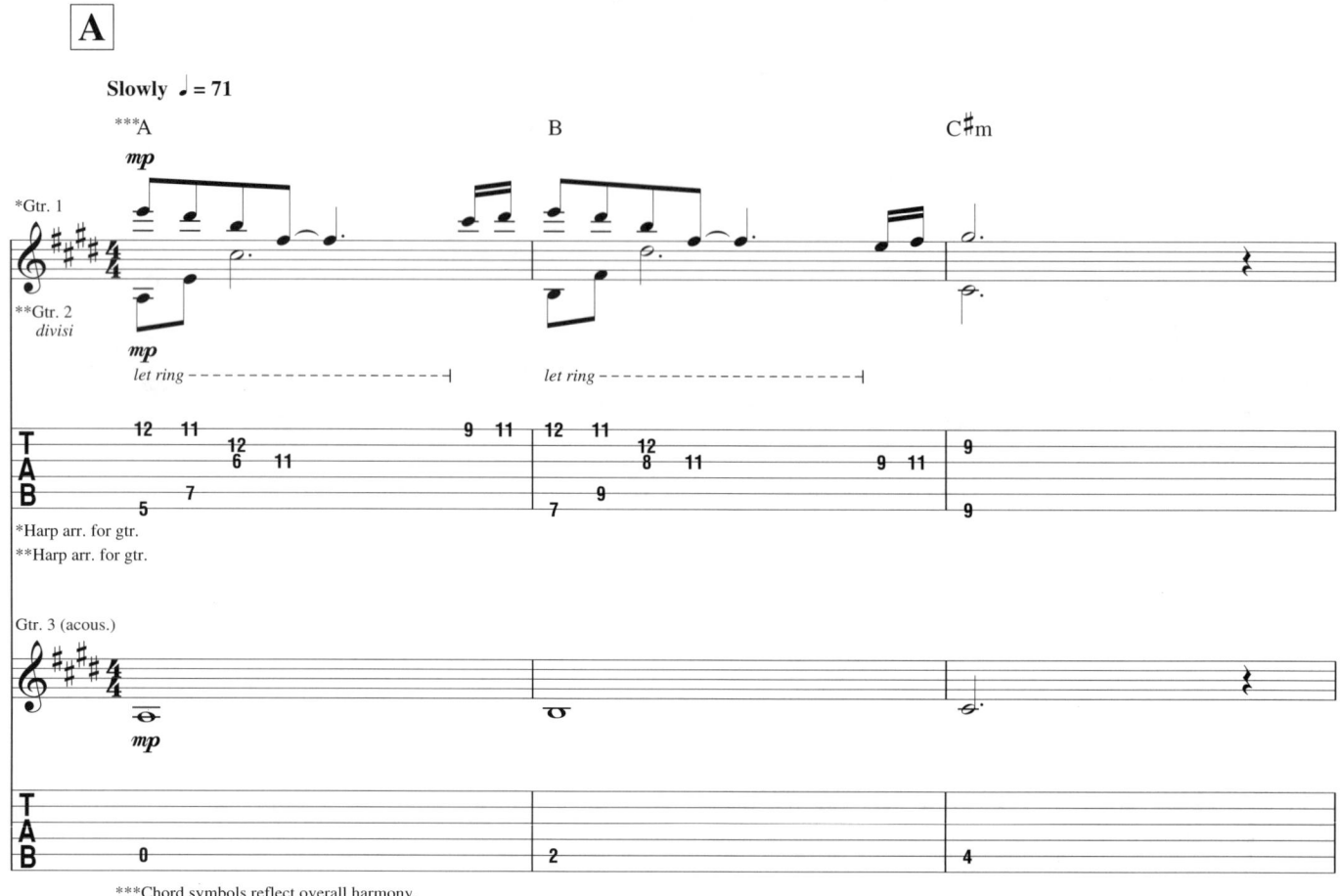

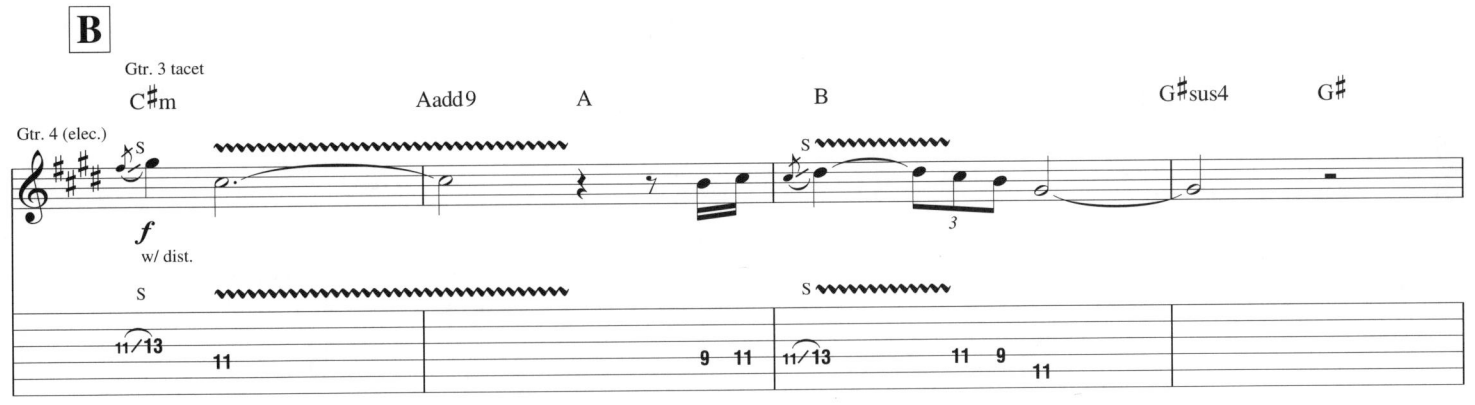
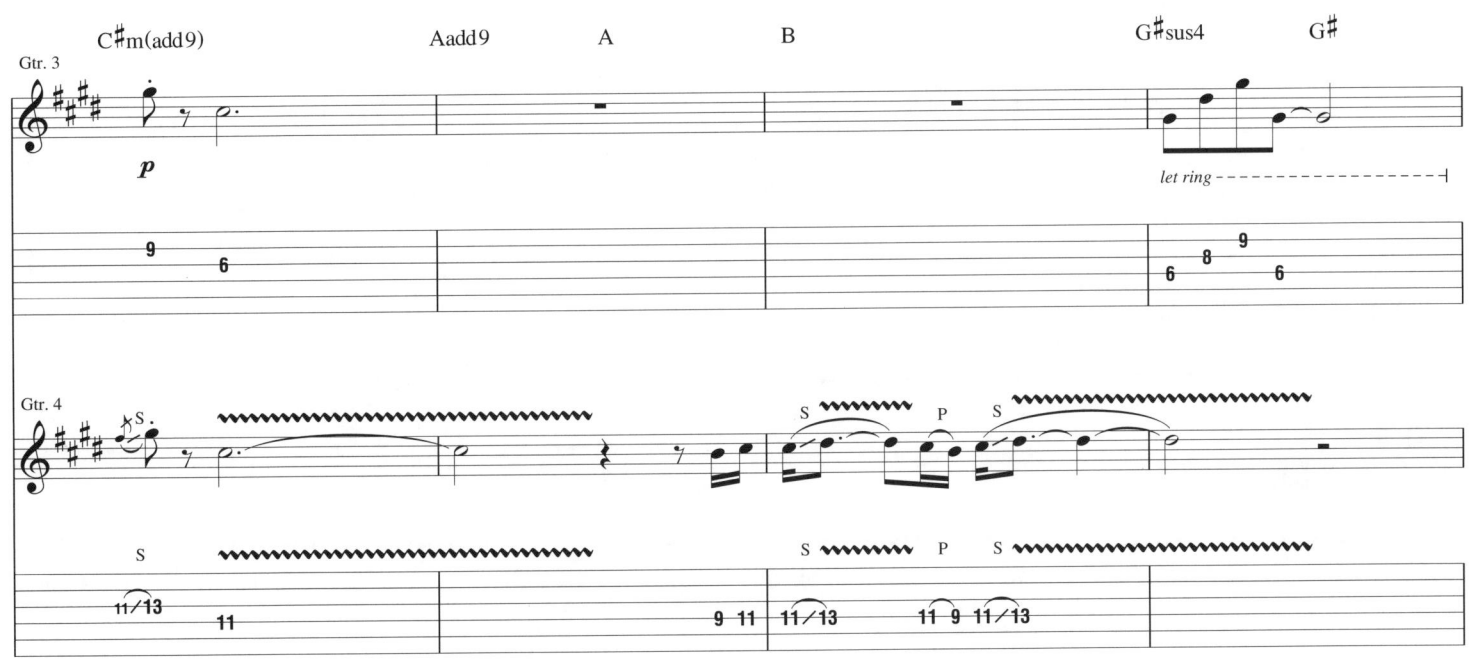

103

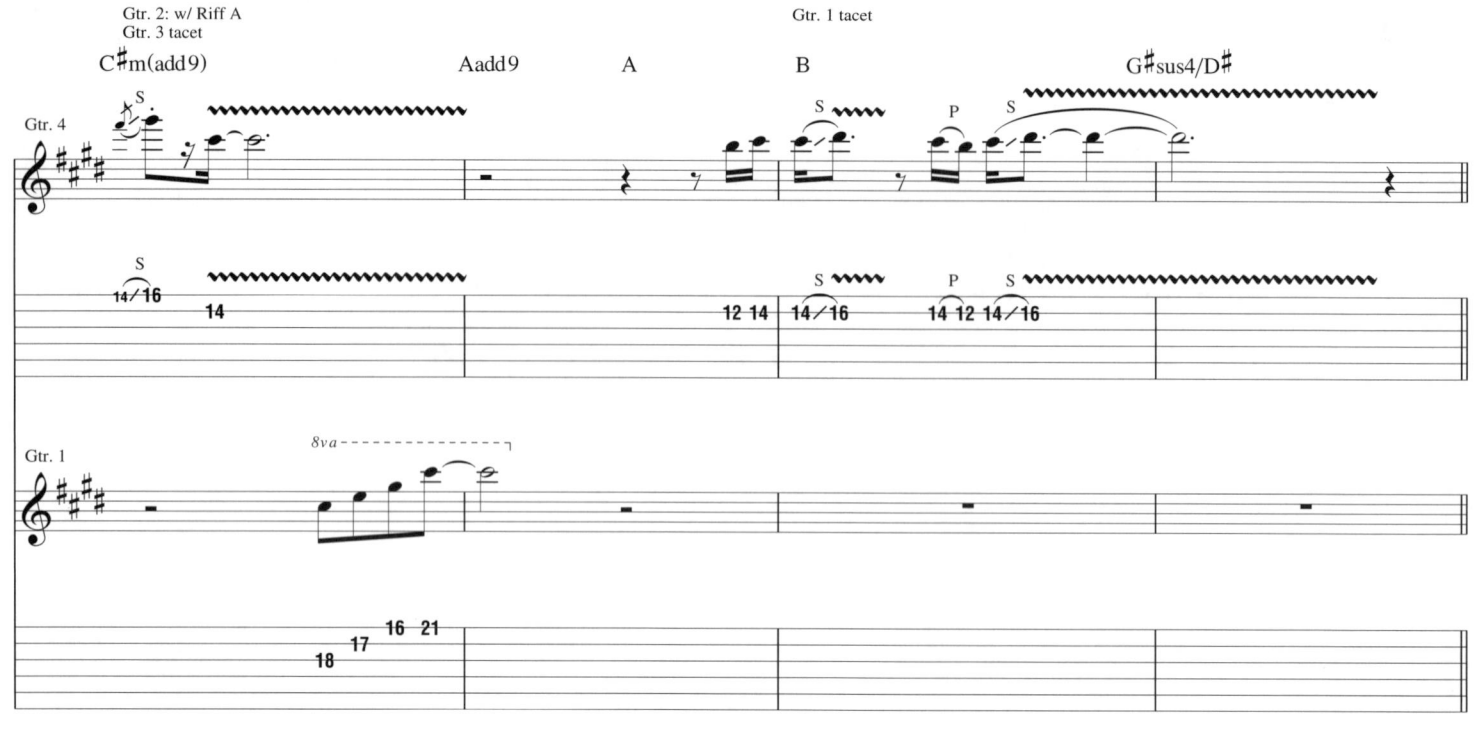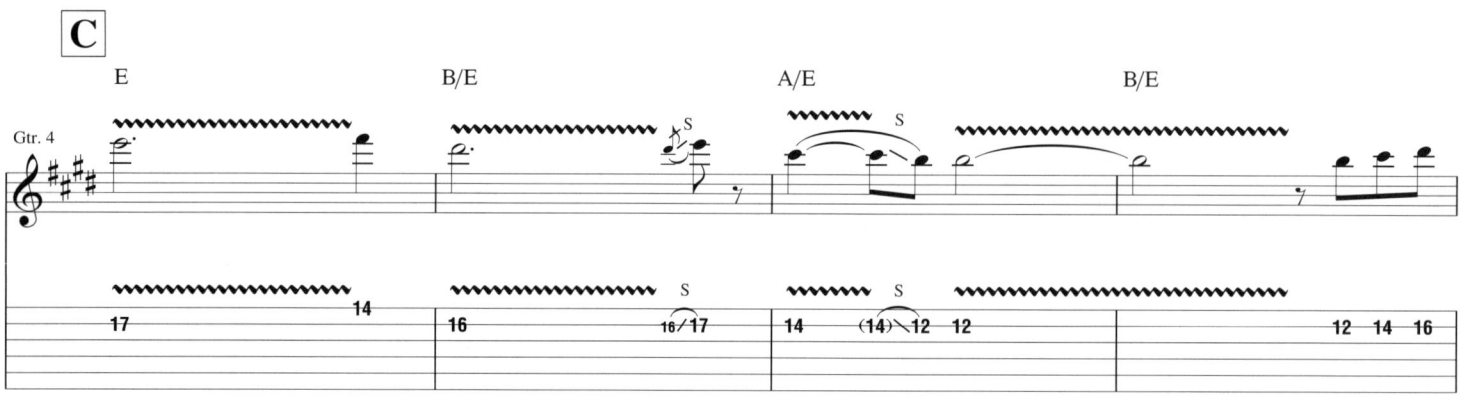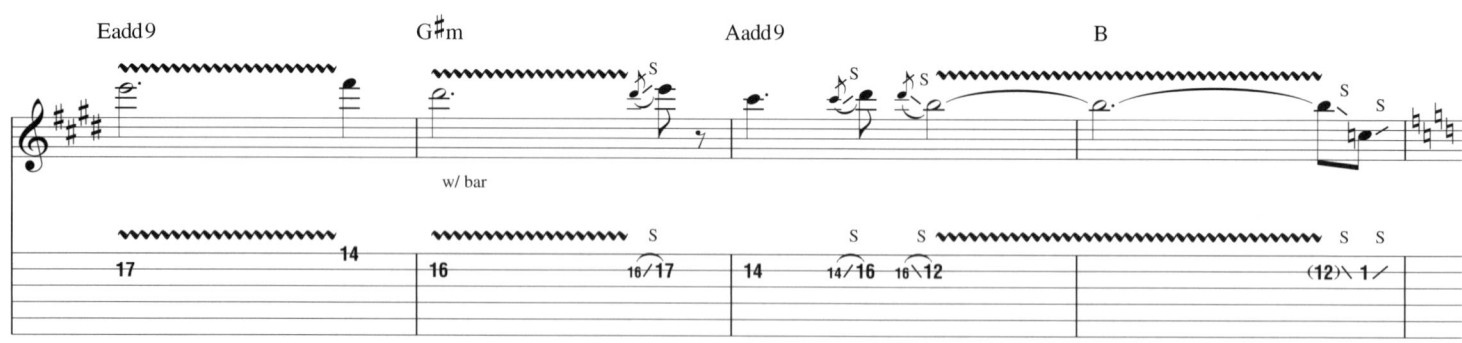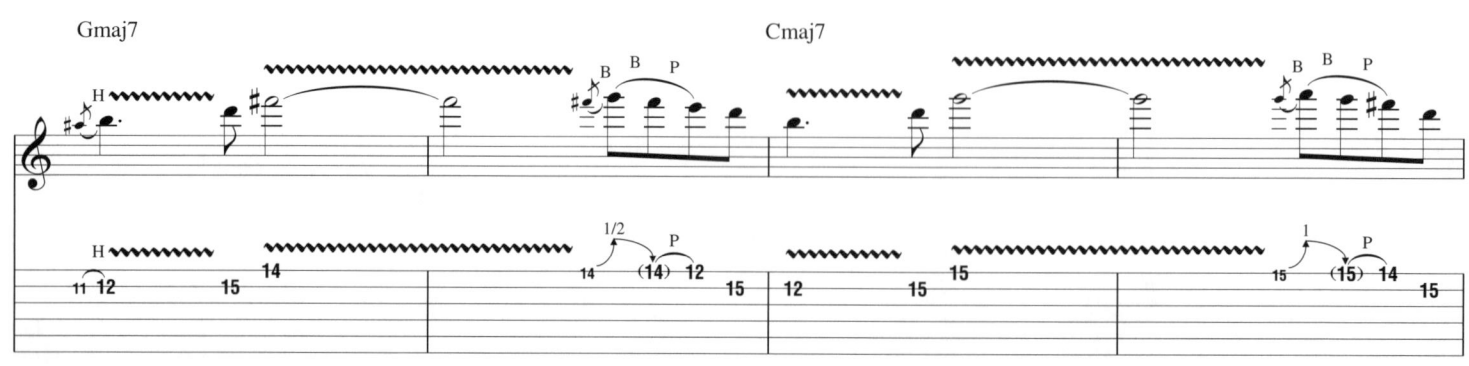

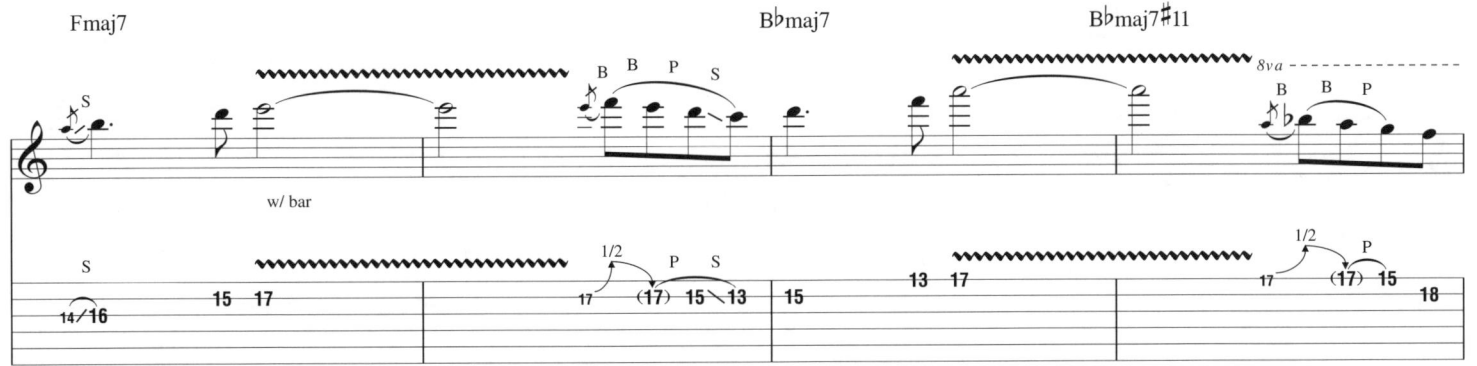
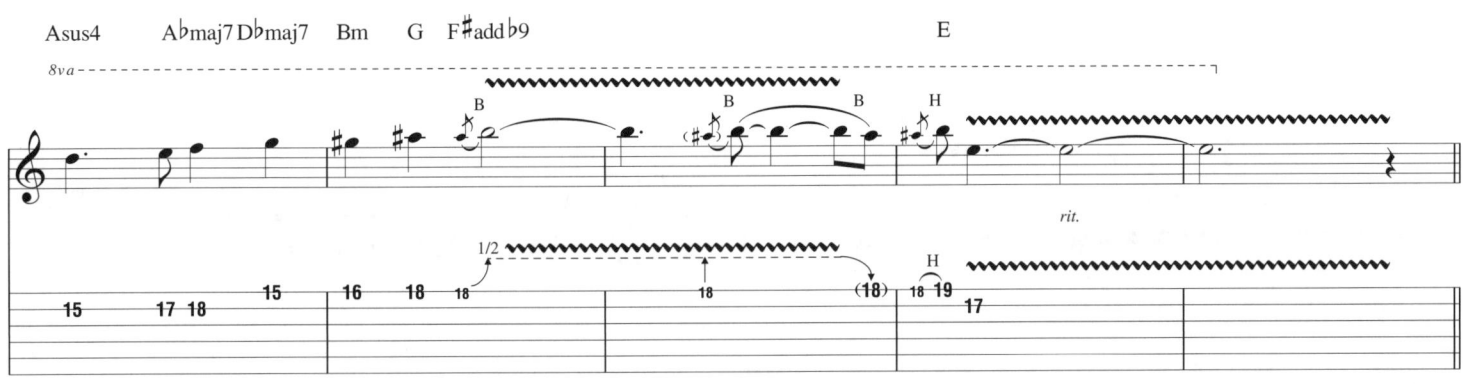
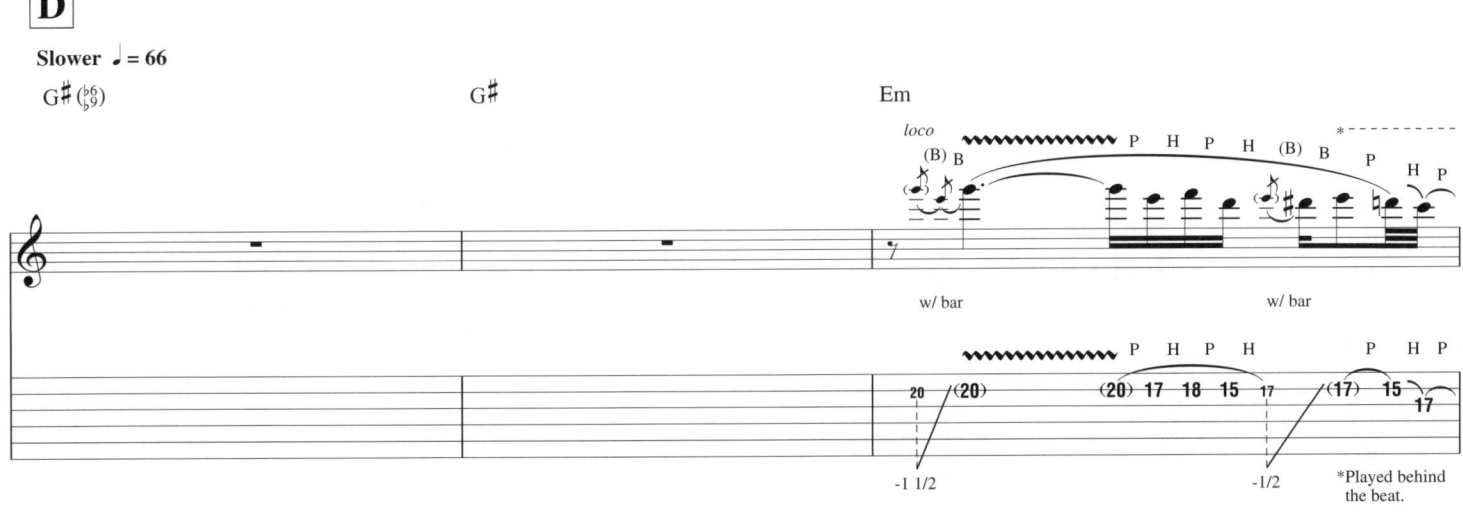
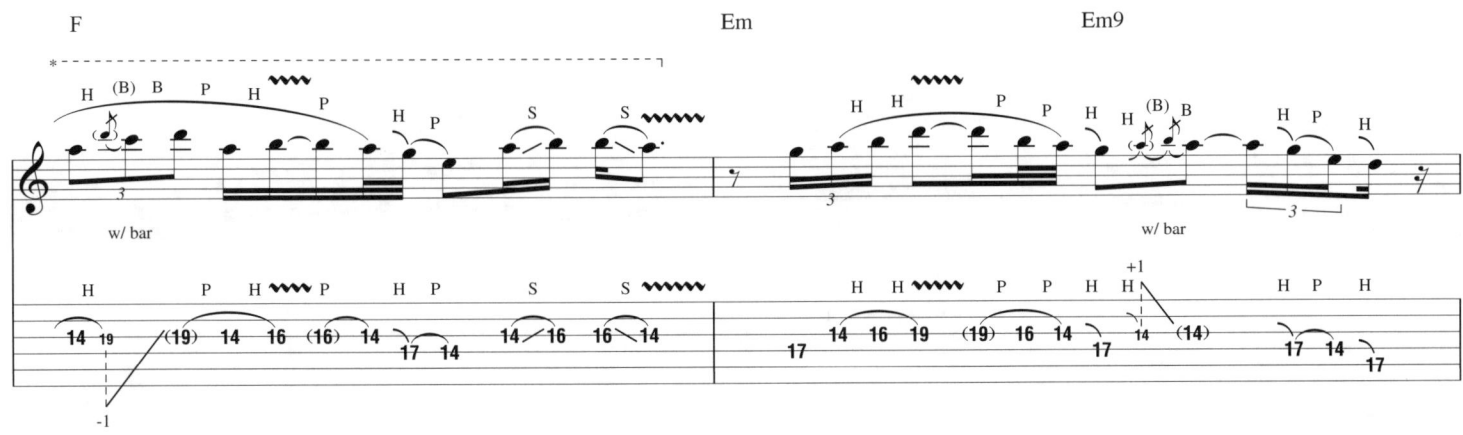

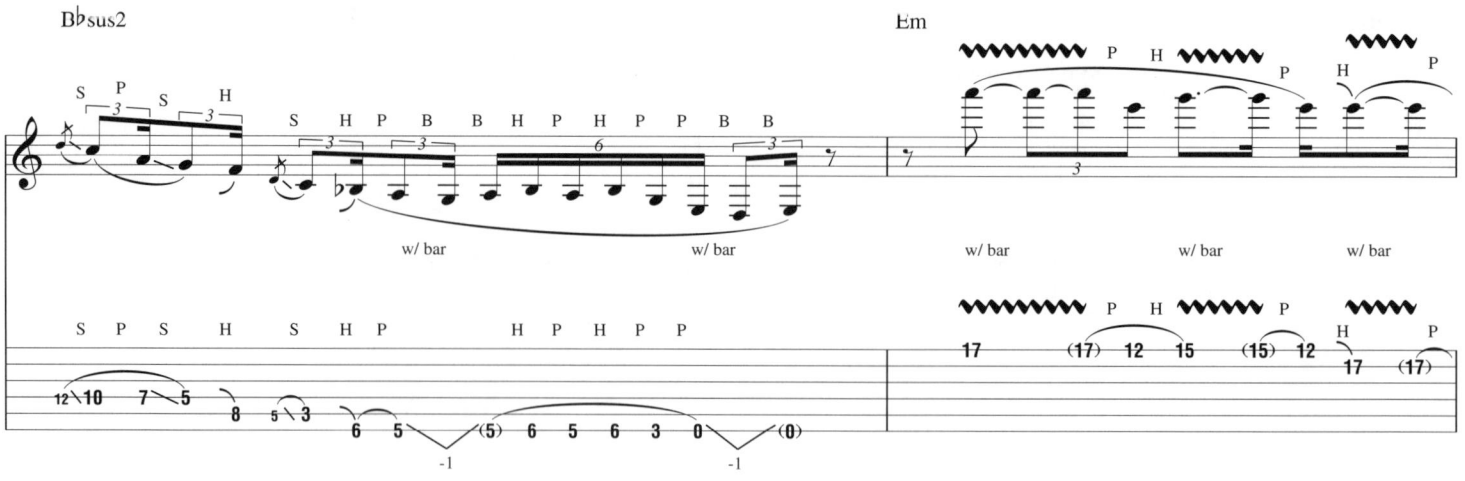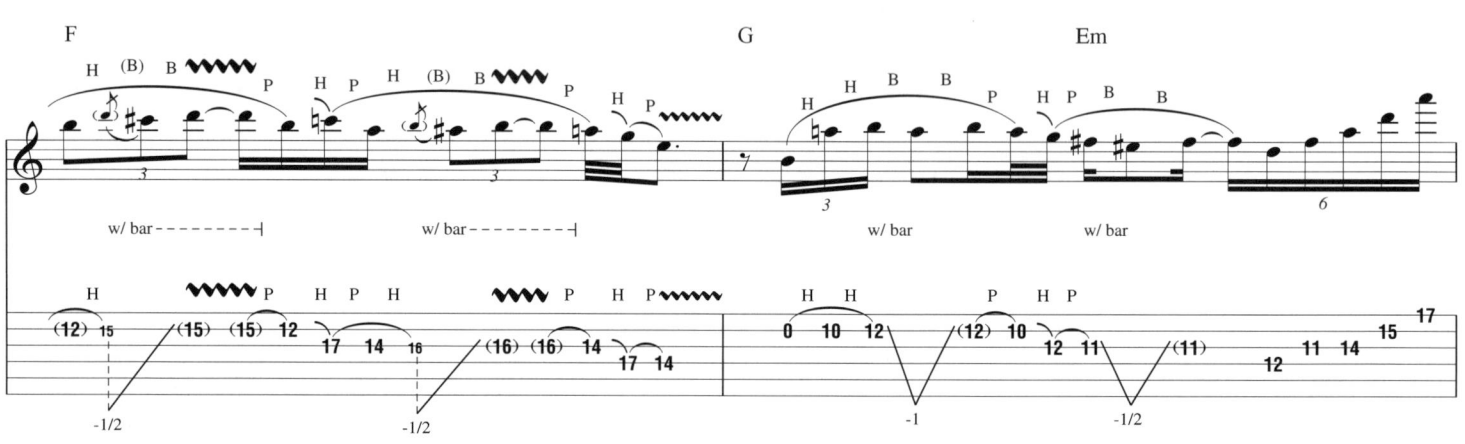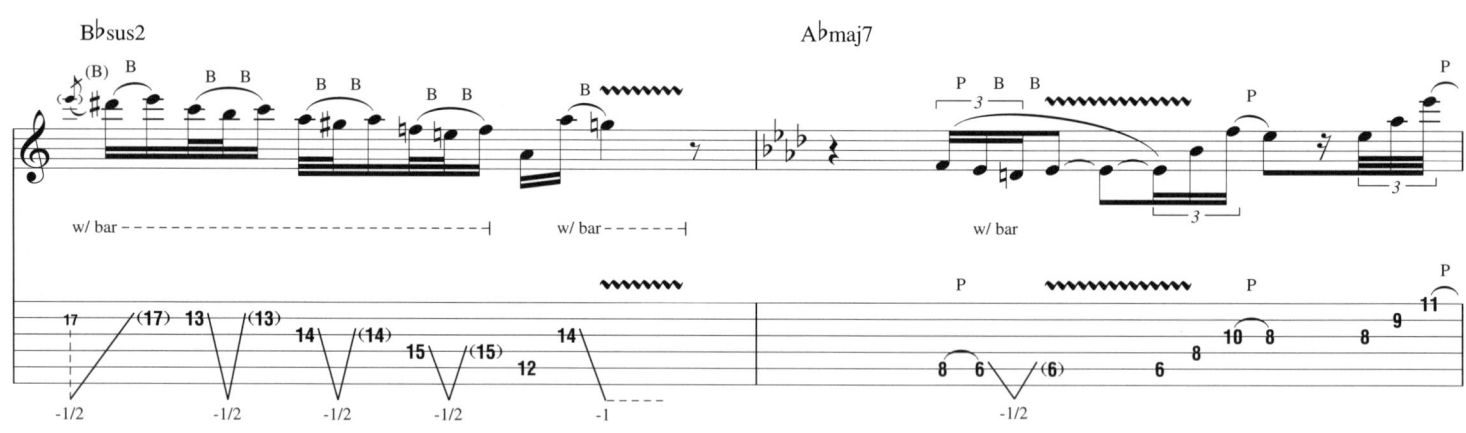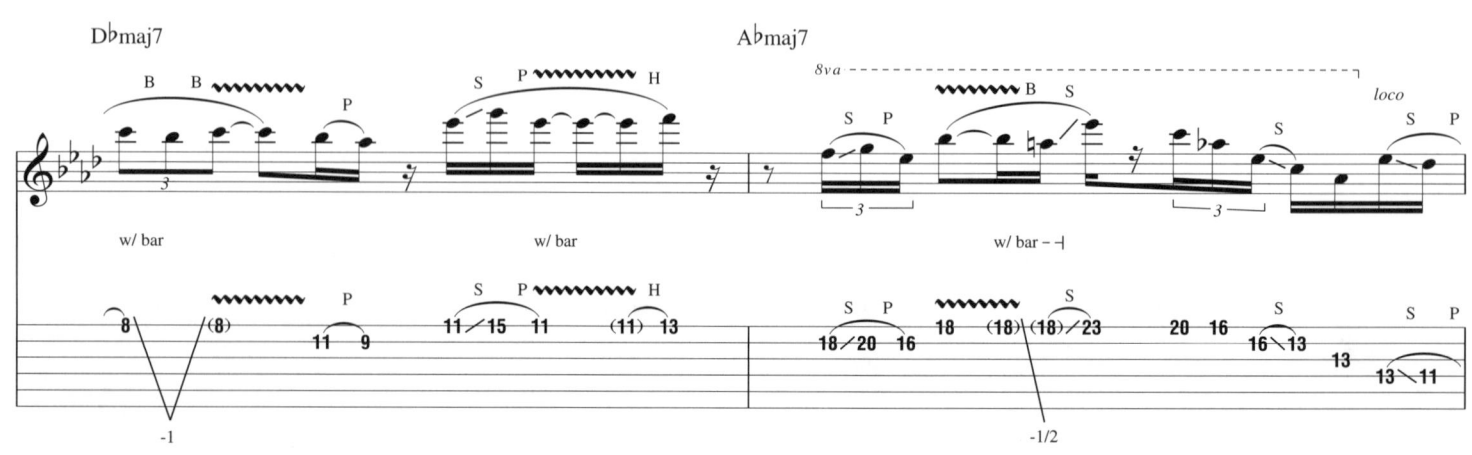

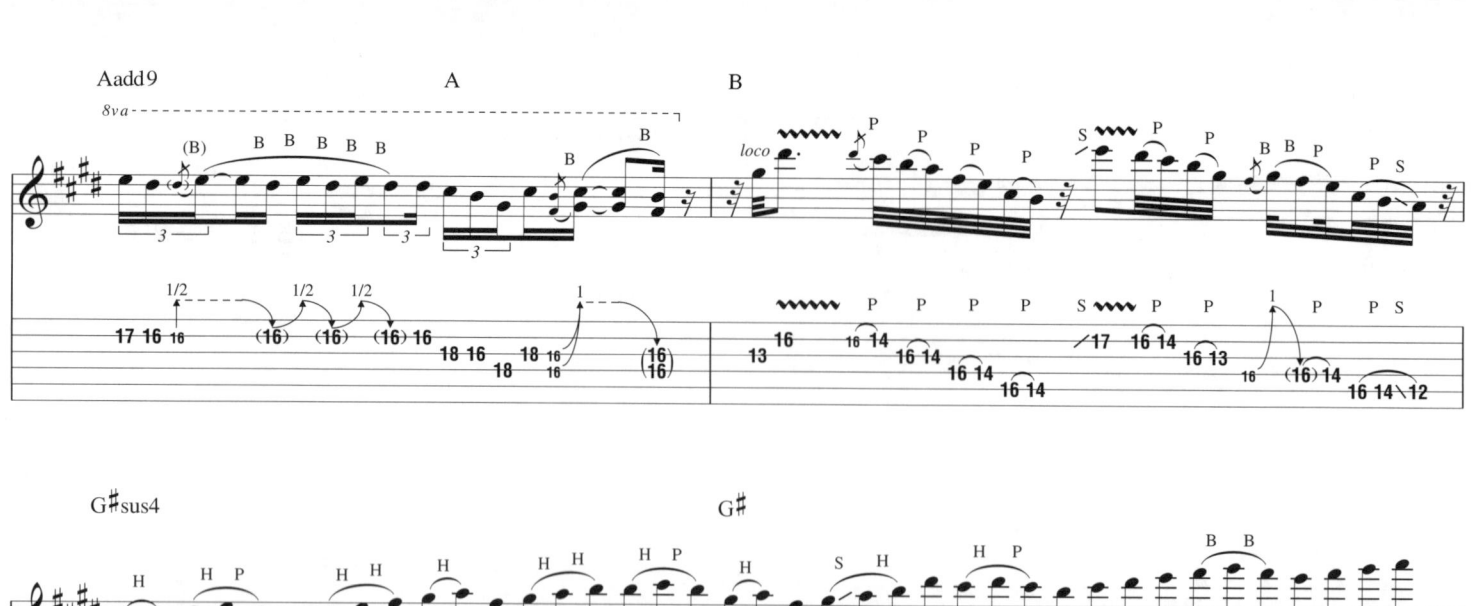
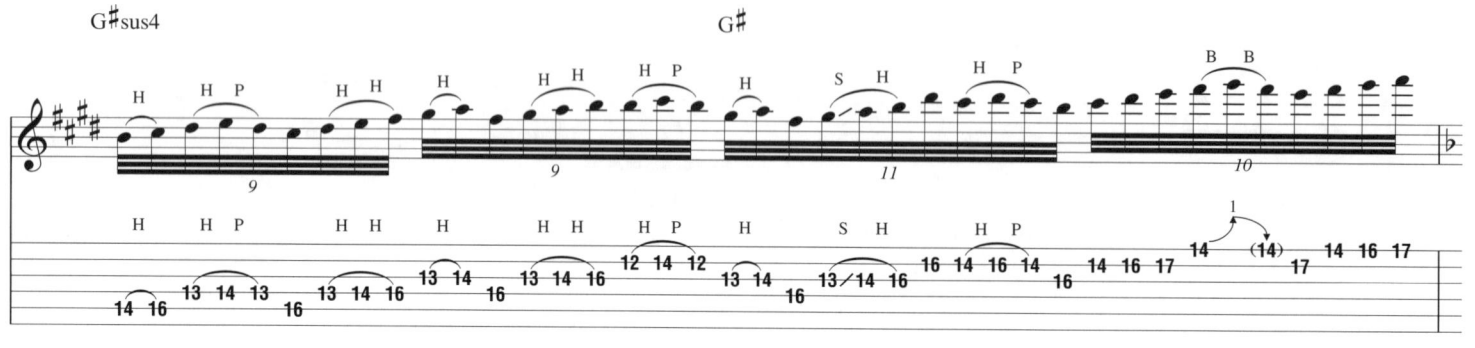
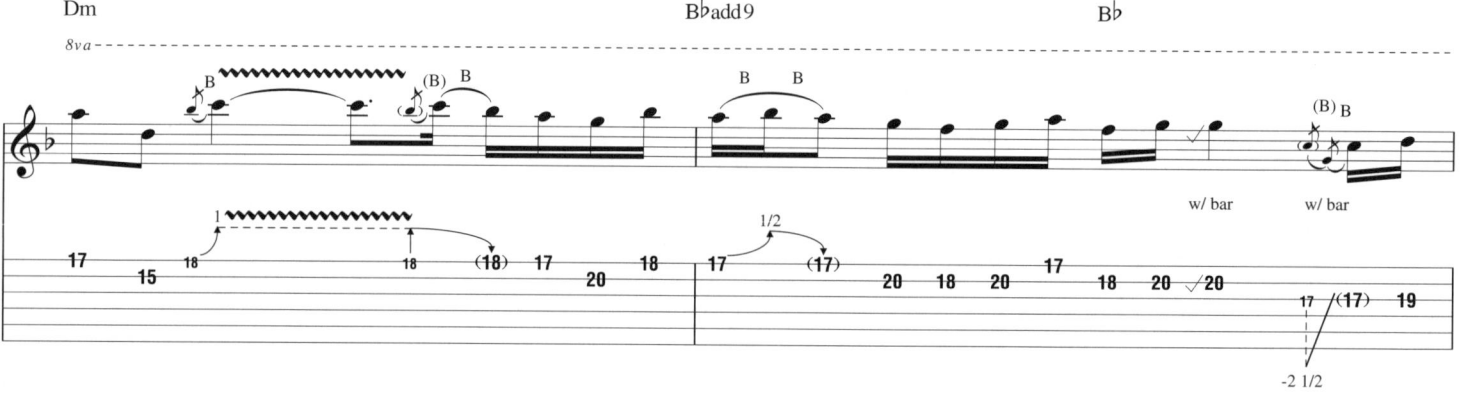
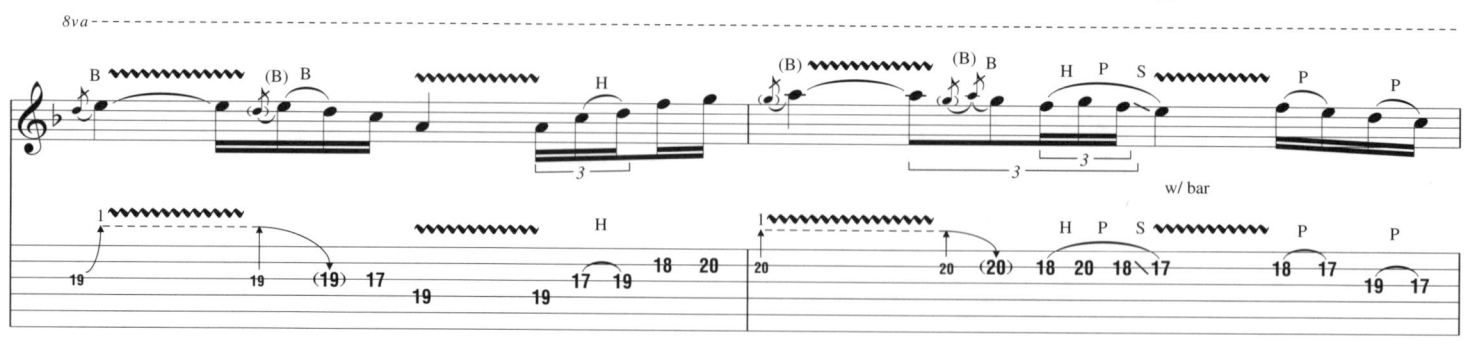
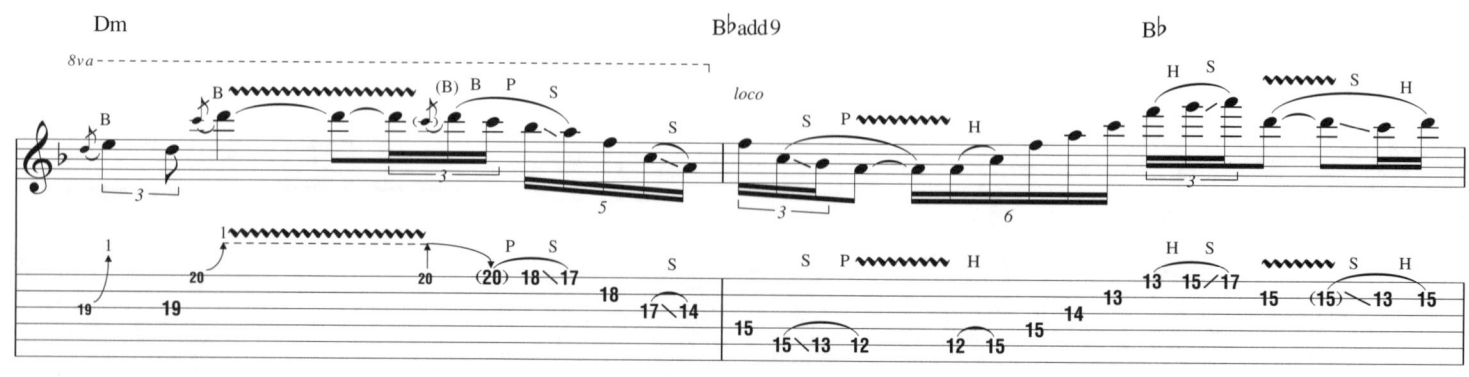

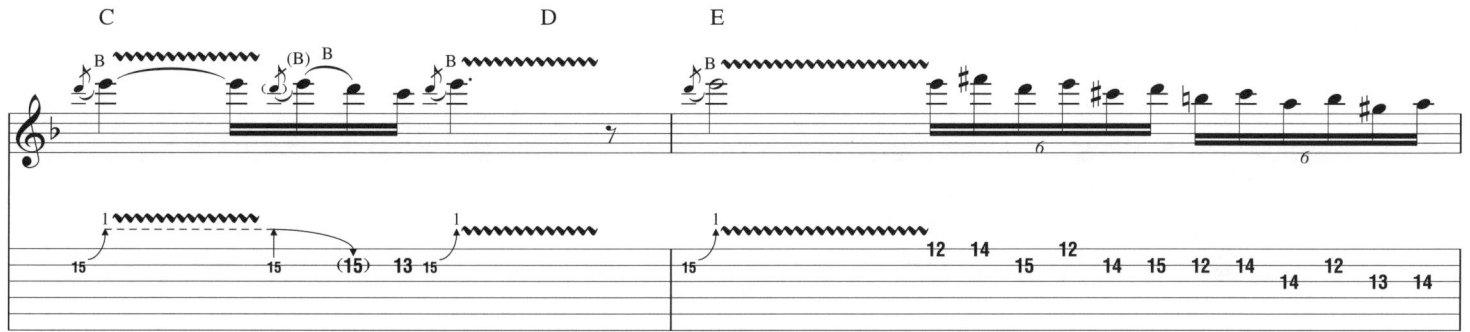

F

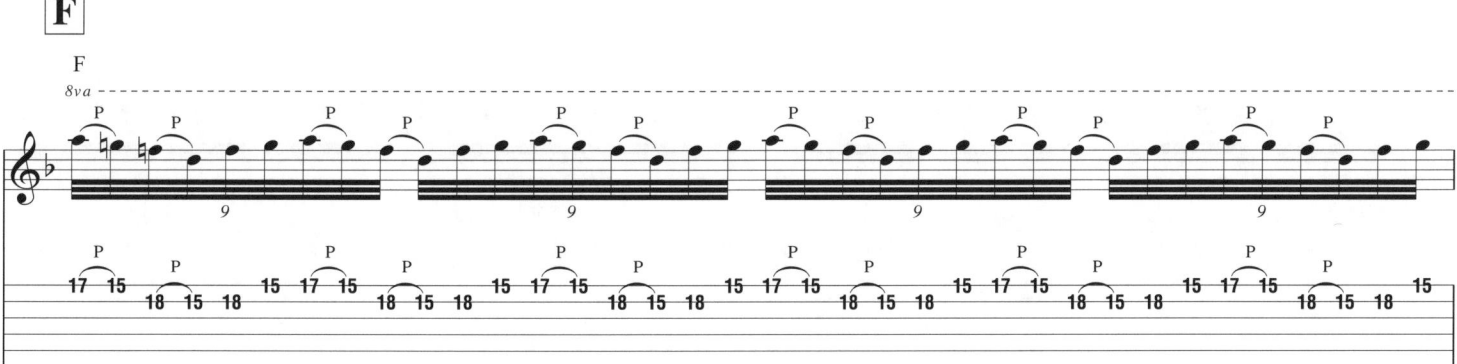
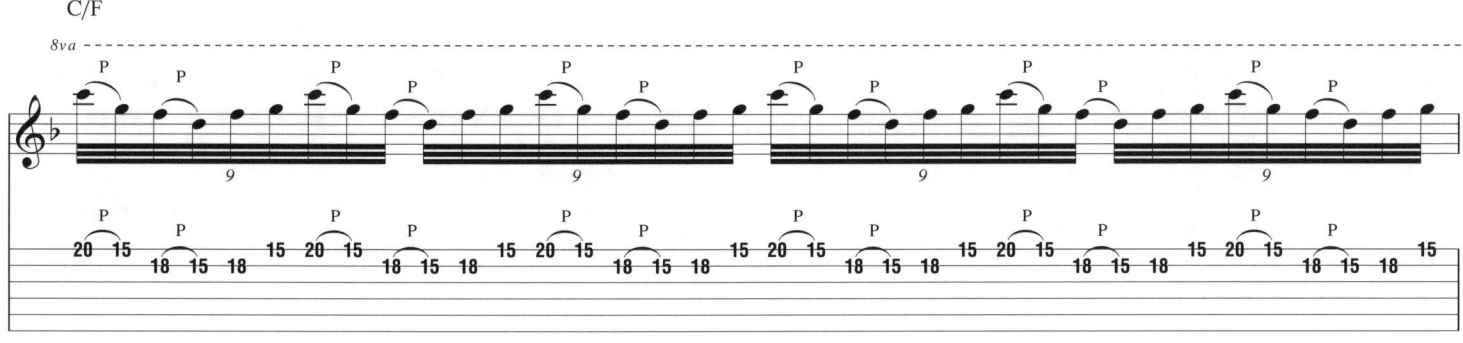
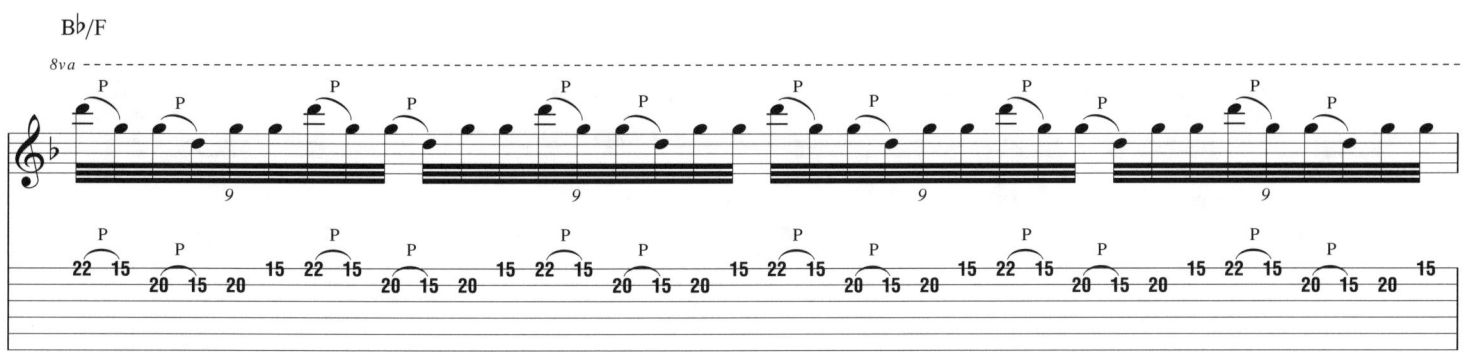

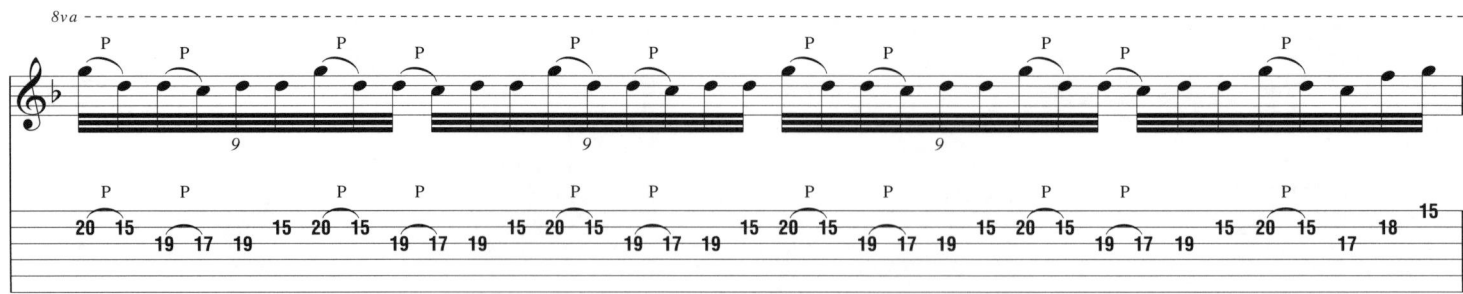
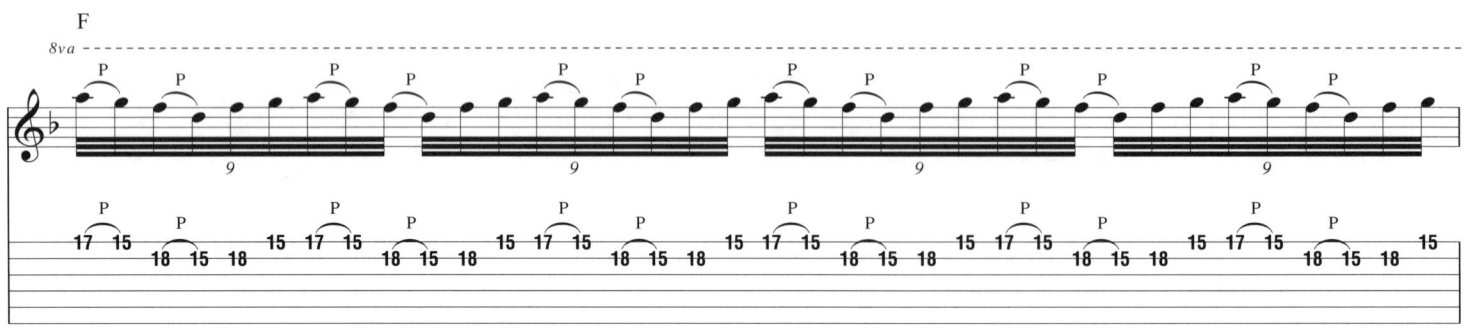
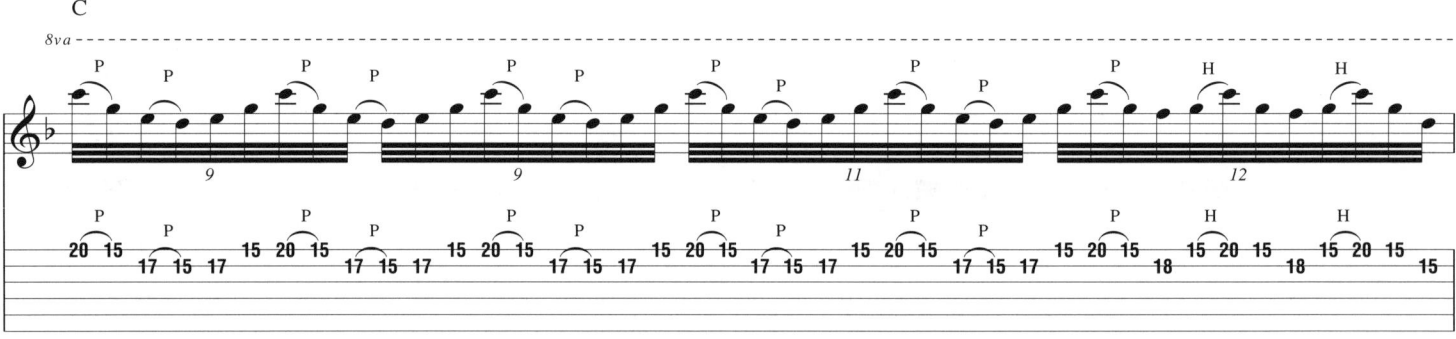
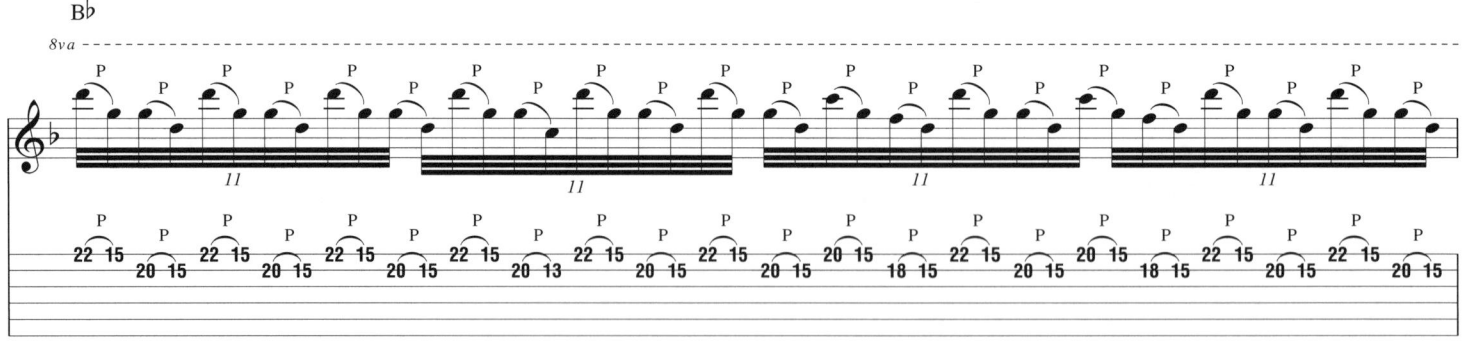
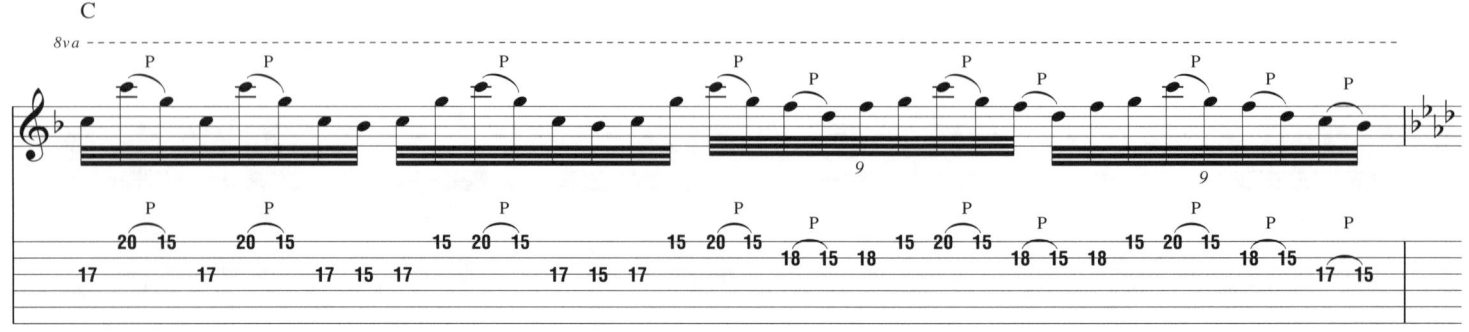

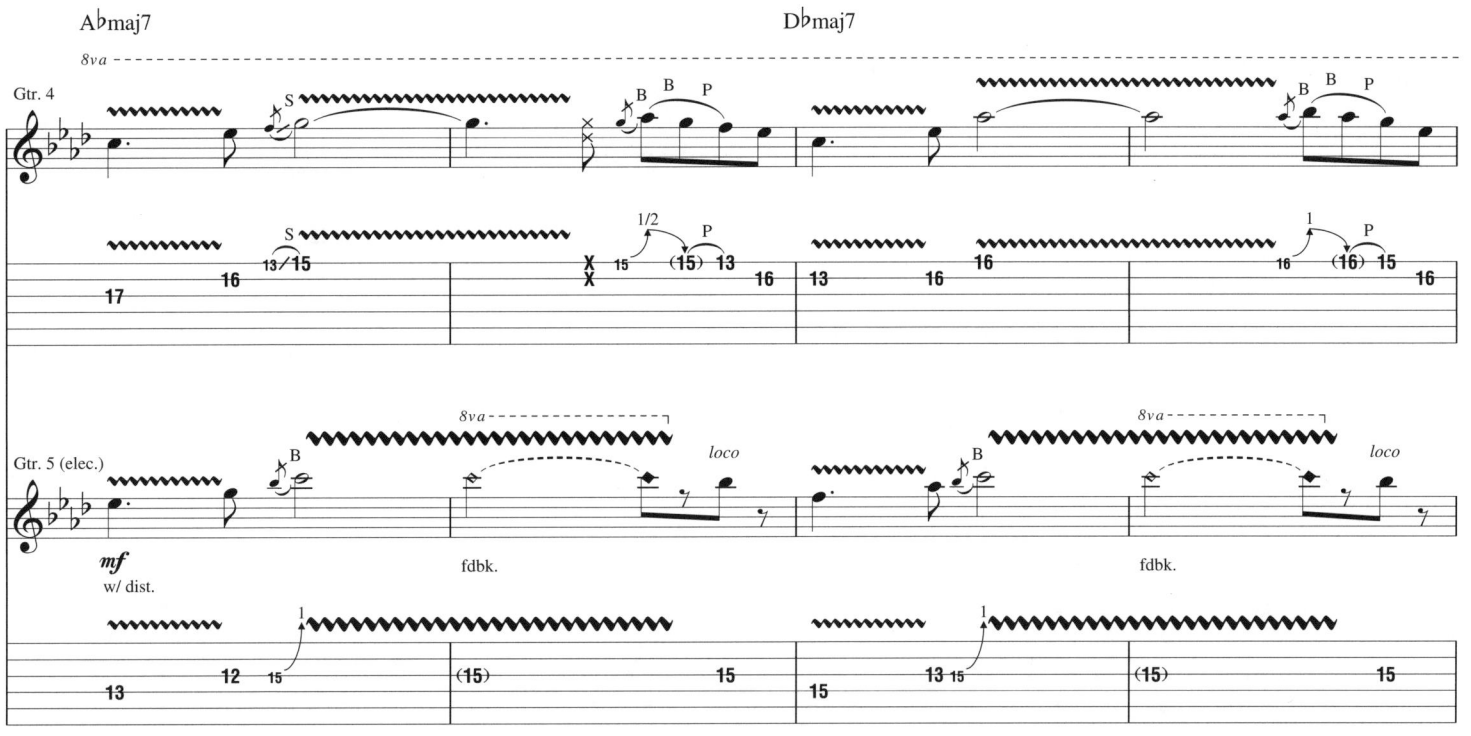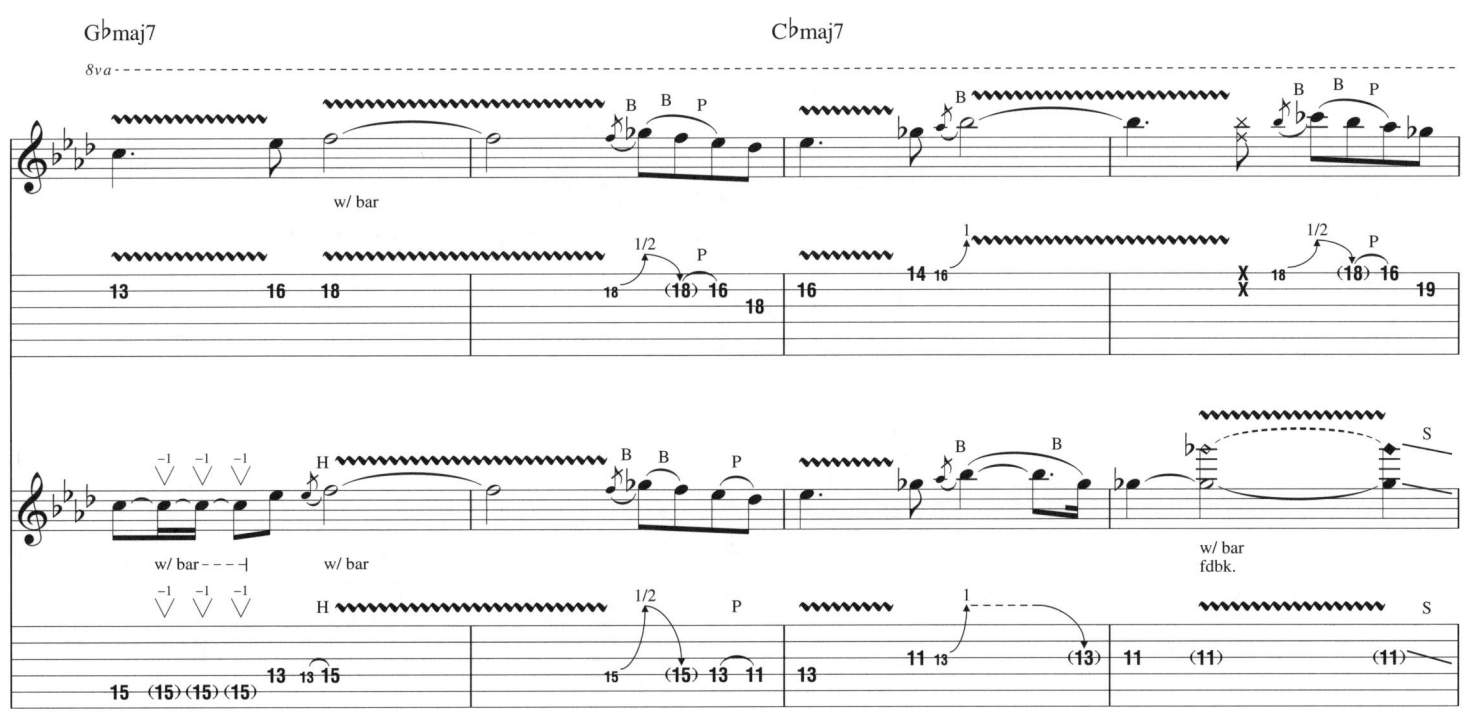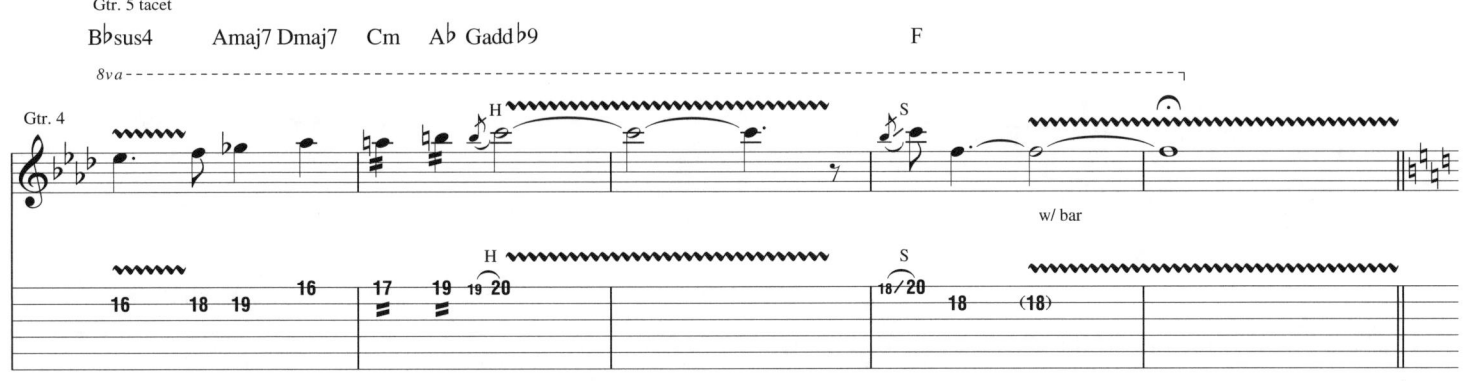

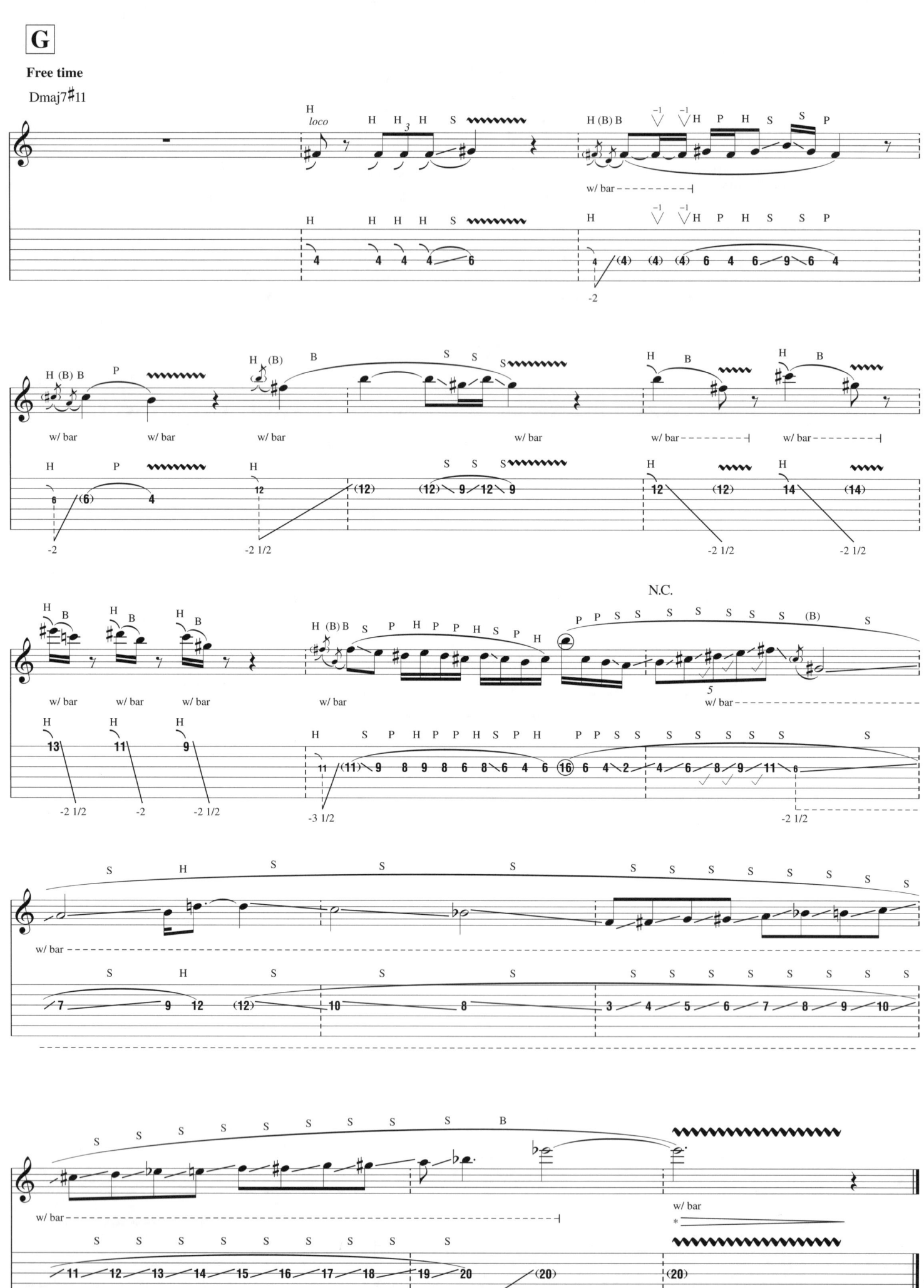

Yai Yai

By Steve Vai

DADGAD tuning, down 1 step:
(low to high) C-G-C-F-G-C

Moderately ♩ = 108

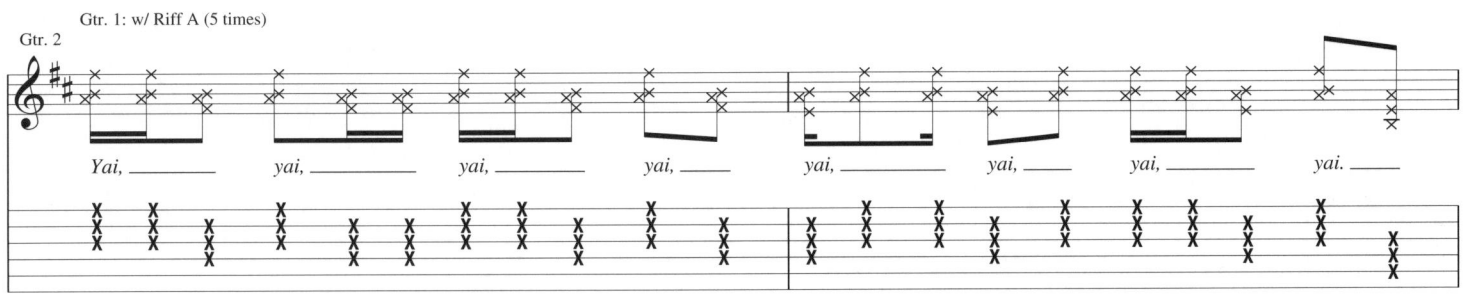

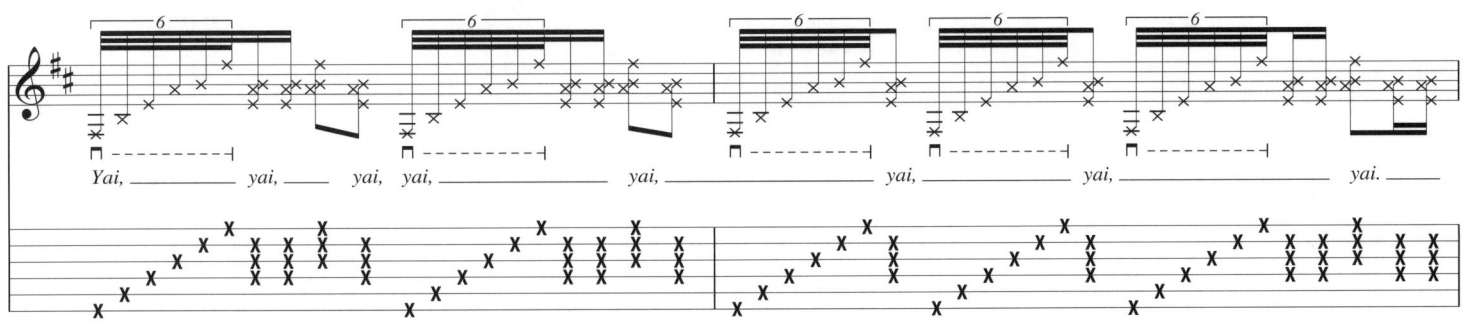

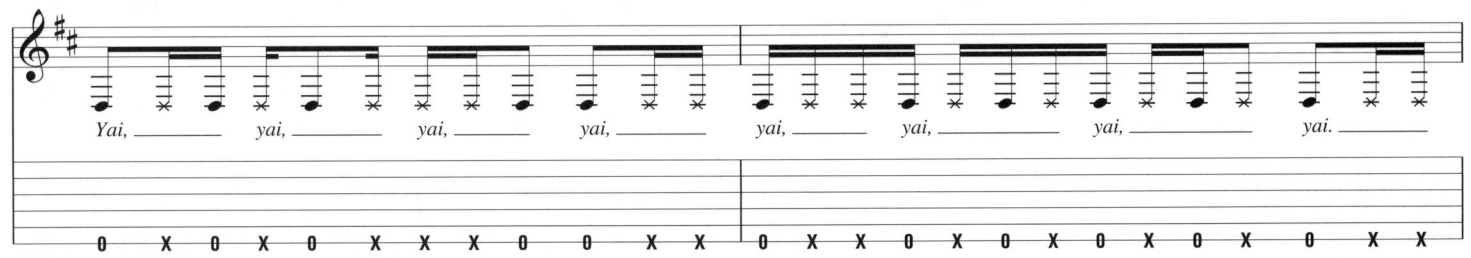

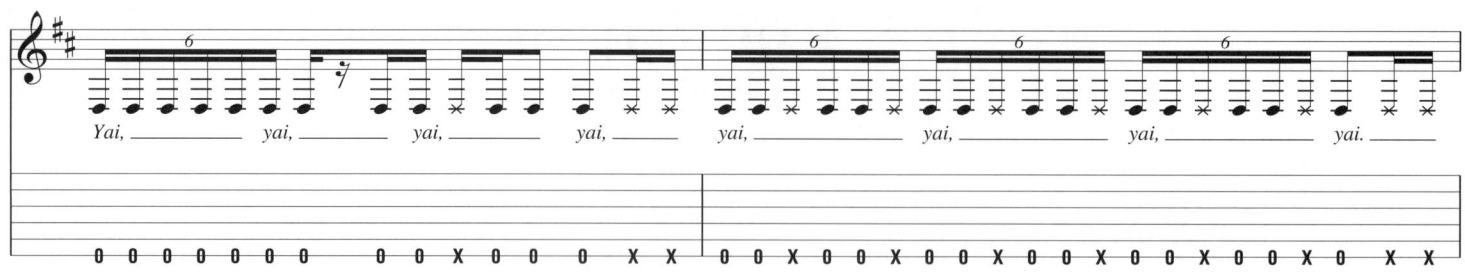
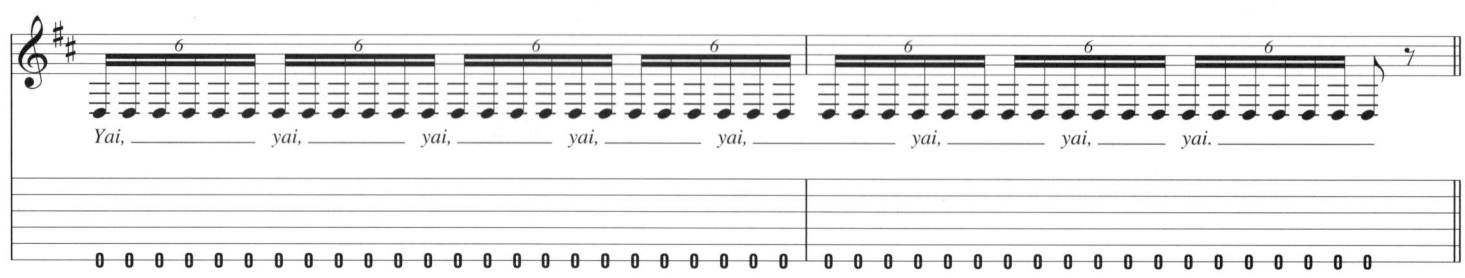

B

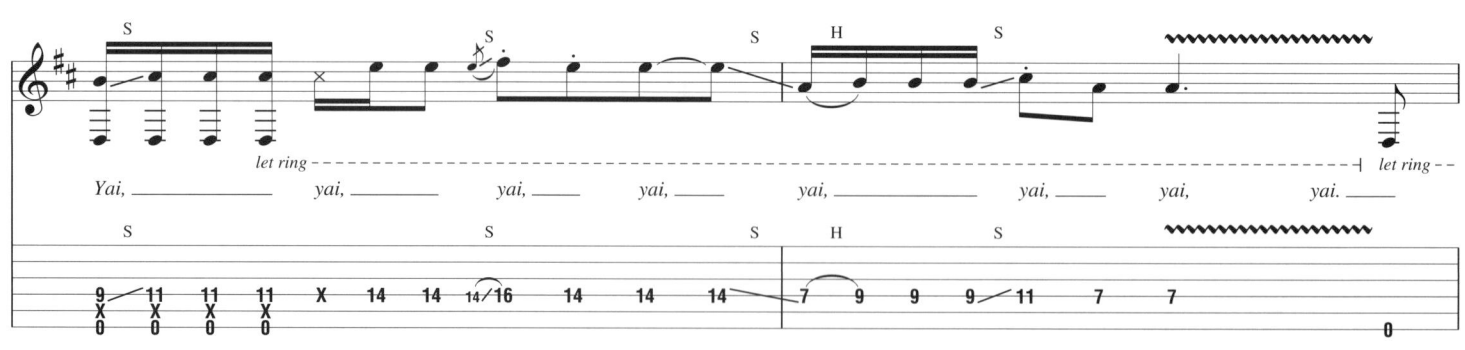
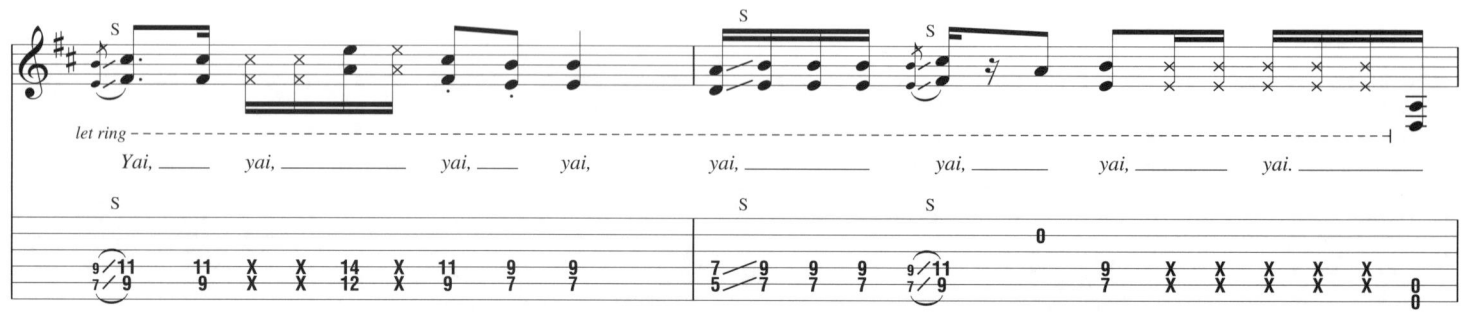

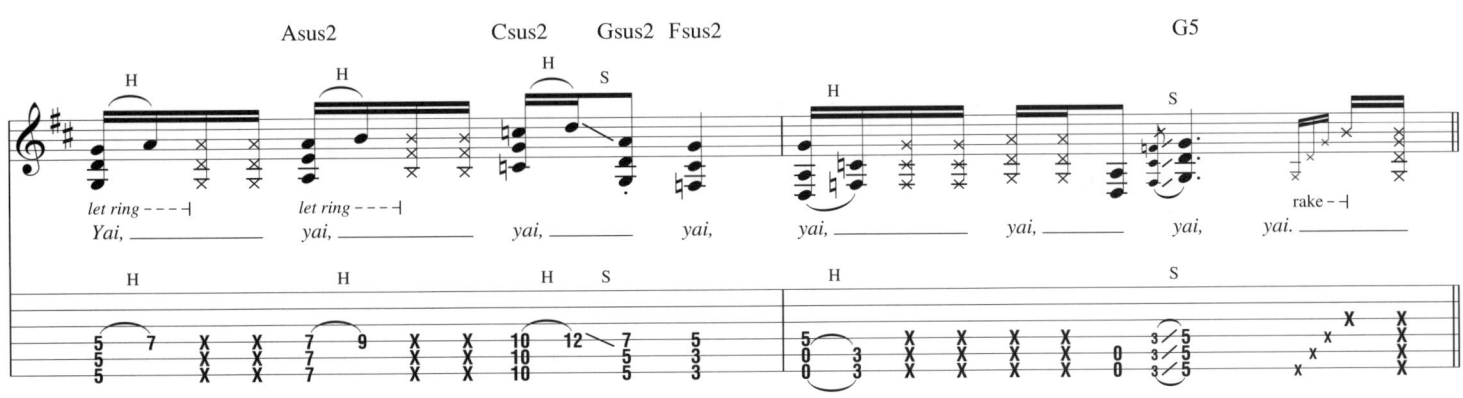

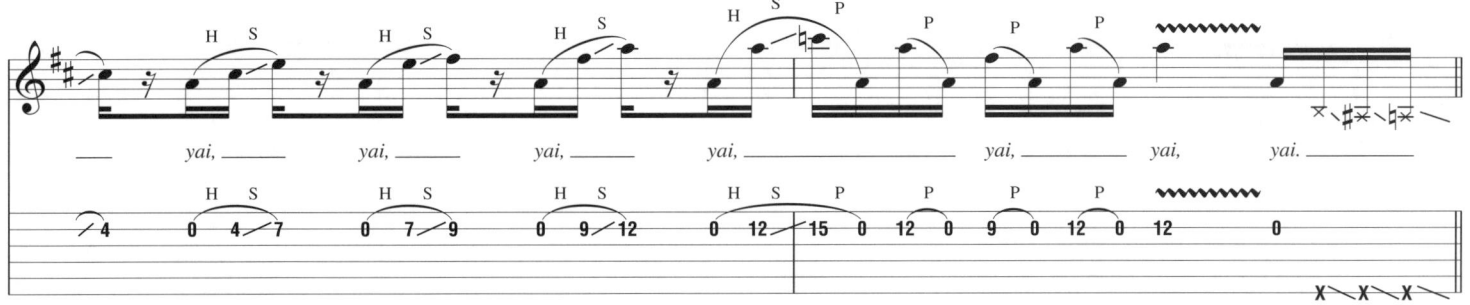

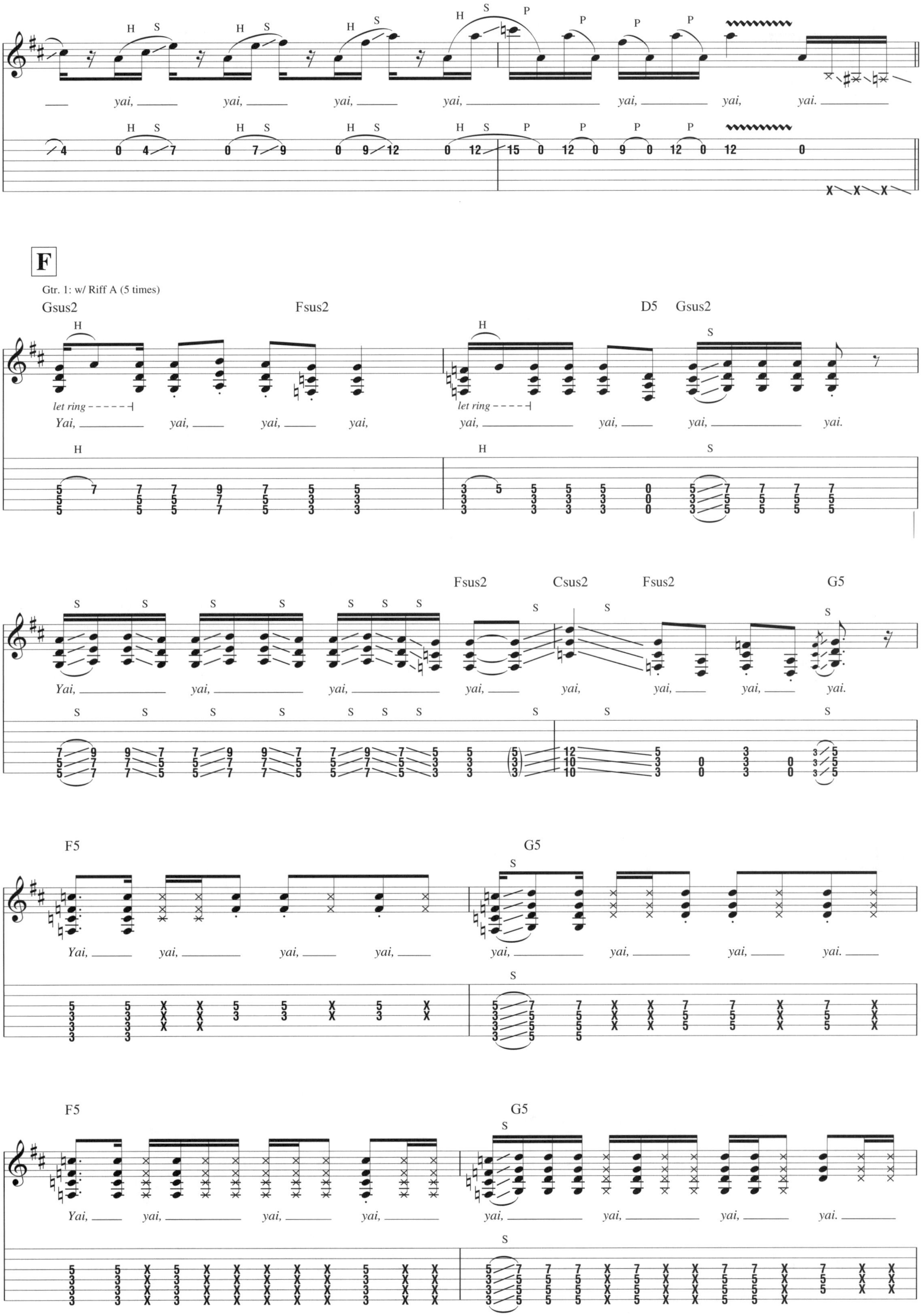

F

Gtr. 1: w/ Riff A (5 times)

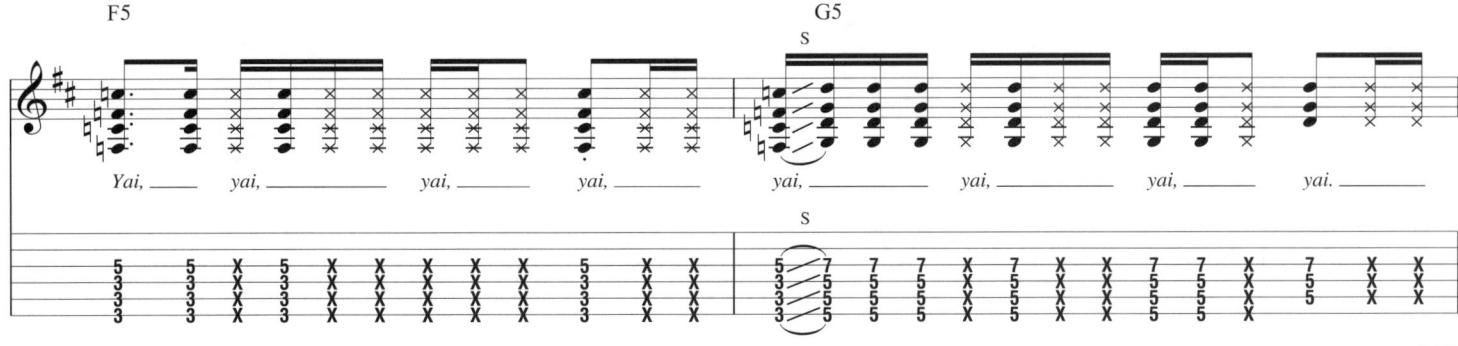

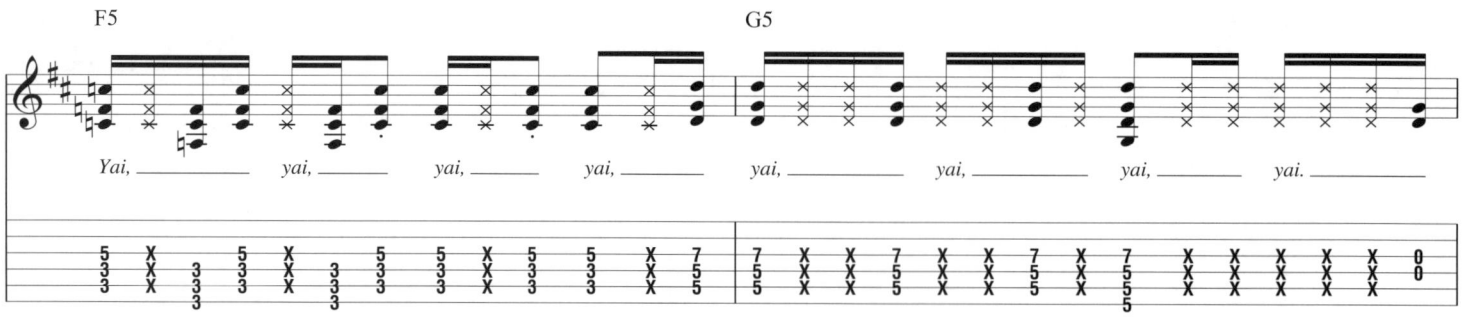
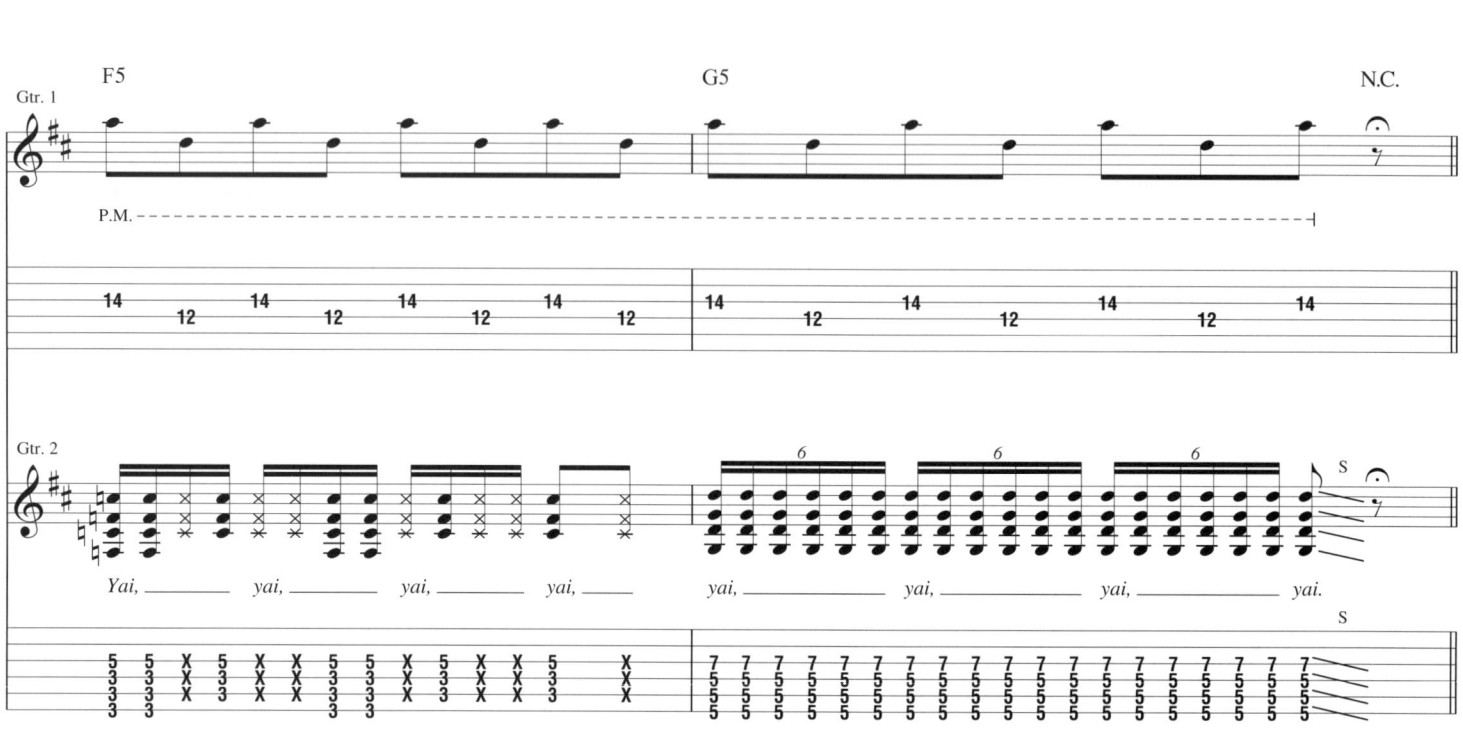
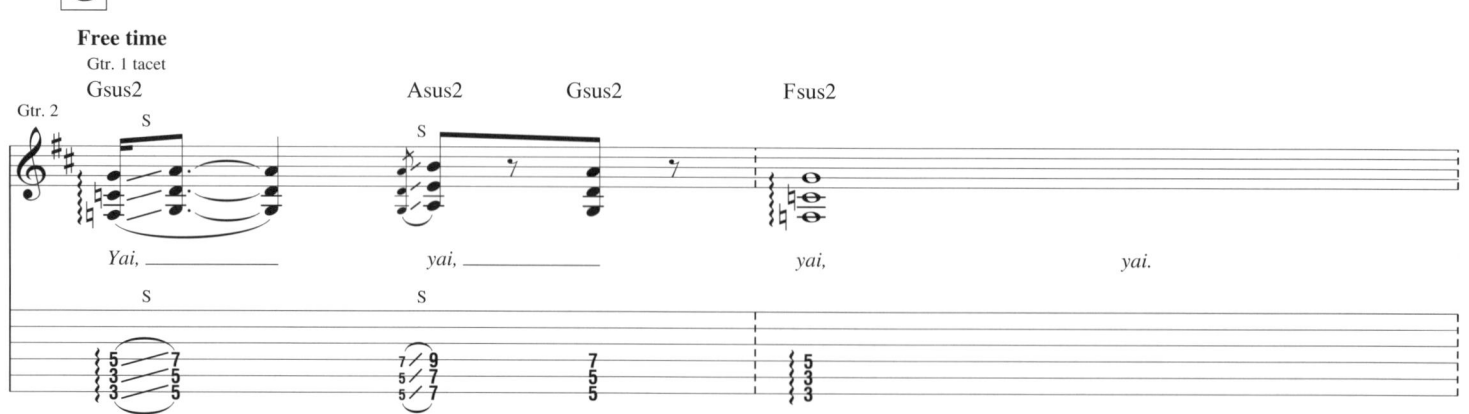
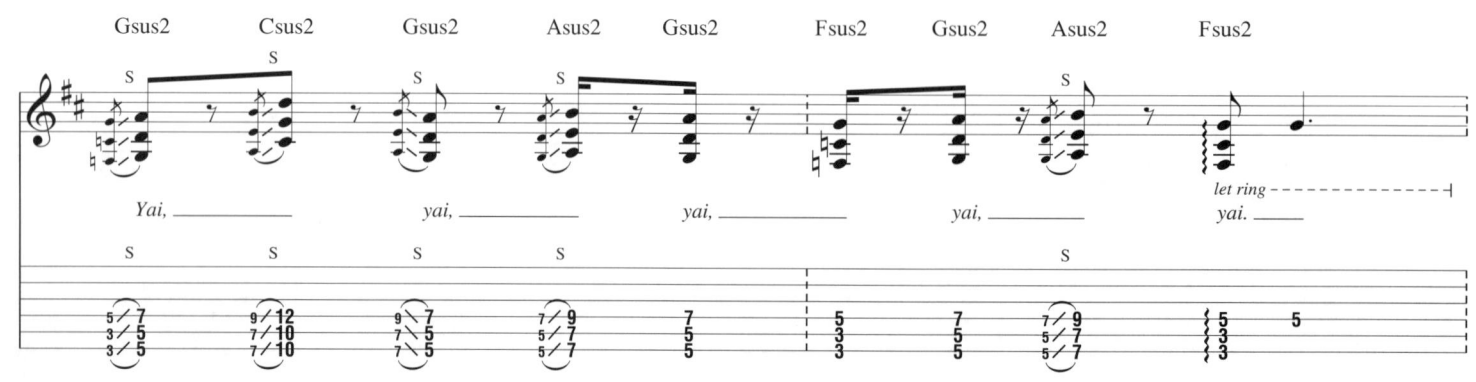

Midway Creatures
By Steve Vai

*Fmaj9

*Chord symbols reflect overall harmony.

121

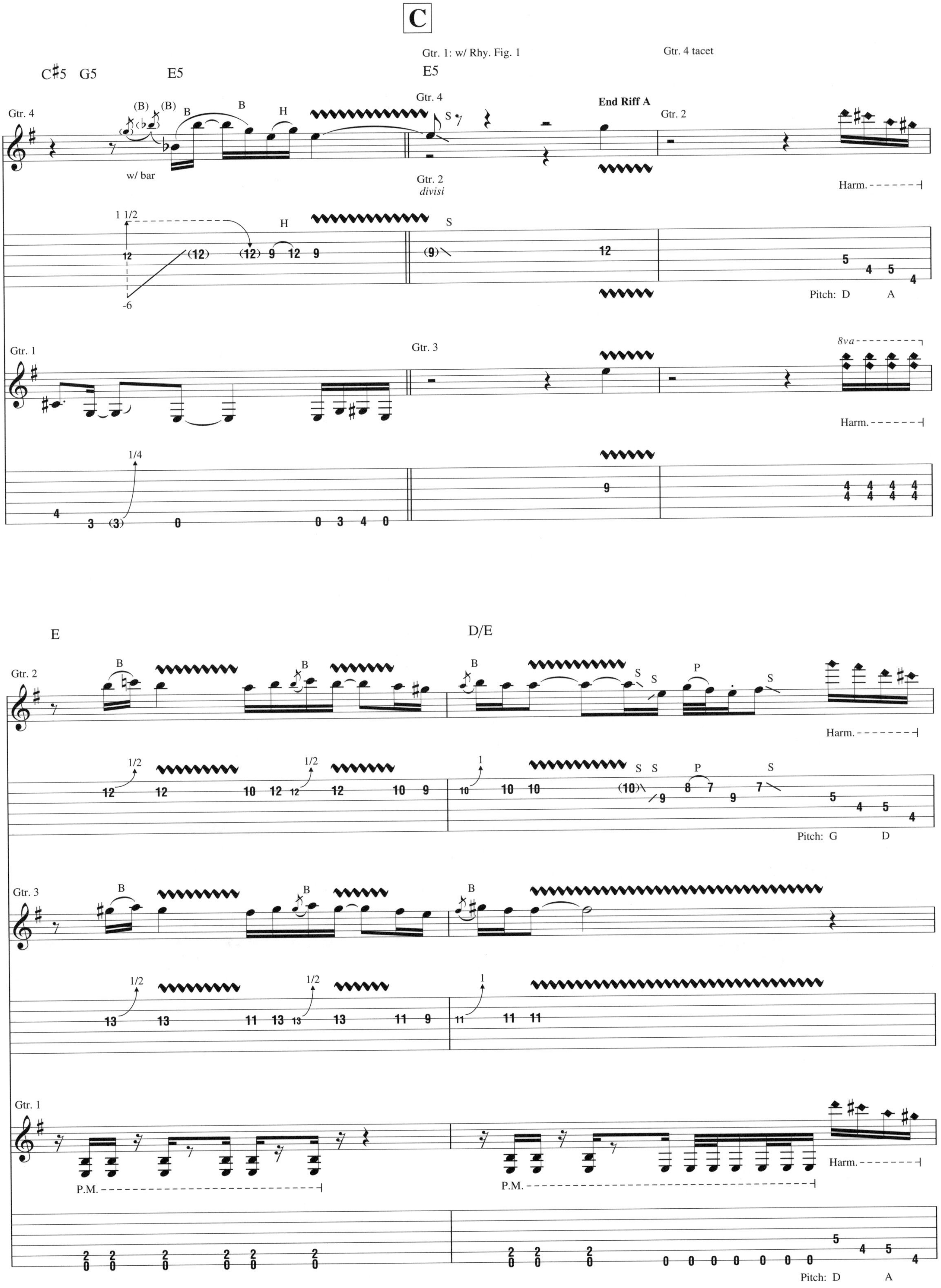

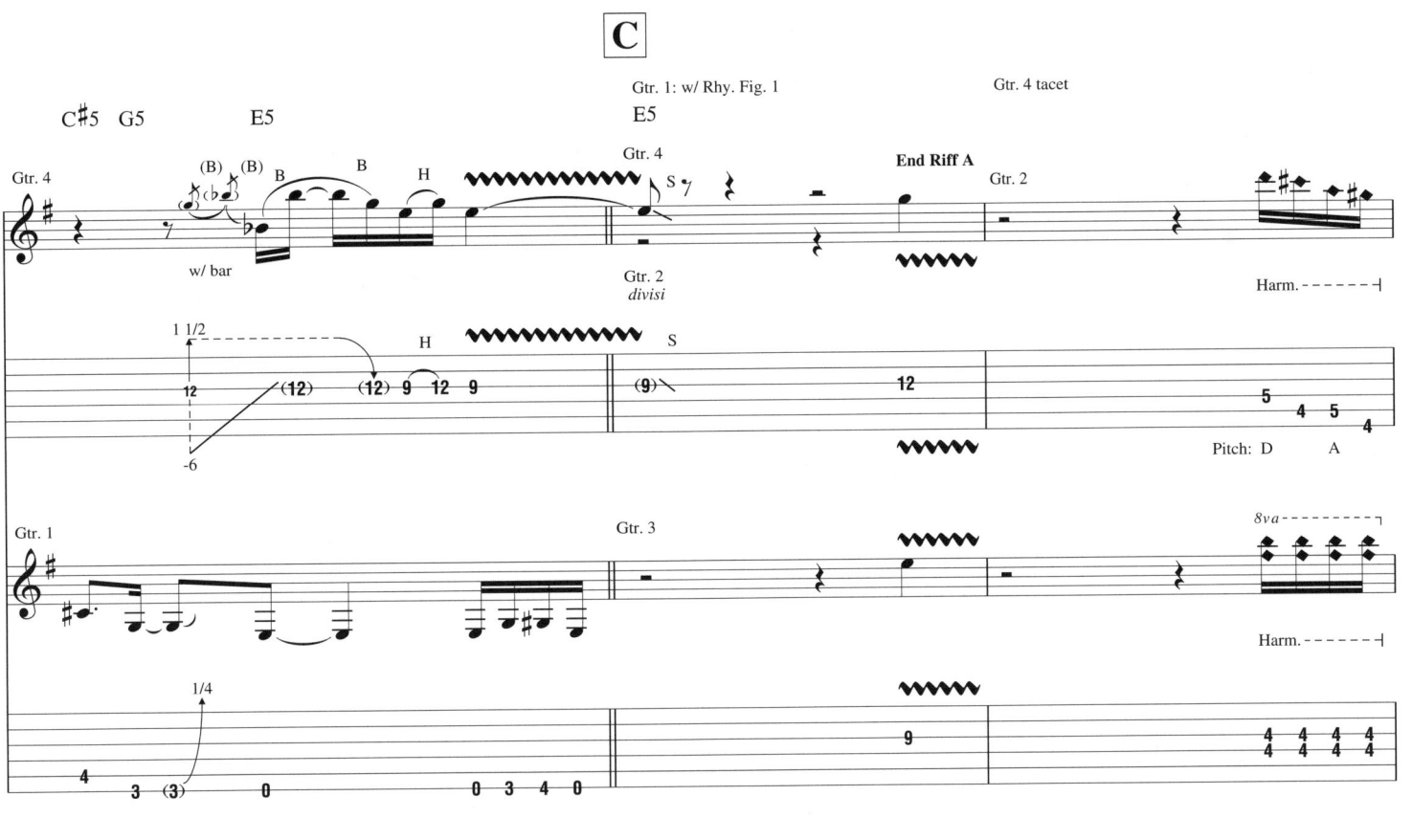

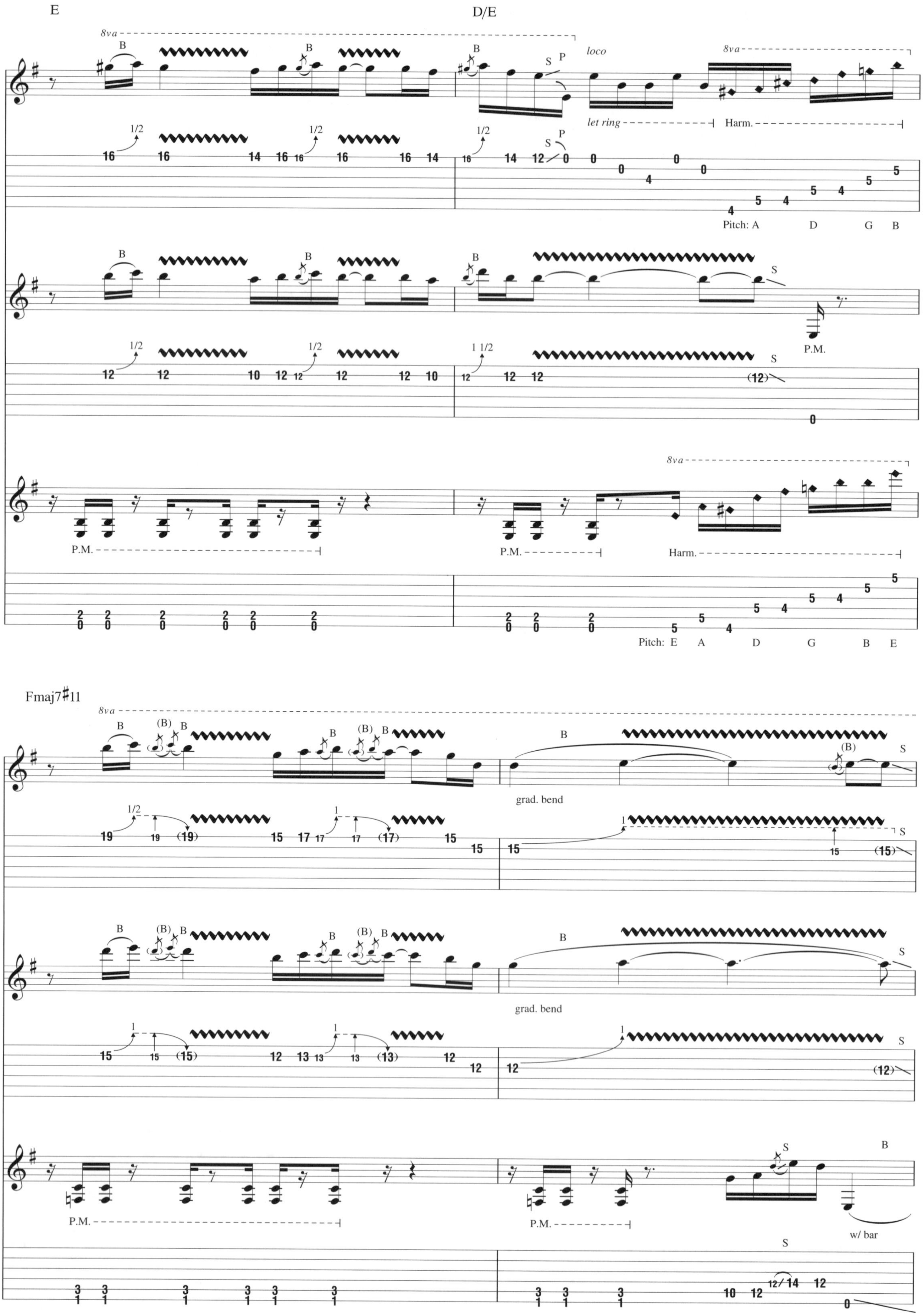

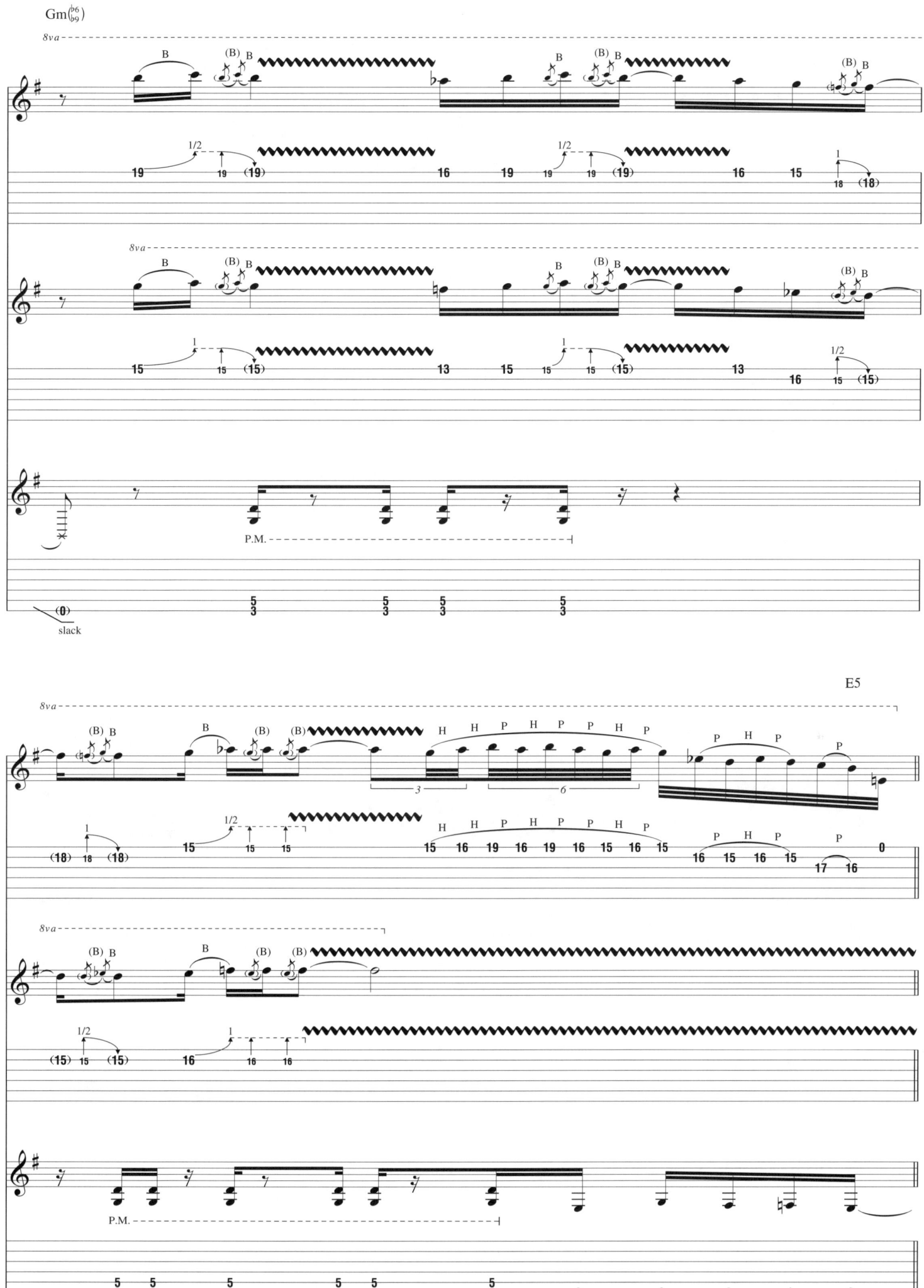

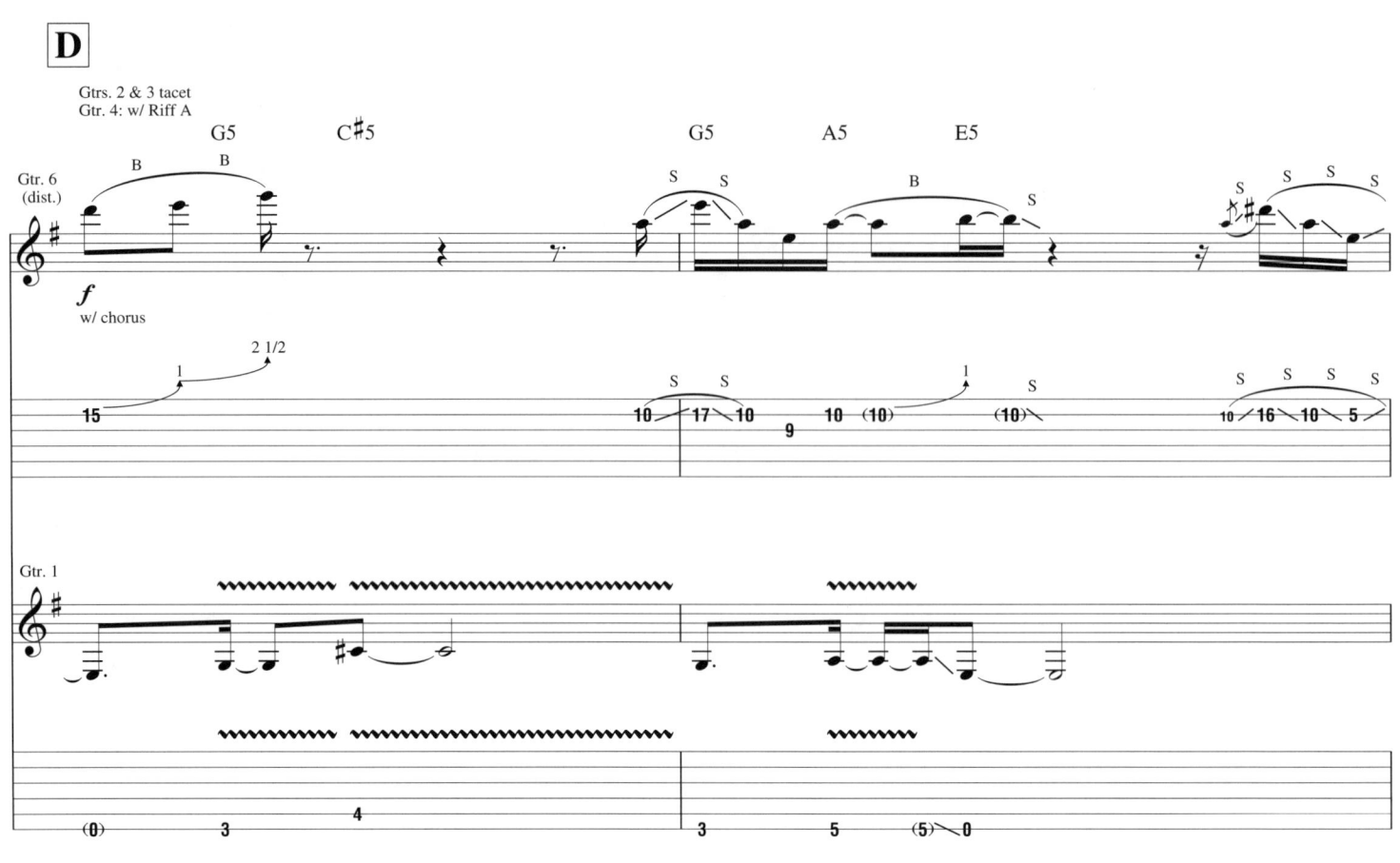
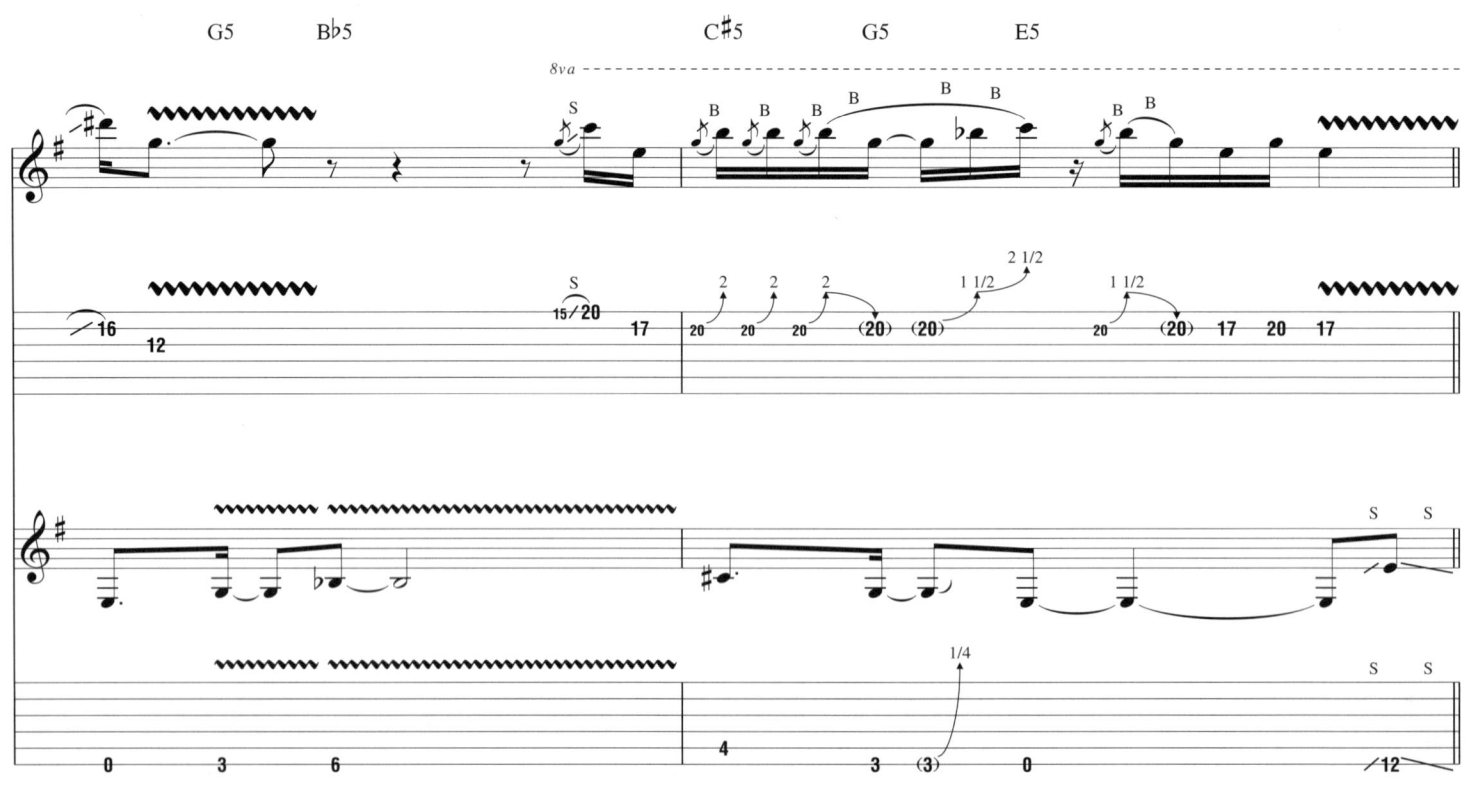

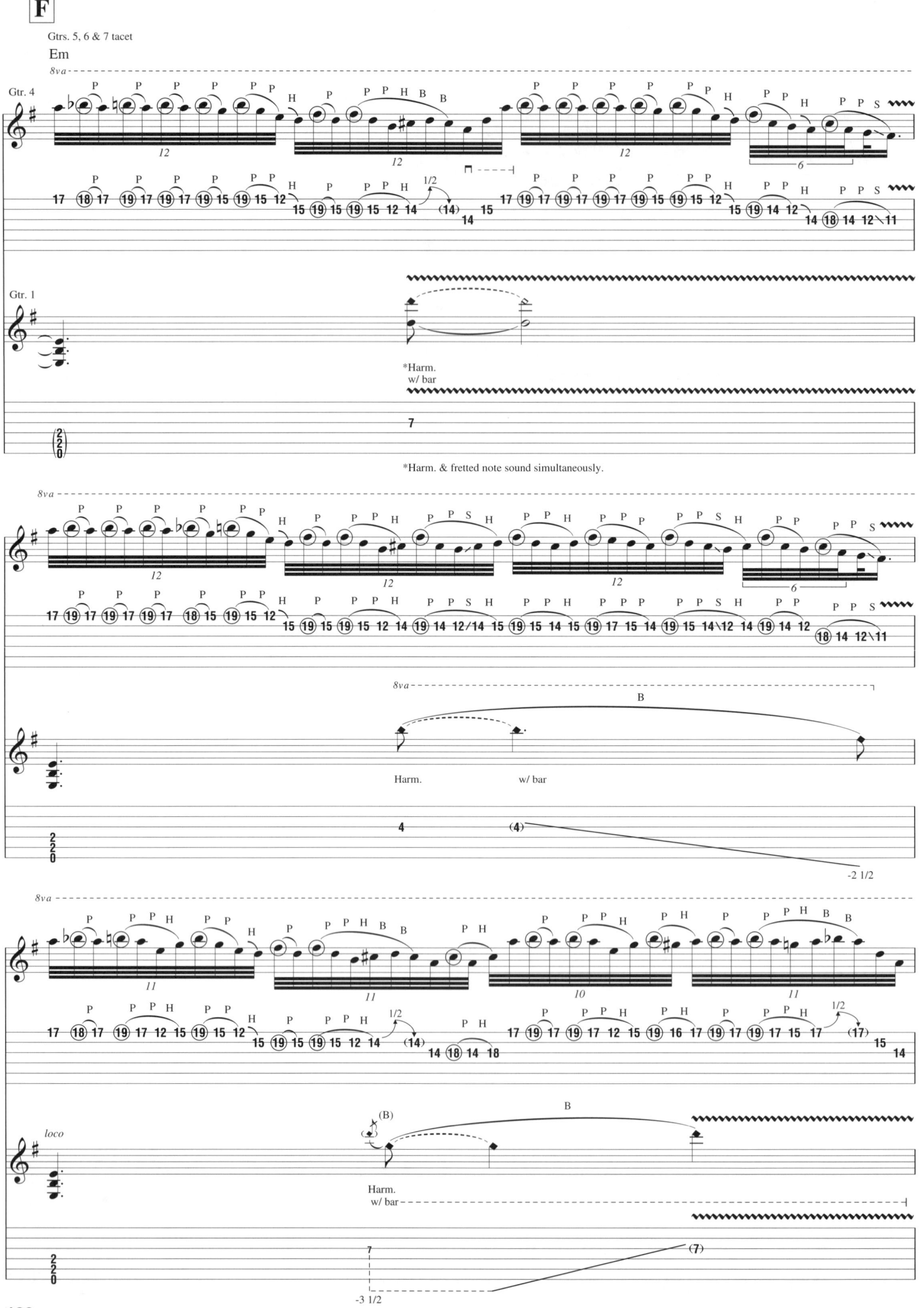

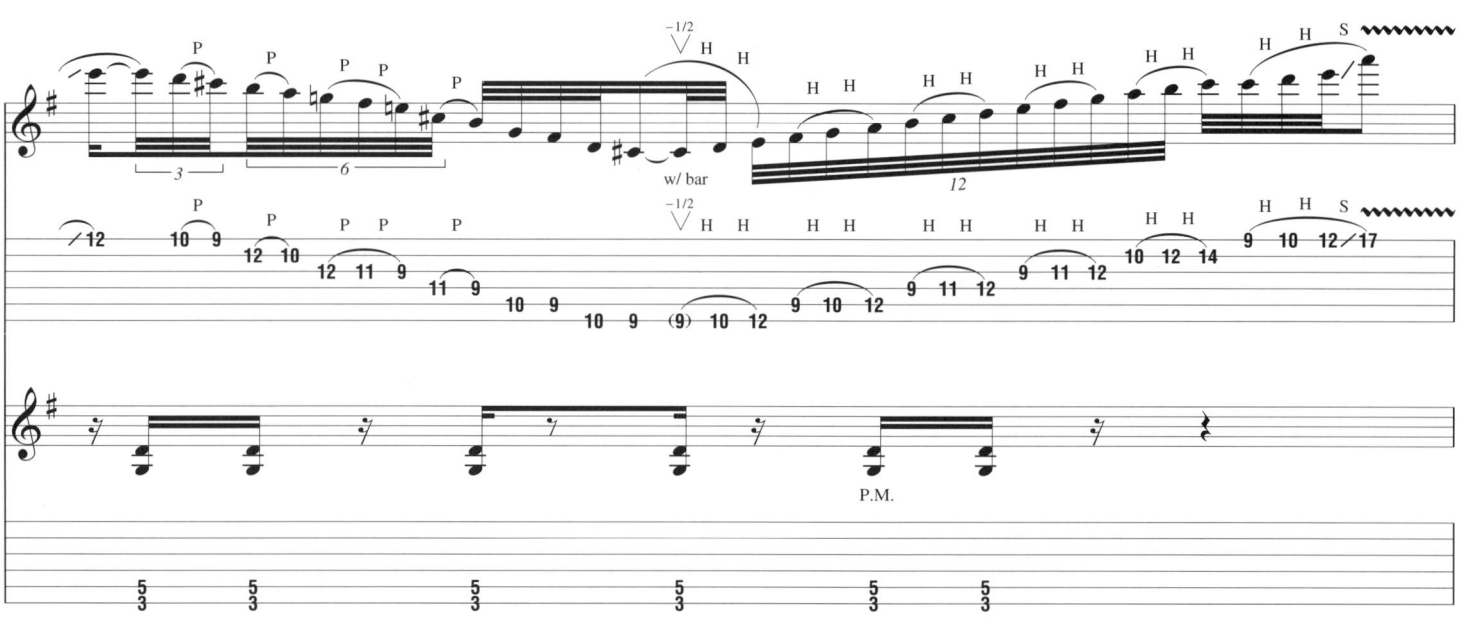

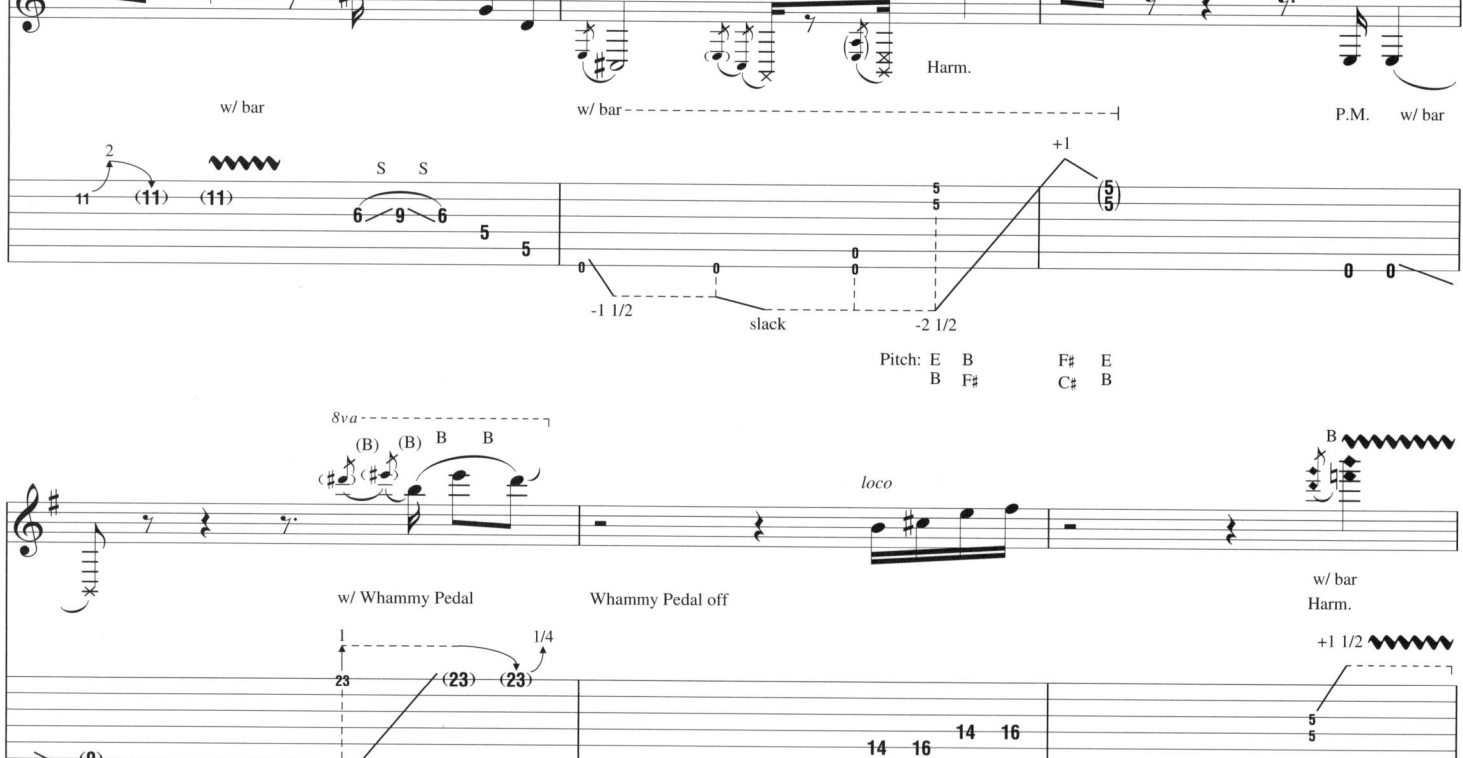
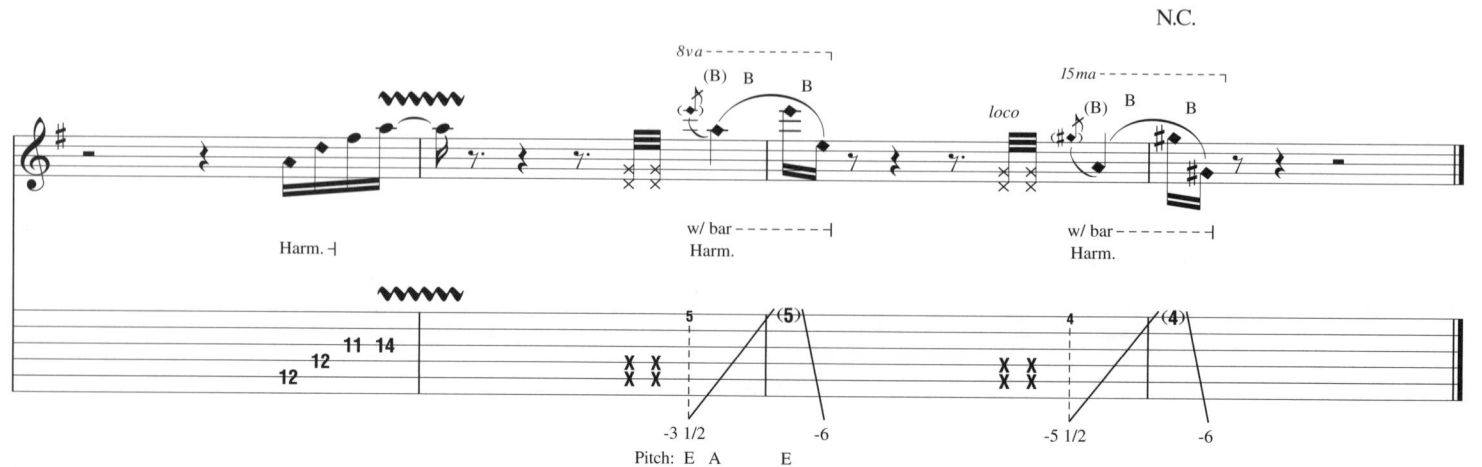

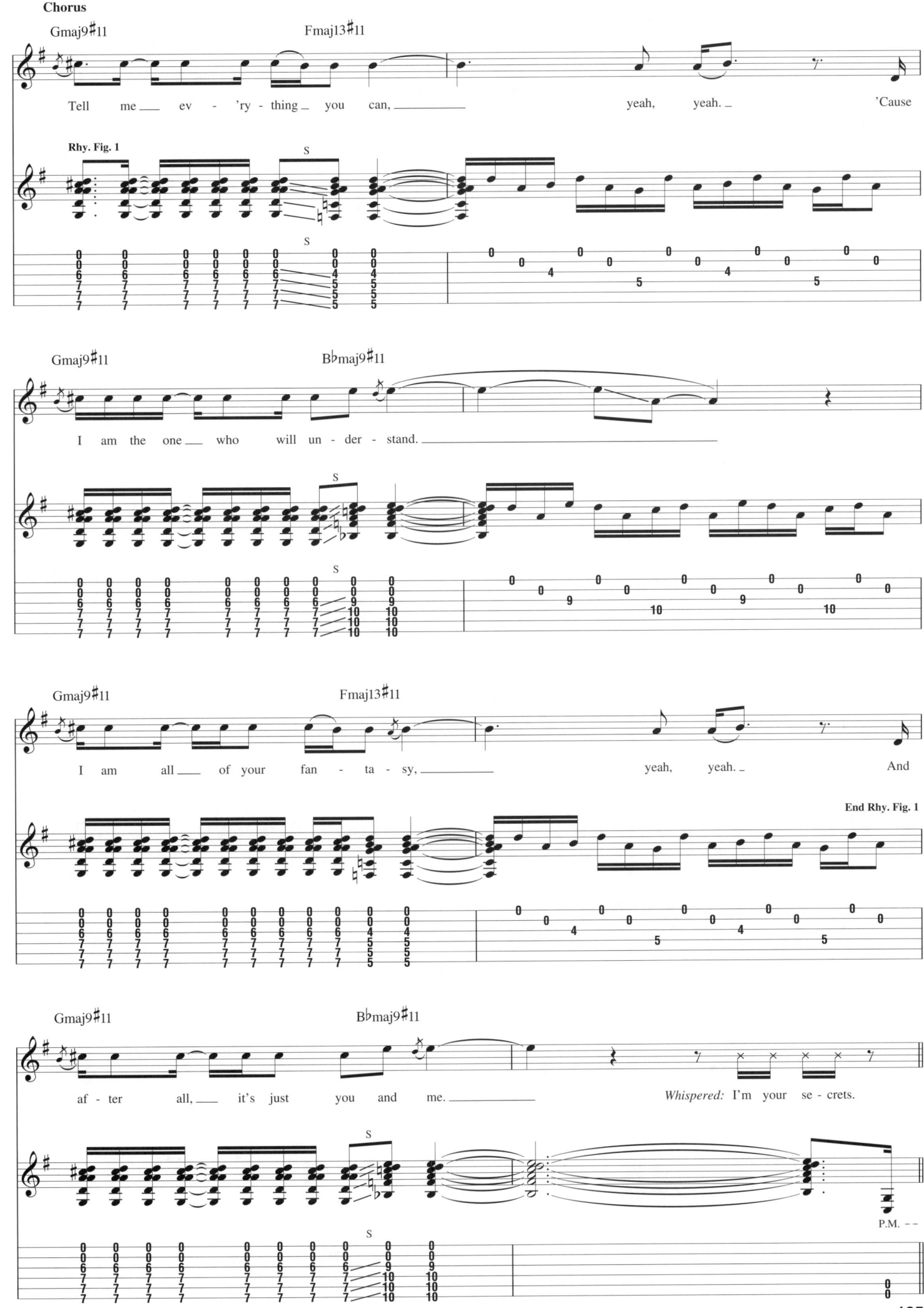

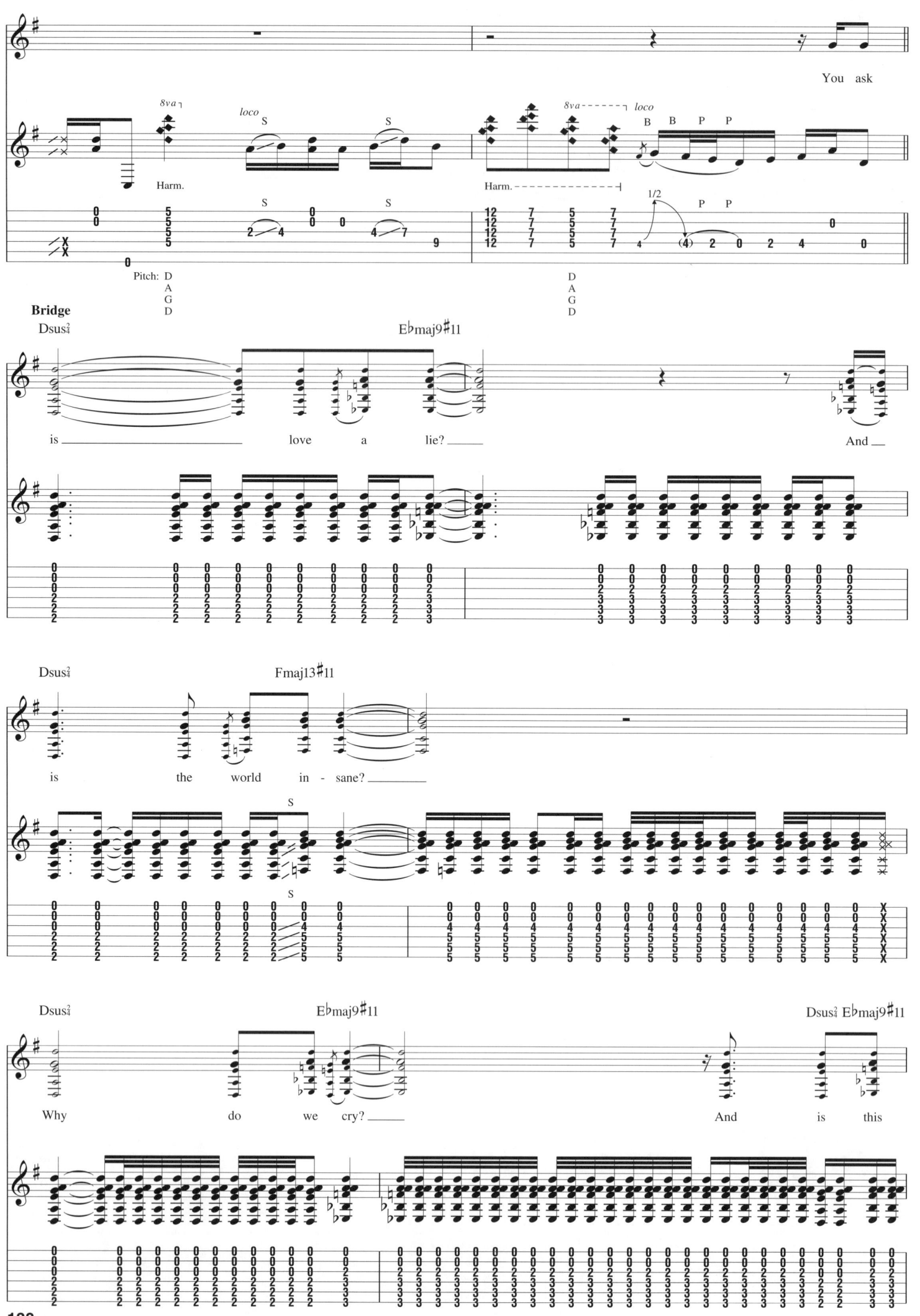

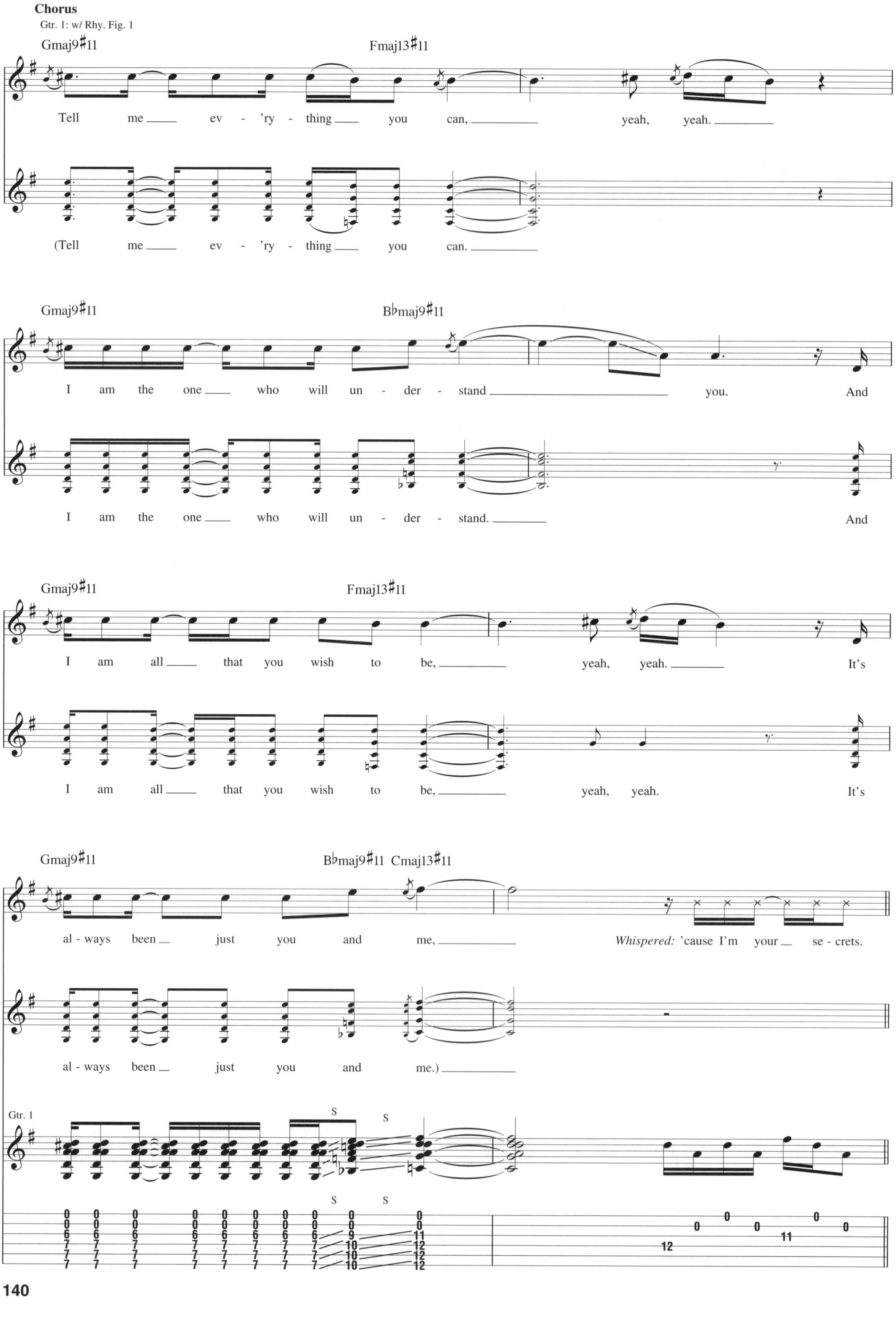

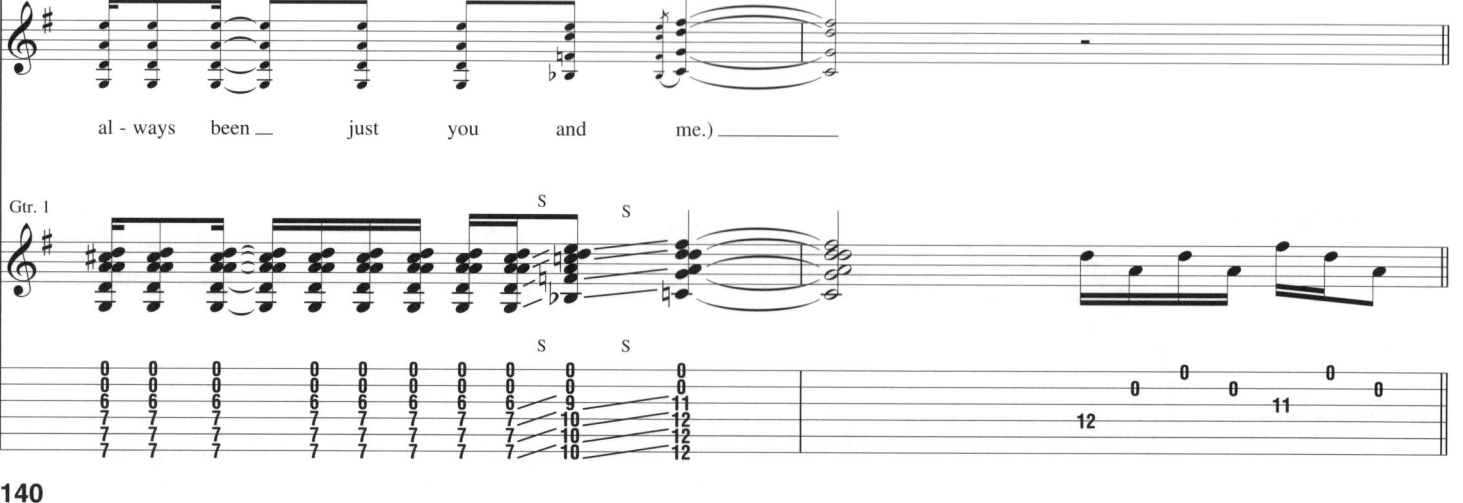

Outro

Cmaj13♯11   B♭maj9♯11

Whispered:
Secrets, secrets, secrets. Secrets, secrets, secrets. Secrets, secrets,
Whispered: Secrets, secrets. Secrets, secrets, secrets. Secrets, secrets.

*Two elec. sitars arr. for gtr.

Cmaj13♯11   B♭maj7♯11   Cmaj13♯11   E♭maj9♯11

Secrets, secrets, secrets. Secrets, secrets.
Secrets, secrets, secrets. Secrets, secrets, secrets.

Under It All

By Steve Vai

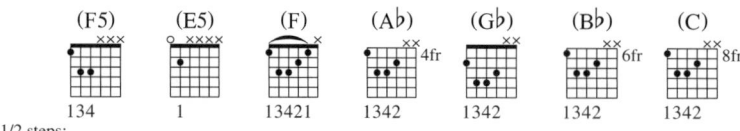

Gtrs. 1, 2, 7, 8 & 9: Tune down 2 1/2 steps:
(low to high) B-E-A-D-F♯-B

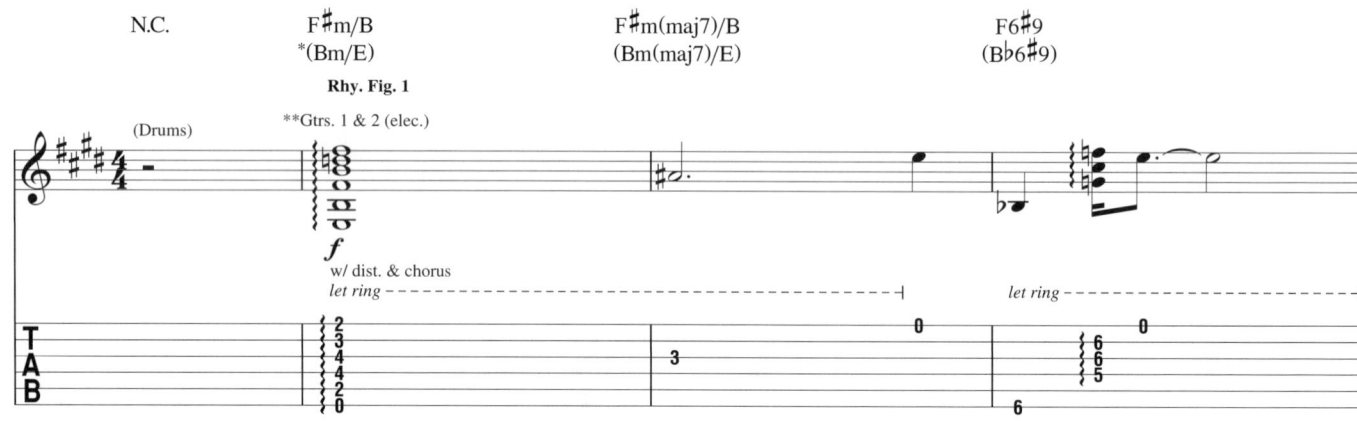

*Symbols in parentheses represent chord names respective to de-tuned guitars.
Symbols above represent actual sounding chords. Chord symbols reflect overall harmony.
**Composite arrangement

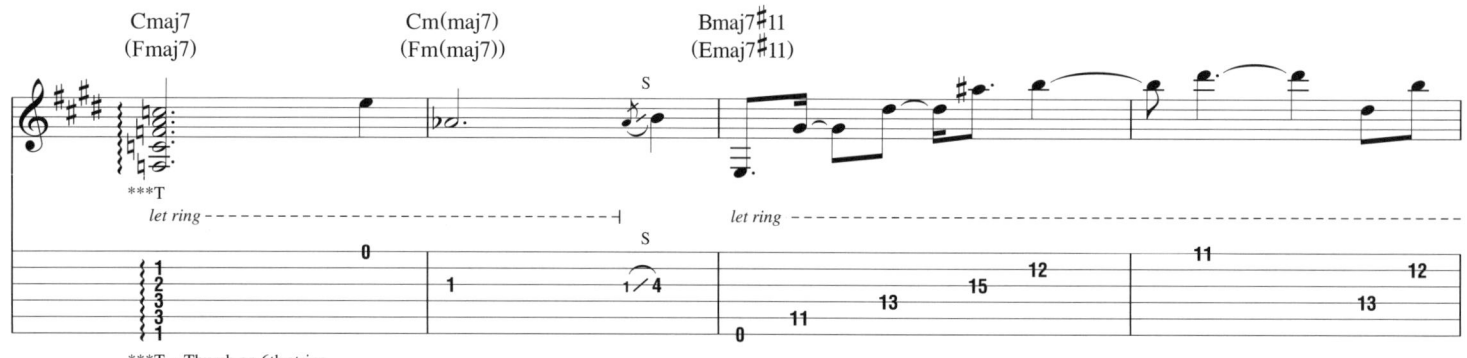

***T = Thumb on 6th string

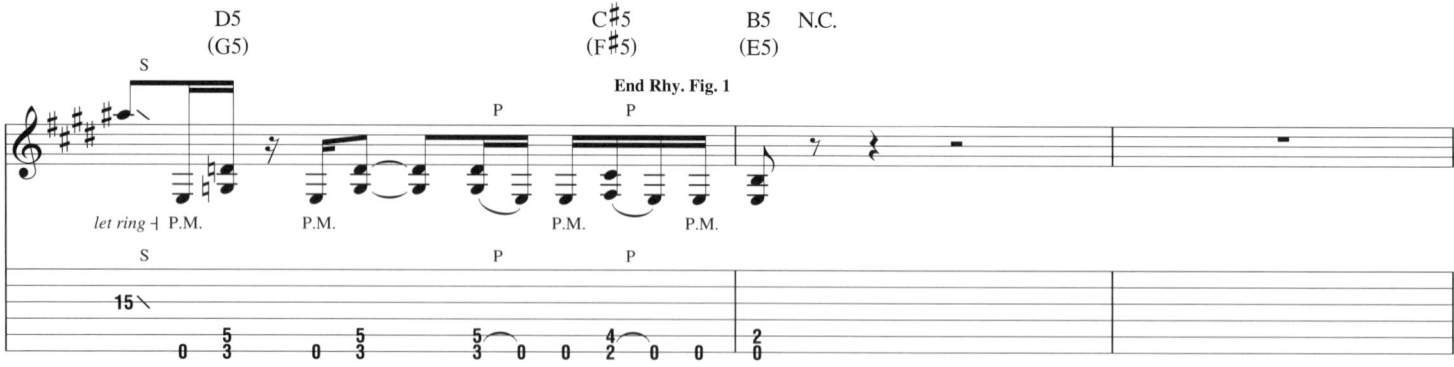

Copyright © 2005 Sy Vy Music (ASCAP)
International Copyright Secured   All Rights Reserved

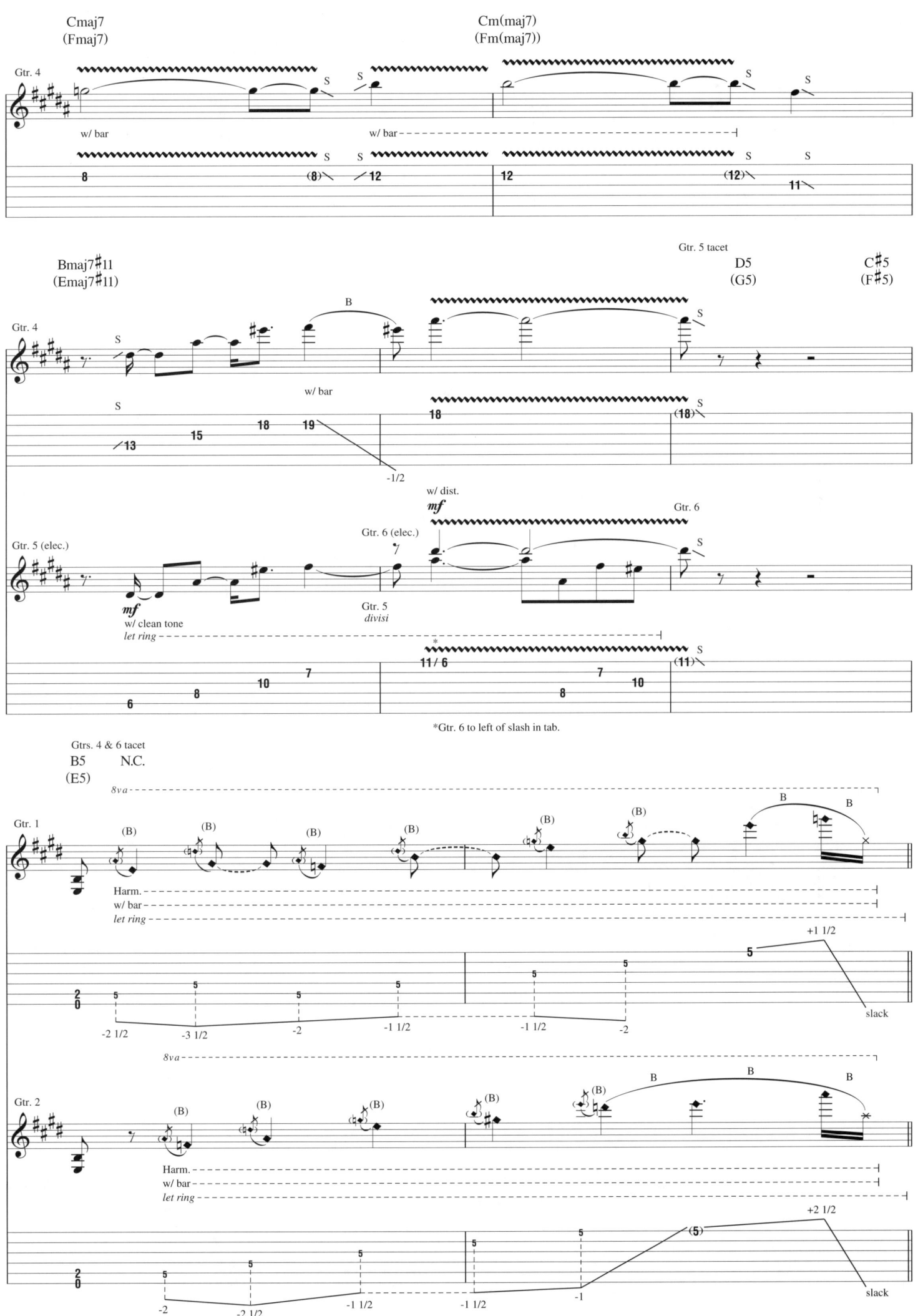

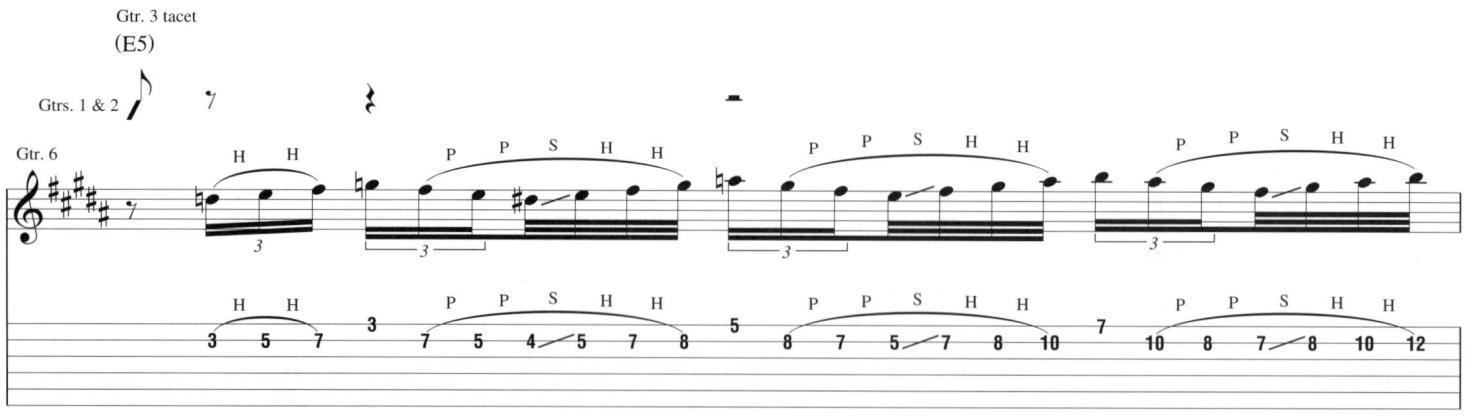

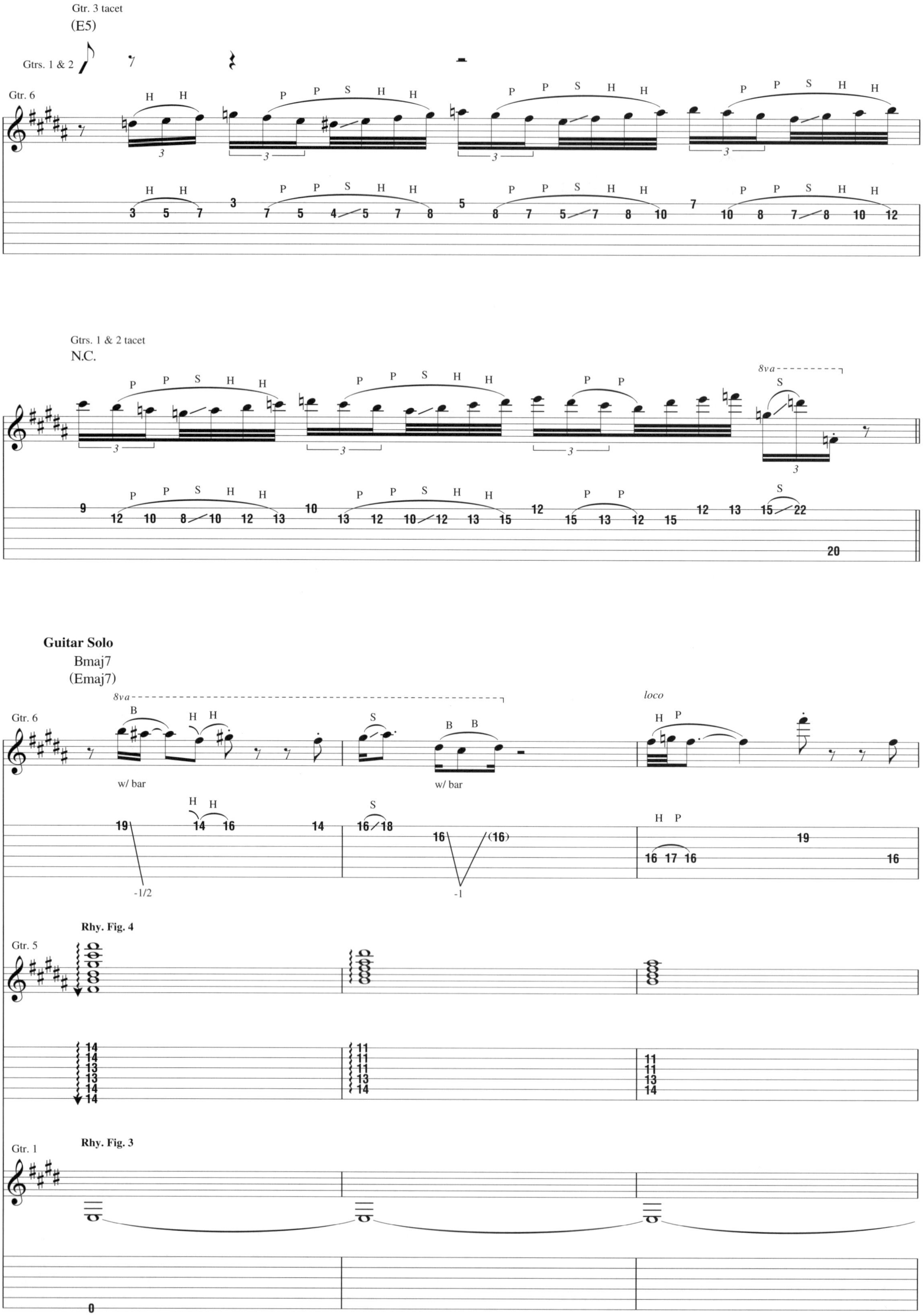

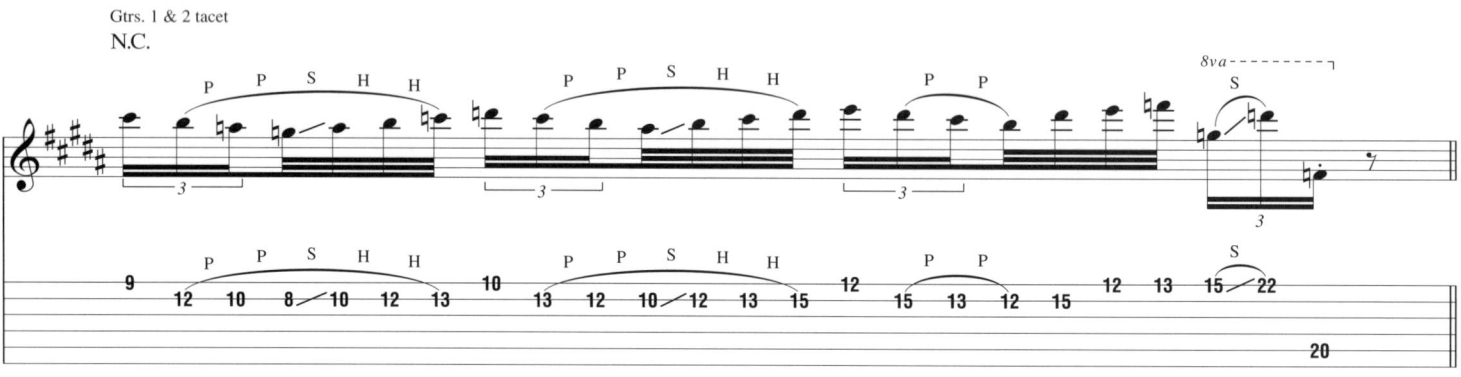

Guitar Solo
Bmaj7
(Emaj7)

152

154

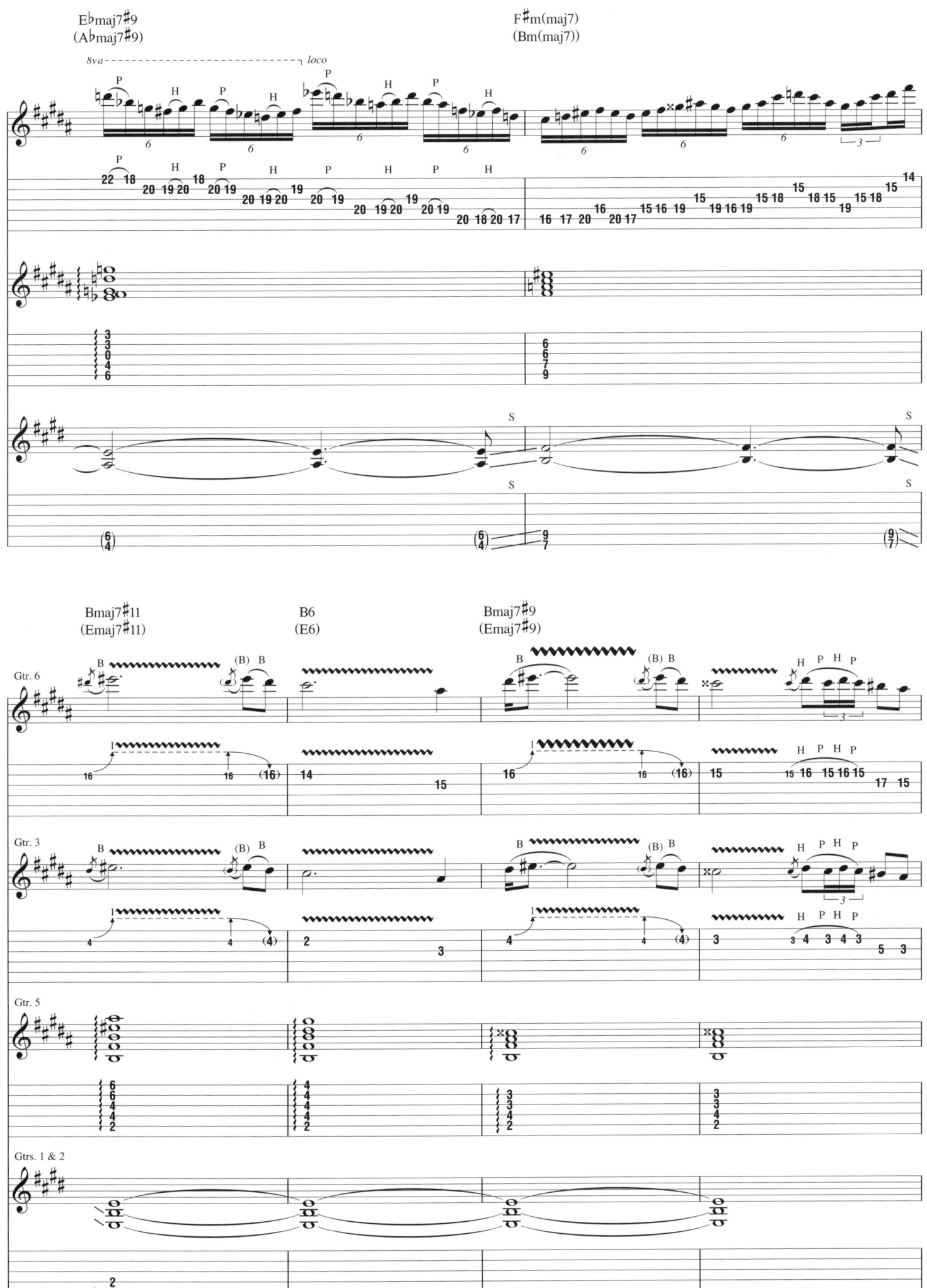

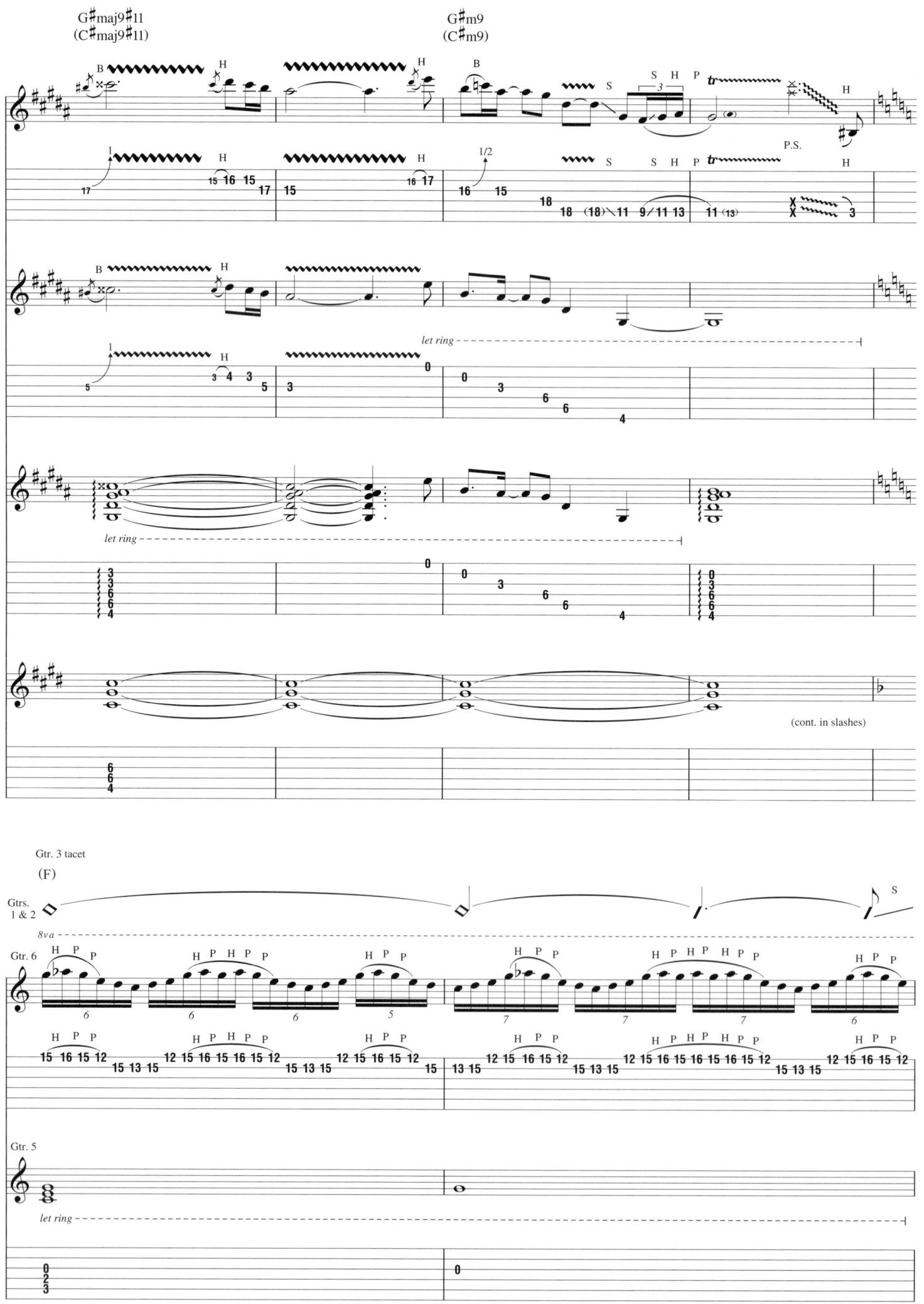

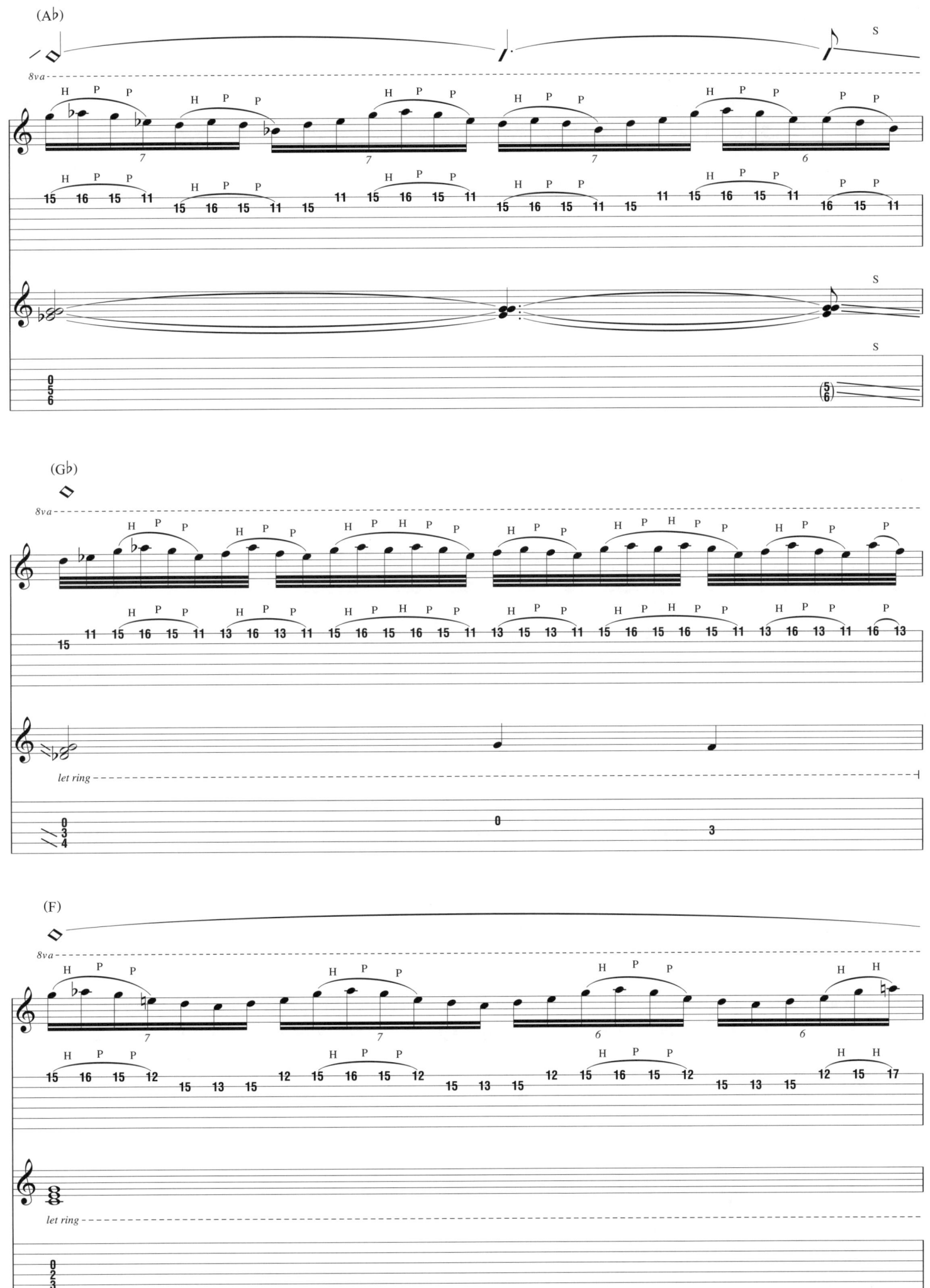

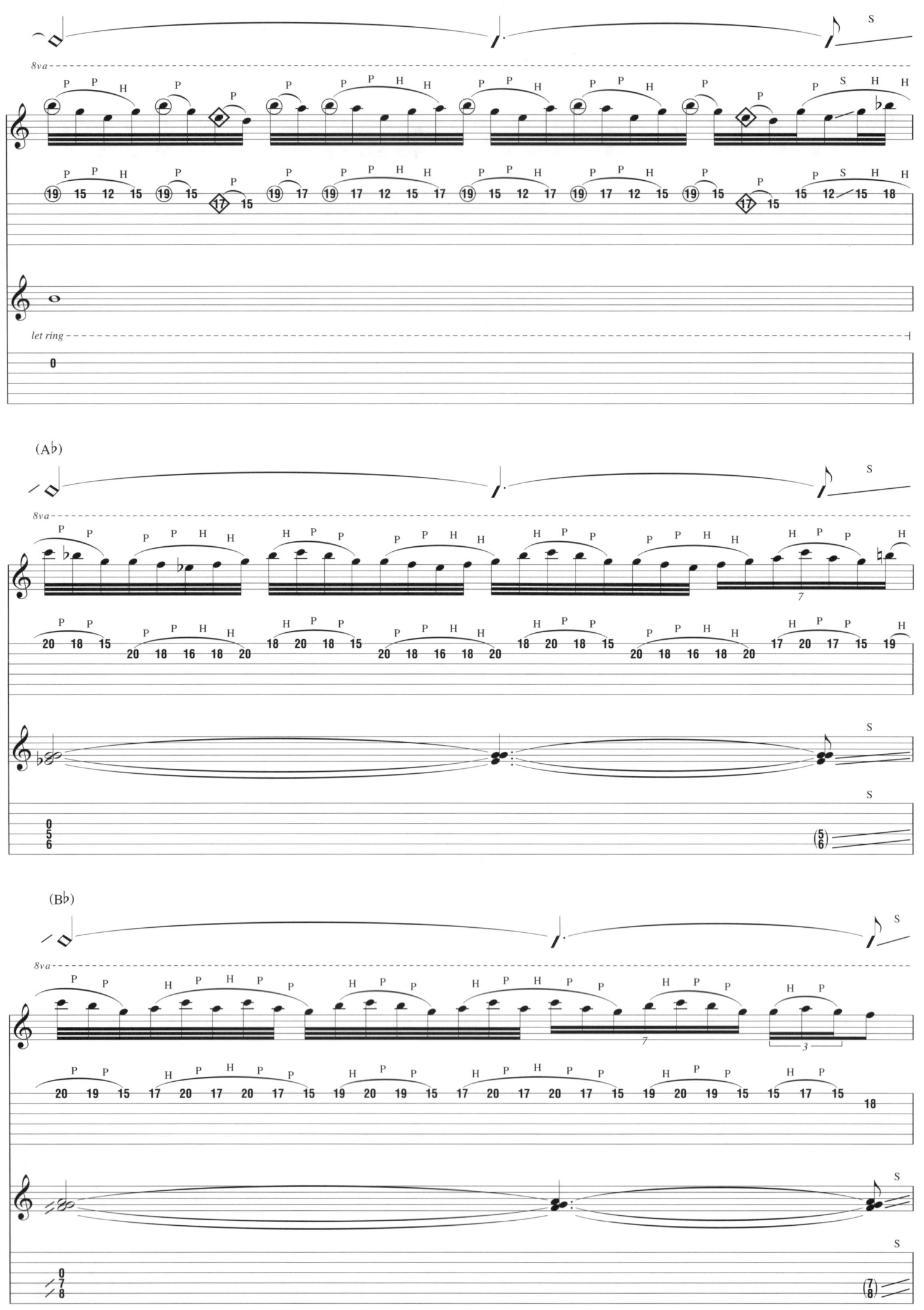

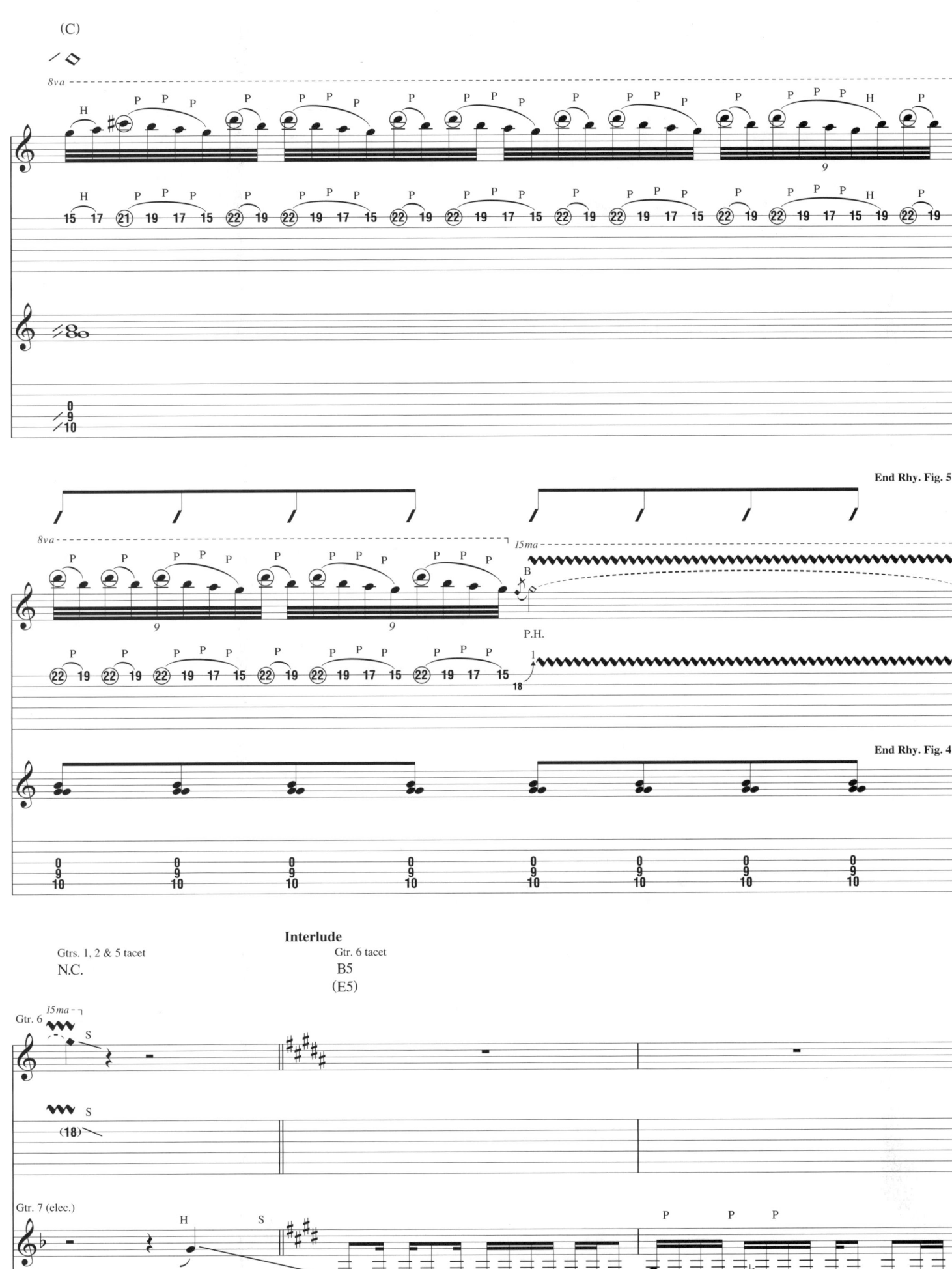

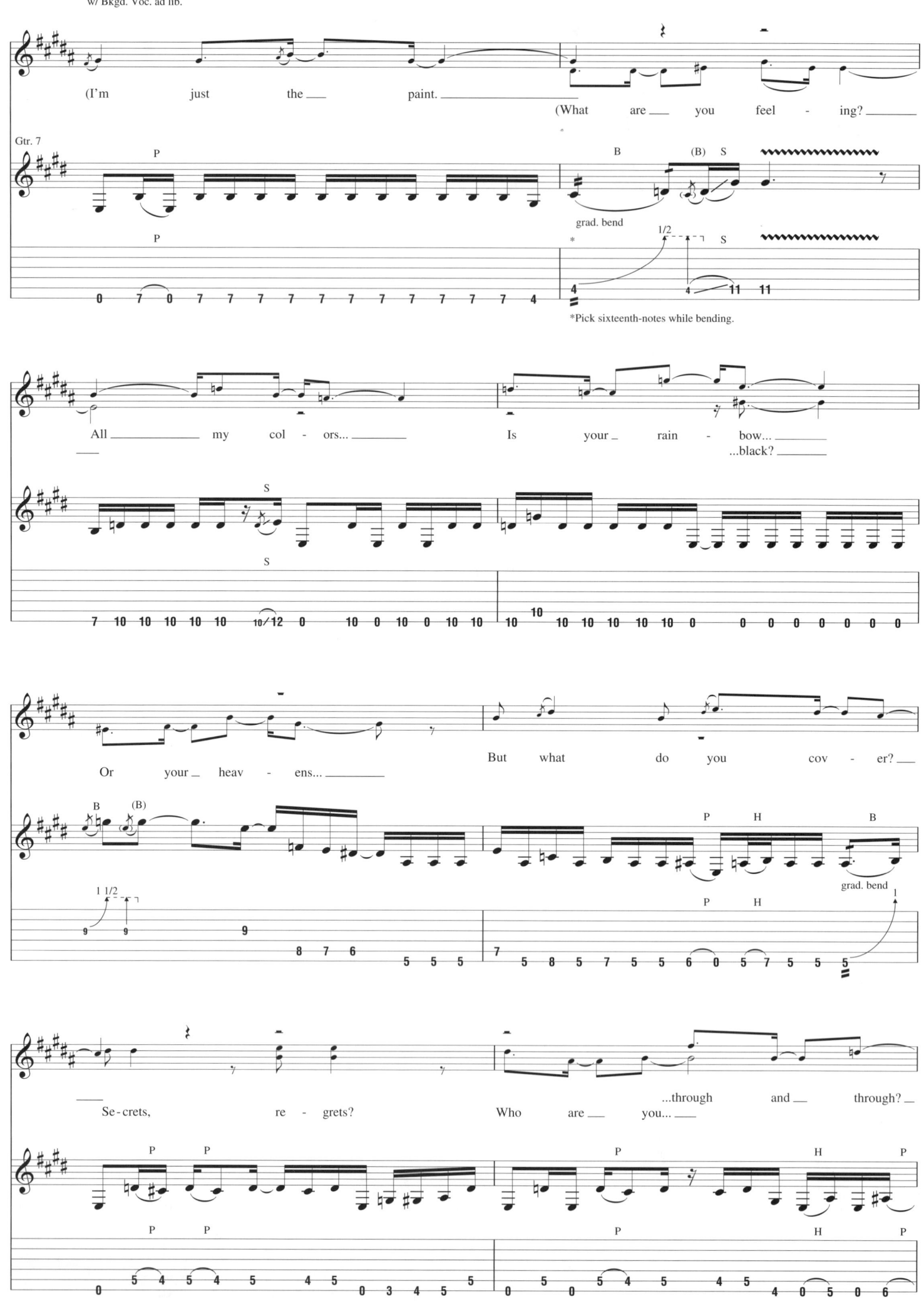

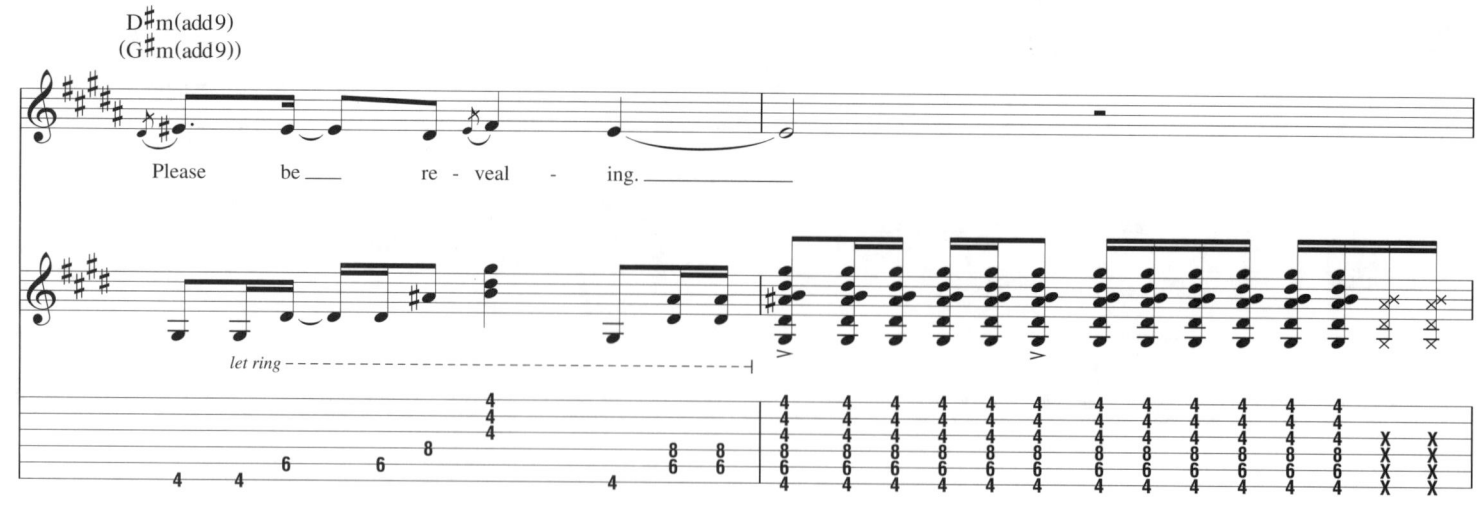
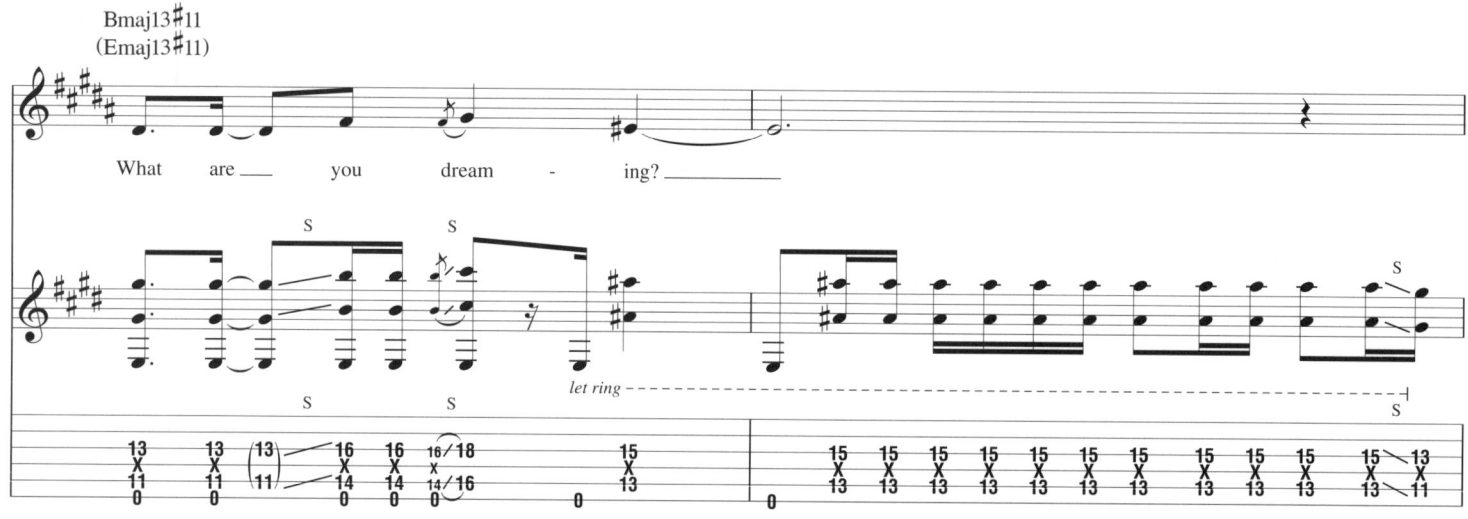

*T = Thumb on 6th string

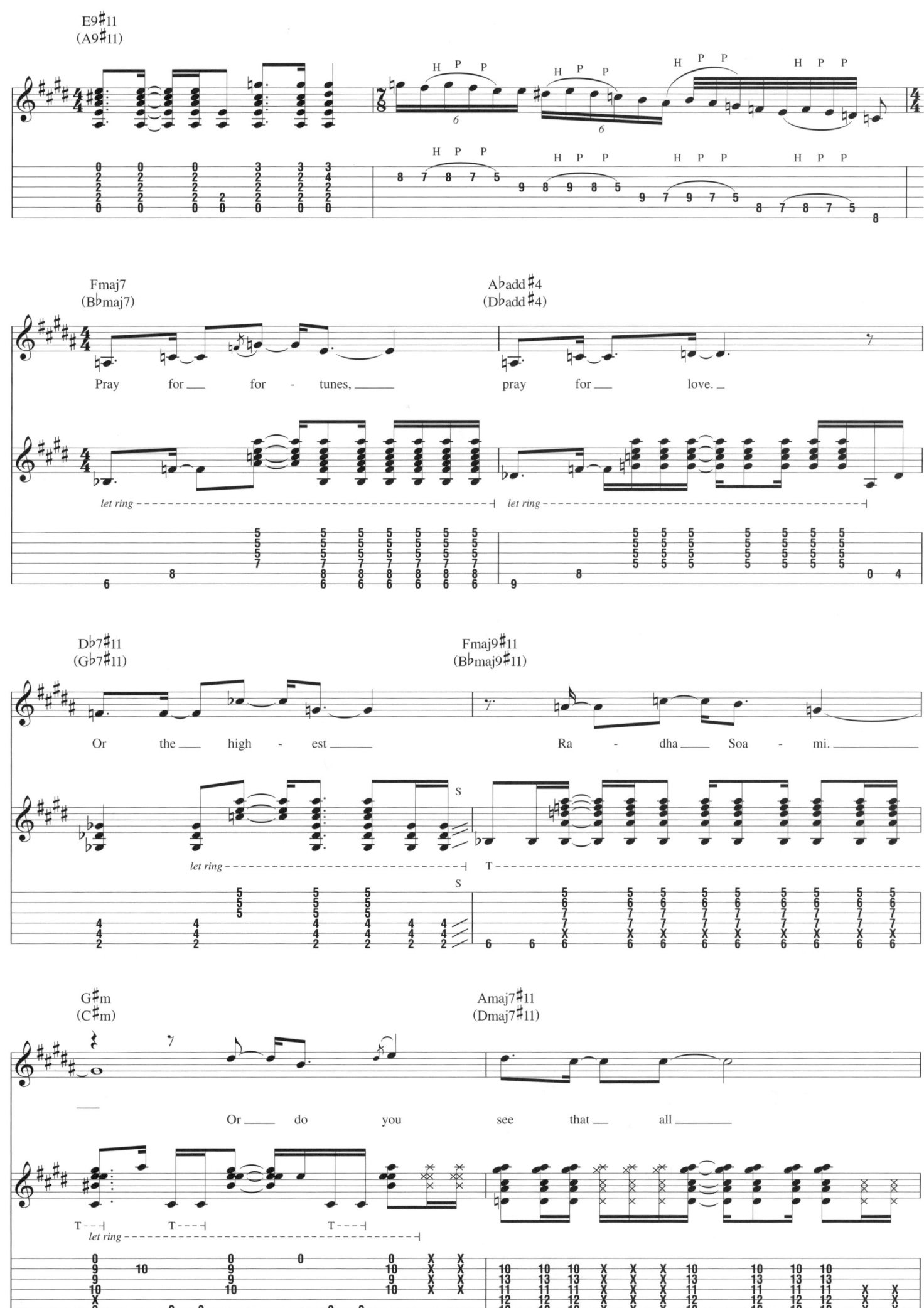

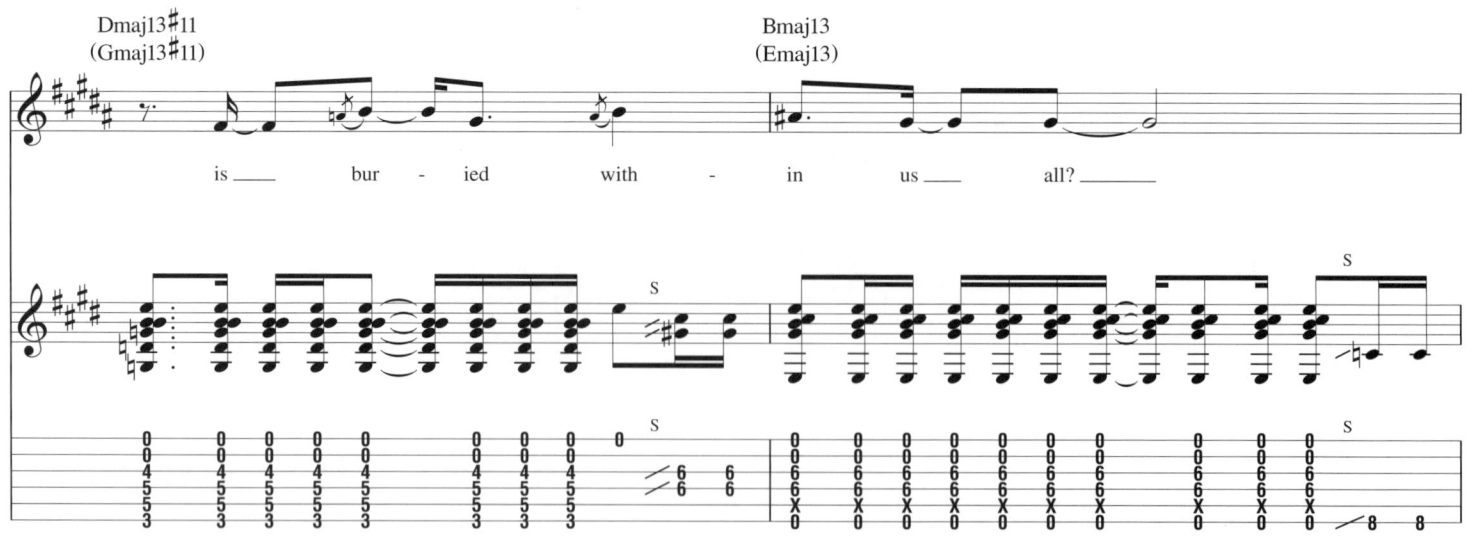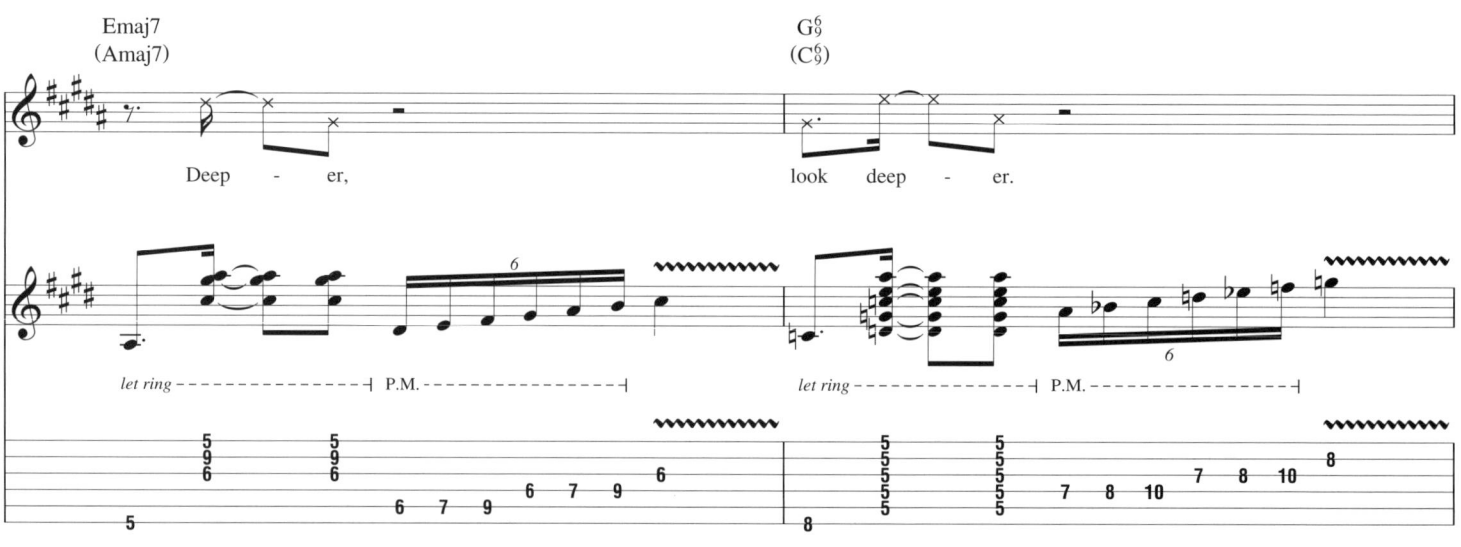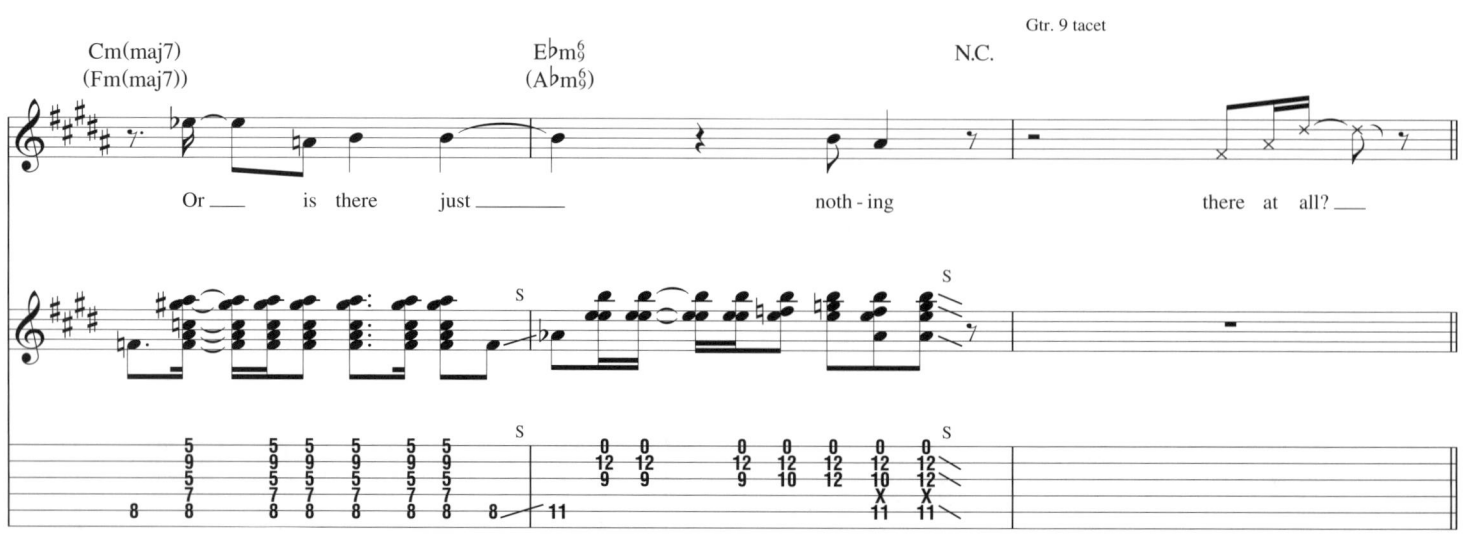

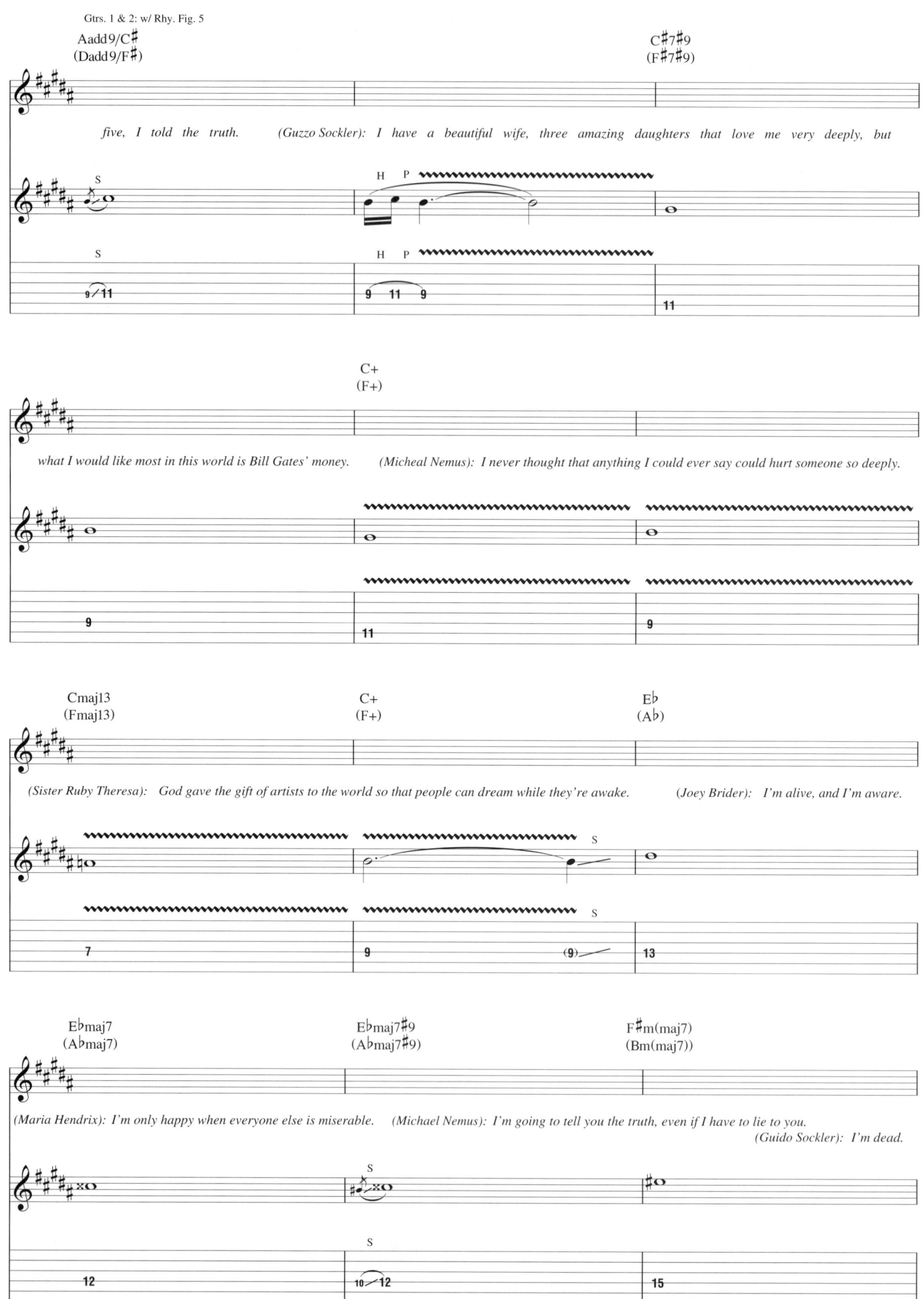

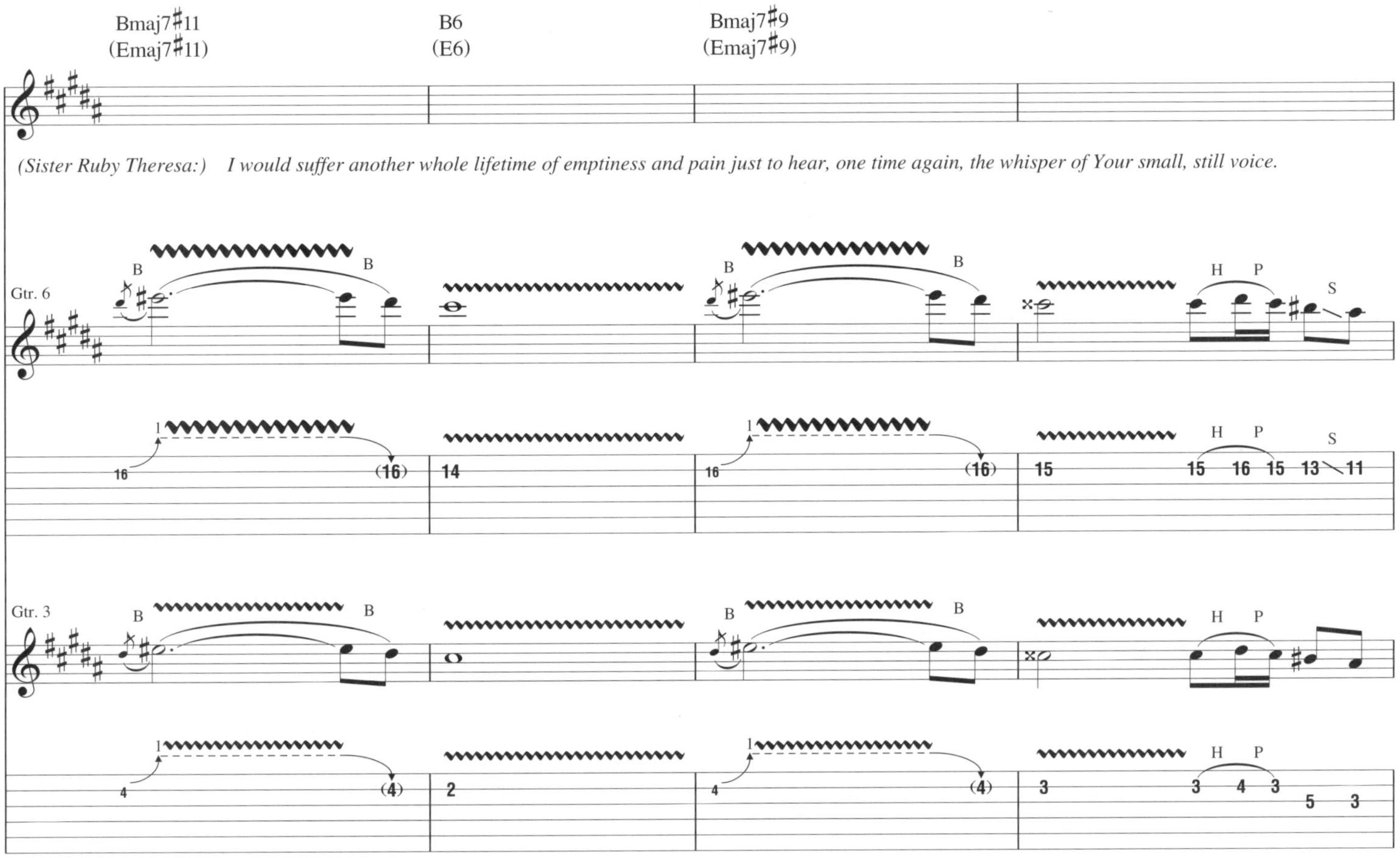

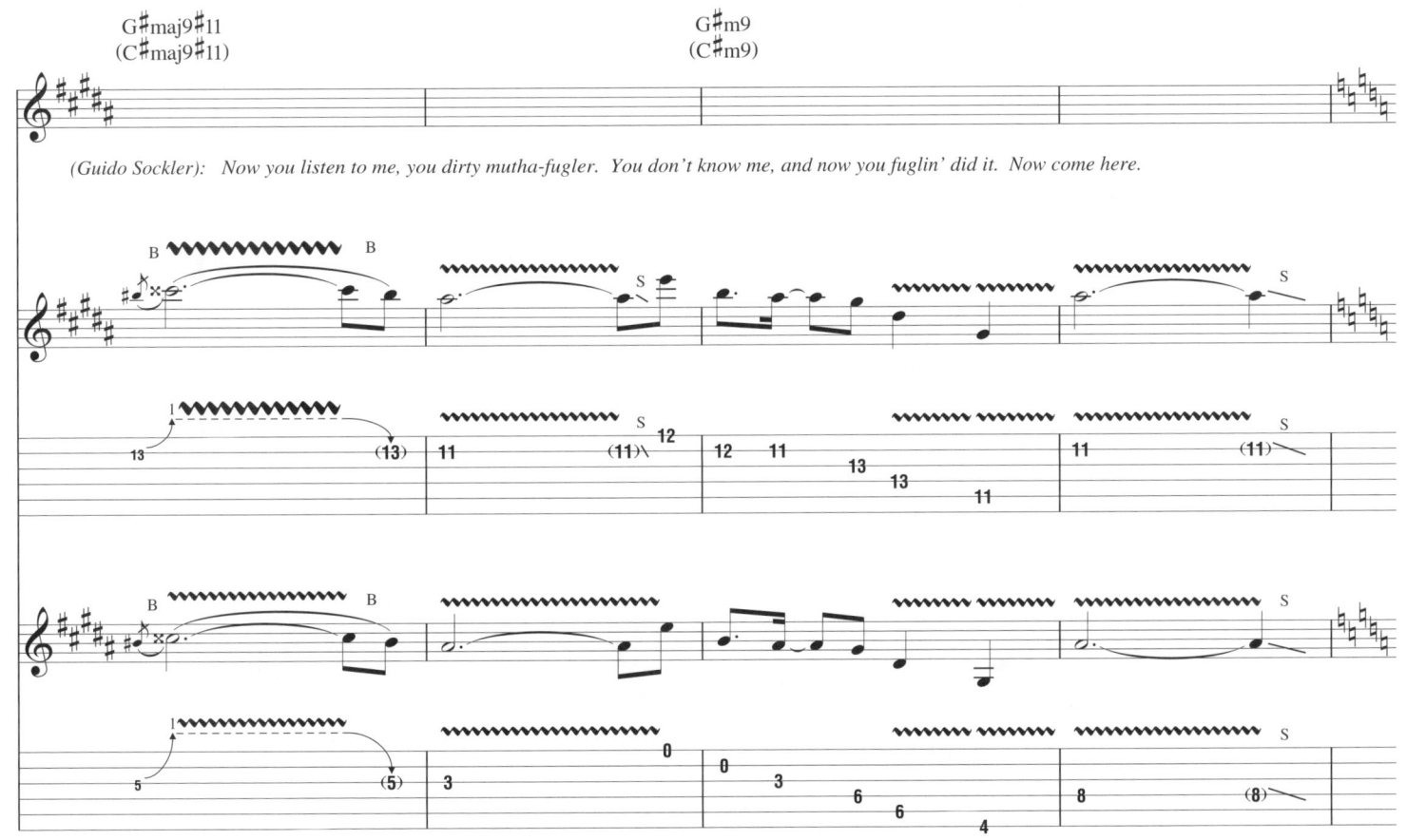

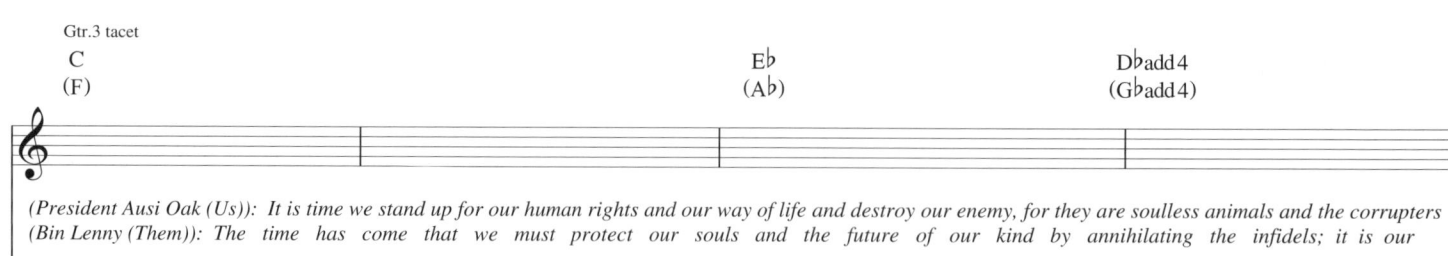
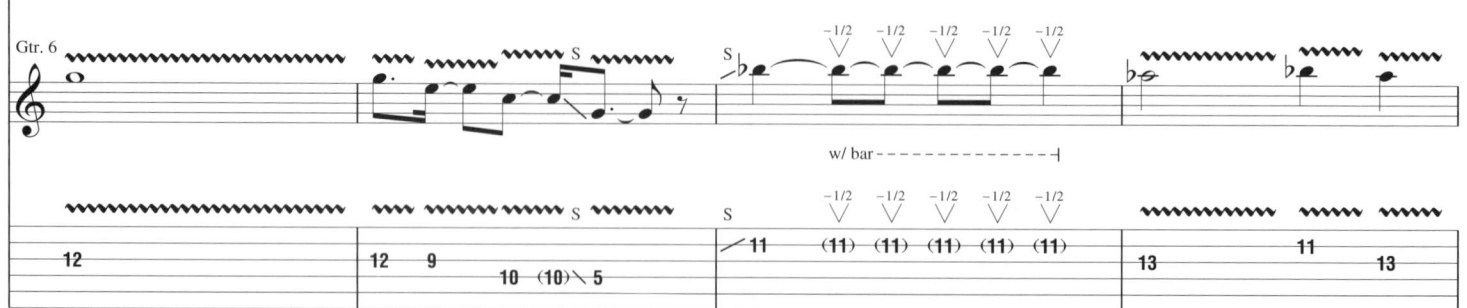
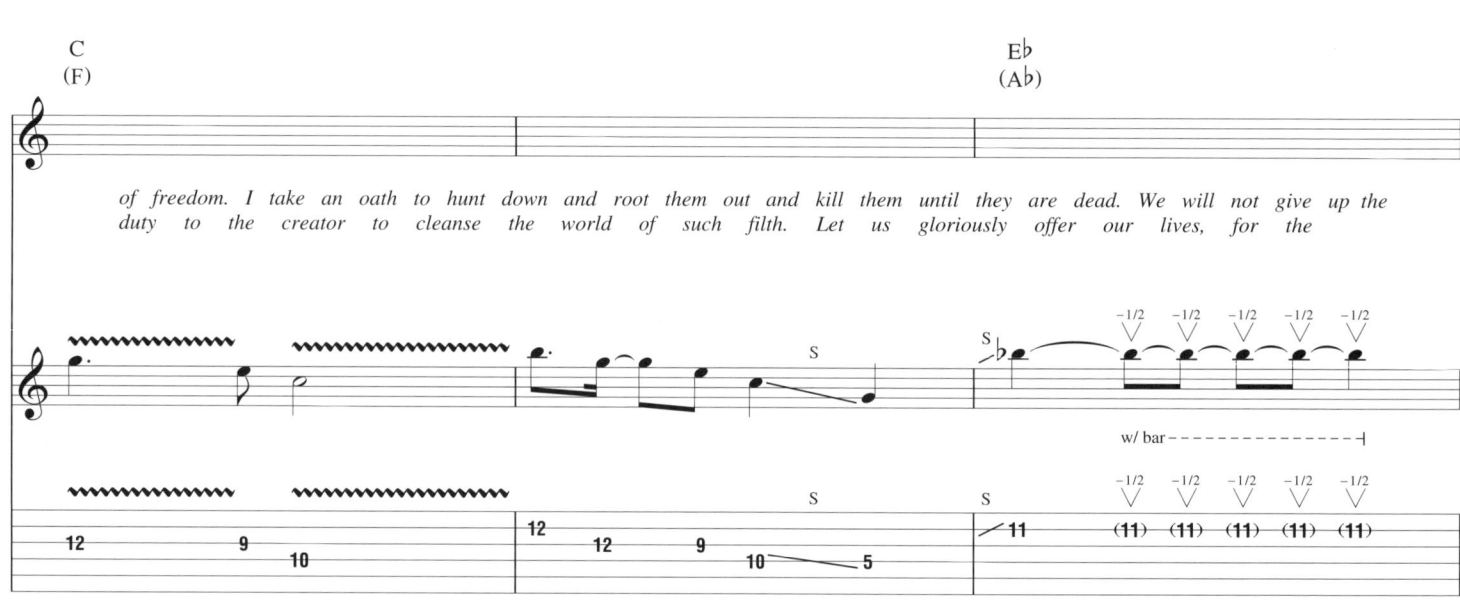
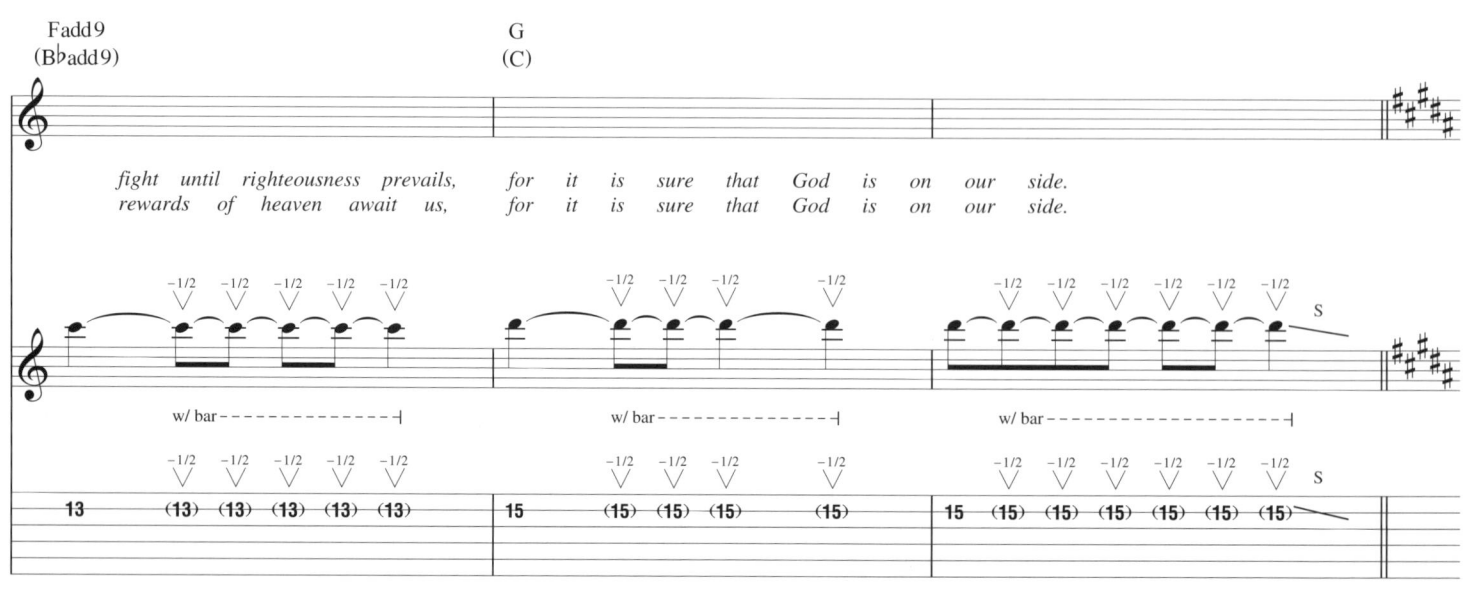

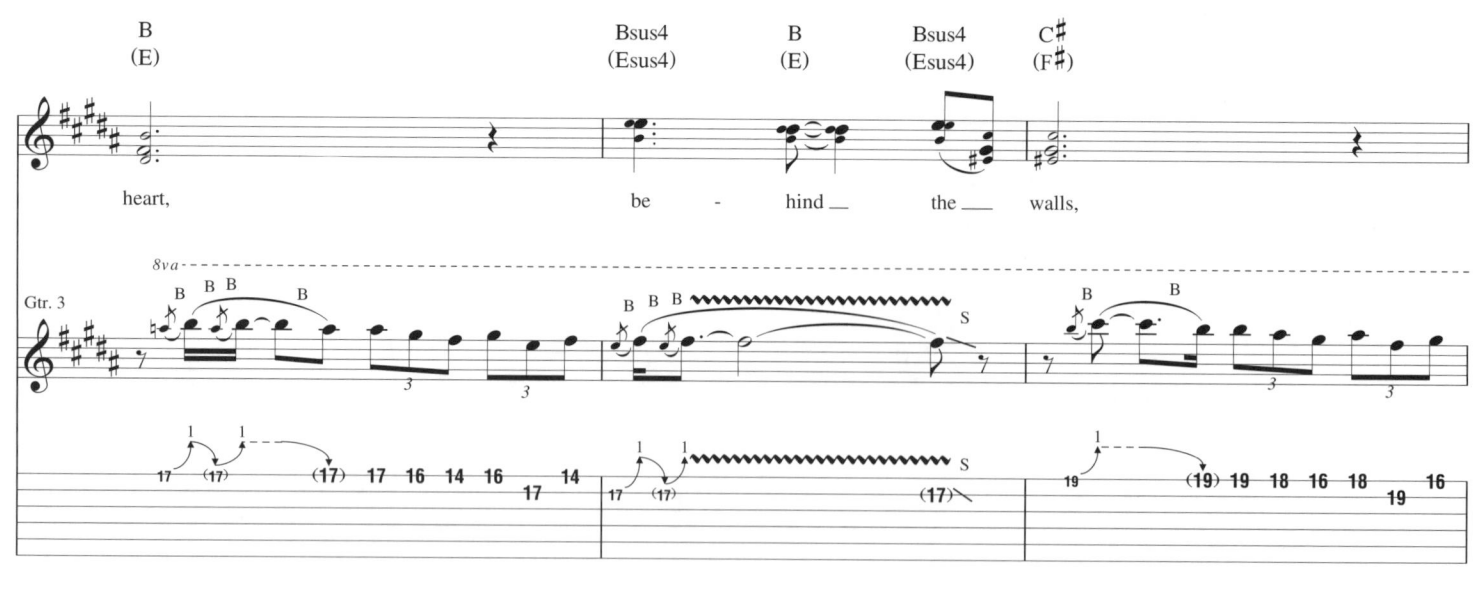

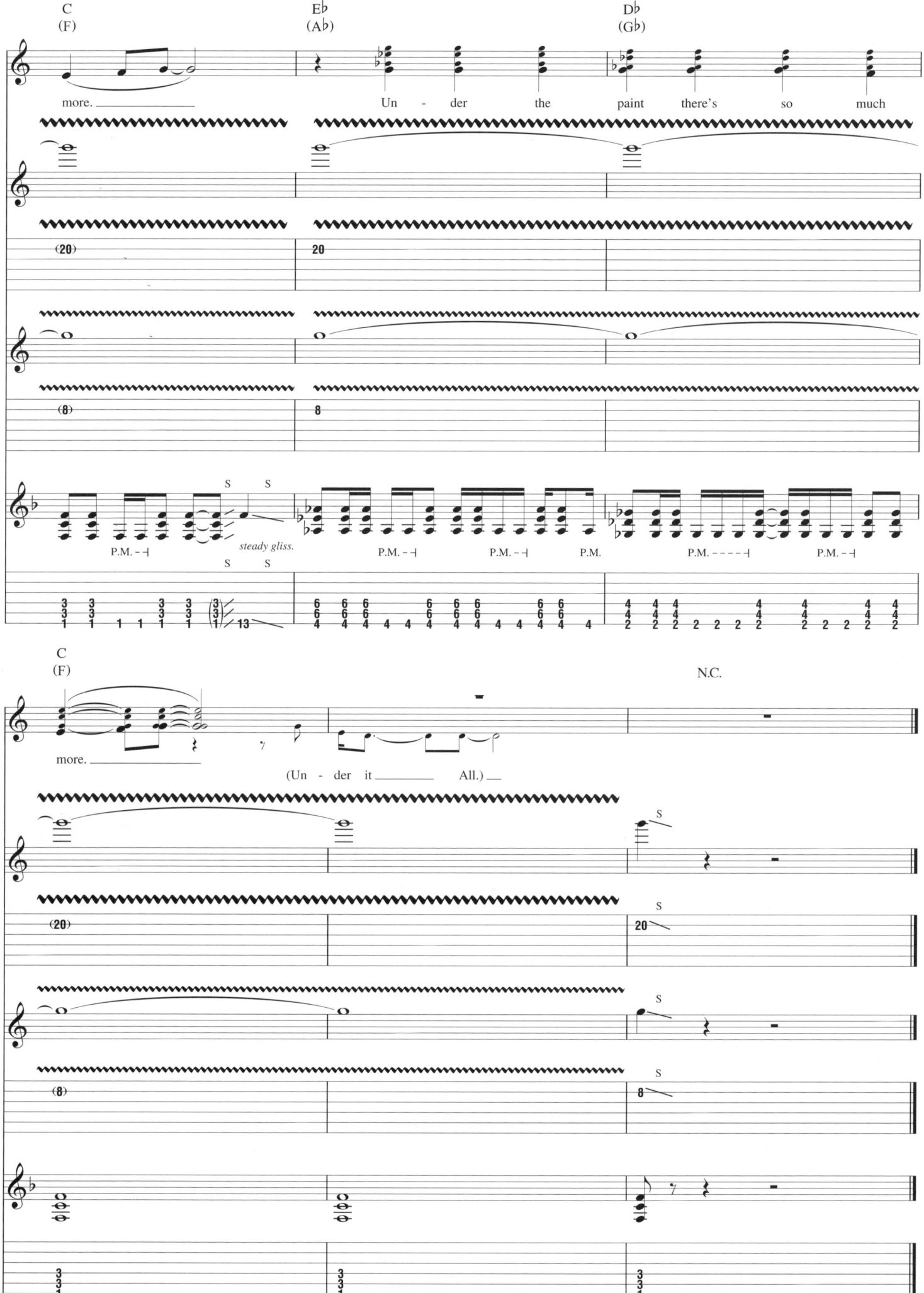

Guitar Notation Legend

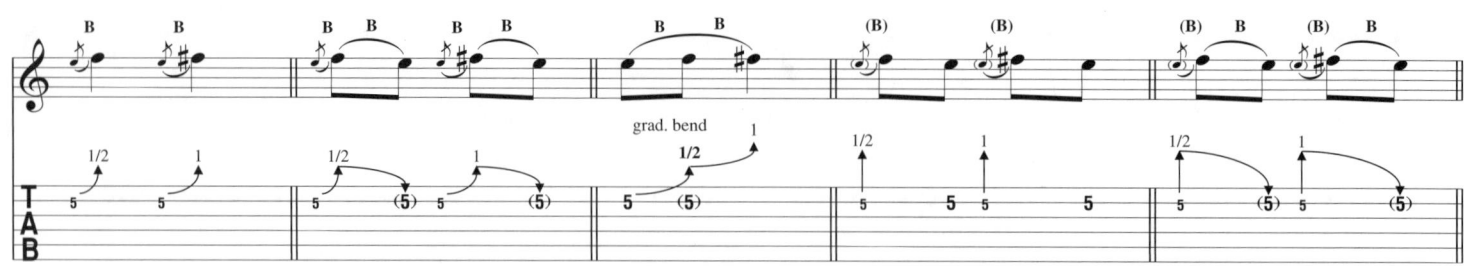

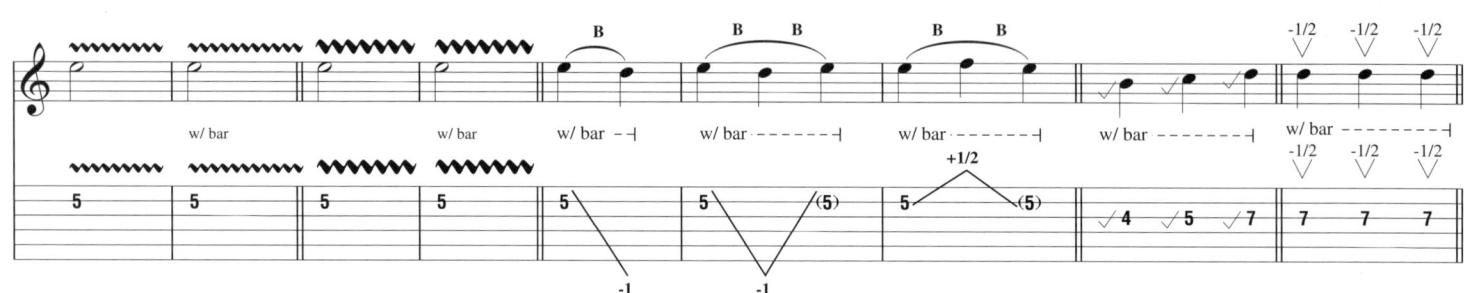

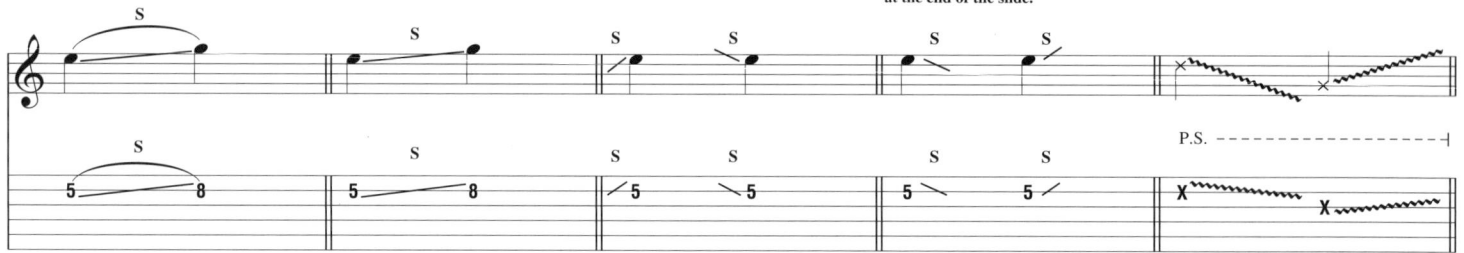

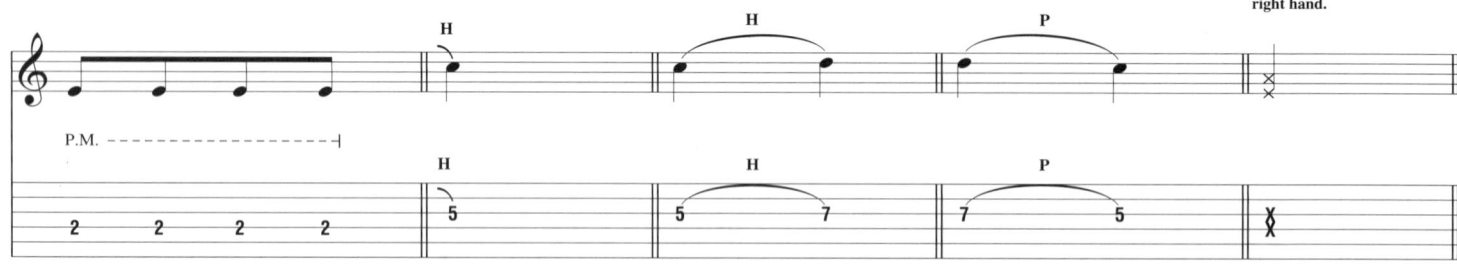

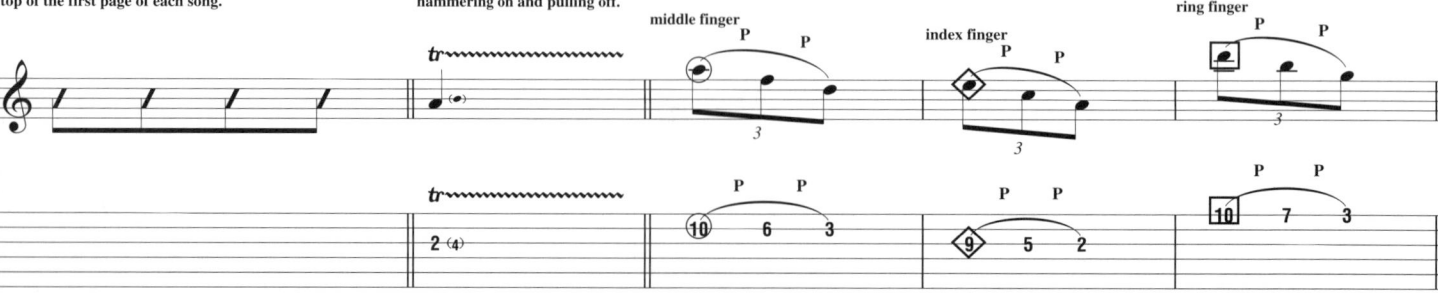

RECORDED VERSIONS®
The Best Note-For-Note Transcriptions Available

ALL BOOKS INCLUDE TABLATURE

00692015	Aerosmith – Greatest Hits	$22.95
00690603	Aerosmith – O Yeah! (Ultimate Hits)	$24.95
00690178	Alice in Chains – Acoustic	$19.95
00694865	Alice in Chains – Dirt	$19.95
00690387	Alice in Chains – Nothing Safe: The Best of the Box	$19.95
00690812	All American Rejects – Move Along	$19.95
00694932	Allman Brothers Band – Volume 1	$24.95
00694933	Allman Brothers Band – Volume 2	$24.95
00694934	Allman Brothers Band – Volume 3	$24.95
00690865	Atreyu – A Deathgrip on Yesterday	$19.95
00690609	Audioslave	$19.95
00690804	Audioslave – Out of Exile	$19.95
00690884	Audioslave – Revelations	$19.95
00690820	Avenged Sevenfold – City of Evil	$22.95
00690366	Bad Company – Original Anthology, Book 1	$19.95
00690503	Beach Boys – Very Best of	$19.95
00690489	Beatles – 1	$24.95
00694929	Beatles – 1962-1966	$24.95
00694930	Beatles – 1967-1970	$24.95
00694832	Beatles – For Acoustic Guitar	$22.95
00690110	Beatles – White Album (Book 1)	$19.95
00692385	Chuck Berry	$19.95
00690835	Billy Talent	$19.95
00692200	Black Sabbath – We Sold Our Soul for Rock 'N' Roll	$19.95
00690674	blink-182	$19.95
00690831	blink-182 – Greatest Hits	$19.95
00690491	David Bowie – Best of	$19.95
00690873	Breaking Benjamin – Phobia	$19.95
00690764	Breaking Benjamin – We Are Not Alone	$19.95
00690451	Jeff Buckley – Collection	$24.95
00690590	Eric Clapton – Anthology	$29.95
00690415	Clapton Chronicles – Best of Eric Clapton	$18.95
00690074	Eric Clapton – The Cream of Clapton	$24.95
00690716	Eric Clapton – Me and Mr. Johnson	$19.95
00694869	Eric Clapton – Unplugged	$22.95
00690162	The Clash – Best of	$19.95
00690828	Coheed & Cambria – Good Apollo I'm Burning Star, IV, Vol. 1: From Fear Through the Eyes of Madness	$19.95
00690593	Coldplay – A Rush of Blood to the Head	$19.95
00690838	Cream – Royal Albert Hall: London May 2-3-5-6 2005	$22.95
00690856	Creed – Greatest Hits	$22.95
00690401	Creed – Human Clay	$19.95
00690819	Creedence Clearwater Revival – Best of	$19.95
00690572	Steve Cropper – Soul Man	$19.95
00690613	Crosby, Stills & Nash – Best of	$19.95
00690289	Deep Purple – Best of	$17.95
00690784	Def Leppard – Best of	$19.95
00690347	The Doors – Anthology	$22.95
00690348	The Doors – Essential Guitar Collection	$16.95
00690810	Fall Out Boy – From Under the Cork Tree	$19.95
00690664	Fleetwood Mac – Best of	$19.95
00690870	Flyleaf	$19.95
00690808	Foo Fighters – In Your Honor	$19.95
00690805	Robben Ford – Best of	$19.95
00694920	Free – Best of	$19.95
00690848	Godsmack – IV	$19.95
00690601	Good Charlotte – The Young and the Hopeless	$19.95
00690697	Jim Hall – Best of	$19.95
00690840	Ben Harper – Both Sides of the Gun	$19.95
00694798	George Harrison – Anthology	$19.95
00692930	Jimi Hendrix – Are You Experienced?	$24.95
00692931	Jimi Hendrix – Axis: Bold As Love	$22.95
00690608	Jimi Hendrix – Blue Wild Angel	$24.95
00692932	Jimi Hendrix – Electric Ladyland	$24.95
00690017	Jimi Hendrix – Live at Woodstock	$24.95
00690602	Jimi Hendrix – Smash Hits	$19.95
00690843	H.I.M. – Dark Light	$19.95
00690869	Hinder – Extreme Behavior	$19.95
00690692	Billy Idol – Very Best of	$19.95
00690688	Incubus – A Crow Left of the Murder	$19.95
00690457	Incubus – Make Yourself	$19.95
00690544	Incubus – Morningview	$19.95
00690790	Iron Maiden Anthology	$24.95
00690730	Alan Jackson – Guitar Collection	$19.95
00690721	Jet – Get Born	$19.95
00690684	Jethro Tull – Aqualung	$19.95
00690647	Jewel – Best of	$19.95
00690814	John5 – Songs for Sanity	$19.95
00690751	John5 – Vertigo	$19.95
00690845	Eric Johnson – Bloom	$19.95
00690846	Jack Johnson and Friends – Sing-A-Longs and Lullabies for the Film Curious George	$19.95
00690271	Robert Johnson – New Transcriptions	$24.95
00699131	Janis Joplin – Best of	$19.95
00690427	Judas Priest – Best of	$19.95
00690742	The Killers – Hot Fuss	$19.95
00694903	Kiss – Best of	$24.95
00690780	Korn – Greatest Hits, Volume 1	$22.95
00690834	Lamb of God – Ashes of the Wake	$19.95
00690875	Lamb of God – Sacrament	$19.95
00690823	Ray LaMontagne – Trouble	$19.95
00690679	John Lennon – Guitar Collection	$19.95
00690781	Linkin Park – Hybrid Theory	$22.95
00690782	Linkin Park – Meteora	$22.95
00690783	Live – Best of	$19.95
00690743	Los Lonely Boys	$19.95
00690876	Los Lonely Boys – Sacred	$19.95
00690720	Lostprophets – Start Something	$19.95
00694954	Lynyrd Skynyrd – New Best of	$19.95
00690752	Lynyrd Skynyrd – Street Survivors	$19.95
00690577	Yngwie Malmsteen – Anthology	$24.95
00690754	Marilyn Manson – Lest We Forget	$19.95
00694956	Bob Marley – Legend	$19.95
00694945	Bob Marley – Songs of Freedom	$24.95
00690657	Maroon5 – Songs About Jane	$19.95
00120080	Don McLean – Songbook	$19.95
00694951	Megadeth – Rust in Peace	$22.95
00690768	Megadeth – The System Has Failed	$19.95
00690505	John Mellencamp – Guitar Collection	$19.95
00690646	Pat Metheny – One Quiet Night	$19.95
00690558	Pat Metheny – Trio: 99>00	$19.95
00690040	Steve Miller Band – Young Hearts	$19.95
00690794	Mudvayne – Lost and Found	$19.95
00690611	Nirvana	$22.95
00694883	Nirvana – Nevermind	$19.95
00690026	Nirvana – Unplugged in New York	$19.95
00690807	The Offspring – Greatest Hits	$19.95
00694847	Ozzy Osbourne – Best of	$22.95
00690399	Ozzy Osbourne – Ozzman Cometh	$19.95
00690866	Panic! At the Disco – A Fever You Can't Sweat Out	$19.95
00694855	Pearl Jam – Ten	$19.95
00690439	A Perfect Circle – Mer De Noms	$19.95
00690661	A Perfect Circle – Thirteenth Step	$19.95
00690499	Tom Petty – Definitive Guitar Collection	$19.95
00690428	Pink Floyd – Dark Side of the Moon	$19.95
00690789	Poison – Best of	$19.95
00693864	The Police – Best of	$19.95
00694975	Queen – Greatest Hits	$24.95
00690670	Queensryche – Very Best of	$19.95
00690878	The Raconteurs – Broken Boy Soldiers	$19.95
00694910	Rage Against the Machine	$19.95
00690055	Red Hot Chili Peppers – Blood Sugar Sex Magik	$19.95
00690584	Red Hot Chili Peppers – By the Way	$19.95
00690379	Red Hot Chili Peppers – Californication	$19.95
00690673	Red Hot Chili Peppers – Greatest Hits	$19.95
00690852	Red Hot Chili Peppers – Stadium Arcadium	$24.95
00690511	Django Reinhardt – Definitive Collection	$19.95
00690779	Relient K – MMHMM	$19.95
00690643	Relient K – Two Lefts Don't Make a Right...But Three Do	$19.95
00690631	Rolling Stones – Guitar Anthology	$24.95
00690685	David Lee Roth – Eat 'Em and Smile	$19.95
00690694	David Lee Roth – Guitar Anthology	$24.95
00690031	Santana's Greatest Hits	$19.95
00690796	Michael Schenker – Very Best of	$19.95
00690566	Scorpions – Best of	$19.95
00690604	Bob Seger – Guitar Collection	$19.95
00690803	Kenny Wayne Shepherd Band – Best of	$19.95
00690857	Shinedown – Us and Them	$19.95
00690530	Slipknot – Iowa	$19.95
00690733	Slipknot – Vol. 3 (The Subliminal Verses)	$19.95
00120004	Steely Dan – Best of	$24.95
00694921	Steppenwolf – Best of	$22.95
00690655	Mike Stern – Best of	$19.95
00690877	Stone Sour – Come What(ever) May	$19.95
00690520	Styx Guitar Collection	$19.95
00120081	Sublime	$19.95
00690771	SUM 41 – Chuck	$19.95
00690767	Switchfoot – The Beautiful Letdown	$19.95
00690830	System of a Down – Hypnotize	$19.95
00690799	System of a Down – Mezmerize	$19.95
00690531	System of a Down – Toxicity	$19.95
00694824	James Taylor – Best of	$16.95
00690871	Three Days Grace – One-X	$19.95
00690737	3 Doors Down – The Better Life	$22.95
00690683	Robin Trower – Bridge of Sighs	$19.95
00690740	Shania Twain – Guitar Collection	$19.95
00699191	U2 – Best of: 1980-1990	$19.95
00690732	U2 – Best of: 1990-2000	$19.95
00690775	U2 – How to Dismantle an Atomic Bomb	$22.95
00690575	Steve Vai – Alive in an Ultra World	$22.95
00660137	Steve Vai – Passion & Warfare	$24.95
00690116	Stevie Ray Vaughan – Guitar Collection	$24.95
00660058	Stevie Ray Vaughan – Lightnin' Blues 1983-1987	$24.95
00694835	Stevie Ray Vaughan – The Sky Is Crying	$22.95
00690015	Stevie Ray Vaughan – Texas Flood	$19.95
00690772	Velvet Revolver – Contraband	$22.95
00690071	Weezer (The Blue Album)	$19.95
00690447	The Who – Best of	$24.95
00690589	ZZ Top Guitar Anthology	$22.95

Prices and availability subject to change without notice.
Some products may not be available outside the U.S.A.

FOR A COMPLETE LIST OF GUITAR RECORDED VERSIONS TITLES, SEE YOUR LOCAL MUSIC DEALER, OR WRITE TO:

HAL•LEONARD® CORPORATION
7777 W. BLUEMOUND RD. P.O. BOX 13819 MILWAUKEE, WI 53213

Visit Hal Leonard online at www.halleonard.com   0607

THE DECADE SERIES

These Guitar Recorded Versions collections feature the top tunes that shaped a decade, transcribed note-for-note with tab.

The 1950s
35 pivotal songs from the early rock years: All Shook Up • Donna • Heartbreak Hotel • Hound Dog • I'm Movin' On • Lonesome Town • Matchbox • Moonlight in Vermont • My Babe • Poor Little Fool • Race With the Devil • Rebel 'Rouser • Rock Around the Clock • Rockin' Robin • Sleepwalk • Slippin' and Slidin' • Sweet Little Angel • Tequila • Wake Up Little Susie • Yankee Doodle Dixie • and more.

00690543...$15.95

The 1960s
30 songs that defined the '60s: Badge • Blackbird • Fun, Fun, Fun • Gloria • Good Lovin' • Happy Together • Hey Joe • Hush • I Can See for Miles • I Feel Fine • I Get Around • Louie, Louie • My Girl • Oh, Pretty Woman • On the Road Again • Somebody to Love • Soul Man • Suite: Judy Blue Eyes • Susie-Q • Wild Thing • and more.

00690542...$15.95

The 1970s
30 top songs from the '70s: Best of My Love • Breakdown • Dust in the Wind • Evil Woman • Landslide • Lay Down Sally • Let It Be • Maggie May • No Woman No Cry • Oye Como Va • Show Me the Way • Smoke on the Water • So Into You • Space Oddity • Stayin' Alive • Teach Your Children • Time in a Bottle • Walk This Way • Wheel in the Sky • You've Got a Friend • and more.

00690541...$16.95

The 1980s
30 songs that best represent the decade: 867-5309/Jenny • Every Breath You Take • Eye of the Tiger • Fight for Your Right (To Party) • Heart and Soul • Hit Me With Your Best Shot • I Love Rock 'N Roll • La Bamba • Money for Nothing • Mony, Mony • Refugee • Rock Me • Rock You Like a Hurricane • Start Me Up • Summer of '69 • Sweet Child O' Mine • Wait • What I Like About You • and more.

00690540...$16.95

The 1990s
30 essential '90s classics: All I Wanna Do • Barely Breathing • Building a Mystery • Come Out and Play • Cryin' • Fields of Gold • Friends in Low Places • Hold My Hand • I Can't Dance • Iris • Jump, Jive an' Wail • More Than Words • Santa Monica • Semi-Charmed Life • Silent Lucidity • Smells Like Teen Spirit • Smooth • Tears in Heaven • Two Princes • Under the Bridge • Wonderwall • and more.

00690539...$16.95

The 2000s
30 songs, including: Alive • All the Small Things • Are You Gonna Be My Girl • Californication • Click Click Boom • Complicated • Drive • Hanging by a Moment • Heaven • If You're Gone • Kryptonite • Lifestyles of the Rich and Famous • Maps • The Space Between • Take a Look Around (Theme from *M:I-2*) • Wherever You Will Go • Yellow • and more.

00690761...$15.95

More of the 1950s
30 top songs of the '50s, including: Blue Suede Shoes • Bye Bye Love • Don't Be Cruel (To a Heart That's True) • Hard Headed Woman • Jailhouse Rock • La Bamba • Peggy Sue • Rawhide • Say Man • See You Later, Alligator • That'll Be the Day • Yakety Yak • and more.

00690756...$14.95

More of the 1960s
30 great songs of the '60s: All Along the Watchtower • Born to Be Wild • Brown Eyed Girl • California Dreamin' • Do You Believe in Magic • Hang On Sloopy • I'm a Believer • Paperback Writer • Secret Agent Man • So You Want to Be a Rock and Roll Star • Sunshine of Your Love • Surfin' U.S.A. • Ticket to Ride • Travelin' Man • White Rabbit • With a Little Help from My Friends • and more.

00690757...$14.95

More of the 1970s
30 more hits from the '70s: Aqualung • Carry on Wayward Son • Evil Ways • Feel like Makin' Love • Fly like an Eagle • Give a Little Bit • I Want You to Want Me • Lights • My Sharona • One Way or Another • Rock and Roll All Nite • Roxanne • Saturday Night's Alright (For Fighting) • Suffragette City • Sultans of Swing • Sweet Emotion • Sweet Home Alabama • Won't Get Fooled Again • Wonderful Tonight • and more.

00690758...$17.95

More of the 1980s
30 songs that defined the decade: Call Me • Crazy Crazy Nights • Heartbreaker • Here I Go Again • It's Still Rock and Roll to Me • Jack and Diane • Jessie's Girl • Once Bitten Twice Shy • Rock the Casbah • Runnin' Down a Dream • Sharp Dressed Man • Smokin' in the Boys Room • Stray Cat Strut • Wanted Dead or Alive • White Wedding • and more.

00690759...$16.95

More of the 1990s
30 songs: Alive • Change the World • Come as You Are • The Freshmen • Hard to Handle • Hole Hearted • Just a Girl • Lightning Crashes • Mr. Jones • No Excuses • No Rain • Only Wanna Be with You • Pretty Fly (For a White Guy) • Push • Shimmer • Stay • Stupid Girl • What I Got • Whatever • Whiskey in the Jar • Zombie • and more.

00690760...$14.95

More of the 2000s
30 recent hits: All Downhill From Here • By the Way • Clocks • Cold Hard Bitch • Drops of Jupiter (Tell Me) • Harder to Breathe • I Did It • I Hate Everything About You • Learn to Fly • Ocean Avenue • St. Anger • Wasting My Time • When I'm Gone • Wish You Were Here • With Arms Wide Open • Youth of the Nation • and more.

00690762...$16.95

For More Information, See Your Local Music Dealer, or Write To:

7777 W. Bluemound Rd. P.O. Box 13819 Milwaukee, WI 53213

Complete songlists available online at
www.halleonard.com

Prices, contents and availability subject to change without notice.

0706